The Ring of Truth

ROGER SCRUTON

The Ring of Truth

The Wisdom of Wagner's
Ring of the Nibelung

ALLEN LANE
an imprint of
PENGUIN BOOKS

ALLEN LANE

UK | USA | Canada | Ireland | Australia
India | New Zealand | South Africa

Allen Lane is part of the Penguin Random House group of companies
whose addresses can be found at global.penguinrandomhouse.com.

First published 2016
001

Copyright © Roger Scruton, 2016

The moral right of the author has been asserted

Set in 10.5/14 pt Sabon LT Std
Typeset by Jouve (UK), Milton Keynes
Printed in Great Britain by Clays Ltd, St Ives plc

A CIP catalogue record for this book is available from the British Library

ISBN: 978-0-241-18855-2

Contents

Preface

This is a work of criticism and also of philosophy. I try to explain Wagner's artistic achievement in his tetralogy of *The Ring of the Nibelung,* and also to use the work as a vehicle for philosophical reflection. I emphasize throughout that the meaning of *The Ring* cannot be understood without appreciating the music. That said, I have kept technical analysis to a minimum, confined detailed description of the music to one chapter (Chapter 4) and placed all musical examples, leitmotifs included, in the Appendix.

The book began life as a series of three lectures delivered in 2005 in Princeton, under the auspices of the Council for the Humanities. Sarah-Jane Leslie attended those lectures and vigorously contested my interpretation of the cycle. I am very grateful to her for her combative encouragement over the years, and for persuading me to take the character of Brünnhilde far more seriously than I was then inclined. I owe a debt of thanks to Paul Heise, whose extraordinary dedication to Wagner's masterpiece has been an inspiration to my work, and whose comments on an earlier version have greatly clarified the argument. I am also indebted to Andreas Dorschel, who put me right on many points both scholarly and philosophical.

I have learned much from the keen and constructive criticism offered by Philip Kitcher and Robin Holloway, and have depended from the beginning on the generous encouragement and insight of two friends, Jonathan Gaisman and Robert Grant, without whose broad knowledge and musical culture I would have been many times led astray. Finally I owe a special thanks to my publisher, Stuart Proffitt, whose attentive criticism of earlier drafts has led to radical changes for the better.

Scrutopia, 2015

I

Introduction:
The Work and the Man

Wagner's *Ring of the Nibelung* is one of the greatest works of art produced in modern times, and in this book I interpret it in terms that I hope will show its relevance to the world in which we live. Enormous obstacles stand in the way of this endeavour, by no means the least of them being Richard Wagner, whose vast ambitions and titanic character have made him into a regular target of denigration in our anti-heroic age. From the point of view of his posthumous reputation, Wagner's life was riddled with mistakes. He made no secret of his anti-semitism, and broadcast it to the world in a notorious pamphlet.* He provided the story and the characters that would, in their Nazi caricature, become the icons of German racism. He scandalously mistreated those who subsidized his extravagant life, including his erratically devoted sovereign, King Ludwig II of Bavaria. He had a penchant for the wives of other men, and in his most notorious tribute to forbidden sexual relations, portrayed incest in terms that were both sympathetic and the raw material for subsequent racist fantasies.

Nor did his mistakes end with his death. Not only did he become Hitler's favourite composer, but the Nazi caricature of the Jew was read back into Wagner's villains. Alberich, Mime and Klingsor were regularly presented on the German stage as though imagined by Dr Goebbels, and his theatre at Bayreuth was used to turn Wagner into the founder and high priest of a new and sinister religion. As a result

---

* *Judaism in Music* appeared in 1850 over the pseudonym K. Freigedank, in the *Neue Zeitschrift für Musik*, but Wagner was soon known to be the author. He reissued it under his own name as a pamphlet in 1869, despite knowing how much it had damaged him.

of these mistakes, only some of which are strictly attributable to Wagner, the tendency has arisen to treat the composer's works as expressions of his personality, to analyse them as exhibits in a medical case study, and to create the impression that we can best understand them not for what they say but for what they reveal about their creator.

The tendency is already present in the polemics with which Nietzsche tried to break from the enchanter who had cast such a spell on him (*The Case of Wagner*, 1888, and *Nietzsche Contra Wagner*, 1895). But it gathered strength in the early years of the twentieth century, when the habit arose of treating works of art as journeys into the inner life of their creator. From the first days of psychoanalysis, Wagner's works were singled out as both confirming and demanding a psychoanalytic reading. Their super-saturated longing, their cry for redemption through sexual love, their exaltation of Woman as the vehicle of purity and sacrifice – all these features have naturally suggested, to the psychoanalytical mind, incestuous childhood fantasies, involving a fixation on the mother as wife. Such is the interpretation maintained by Max Graf and Otto Rank, both writing in 1911.[1] Thereafter the habit of reading the works in terms of the life became firmly established in the literature, not only among Wagner's detractors, but also among his admirers, as we find in Paul Bekker's sympathetic study of 1924, *Wagner: Das Leben im Werke*.

Later, writing in reaction to the Nazi cult of Wagner, and using the heavy machinery of Frankfurt-school Marxism, Theodor Adorno attacked the composer as a symbol of all that was hateful in the culture of nineteenth-century Germany, a purveyor of 'phantasmagoria' whose aim and effect are to falsify reality.[2] More recently Robert Gutman, in his comprehensive study of 1968, *Richard Wagner: The Man, His Mind and His Music*, presented Wagner as a proto-Nazi and a 'characterless ogre'. The accusation was rubbed in obsessively by Marc A. Wiener in his book of 1995, *Richard Wagner and the Anti-Semitic Imagination*. And the habit of psychoanalysing the composer through his works has continued. The most influential recent examples of this – Jean-Jacques Nattiez's *Wagner Androgyne* and Joachim Köhler's *Richard Wagner: Last of the Titans* – see anti-semitism as the meaning and Oedipal confusion as the cause of just about everything the master composed.³ Even Barry Millington, otherwise alert to the musical argument, can write as though anti-semitism is somewhere near the top of Wagner's musical and intellectual agenda.⁴ This reading has strongly influenced the discussion and performance of Wagner's works in France, where revenge on Wagner was for some time an almost obligatory part of the intellectual's apprenticeship.⁵ Although the charges against Wagner's art have been powerfully rebutted by Michael Tanner and Brian Magee,⁶ something needs to be added to the case for the defence, if we are to treat Wagner's works for what they are, rather than for what they reveal, or are thought to reveal, about their creator.

Wagner himself wrote a striking autobiography. It tells the story of a fraught and difficult life and abounds in expressions of love and gratitude, as well as self-praise. The book reinvents its author as a symbol of the emerging Germany, is catty and mendacious about Meyerbeer, and is less than generous to Mendelssohn.⁷ But it steers clear of ardent nationalist and anti-semitic sentiments. Written at the request of King Ludwig II and dictated to Wagner's second wife Cosima, it was issued in a small edition to be circulated among Wagner's friends. But it is now regularly mined for the hidden flaws in the composer's character, and for the proof – however fleeting and arcane – that in this or that respect he was just as ordinary as the rest of us, even though the mind revealed in the book is one of the most extraordinary and comprehensive that has ever existed. Its failure to protect Wagner's reputation, either from false friends or from implacable enemies, is reflected in modern productions of Wagner's one attempt to portray the day-to-day life of the German people: *Die Meistersinger von Nürnberg*, now routinely understood as an apology for all the things that are alarming in the popular caricature of Germany.

Such a reading reflects the lamentable triumph of Hitler's view of Germany over Wagner's: a triumph reflected in our school curriculum, in university courses, in popular culture and in the media. It ought to be clear to every educated listener that *Die Meistersinger*, completed in 1867, is not about the new Germany of the nation state, which, through an unexpected turn of history, came into being in 1871, but about the old Germany of the Holy Roman Empire. (Alas, it wasn't clear to Dr Goebbels, who allegedly attended 100 performances of the work, surely without understanding what it means.) Wagner's Nuremberg is a self-contained city, in which autonomous corporations maintain order and meaning without depending on a centralized nation state, in which local ties are sustained by religion, family and the 'little platoons' of civil society, and whose peace is symbolized in the serene F major melody of the night-watchman, as he obstinately disregards the dissonant G flat of his own policeman's horn. *Die Meistersinger* is one of the few great works of art in which the central character is a corporate person rather than an individual,* and it paints a moving portrait of all that the Germans lost when Napoleon forced them to join the modern world – the world made in France. The destruction of the old Germany is one of the critical factors to take into account if we are to understand not only Wagner's philosophy, but the real meaning, for us as much as for him, of the *Ring* cycle.

Wagner extracted his heroes from the archetypes of folk tales. As in so many 'rags to riches' children's stories, they tend to be orphans, or else to arrive, like Walther von Stolzing in *Die Meistersinger* and Lohengrin and Parsifal in the eponymous operas, from an inexplicable 'elsewhere'. They are on the surface antagonistic to the existing social order; but their antagonism is gradually overcome, often by some wise father-figure like Sachs or Gurnemanz, who is able to understand and forgive. Modern commentators seem to prefer the revolutionary philosophy of Wagner's Dresden years to the later endorsement of civil society and the ethic of renunciation. But that endorsement, made explicit in *Die Meistersinger* and *Parsifal*, is the true tendency of all the mature dramas, and is evinced in a final reconciliation between youthful adventure and aged restraint. The outward form of this reconciliation is presented in the last act of *Die Meistersinger*, and its inner price is the theme of *Parsifal*. If we wish to read those works psychoanalytically, then they should be interpreted, not as expressions of Oedipal confusion, but as tributes to the rediscovered father – a wanderer's attempt to come home. If Wagner's

---

* In my view it is as a member of that corporate person, the Guild of Mastersingers, and as the one who most clearly expresses the pathos of membership, that Hans Sachs assumes his leading role in the drama.

stepfather, Geyer, lies at the back of this, that only confirms the account of him given in *My Life*, as an object of love.

In the human relations that mattered to him, Wagner's first concern was to dominate. But there are human beings who flourish under domination and who also encourage it – Cosima Wagner was one of them. And it was only by dint of his overpowering ego that Wagner was able to bring his astonishing artistic projects to completion. It is also true that Wagner suffered, both from his own bad behaviour and from the incomprehension with which he was treated. In his creative work he devoted himself to the highest of ideals, with no special pleading on his own behalf and with an urgent and objective vision of what is at stake in human life. Indeed, he was a great moralist, and the lessons expounded in his later works are as pertinent today as they were when he first announced them. He worked conscientiously on behalf of a vision that he wished urgently to share, and gave time and energy not merely to projects of his own but to the works that he admired, and to the public culture which for so long refused to admit him. He inspired love in both men and women, and was as likely to squander his borrowed money on others as on himself. All in all, and putting the supreme achievement of Wagner's works against the wrongdoings of his life, I would say: how lucky were those who paid his debts. Alas, this is rarely the expressed opinion of the experts and the impresarios, and Wagner's character continues to stand as an obstacle before all who attempt to understand his art.

The antagonism has made it almost impossible now to experience these works as their creator intended, since they are regularly produced in such a way as to satirize or deny their inner meaning. No work of Wagner's has suffered more from this form of creative censorship than *The Ring of the Nibelung*, which tells the story of civilization, beginning at the beginning and ending at the end. In the immediate post-war years its pagan setting, its focus on the incestuous race of the Volsungs, and its vivid depictions of blond beasts in action were understandably hard to stomach. Even without the spectre of anti-semitism, its world of sacred passions and heroic actions offends against the sceptical and cynical temper of our times. The fault, however, lies not in Wagner's tetralogy, but in the closed imagination of those who are so often invited to produce it.

The Ring began life as a single drama, devoted to the story of Sieg-fried's death as Wagner had extracted and embellished it from his reading of the old German *Nibelungenlied* and the Icelandic *Volsunga-saga*. As he worked on the dramatic poem and the music, over a period of twenty-five years, it was re-conceived as a religious festival, with the *Oresteia* of Aeschylus in mind. *The Ring* was to unfold a world-embracing myth, through intimate human dramas. Its charac-ters were conceived both as believable people and as symbols of universal powers. By following their fate the audience would be led by natural sympathy towards a vision of redemption, in which human beings stand higher than the gods.

This is the aspect of the cycle that we modern listeners most need to appreciate. In recent years, however, the fashion has been to follow the famous Bayreuth production of 1976, when Pierre Boulez sani-tized the music, and Patrice Chéreau satirized the text. Since that ground-breaking venture, *The Ring* has been regarded as an oppor-tunity to deconstruct not Wagner only but the whole conception of the human condition that glows so warmly in his music. *The Ring* is deliberately stripped of its legendary atmosphere and primordial set-ting, and everything is brought down to the quotidian level, jettisoning the mythical aspect of the story, so as to give us only half of what it means. The symbols of cosmic agency – spear, sword, ring – when wielded by scruffy humans on abandoned city lots, appear like toys in the hands of lunatics.[8] The opera-goer will therefore very seldom be granted the full experience of Wagner's masterpiece. One reason for writing this book, and adding to what many might think to be the quite excessive literature devoted to its subject, is to enter a plea on behalf of a work that is more travestied than any other in the operatic repertoire, but whose vision is nevertheless as important to the times in which we live as it was to those of its creator.

The tetralogy presents a space on the very edge of history, fading here and there into hunter-gatherer darkness, emerging elsewhere into the crepuscular light of a civilization in which land has been claimed as property, and loyalty shaped by feudal ties. From the outset it is clear that nature and ambition are in conflict, and that the primordial equilibrium could be recovered only if our human dominion were relinquished. This overcoming of the will to power demands sacrifice of a kind that love alone can accomplish. That is what Brünnhilde – the Valkyrie who has, through compassion, fallen into the human world from the cold realm of the immortals – finally understands, as she joins her beloved Siegfried in death. The self-sacrifice of the individual rearranges the world, atones for the original sin of existence and in some way fulfils what we are. But whether it returns us to the natural order and whether that return is in any case desirable are questions to which the drama gives only ambiguous answers.

Primeval nature is invoked in the very first bars of *Das Rheingold*: a single chord, sustained for three minutes in root position, constantly mutating and yet endlessly the same. Soon we witness the gold of the Rhine, guarded by the Rhine-daughters, and stolen by Alberich the Nibelung, who forswears love in order to obtain it. In forging the gold as a ring, Alberich creates the power upon which civilization will come to depend – the power that sustains both law and leisure, but which shows itself more directly as servitude, labour and the 'hoard' of Alberich's possessions.

Wagner goes on to tell the story of three worlds, which are also three regions of the human psyche: Nibelheim, the underworld, governed by power and exploitation; Valhalla, the realm of the gods, governed by law and treaty; and, in *Die Walküre*, the human world, in which love battles with law, and freedom with resentment. The music of *Die Walküre* expresses the work of love, and dramatizes the price that must be paid for love when we surrender to its claims on us.

Wagner was not in any straightforward sense a religious believer; but he took a profoundly religious view of the human condition. His aim in all the mature works was to give credibility to the thought that we are rescued by our ideals, despite their purely human origin, and also because of it. The gods, demi-gods and goblins portrayed in *The Ring* are personifications of our unconscious needs and strivings – they are thrown off by that great explosion of moral energy, whereby the human community emerges from the natural order and becomes conscious of its apartness. They therefore bear the marks of a deeper nature – a nature that is pre-conscious, pre-moral and un-free. Examine them too closely and their credentials dissolve. This Wagner wonderfully shows in the character of Wotan, chief of the gods, and also in the narrative that continuously questions him.

Christian doctrine holds that man was redeemed by God, when God took on our humanity. Wagner suggests rather that God is redeemed by man, who expiates the crimes required by the bid for eternal government. The gods are bound by the laws that they lay down for us. But we humans belong in the stream of time and change, and can act outside the law. Indeed, love requires us to do so, and the 'law versus love' theme, which Wagner and many of his contemporaries read into the ancient drama of *Antigone*, is one to which the composer constantly returned, always embellishing and qualifying, but never quite relinquishing it. The highest love, Wagner believed, is a relation between dying things, and also the only redeeming power. There is no redemption *from* death, but there is a kind of redemption *in* death. Hence it is only through incarnation in a human being, and through the enjoyment of a human freedom, that the gods can be rescued from their immortal remoteness, stepping from their altars to die beside the mortals who created them.

To realize that high romantic vision, the Wagnerian drama creates its own religious background, its own awareness of an ideal cosmic order. And this awareness shines through the deeds of god and hero in much the way that it shines through the actions on the Greek tragic stage. Who is to say whether Aeschylus or Sophocles really believed in the gods whom their characters worship and upon whose will they depend? What is sure, however, is that the tragedians believed in the religious need of their audience, and in the possibility that drama might speak to that need and offer consolation for our guilt and suffering. Just so with Wagner, who recognized that modern people, having lost their faith in the divine order, need another route to meaning than that once offered by religion. This is what *The Ring* aims to provide: a vision of the ideal, achieved with no help from the gods, a vision in which art takes the place of religion in expressing and fulfilling our deepest spiritual longings.

In the course of this book I naturally touch on the question of artistic meaning. When we elucidate the meaning of a work of art what exactly are we doing? What is the difference between discovering meaning *in* a work, and attaching meaning *to* it? And in what way does a work of art justify what we find in it, so as to give force and credibility to its inner vision? Those questions can be asked of any serious work of art. But they are especially difficult to answer in the case of Wagner, since the emotions in his dramas develop simultaneously in three ways: through the action on the stage, through the words of the principal characters, and through the music that binds everything together in a symphonic unity. The extraordinary process whereby events are captured from the stage and distilled into orchestral sound, there to be developed through their own musical logic and returned to the action in a transfigured form – this unsurpassed musical chemistry which is Wagner's highest claim to genius – has never been fully elucidated. Yet it must always be kept in mind by anyone who wishes to know what the dramas really mean. In what would surely have been one of the most illuminating of all commentaries on *The Ring* had he lived to complete it, Deryck Cooke complains that the then existing accounts of the tetralogy refer only casually to the music, and expound the work as though the text alone were sufficient to present what happens.[9] Moments of inner reflection, such as Wotan's confession to his daughter in Act 2 of *Die Walküre*, or Siegfried's soliloquy in the forest in Act 2 of *Siegfried*, are passed over as though the schematic words uttered by the characters contain a full account of their emotion. In fact these are moments of transition, in which the profoundest and most far-reaching psychic changes are accomplished – but accomplished in the music, with little or no help from the words.

In an intriguing chapter, Cooke addresses the question of the leitmotifs and their meaning, and I take up his argument in Chapter 4 of this book. There is also available, on the Decca label, the introduction prepared by Cooke for the Solti recording of the cycle, in which he clearly and genially explains the relations between leitmotifs and their role in shaping the drama. As he points out, there is no one-to-one correspondence between a leitmotif and the concept, idea or emotion that is first attached to it. The leitmotif has a potential to develop – but to develop musically. And it is by implanting the principal of musical development in the heart of the drama that Wagner is able to lift the action out of the events portrayed on the stage, and to endow it with a universal, cosmic and religious significance. Reflecting on his art in his later years Wagner insisted on this aspect, suggesting that what passes on the stage is nothing but 'an act of music made visible'.[10]

Wagner's treatment of his story is therefore replete with musical symbolism, and raises the question of how symbolism works. This question will occupy me in much of what follows, but it is perhaps worth pointing out at this stage that symbolism is not the same as allegory, even if allegory is a form of it. In allegory a story is told in which each character, each object and each action stands for something else – usually a universal concept – so that a narrative of concrete episodes forges a connection between abstract ideas. Much medieval literature is allegorical in that sense, and in an early and highly influential commentary Bernard Shaw gave an allegorical reading of the *Ring* cycle.[11] More recently, in one of the most thorough accounts of *The Ring* to date, Paul Heise has defended a comparable allegorical interpretation, aligning the characters and actions of the drama with the forces at work in forging civilization from the raw material of nature.[12] Heise derives his allegory from a close reading of the philosophy of Wagner's early mentor Ludwig Feuerbach, as well as from the text and music of *The Ring* and Wagner's own voluminous writings. The allegory is spelled out carefully, with the leitmotifs identified at every occurrence, so that the reader can click on to the score and hear the music. This invaluable aid to understanding the tetralogy has made it far easier for me to embark on my own account, by providing a step-by-step guide to the leitmotifs as they appear.

Heise's allegory does, I believe, contain a core of truth: but it is a truth about *The Ring* as Wagner originally conceived it. *The Ring* as it finally emerged tells a rather different story, and tells it not through allegory but through a kind of concentrated symbolism that admits of no simple stepwise decipherment. Several recent commentators have explored the deeper meaning of this symbolism. Light has been cast by the Jungian account offered by Robert Donington, by the patient but incomplete work of Deryck Cooke, by the listener's companion and concordance of J. K. Holman, by the engaging radio talks of Father Owen Lee and by the fascinating study of Wotan's search for an ending by Philip Kitcher and Richard Schacht.[13] Thanks to such works of criticism and analysis, some of which I consider in more detail in Chapter 5, Wagner's artistic aims and musical language are beginning to be accorded their true artistic significance. The commentators just mentioned all agree that the music of *The Ring* is the wellspring from which the motives and emotions of the characters are drawn and their work encourages me to direct the reader to salient musical details whenever this casts light on the drama.

Among the many early commentaries one stands out, to my mind, as indispensable and that is the record of Wagner's directions at the first Bayreuth performance, written down by the composer's intimate friend and disciple, Heinrich Porges.[14] Porges's work offers a unique insight into Wagner's own understanding of his masterpiece, and a moving account of a young musician's response to its message. Although Porges did not venture a comprehensive analysis, he recounts, in his own words and also in Wagner's, the dramatic significance of crucial passages in the score. All too brief, the book nevertheless shows that every note in the score was precious to the composer, had been thought over with the utmost care, and was accorded a definite dramatic significance.

It is ironic that Wagner's detractors have had so little to say about this work, which was largely ignored by German musicologists and in due course suppressed by the Nazis. For Porges was one of many Jewish friends who regarded Wagner's anti-semitism as a regrettable weakness rather than the heart of what he was as an artist and a man. Porges brings home to us the universal significance of a work in which the central motive is not German nationalism, racial supremacy, heroic triumph or any other of the bombastic themes foisted on Wagner by his false friends and real enemies, but a boundless sympathy for innocent suffering, whoever the victim might be.

2

History and Culture

Like all great works of art, *The Ring* bears its meaning within itself, and can be understood by a musical person without enquiring into its origins or the life and ideas of its creator. However, it did not appear from nowhere, and some aspects of its meaning become easier to grasp when it is seen in the context from which it arose. Wagner lived at the end of cultural movements that have had a lasting impact on the way we see ourselves, as well as on the history and identity of Germany. In this chapter I summarize some of these movements, and the traces they left in Wagner's outlook, as poet, philosopher and musician.

Wagner began writing the poem of *The Ring* in 1848, the year of revolutions across Europe, in one of which he played an active part. In the German-speaking lands these revolutions were inseparable from the growing nationalist feelings of the people, and the search for political identities that would coincide with perceived national borders. Wagner shared these nationalist feelings and saw his own art as a vindication of their legitimacy.

Nevertheless, we should bear in mind that German nationalism had only recently become overtly political. Before the French invasions of 1806/7 there had been no serious attempt to form a unified German state, and until the early years of the nineteenth century the geographical region that we now know as Germany was composed largely of cities and princedoms of the Holy Roman Empire, in which German was the vernacular language, and Christianity the established faith.

The Thirty Years War, precipitated by the religious conflict between Catholic and Protestant, had devastated Central Europe in the first part of the seventeenth century, and was brought to an end in the middle of that century by the Peace of Westphalia, which reshaped the German-speaking lands as a loose alliance of sovereign entities. The established religion of each such entity was to be decided by the secular power, choosing between Catholicism, Lutheranism and Calvinism, and forgoing any intention to impose that choice upon its neighbours.

In the German city-states there emerged thereafter a high culture, in which literature, philosophy, music, art and architecture were all spurred on by the rivalry of local sovereigns and the spread of Enlightenment ideas. By the last decades of the eighteenth century, during the so-called *Goethezeit*, when Goethe, Herder and Schiller flourished in Weimar, when Kant was at the height of his powers in the Prussian university of Königsberg, when Haydn and Mozart had established the classical style as the musical lingua franca of the German-speaking people and when the many sovereigns were vying over orchestras, universities, theatres and rococo palaces, the German lands were more than a match for France and Britain in their cultural and scientific accomplishments. In one matter, however, they were radically deficient, and that was military power. With the exception of Prussia, which had been only partially included in the Holy Roman Empire, and whose French-speaking King Frederick II (Frederick the Great) had devoted the resources of the state to building a disciplined army, the military arms of the German princedoms were more ceremonial than practical, and following the death of Frederick the Great in 1786 the Prussian army also entered a state of decline.

The Enlightenment loosened the hold of the Church and dimmed the aura of monarchical power. Educated people therefore began to define their attachments in other ways, many of them moved by the romantic national sentiment that focused on the folk poetry and folk tales of the German people. This sentiment was later to inspire the nostalgic feelings for home and landscape that were so memorably expressed by Hölderlin in poetry, Friedrich in painting, Weber in opera and Schubert in song. In its beginnings, however, in the late eighteenth century, romanticism served to create a false sense of security. Educated Germans were uniting around the idea of a land and a way of life that they were more able to rhapsodize over than to defend, and living within borders that would collapse at the first impact from outside. Only after Napoleon's coup d'état did they begin to become aware of this.

By 1803 Napoleon, pursuing his grand strategy of European domination, had acquired all German territory on the left bank of the Rhine and abolished most of the smaller states and free cities of the Holy Roman Empire. Thereafter the princes had no choice but to accept what Napoleon offered, since they lacked the means to oppose it. Following his seizure of Hanover in 1803 (undertaken in the course of the war with England), Napoleon became the effective master of Germany. Austria and Russia were defeated at Austerlitz in December 1805, and in 1806 a Deputation representing the Empire agreed to a new confederation of southern German States (the Confederation of the Rhine) in alliance with Napoleon. Only Prussia maintained a quixotic resistance, which was decisively crushed in 1806 at the battles of Jena and Auerstedt. The Holy Roman Empire ceased thereafter to exist, with the dismembered remnants of Prussia forced into alliance with Napoleon and compelled to pay exacting reparations to France.

Prussian and Austrian troops fought in Napoleon's army during his march on Moscow, and were released from this painful bondage only by the reversal of Napoleon's fortunes there. The diplomacy of Metternich in Austria and Hardenberg in Prussia led eventually to an effective alliance and the defeat of Napoleon at the battle of Leipzig in 1813. Thereafter, following Napoleon's abdication, the Treaty of Paris confined France within its pre-Napoleonic borders. And in 1815 the Congress of Vienna again rewrote the map of Germany, Prussia emerging greatly enlarged and the Confederation of the Rhine replaced with a new Confederation of German States.

During that tumultuous period, despite subjection to France, and also because of it, the German people enjoyed an extraordinary cultural flowering. The Romantic Movement gathered strength in art, literature and music, and Herder's concept of the *Volk* and its natural gifts and entitlements became the foundation of a new national consciousness. Social and legal reforms loosened the power of the aristocratic estates and the feudal subjection of the peasant farmers. The universities flourished and in 1810 a new university was founded, under the enlightened leadership of Wilhelm von Humboldt, in Berlin. This university consciously identified itself as the educator of the emerging nation, and through its flexible curriculum and emphasis on research was able to attract some of the ablest minds from all over Germany, and from the rest of Europe too.

In 1762, as a teenager, Herder had attended Kant's lectures in Königsberg, and he wrote partly in reaction to the philosopher's reason-based vision of the moral life. For Kant Enlightenment was the moment of mankind's moral maturity, when the free individual emerges from the prison of custom and superstition. Guided by the light of reason, such an individual will adopt the universal moral law that reason commands. Kant's argument for this position was to have a lasting impact on German philosophy, and in due course on Wagner. But it did not persuade Herder, who believed that it gave too thin a description of the moral motive, reducing human beings to their over-civilized shadows. For Herder there was a deep distinction in the human psyche between Civilization, which is the sphere of rational calculation and institution-building, and Culture, which is the shared temperament of a *Volk*. Culture is what unites human beings in mutual attachment, and consists of language, custom, folk tales and folk religion.

In the course of expounding that idea Herder proposed medieval Germany as a cultural icon in the place of the hitherto adopted classical Greek ideal. He also began the practice of collecting and publishing folk poetry and folk tales, and thereby inspired the subsequent work of Achim von Arnim and Clemens von Brentano (*Des Knaben Wunderhorn*, 1805–8) and the folk-tale collections of the Brothers Grimm (1812).

Herder was a Protestant clergyman, and his romantic nationalism was inseparable from his attachment to Martin Luther's Bible, the great work that taught ordinary Germans to read, and which endowed their language with its lasting spiritual resonance. Herder regretted that Luther had not founded a national church, which would have provided durable foundations to a unified German culture. Subsequent nationalist writers saw national sentiment more as an alternative to religion than a form of it, and recognized that Luther had been as much responsible for the divisions among the German people as for the language that united them. It was another reader of Kant, J. G.

Fichte, who made the non-religious form of nationalism explicit, and it was his *Addresses to the German Nation*, delivered in occupied Berlin in 1807 and published in 1808, that helped to inspire the Germans to join together against Napoleon.

Fichte's importance for the student of Wagner is twofold. He was the most philosophical among the founders of German nationalism in its political form; and he was also the thinker who took Kantian idealism in the direction that was to change the worldview of the German educated elite. Kant begat Fichte, who begat Hegel who begat Feuerbach; and Feuerbach begat both Wagner and Marx, the two most influential minds of their time. It is well to understand this episode in intellectual history if we are to grasp the full repertoire of ideas behind Wagner's masterpiece.

Fichte's philosophy begins from the critical philosophy of Kant, expounded in the three great *Critiques* – *The Critique of Pure Reason* (1781), *The Critique of Practical Reason* (1788) and *The Critique of Judgement* (1790). Kant argued that self-consciousness presents us with a world of appearances, organized by scientific categories such as substance and causality, and arranged according to the forms of space and time. All attempts to transcend the limits of experience, and to know the world as a whole and as it is in itself, are bound to end in contradiction. The critical philosophy, which Kant called 'transcendental idealism', therefore denies the possibility of a positive theology, regards the traditional arguments for God's existence as sophisms, and finds the meaning and purpose of human life in morality alone.

From the perspective granted by self-consciousness, Kant argued, I see myself as the free originator of my own actions. But I also see myself from outside, as one object among others, a part of nature, bound by the law of cause and effect. I am both a free subject and a determined object, and this defines the deep paradox of the human condition. Freedom requires the ability to act from reason alone; reason must therefore provide a motive to action. This motive is the so-called categorical imperative, which tells me to act only on that maxim that I can will as a law for all rational beings. The categorical imperative commands me to recognize and respect the dignity of all who are governed, as I am, by the laws of practical reason. I must therefore live by the rule of justice; any other course is incompatible with a fully free and responsible life. This is what is involved in being a *person* – that I respect other persons as ends in themselves.

Self-consciousness is identified by Kant with the so-called 'transcendental unity of apperception'. By this he meant my ability to attribute my own subjective states to an enduring subject of consciousness. This unity is 'transcendental' in two senses: it is not arrived at by deduction from experience but presupposed in understanding experience. And it involves a peculiar non-empirical perspective on the world – a perspective from a point of view that is neither in the world nor out of it. This 'transcendental' perspective – what Thomas Nagel calls 'the view from nowhere' – is adopted whenever we reflect upon our own experience, and whenever we address the question of what to do.

Philosophers will be aware of the many intricate arguments that Kant advances for his position, and the many objections which have since been levelled against it, especially in recent times. However, it is a position that is deeply embedded in the idealist thought that influenced Wagner, and it is deeply embedded too in the Wagnerian music dramas, all of which focus on the trials of individuals, as they affirm their freedom in heroic action, or over-reach it in love.

For Fichte, Kant's vision of the moral life showed the deep truth of our condition, that we are subjects of consciousness, who shape ourselves by creating the world from our own subjective resources. And the process of self-realization, which governs the life of the individual, governs the life of nations too. Fichte was an admirer of the French Revolution, which he saw as a liberation of humanity from servitude and darkness. His provocative stance towards the world in general and his opponents in particular led to his dismissal from the University of Jena in 1799 on a charge of atheism, and he was widely regarded by his contemporaries as a Jacobin. It was only when witnessing the impact of Napoleon's occupation that he recognized that the French Revolutionary idea of citizenship was as likely to destroy national attachments as to protect them. To be a citizen was a luxury; to be a patriot a necessity. Only through a shared national loyalty, he concluded, could people come together in a spirit of sacrifice, so as to defend their material and spiritual assets. Although Fichte shared Herder's view of language, as fundamental to the spirit of the *Volk*, he had no time for organized religion, and advocated a form of nationalism that was overtly political, being a call to militant action against the occupying power.

When the new University of Berlin was founded in 1810, Fichte was appointed as its first Rector, a post from which he resigned in a characteristic huff in 1812, soon afterwards joining the war effort as a medical officer, to die of typhus in 1814 on the eve of Napoleon's final defeat. During the twenty years of his intellectual maturity he devoted himself to expounding and refining his *Wissenschaftslehre* (*Theory of Knowledge*), which was to inspire Schelling and Hegel and to make idealism into the academic orthodoxy in Germany. And the central argument of this philosophy, expounded again and again in Fichte's lectures, constantly refined and amended but never clarified to its author's (or to anyone else's) satisfaction, adopted nevertheless by Hegel and shaped as a credo by his 'Young Hegelian' disciples, reappears in new guises in Wagner's masterpiece.

The premise of our knowledge, Fichte argued, is the self, the transcendental subject whose freedom is the anchor of all that he thinks and does. Such, he believed, was the enduring lesson of Kant's 'transcendental idealism' – namely that knowledge begins and ends in the consciousness of self, and that the self is 'transcendental', with no place in the empirical world. Fichte went on to draw the conclusion that we live in a spiritual and not a material universe. 'The I freely posits itself', and it is from this self-positing that the subject constructs the objects of its knowledge. In the act of self-positing I am aware simultaneously of the self and its limits – of the I and the not-I that stands over against it. Yet this not-I owes its being and its nature to the I that posits it. Subject and object exist in mutual dependence, and the freedom of the one implies the necessary laws that bind the other.

I act freely in the world, however, only when I recognize the presence of other free subjects who call on me to limit my freedom. This is the origin of political life, namely that we live in mutual dependence, each freely limiting his own freedom in order that the other can exist freely too. Hence political order is a realm of 'right', 'law' and 'contract', all of which are presupposed in the self-conscious existence of the human subject. I come to self-knowledge and free-dom through the process of '*Selbstbestimmung*', that is, the self-definition and self-limitation that marks out for me a place in an objective order in which others too have a share.

Those ideas are spelled out in highly abstract arguments that are difficult to translate from the idiosyncratic language of their author. Nevertheless they had an enormous and immediate influence, since they were offered and received as a defence of 'idealism' against mat-erialist 'dogmatism', and hence as a way of continuing the critical philosophy of Kant, which had knocked theology from its throne in the German universities, and put the study of freedom, subjectivity and the moral law in its place. In the wake of Kant and Fichte phil-osophy took up the central place in German intellectual life that it was not to lose for half a century, and it did so in the name of ideal-ism, by which its readers understood a comprehensive view of the world in which the human subject is discovered in the place that had been reserved by history for God. According to the post-Kantian vision, adopted in one form or another by Schiller, Schelling and Fichte, our world is a world of appearances, organized by our mental faculties; we have no knowledge of things in themselves, and the one certain reality is the self and its freedom.

Georg Wilhelm Friedrich Hegel succeeded Fichte as Berlin's profes-sor of philosophy in 1818, after a brief period in which the professorship was in abeyance. He had begun his academic career as a student of theology, and aimed to rescue the Christian faith from Fichte's excesses, while accepting that idealism in some form must be true. Schopenhauer, Hegel's curmudgeonly opponent at the Univer-sity of Berlin, is often singled out as the most important intellectual influence on Wagner, since it was the reading and rereading of Scho-penhauer that helped to crystallize the pessimistic vision of Wagner's later years. But when Wagner enrolled at the University of Leipzig in 1831, the year of Hegel's death, it was the Hegelian philosophy that dominated the faculties and captured the imagination of the young. And it was a reading of the Hegelians that opened Wagner to philos-ophy. Like the Hegelians, Wagner saw the contest over religion as the decisive episode in the emergence of the modern world. And he under-stood the human condition in terms of two great processes in the life of the individual – the process of *Selbstbestimmung*, whereby the free individual emerges from the condition of nature; and erotic love, in which the self encounters that which is wholly Other. In both of these conceptions Wagner was profoundly influenced by ideas that originated in the writings of Hegel.

For Hegel the ultimate substance of the world is spirit, or *Geist*. Spirit achieves individuality in you and me, but in itself is greater than all of us. Science, religion, politics and art are ways that spirit realizes itself in objective form. All ventures of the spirit are movements towards the Absolute Idea, in which the world achieves full consciousness of itself. In every sphere, therefore – in science, religion, politics and art – old forms of understanding die and new forms come in their stead. All our attempts at order must meet with their own negation, and so give way to the higher forms that replace them. Nothing human is permanent, and all must perish in the spirit's on-going search for self-knowledge.

Hegel wrote *The Phenomenology of Spirit* in Jena in 1806 as Napoleon engaged the Prussian forces in the decisive battle outside the city walls. At the time Hegel, like Fichte, was in sympathy with the French Revolution, and although forced to leave Jena by Napoleon's occupation, he observed the great general's entry into the town with admiration, describing Napoleon subsequently as 'the World Spirit on Horseback'. In later years Hegel's political views moved in a conservative direction. But he never lost his belief in heroes, writing, in his *Philosophy of History*, published posthumously in 1834, that 'this is the role of heroes in the history of mankind: it is through them that a new world comes into being'. Wagner was reading Hegel's *Philosophy of History* when he began the poem of *The Ring*, and at first conceived the work as the story of just such a hero, Siegfried, who was to usher in the new world of human freedom after the downfall of the gods.

In *The Phenomenology of Spirit* Hegel adopts Fichte's idea of the subject of consciousness, striving to realize its freedom from its own subjective resources. But for Hegel the primordial subject is not yet an individual. The starting point of all history, all knowledge and all institutions – even of nature itself – is the universal *Geist*, the world-spirit intent on *realizing* itself as an object of its own awareness. Through successive 'moments of consciousness', *Geist* shapes itself as the free individual, and these moments of consciousness are reflected not only in our individual development as persons, but also in the movement of human history.

A famous passage in *The Phenomenology of Spirit* describes a transition from the 'life-and-death struggle' in the state of nature, to the acceptance of universal moral law. The transition is described as the 'moment' of lordship and bondage, or master and slave. One party to the original struggle overcomes and enslaves the other, so as to use the other as a means to his ends. The result is that the victor (the master) retires into a life of leisure and consumption which distances him from reality, while the loser, the slave, continues, even in his bondage, to imprint on the world the mark of his individual will. As producer, the slave is able to acquire a consciousness of himself as agent, and a sense of the world as containing not only means but also ends; as consumer, the master loses that consciousness, and with it the sense of the ends of his existence. The 'inner freedom' of the slave grows with the 'inner bondage' of the master, until the slave is in a position to rise up and bind his oppressor, so beginning the process again with a reversal of roles. The toing and froing between command and obedience is resolved only by the transition from this 'moment' of consciousness to a higher 'moment', in which each party sees the other as end and not as means, recognizing freedom as their shared condition, and thereby accepting the governance of a universal moral law.

The process whereby freedom and mutual respect emerge from the condition of slavery illustrates the Hegelian 'dialectic' – the emergence from opposition of a new condition that transcends and resolves the conflict. The dialectic can be discerned not only in the growth of the individual but also in the movement of history – both of which evolve by 'the labour of the negative'. Thus freedom and self-knowledge are achieved only through the resolution of conflict, when the other acknowledges my right to them, and when I acknowledge the other's right in turn. It is only in the moment of recognition that I become a full-fledged individual, with a will, a destiny and a self of my own. And recognition must be mutual. I can be truly free only if I recognize the freedom of others.

Hegel's argument was to form the philosophical core of Marx's critique of capitalist society, Marx distinguishing between labour as self-creation and 'alienated labour' under the rule of private property. But Hegel's argument also makes a connection between individuality, freedom and self-consciousness, and gives a profound insight into the need of the free individual for a shared rule of law. Both those ideas were to find artistic expression in Wagner.

The Ring tells the story of Siegfried's quest for freedom and individuality through contests with a dwarf, a dragon, a god and the woman who teaches him fear. It tells the story of his self-betrayal when he enslaves the one he loves and trades her for a substitute. It dramatizes the corruption of Siegfried, when conventional bonds of honour displace the spontaneous self-giving in love. And it shows that, in a world of manipulation and distrust, the freedom of the individual can be as easily lost as won. Only at the moment of death does Siegfried regain the path to individuality and freedom; but by then it is too late.

The reverberations of Hegel's argument can be felt not only in that central story but throughout the *Ring* cycle: in the self-torment of Alberich, who has forsworn love for the sake of power; in the dark underworld of Nibelheim, whose subjugated people are instruments of a will that they cannot influence; in the tragedy of *Die Walküre*, in which two suffering humans win through to freedom only to find that the god who planned this can no longer permit it. And Hegel's account of law and its indispensable presence in the life of the free being is embodied in the character of Wotan, king of the gods.

After Hegel's death his followers divided into the Old Hegelians, who saw idealism as laying the foundations for the Prussian monarchy, and the Young Hegelians, who were for the most part anti-religious and leftist critics of the emerging bourgeois order. The Old Hegelians adopted the conservative conclusions beautifully spelled out by Hegel in his *Elements of the Philosophy of Right*, published in 1820. In that work Hegel tries to show that the process whereby human beings realize their freedom also builds the institutions of law, property, family, civil society and the state. These are not things that we freely choose from a position of detachment, but things through which we *actualize* our freedom, and without which we could not exist as fully self-conscious agents. Hence they are the goal and the bequest of political life, permanent features of a free society. For the Old Hegelians, that argument left the liberal philosophy of the social contract in ruins.

The Young Hegelians were more interested in the argument about individual freedom than in the defence of institutions. Following Hegel's death they met and published in Berlin, and their influence spread rapidly through society. To be a German intellectual at that time was to be a Hegelian of one kind or another. But it was not necessarily to be an idealist. The greatest of the Young Hegelians, Ludwig Feuerbach, attempted to turn Hegel's philosophy upside-down, or rather to set it on its feet. He wanted to rewrite Hegel's idealist philosophy as a form of materialism. It was this that inspired his two most influential readers – Wagner and Marx.

Feuerbach agreed with one aspect of the idealist philosophy. He agreed that our world is one of conflict, in which we strive to assert our power, to achieve knowledge of our capacities, and to win recognition and respect from others. And he agreed that history is an on-going process, which moves constantly towards greater freedom, greater self-knowledge, greater emancipation from the superstition and fear that first enslaved us. But he disagreed with the idealist premise. Reality, he asserted, is material, not spiritual. The self is not the creator of the objective world but simply one of its by-products. Consciousness arises from life. And life is a material, not a spiritual, fact.

From this premise Feuerbach mounted a critique of religion. In his exploration of the 'unhappy consciousness' – 'spirit in self-estrangement' – Hegel had many interesting things to say about religion. He argued that a particular kind of religion is the reflection of a 'self-alienated spirit'. This is the religion that regards God as irremediably transcendent, the locus of all virtue and holiness, and the world as eternally separated from God: the religion that tells the story of man's 'fall'.

Feuerbach applied that observation to all religion, and to Christianity in particular.[1] In Christianity human beings locate all virtue in a heavenly sphere and therefore find no virtue in themselves. Feuerbach here borrows from Kant's philosophy of religion the crucial concept of the 'fetish'. In fetishism, Kant argued, human beings attribute their own powers to objects that are outside them and are therefore set at one remove from their own will. Christianity too is fetishism, argued Feuerbach, in which human beings attribute their virtue, freedom and happiness to an unreal 'spiritual' realm, and so live out their material existence in a state of hopeless separation from their true nature and powers. Virtue could be regained, were we to recognize that its reality lies here, in our material, social existence – in our 'species-being' (*Gattungswesen*) as Feuerbach tendentiously described it. In religion we make our virtue into an object, and then worship it as our master. Hence we are 'alienated' from ourselves and separated from our fulfilment. In this way our fetishistic conscious-ness deprives us of our powers, by investing them in unreal objects.

Since the world is material, there are no spiritual realities. Religion conjures a world of illusions. In the Virgin Mary, in Christ and in God the Father Christians idealize aspects of the human condition, endowing them with a fictitious life. They then bask in the excuse that this gives them to be morally inferior to their own fictions. The result of this is to alienate believers from the moral qualities that they need if they are to live fully and freely in society. Religion is part of the long story of man's self-enslavement.

Wagner created the supernatural beings of *The Ring* on Feuerbach's model. They are personifications of human characteristics – both good and bad. But, unlike the Christian pantheon mocked by Feuerbach, Wagner's gods are far lower in the scheme of things than the humans over whom they exert their dwindling authority. Indeed, as Brünn-hilde realizes in the great scene in which she announces death to Siegmund, the human world exhibits the virtue that the gods lack and without which life is deprived of its meaning – the willingness to sacrifice everything, even life itself, for the other's sake. Thereafter Brünnhilde enters a conflicted condition, torn between the uncon-scious wish to descend into the world of mortals so as to share their fate and the conscious desire to fulfil Wotan's deeper purpose, albeit in a way that the god had forbidden. In attempting to rescue Sieg-mund, she risks her immortality. But when the crisis comes she embraces death, knowing that death is the price of love, and that love is her salvation, and the world's salvation too.

The theological background of the *Ring* cycle, while influenced in that way by Feuerbach, was also the crystallization of another powerful intellectual movement in the Germany of Wagner's youth. The Enlightenment had pitted the scientific against the religious worldviews, and science had scored the major victories. Diderot, Voltaire and Rousseau in France, Hume and Smith in Britain, Goethe, Schiller and Kant in Germany – many of the most influential thinkers of the second half of the eighteenth century – adopted a secular view of the human condition, and regarded religion as acceptable only if confined 'within the limits of reason alone', as Kant was to put it in the title of his most controversial work. At the same time voyages of discovery, the romantic interest in indigenous myths and fairy tales, and a new scientific approach to the gods of Greece and Rome led to the first attempts to explore religion as a natural phenomenon, a pre-scientific residue in the human psyche, to be understood for what it says about *us*, rather than for the truth or otherwise of its doctrines.

The study of comparative religion took off with the survey of tribal religions by Charles de Brosses (*Du culte des dieux fétiches*), which appeared in 1760, arguing that practices dismissed as 'idolatry' by the Christian missionaries were in fact addressed to beings with all the divine attributes of the ancient gods. Karl Philipp Moritz's *Götterlehre*, published in 1791, saw those ancient gods, and the myths surrounding them, as a 'language of the imagination' – not simply allegories, but a way in which people made sense of themselves and their world. This idea was taken up by the idealist philosopher Friedrich Schelling who argued in his lectures on the philosophy of art (1802–3) that mythology is not allegorical but 'tautegorical'. The term comes from Coleridge, himself strongly influenced by Schelling, and means 'saying the same thing in another way', as opposed to 'allegorical' – saying another thing in the same way. From the point of view of the myth, Schelling insisted, the gods are actually existing entities. The gods do not mean something else: they mean what they are, while at the same time corresponding to 'potencies' in human nature.

In 1784 Sir William Jones founded the Asiatic Society in Bengal, and he and his colleagues began the collection of Sanskrit texts that initiated the scientific study of the Vedas and the Indian religions. This study led to the highly influential work of Karl Friedrich von

Schlegel, *Über die Sprache und Weisheit der Indier* (1808), arguing that people from India were the originators of European civilization. Schlegel explored the common roots of Sanskrit and the European languages, and presented Indian civilization as a source of the wisdom for which the German romantics hungered. Schlegel's book was followed by the great work of Georg Friedrich Creuzer, *Symbolik und Mythologie der alten Völker, besonders der Griechen*, which appeared in 1810 and which argued (against Herder's view of folk religion as the pure expression of the collective soul) that gods travel from people to people, and that those worshipped by Homer and Hesiod were of oriental provenance. By the early 1820s, when Schopenhauer was a *Privatdozent* (a lecturer funded by fees collected from his students) in the University of Berlin, eclipsed but not quite extinguished by Hegel, the sacred texts of the East were becoming known in Germany, and Schopenhauer was writing of Hinduism as the closest to the truth among existing religions.

Meanwhile the Brothers Grimm continued the work of Herder in collecting the fairy tales of the German-speaking people, and exploring the history of their language. In the work of Jacob Grimm philology, etymology and the study of myth were combined with the search for pagan residues interred beneath the soil of German literature. Grimm influenced the whole course of German thought during Wagner's youth, and inspired new and scholarly editions of medieval literature, including the stories of Tristan, Tannhäuser, Lohengrin and Parsifal, along with that of Siegfried as recounted in the medieval *Nibelungenlied*. These stories, which provided Wagner with his primary material, persuaded him that he could rise free of the present moment and explore what is permanent and universal in the German experience.

The *Nibelungenlied* is an early thirteenth-century epic set on the Rhine in the Christian Middle Ages. It tells the story of Siegfried the Nibelung, his wife Kriemhild, and the bitter and rejected Brünhild, climaxing with Siegfried's murder in the cathedral city of Worms. Although it contains in embryo much of the plot of *Götterdämmerung*, it is a far cry from the masterpiece that Wagner eventually composed from its usable fragments. Enthusiastically welcomed when the modern translations began to appear in Wagner's youth – with Thomas Carlyle characteristically praising it as 'our northern *Iliad*' – the poem is a Christianized rehash of pagan myth which only here and there rises to the kind of grandeur that Homer sustains for book after book. Of course, the existence of a true German epic could not fail to inspire those who were looking for the deeper history of the emerging nation, and two great composers – Schumann and Mendelssohn – both contemplated making it into an opera, with Wagner's rival Heinrich Dorn actually producing a *Die Nibelungen* in 1854. But Wagner, much as he esteemed the *Nibelungenlied* as a national epic, rightly perceived that it is a reworked version of more interesting originals.

He therefore turned to the study of the surviving literature in the ancient Teutonic languages – Old Norse, Old High German and Anglo-Saxon. This literature included the Poetic Edda (or Elder Edda) of Iceland, a collection of poems in alliterative verse, which record the religious traditions of the Vikings, and the Prose Edda in which the same material is summarized by Snorri Sturluson, a twelfth-century poet, historian and politician who was twice elected lawspeaker of the Icelandic Parliament. Although the codex containing the Edda was written down in the twelfth century by a Christian scribe, the poems themselves are thought to have originated before the settlement of Iceland in the ninth century, retaining the stories of the old gods in an unexpurgated form. The codex was given by an Icelandic bishop to the Danish King in the seventeenth century, and tucked away in the royal library. In the wake of Grimm's researches scholars began to study it, along with the other surviving fragments of the old Teutonic literature. Siegfried, the hero of the *Nibelungenlied*, appears in the Icelandic literature as Sigurd, and the story of the Niflungs or Nibelungs is given in the *Volsungasaga*, a thirteenth-century epic in prose.

The enterprise of combining the *Nibelungenlied* with the Icelandic saga in a single dramatization was first undertaken by one of Wagner's literary heroes, the romantic poet Friedrich de la Motte, Baron Fouqué, whose *Sigurd the Dragonslayer: A Heroic Drama in Six Adventures*, appeared in 1808. In the epilogue to the *Ring* cycle, published in pamphlet form in 1872, Wagner writes that, when he printed his own Nibelung poem in 1853, the 'stuff' of the medieval *Nibelungenlied* had only once, so far as he could ascertain, 'been turned into a stage-piece; that was a long time ago, by Raupach in his prosy fashion'.[2] However Wagner knew Fouqué's work, which contained much of his cast of characters, both heroic and divine, as well as some of the plot in outline.[3] He must also have been aware of the seven-act *Nibelungenlied* tragedy, *Der Hürnen Seufrid*, by the sixteenth-century mastersinger Hans Sachs, from whose life and circumstances Wagner composed his own great mastersinger drama.

Wagner began work on the poem of *The Ring* in 1848 and finished it in 1852; meanwhile Karl Simrock, who had published a popular modern rendering of the *Nibelungenlied* in 1827, and then, between 1843 and 1849, a series of volumes on the German heroes, issued a German translation of the Eddas in 1851. He followed this in 1853 with the first volume of his *Handbuch der deutschen Mythologie*. By the time Wagner was able to secure a performance of *Das Rheingold*, in 1869, the Icelandic originals of his gods and goblins had become familiar characters in an emerging national legend.

Wagner reimagined the Volsung saga as an account of the birth and death of our world. The resulting story is far from authentic as an account of the Viking theology; but it is a remarkable attempt to give coherence and meaning to the pagan narratives. Picking from all the surviving sources, and also from the *Nibelungenlied*, Wagner set out to create a vast and living symbol of the price we humans pay for civilization, by showing a world in which that price has yet to be paid.[4] At almost every turning point in *The Ring*, and in every place where a light of meaning is suddenly sparked in the narrative, Wagner has discovered a dramatic use for some fragment of the original literature. From *Gripir's Prophecy*, telling the story of Sigurd's visit to the hall of Gripir, Wagner took the skeleton plot of *Siegfrieds Tod*, which was to become *Götterdämmerung*. The story of Mime is contained, in embryo, in the Lay of Regin, and that of the slaying of the dragon, and the voice of the wood-bird (here a pair of nut-hatches), in the Lay of Fafnir. Brünnhilde's morose and silent tormenting of self and other in *Götterdämmerung* is a central theme of the *Volsungasaga*, while the wisdom contest between Mime and the Wanderer in *Siegfried* Act 1 is foreshadowed in the 'Allwise Sayings', which contain a similar contest about the knowledge of names between Thor and a dwarf.

In the originals all those suggestive fragments are buried in tributes to the gods that are singularly off-putting to the modern reader. Here, for example, is a poem commending the god Thor, by Vatrliði Sumarliðason:

> You smashed Leikn's limbs,
> You bashed Thrívaldi,
> You knocked down Starkað
> You trampled Gjálp dead . . .[5]

Wagner's triumph is to have discovered, buried in the heart of this literature, symbols of lasting human passions and predicaments. It suffices to give one example.

The Eddas tell of Valholl, the fortress that the god Odin builds to fend off the day of Rognarök (in which the gods will be destroyed in their final battle).* They also introduce the Valkyries, warrior demi-goddesses who secure the death of heroes, in order to assemble them in Valholl as a shield. In this story we witness the pitiless savagery of the Viking worldview, personified in the god who endorses pillage, rape and murder whenever needed, and who rejoices in the bloodshed that creates his conscript army. However, in the Ballad of the Victory-bringer (*Sigrdrífumál*) in the Poetic Edda, there is a brief narrative telling the story of the sleeping Sigrdrifa ('victory bringer'), who has been awoken by Sigurd:

> She gave her name as Sigrdrifa, and she was a Valkyrie. She told how two kings warred with each other: one was called Hjalmgunnar, an old man and a great warrior, and Odin had promised him the victory; the other was Agnar, the brother of Auda – there was no one willing to shield him. Sigrdrifa slew Hjalmgunnar in the battle; but Odin, as a punishment for this, pricked her with a sleep-thorn, and said that

---

* Rognarök means the doom of the gods; but in some sources (e.g. stanza 39 of the poem Lokasenna in the Poetic Edda, and in the Prose Edda of Snorri) it is spelled 'rognarøkkr', meaning twilight of the gods, a meaning also given by Zoega's Old Icelandic Dictionary. This may have been the result of a spelling mistake; nevertheless, it gave Wagner the idea for one of the most poetic titles ever conferred on a work of dramatic art.

from then on she should never again win victory in battle, but should be married. 'But I said to him that I had made a vow never to marry a man who could be afraid.'

In one almost buried sentence – 'there was no one willing to shield him' – Wagner discerned the place where sympathy shone dimly in the dark world of the Viking gods. And so it was, in Act 2 of *Die Walküre*, that love and compassion were planted in the drama, the seeds that would grow to overturn all Wotan's projects, and to achieve for the god a kind of redemption beyond anything that could be gained by power and trickery. Having seen this implication, the rest of Sigrdrifa's story became immediately clear to Wagner, and with it the character and role of his own Valkyrie heroine. It is as though Wagner had asked himself 'How could it be that a Valkyrie should take the side of the unprotected warrior whom she is to cull from the battlefield?' And in answering that question he saw the *inside* of that bleak Viking world, the reality of love and compassion that all these hammer-throwing and skull-smashing gods concealed. That brief stab of pity in a Valkyrie spelled the *real* Rognarök: this, for those cruel deities, was the beginning of their end.

We might ask, why did Wagner scour the myths and the legends in this way, for the little details that fitted his dramatic intuition? Why not simply start again from the beginning, inventing the characters of both gods and heroes, and also the story that brought them together? Why hamper your creative instinct with the residues of stories whose context has been largely forgotten, and which address the concerns of a barbarous people with whom we no longer have much in common? The question is important, because it points to an idea of myth that was current in Wagner's day, and which he above all others helped to make current too in ours.

The monotheistic faith of Europe abounds in stories, but they are stories of supposedly real people, responding in this world to the designs and demands of a transcendent deity. Even the story of Adam and Eve was accepted as literal truth, the first chapter of a continuing narrative of which we are the current episode. Classical scholarship showed another kind of religion, in which the sacred stories are not directly related to events in our world, but describe how things were *in illo tempore*, as Mircea Eliade puts it,[6] in that stationary moment when the course of history was yet to be established and when things stood outside the stream of time. Readers of Greek and Roman literature – of whom there were many in nineteenth-century Europe – were acquainted, therefore, with another kind of story-telling, not distinct in its methods from poetic invention, but nevertheless conveying insight into the deeper meaning of the human world. How are such myths to be understood, and how were they understood by those who repeated them, learned them and lived by them?

Writers and philosophers of the Enlightenment were largely agreed that myths of that kind are not merely fictions. They represent another way of conceiving the world, and one that is directly connected with the religious way of life. Myths are not literally true; but they are not false either. They symbolize human passions and states of character, elevated to a sphere beyond the reach of chance events. By seeing their own nature symbolized and purified in mythic form, ordinary people were able the better to understand their fate. Hence, myths formed a kind of spiritual *bequest*, a language of symbols through which the adherents of the ancient religions could both understand the permanent features of the human condition and also rehearse their membership of the tribe, the community, the *Volk* that included them. That, roughly, was the view of myth propagated by Herder, and in one way or another it was to influence anthropologists throughout the nineteenth century.

When Wagner became interested in myth, however, that view of things was beginning to appear too simple. Researches into Eastern and other religions brought home to the world of scholarship that the mythic way of thinking is a human universal, something that may be superseded by a reasoned theology and a narrative of God's presence, but which precedes all such rational attempts to make sense of things. In myth we find an older, purer, less conscious expression of man's religious need. For Schelling, myth was not to be understood merely as a symbolic representation of the life of the tribe, but as a direct intuition of God: in myth, Schelling suggested, the Absolute is made present in imagined form. Myths are a form of *knowledge*, expressed in narratives of another and inaccessible time. And this view of myth as a kind of obscure revelation, a precursor of philosophy and an insight into the destiny of the world, is further developed in Hegel's lectures on the philosophy of religion.

By the time of the appearance in 1829 of Wilhelm Grimm's *Die deutschen Heldensagen* (Sagas of the German Heroes) and his brother Jacob's great work *Deutsche Mythologie* in 1835, it was therefore widely accepted that the religions suppressed by the Christian faith embodied another and earlier form of knowledge. Paradoxically the Enlightenment, which had scorned rational theology as a feeble refuge from science, fostered a new respect for myth, as a genuine *alternative* to science – a pre-scientific vision of the world that revealed its own truths in its own way, touching on things that lie deep in the human psyche and which science has yet to explore. Moreover – and this was Jacob Grimm's special contribution – these ancient forms of knowledge were held to be reflected in all the products of a folk culture, most notably in language and the legacy of names. Through etymology and comparative linguistics we can trace the thinking of a people back to its original form, as a primordial attempt to give meaning to experience. The old religion emerges from Grimm's account as the first attempt by the Teutonic people to become conscious of their world. It records the momentous transition from unconscious nature to conscious reflection, and in its many strata lie buried the ordeals and triumphs of a human community as it strove to make a place for itself in a hostile world.

As a young man Wagner had been caught up in the romantic nationalism of the 'Young Germany' movement, which combined revolutionary politics with an idealization of German culture, and which aimed to unite the German lands under a single democratic government.[7] The most important effect of this movement on Wagner's art was to inspire his research into the remains of the pagan culture of Germany. Like Grimm he believed that he was discovering an older form of knowledge, one implanted in the unconscious memory of the Germans and preserved in their language and in the stories of dimly remembered heroes. For Wagner, therefore, the gods and goblins of the *Ring* cycle were not simply representatives of religion and its place in the human psyche. They were ancestral voices, speaking of values and aspirations that the German people had to repossess as their own, if they were to emerge as a unified nation. Wagner has this to say of the impact of Grimm's *Deutsche Mythologie*, which he discovered in 1843, while meditating the music for *Tannhäuser*:

> I was firmly in the power of its strange enchantment: even the most fragmentary legends spoke to me in a profoundly familiar tongue, and soon my entire sensibility was possessed by images suggesting ever more clearly the recapture of a long lost yet eagerly sought consciousness. There rose up in my soul a whole world of figures, which yet proved to be so unexpectedly solid and well-known from earliest days, that when I saw them clearly before me and could hear their speech I could grasp the source of the virtually tangible familiarity and certitude of their demeanour. The effect they produced upon my innermost being I can only describe as a complete rebirth . . . [8]

The exalted state of mind into which Grimm thus lifted him was to endure throughout the rest of Wagner's life.[9] And it was in this state of mind that *The Ring* was conceived.

From his often contradictory and in any case frequently mysterious sources Wagner was able, with astonishing insight and serendipity, to assemble a story that makes sense on every level of interpretation: literal, metaphorical, symbolic and mythical. And he used the raw material of Germanic myth to compose a new myth of his own. A myth, for Wagner, acquaints us with ourselves and our condition, using symbols and characters that give objective form to our inner compulsions. Myths are set in the hazy past, in a vanished world of dark forces and radiant deeds: *in illo tempore*. This obligatory 'pastness' places the myth and its characters before recorded time, and therefore in an era that is purged of history. It lifts the story out of the stream of human life, and endows it with a meaning that is timeless. Myths do not speak of what was but of what is eternally. They are magical-realist summaries of the actual world, in which the moral possibilities are personified and made flesh.

For Wagner, therefore, as for the Greeks, a myth is not a decorative fairy tale, but the elaboration of a secret, a way of both hiding and revealing mysteries that can be understood only in symbolic terms. Like the story of original sin, as told in Genesis, a myth is giving symbolic form to a permanent feature of consciousness, manifest in you and me as in all our ancestors, and presented as a single occurrence only by way of dramatizing its mysterious 'pastness'. This sense of being lost in the mists of time, barely recoverable from the great sea of forgetting, is a character of every true myth, which points always to the deep psychic residues on which the freedom and self-consciousness of the individual are built.

Wagner's works are therefore more than mere dramas: they are revelations, attempts to penetrate to the mysterious core of human existence.[10] They are not unique in this: Aeschylus and Shakespeare (to both of whom Wagner was greatly indebted) also present dramas that are shaped as religious epiphanies. But Wagner worked in another medium, which enabled him to present the conscious and individual passions of his characters simultaneously with their universal and unconscious archetypes. The orchestra does not merely accompany Wagner's singers, nor are they merely singers. The orchestra fills in the space beneath the revealed emotions with all the ancestral fears and longings of our species, irresistibly transforming these individual passions into symbols of a common destiny that can be sensed but not told. Wagner acquaints us with our lot, and makes available to an age without religious *belief* the core religious *experience* – an experience that we need, but which we also flee from, since it demands from us even more than it gives.

In order to present his drama as myth, therefore, Wagner recognized that he must respect those moments of unconscious knowledge that shine in the darkness of the old Teutonic poems. The point of lifting these moments from the myths was not to explain them, but to bring them to life, to convey their untranslatable spiritual meaning, and to incorporate them into a drama in which character and action take on a believable and engaging form.

The influence of Grimm was not confined to the theory of myth. Wagner took seriously the view that the stories are inextricably bound up with the original forms of language. 'If we look closely at the evolutionary history of (modern) languages,' he wrote, 'we meet in their so-called word-roots a rudiment that plainly shows us how at the first beginning the formation of the mental concept of an object ran almost completely parallel with the subjective feeling of it.'[11] Early language must therefore have resembled song, and in the 'Weia! Waga!' of the Rhine-daughters that opens the *Ring* cycle Wagner presents a compelling image of this primordial musical babble: the lullaby that precedes the great awakening that the Rhine-daughters fail to prevent. Grimm's scholarship, which unearthed a common cognitive bequest in the shared roots of Indo-European words, profoundly influenced Wagner. By returning language to its roots, he thought, we purify our vision, discover the world as it appeared to our forebears, when the corruptions of civilization had not rubbed away its clear emotional contours.

It is in this connection that we should view one of the most remarkable features of the poem of *The Ring*, which is Wagner's return to the alliterative verse forms used by the pre-Christian poets of the Teutonic peoples. We know these forms from the Anglo-Saxon as well as the Icelandic literature, and they convey to modern readers a sense of the stark and cheerless realities that formed the background to daily life, in those days when a ship on the horizon so often meant death. In his *Eddic Songs of the Nibelungs*, published in 1837, Ludwig Ettmüller had already tried to reproduce the old verse forms in translating from the Norse originals, and it was from Ettmüller that Wagner borrowed the metrical and alliterative devices of his own dramatic poem, having first discussed the matter with Ettmüller in Zurich in 1849. To use alliterative verse – *Stabreim* – in operatic dialogue was, however, a remarkable innovation, even without the difficulties posed by the form itself, since it demanded a new relation between words and music, and a new way of shaping the melodic line. The result was, for all the occasional clumsiness and the overuse of superlatives, a triumph of characterization, and a poetry that contributes immeasurably to the primordial atmosphere of the events on stage.

The emphasis on consonant rather than vowel (as distinct from Italian opera) suits the harsh realities of a world in which suspicion is so often the first move in an encounter.[12] And it results in verse that is immediately intelligible when sung, however complex the subject matter. End-rhymes require metrical regularity, in order to prepare the place where the rhyme is to fall. Not so *Stabreim*, in which metre is left comparatively free by the rhyming consonants, and in which the number of accented syllables per line can vary without destroying the rhyme. The verse can therefore move as the music moves, the result being sometimes described (borrowing Wagner's own words in *Opera and Drama*) as 'musical prose'. The music therefore leaves behind the 'periodic' structure of the Italian aria and builds the melodic line from irregular feet and shifting stresses.[13]

I mention this point now since it should be understood how complete was Wagner's immersion in the current of ideas launched by Herder and brought to their creative climax by Jacob and Wilhelm Grimm. Wagner had been granted a vision of the time before time, of the primordial story of the human race, and of the layer upon layer of pre-conscious realities from which we frail beings have grown. The little German prefix 'Ur', signifying an origin before origins, a pre-human archaeology of all that we are, had a special meaning for Wagner. He had understood that, even in the most stark and individualized religion, there are gods before gods. No god represents more than one stage in the journey of consciousness towards the final knowledge that we are here on earth without an explanation and that if there is meaning, we ourselves must supply it. Hence the archaic verse of the *Ring* cycle is itself a symbol both of that time before time, when things lie dormant in their essences, and the time after time, when the bleak truth is known.

There is one further point to add to that observation. In Wagner's remarkable mind the scientific and the poetic outlooks converged. There have been few such minds in the history of civilization – Plato, certainly, Dante and, more recently, Diderot and Goethe. But it is not usual for a work of art to anticipate the results of science, or to present them in poetic form in full consciousness of what they mean. It is clear nevertheless, from Wagner's remarks about Darwin, as recorded in Cosima's diary,[14] from his emphasis, in all his theoretical writings, on the evolved nature of the human being, and from the prehistory encoded in the drama of *Die Walküre*, that Wagner had intuitively grasped what was involved in the transition from hunter-gatherer to farmer. He had recognized that our minds are shaped by adaptations that belong to an era of which we retain no consciousness. Throughout the *Ring* cycle we see human beings balanced on the edge between prehistory and time. In the music of Sieglinde's dream in *Die Walküre* Act 2 we encounter – returned to the archaeological stratum where they belong – those fears that none of us can easily explain although we all intimately know them.[15] In what follows we should bear this point in mind, since it will help us to understand some of the 'Ur' emotions and 'Ur' events in the drama. It will also remind us of how absurd are those many productions of *The Ring* that excise all reference to the natural world – the world before consciousness clamped its fetters around it.

The influence of Grimm was enormous; but Wagner also belonged to a contrasting intellectual current. In one of the first German books to become a classic of European literature, the *History of Ancient Art* (1764), Johann Joachim Winckelmann presented an image of ancient Greece that was to have a lasting influence on intellectual life in Germany. For Winckelmann and his disciple Gotthold Ephraim Lessing the art and literature of Greece presented the human condition as god-like, both part of nature and above nature in its calm acceptance of suffering. Winckelmann's classical ideal, of the free being serenely confronting his fate, influenced Goethe, and the latter's play, several times reworked, of *Iphigenia auf Tauris* (1779), became a cult work, suggesting to some a model for the new forms of German drama.[16] Such was not the attitude of Goethe himself, who was torn between the reversion to classical forms and the development of a purely German drama, as in *Faust*, a play whose leading character is neither king nor nobleman nor Greek but a seeker after knowledge in an ordinary German city. Faust's situation is bound up with the German inheritance: Christianity, university learning, the bourgeois conscience, and the ambition of the self-made man all make their presence known in this poetic *tour de force*. However, while it changed the course of German literature, *Faust* did little or nothing for the German stage. For all its great merits as poetry, it is less a drama than a sequence of lyrical tableaus, loosely assembled around a central philosophical idea.

Winckelmann never visited Greece and his knowledge of Greek art was based largely on plaster casts of Roman reproductions. His vision of Greece was dismissed by Nietzsche as wishful thinking, an Apollonian fantasy with which to disguise the roots of the tragic art in the cult of Dionysus. Nietzsche's dismissal was in turn dismissed, in a striking book published by E. S. (Eliza) Butler in 1935, entitled *The Tyranny of Greece over Germany*. Thanks to Winckelmann and Lessing, Butler argued, German art, literature and architecture had been held in thrall by a constantly reworked image of the Greek ideal. Whether an ideal of classical serenity or one of Dionysian frenzy, it was more the invention of the German imagination than a record of a real historical culture.

Butler's thesis is exaggerated, a reaction in part to the cult of physical beauty, which was being promoted, at the time when she wrote, by the Nazis, with kitsch statuary of the ideal Aryan, modelled on the Apollo Belvedere and the Venus de Milo. Nevertheless, it is undeniable that Greek art, literature and architecture helped to define the aims of German writers and artists throughout the late eighteenth and nineteenth centuries, and Wagner was open to this influence.[17] He studied the plays of Aeschylus in Droysen's edition, in which the facts of German politics were read back into the Athenian politics of Aeschylus' day, and also into the *Oresteia*, which therefore became a kind of spiritual parable for Wagner.[18] But as well as reading the tragedians as political commentators, Wagner was one of the first writers to understand Greek tragedy as a religious institution. The *Oresteia* begins from a fault in the divine scheme of things, which slowly reveals itself in the human world, bringing tragedy and fear until resolved in a new order of justice – which will prove just as flawed in the long run as the old order of revenge. In the same way the *Ring* cycle begins from a fault in Wotan's lawful government, which percolates through the world of mortals until healed by human sacrifice.

'Tragedy,' Wagner wrote, 'was the religious rite become a work of art, by side of which the traditional observance of the genuine religious temple-rite was necessarily docked of so much of its inwardness and truth that it became indeed a mere conventional and soulless ceremony, whereas its kernel lived on in the art-work.'[19] In other words the Greek tragedians set the pattern that Wagner was consciously following, of replacing a defunct religious practice with its rebirth as art – art whose ultimate meaning was to be sacramental. Wagner also saw Aeschylus's tragedies as the model for the *Gesamtkunstwerk*, the total work of art, announced in his 1849 essays on 'Art and Revolution', and 'The Art-Work of the Future'. The four-part structure of the *Ring* cycle owes much to the *Oresteia*, and Wagner's gods, while named after the Viking pantheon and situated in the enchanted world of the north, take some of their character from

Greek originals. This is especially true of Wotan and Fricka, clearly influenced by Zeus and Hera as Homer describes them.[20]

Winckelmann's advocacy of the classical ideal in the plastic arts was echoed by Lessing, in his famous study of the ancient sculpture of the suffering Laocoon. And from Lessing the obsession with Greece was inherited by Goethe and Schiller. However, when it came to literature, and drama in particular, Lessing was moved in another and opposite direction. It was largely thanks to Lessing that Shakespeare became a towering presence in German literature. Plays based on classical originals dominated the French court during the reign of Louis XIV, and out of the French theatre had come the *opera seria* of Handel and his contemporaries: noble and statuesque dramas in which the characters rarely address each other in natural language, but constantly declaim to the audience in ritornello arias or retreat into ensembles that often seem more to shield the characters from each other than to bring them into an active relation.

The break from the classical theatre began with a journal article by Lessing that appeared in 1759. Lessing praised Shakespeare's tragedies, despite their irregularities and vernacular characters, as truer to the spirit of Aristotle's *Poetics* than the courtly classicism of the French.[21] The article was immensely influential on the emerging *Sturm und Drang* movement, and in due course its effect was felt on the operatic stage. Lessing's article was followed by the magnificent translation of the Shakespeare plays by August Wilhelm von Schlegel (Karl Friedrich's brother). Thereafter Shakespeare was not merely a source of subject matter, imagery and inspiration but a model to be followed, Goethe himself leading the way in his play *Götz von Berlichingen* of 1773. In Shakespeare Germans of Wagner's generation found a theatrical art that combined realism and magic, intelligence and feeling, in ways that spoke directly to the romantic imagination.

Wagner's first performed opera, *Das Liebesverbot*, was adapted from Shakespeare's *Measure for Measure*, and Shakespeare remained throughout his life a model to be emulated and the pinnacle of dramatic art. As we know from Cosima's diary, he esteemed Shakespeare not merely as a consummate dramatist, but as a writer who tried to capture the ideal in the real. The great spiritual task that he entrusted to Brünnhilde – the task of representing feminine purity in a world spoiled by the lust for power – had already been given, Wagner knew, to Cordelia. Wagner searched for a new conception of opera, which would enable it to be as true to the world of modern people as Shakespeare had been true to the world of the late Renaissance. He sought to rescue opera from the empty grandiosities of the Parisian stage and also from the muddled amalgam of the German *Singspiel*, and therefore set about developing a new theory of operatic dialogue. The result was *Opera and Drama*, 1851, in which he presented the aspirations that were to guide him through his future compositions and eventually lead to the construction of Bayreuth. I return to this aspect of Wagner's mission below.

The remark about tragedy that I quoted above reveals Wagner's deep concern throughout his creative life with the nature of religion. The core religious phenomenon, Wagner believed, is not the idea of God, but the sense of the sacred. The great Wagnerian music dramas are built around that belief. Although Wagner accepted Feuerbach's view of the gods, as illusions born of our social needs, he believed in the sacred as an independent force in human affairs. In an essay on 'Art and Religion', 1880, Wagner tells his reader that 'It is reserved to art to salvage the kernel of religion, inasmuch as the mythical images which religion would wish to be believed as true are apprehended in art for their symbolic value, and through ideal representation of those symbols art reveals the concealed deep truth within them.'[22] In other words, religion contains deep truths about the human psyche; but these truths become conscious only in art, which captures them in symbols. Religion conceals its legacy of truth within a doctrine. Art reveals that truth through symbols, as in a tragedy, in which the sacred event is enacted before our eyes.

In all of Wagner's music dramas sacred moments are therefore framed and displayed in their full human significance. They are moments of sacrifice, like the deaths of Tristan, Isolde and Siegmund, like the ritualized murder of Siegfried and the immolation of Brünnhilde. And a vindication of the human is somehow figured in these moments. In the unity of love and death, in the willing acceptance of death for love's sake, and in the renunciation of self for other we glimpse the meaning of human life. We understand that life lived in a spirit of sacrifice is worthwhile despite the enormous cost of it.

In one sense, this is not far from Feuerbach's materialism, since it presents the sacred as a purely human phenomenon, one that might be looked upon by a god with envy and awe, as in *The Ring*, but which needs no god to complete it. But it is also a long way from Feuerbach, since it takes the sacred, the spiritual and the sacrificial as fundamental aspects of the human condition, and necessary to our fulfilment. Like Hegel, who had seen religion as a stage on the way to self-knowledge rather than the final goal of it, Wagner sees his art as expressing and completing our religious emotions. Art shows the believable moral realities behind the unbelievable metaphysics. Hence *Tristan und Isolde* and *Parsifal* are often described as religious works, to be compared in this respect to Bach's *St Matthew Passion*.

Wagner was to the end of his life a philosophical thinker, whose ideas, expressed with hectic impetuosity in his letters and prose writings, were delivered with a concentrated steadiness in his works of art. All the currents of philosophical thinking that were important in his day, from Fichte's notion of the self to the Young Hegelian critique of the capitalist economy, and from Feuerbach's repudiation of religion to Schopenhauer's theory of the will, left traces in his dramas. There are surely few works of philosophy that delve so deeply into the paradoxes of erotic love as *Tristan und Isolde*, few works of Christian theology that match Wagner's exploration of the Eucharist in *Parsifal*, and few works of political theory that uncover the place of power and law in the human psyche with the perceptiveness of *The Ring*. While taking us into the heart of philosophical concerns, however, Wagner never sacrifices concrete emotion to abstract ideas, and in considering all those influences it is important to remember that they are not what the works themselves are about: the true subject matter of a Wagner opera is always the drama and the characters whom it puts to the test.

During the course of writing *Tristan* (1859) Wagner fell under the spell of Schopenhauer, the last great representative of post-Kantian idealism. Schopenhauer's philosophy fitted the contours of the Wagnerian music dramas, and in particular gave an articulate justification of what, to many people, was their pessimistic message. Taking over Kant's distinction between appearance and thing-in-itself, Schopenhauer identified appearances as 'representations' (*Vorstellungen*), which are subjective states, ordered by the concepts of space, time and causality. Every argument and every experience leads only to the same end: the system of representations, standing like a veil between the subject and noumenal reality. No scientific investigation can penetrate the veil; and yet it is only a veil, a tissue of illusions that we can, if we choose, penetrate by another means. This is what the Hindu writers have in mind when they refer to the 'veil of Maya': so Schopenhauer argues in his magnum opus, *The World as Will and Representation* (1818/1819, vol. 2 1844).

In our own case, according to Schopenhauer, we have only to look inwards to encounter the reality behind the veil of appearance. 'We ourselves are the thing-in-itself,' Schopenhauer wrote. 'Consequently, a way from within stands open to us to that real inner nature of things to which we cannot penetrate *from without*.' Hence we discover that the thing-in-itself is will, the endlessly restless, yearning, unsatisfied and disruptive tumult within, which we know without concepts, and which has no place in the empirical world. Existence is a mistake, a way in which the will is trapped in the spatio-temporal framework, longing to escape, endlessly wrestling with its prison of flesh. The only solution to the torment of existence is renunciation – the setting aside of the will.

Exactly what renunciation is and how it is achieved were questions that Schopenhauer addressed at length, arguing that the solution to our predicament is neither suicide (which is just another surrender to the will) nor religious resignation, but a stepping away from the tumult of life, as we step away through art, to become 'pure subjects of knowing'. Art offers us 'the Sabbath of the penal servitude of willing'. In aesthetic experience 'the wheel of Ixion stands still'. (Ixion, punished by Zeus for a variety of transgressions, was bound to a flaming wheel, which spins through the heavens and the underworld for all eternity. Only when Orpheus played his lyre, during his trip to the underworld in search of his dead wife, Eurydice, did the wheel briefly come to rest.) And this is a premonition of that higher abdication of the will, in which we stand back from the world of representation entirely, and recognize the whole thing as a mistake – though a mistake made by no one in particular, since being a person in particular is what the mistake amounts to.

Schopenhauer raises questions that are of the first importance to the understanding of Wagner's cycle, not least the question of music itself – what it means and how – to which I return below. He astutely recognized that idealism, which identifies the self as subjectivity, raises a deep problem of identity – what makes me the individual that I am? Only in space and time can a principle of individuation be defined; hence it is only as object, and never as subject, that I have an identity. But in the nature of the case that identity is fleeting, without permanent foundation, destined to be reabsorbed into the oceanic will that comprehends us all. How, then, can I be the free individual that I am in the moment when I renounce my empirical existence, as Isolde and Brünnhilde renounce it, for the sake of love? This metaphysical conundrum underlies the drama of *Tristan und Isolde* and is also central to a full understanding of *The Ring*.

It is clear, therefore, that Schopenhauer's vision is of deep relevance to the later parts of the *Ring* cycle. However, we should remember that the cycle was conceived, as was *Die Meistersinger*, much earlier, at a time when Hegel and the Young Hegelians were setting the agenda of German philosophy. During the 1849 revolution in Dresden, when Wagner was appointed by the revolutionary faction to keep watch from the Frauenkirche, he was discovered at his post deeply immersed in Hegel's *Phenomenology of Spirit*. *The Ring* itself is a post-Hegelian, rather than a Schopenhauerian, work. In the descent into Nibelheim, Wagner gives us an image of industrial production that stems directly from the Young Hegelian critiques of the new capitalist economy. In the character of Wotan he presents a brilliant summary of the vision underlying Fichte's political philosophy. And although Wotan eventually follows the path marked out by Schopenhauer, so as to renounce the will, he is to the end a robust individual, clinging to the identity that is conferred by his real presence in the empirical world.[23] Likewise, in the drama of Siegfried and Brünnhilde Wagner unfolds an epitome of the idealist philosophy of self-knowledge, and one that transforms Brünnhilde's final act of suttee into an affirmation rather than a denial of the will.

This brings me to what many see as the most important aspect of the context in which *The Ring* was created: the revolutionary politics that culminated in the Dresden revolution of 1849. As I mentioned earlier, Wagner had, in his youth, been part of the Young Germany movement, and a disciple of its leading figure, the radical young jour-nalist Heinrich Laube (1806–84). Young Germany aimed to unite the German princedoms under a national and democratic form of gov-ernment, and saw cultural innovation and revolutionary politics as two sides of a coin. It was also entwined, during the 1840s, with the Young Hegelian philosophy, so that for leftist thinkers of Wagner's generation nationalism, revolutionary socialism and the Hegelian dialectic were all absorbed into a single image of progress.

It is not certain that Wagner read the works of Marx; but at the time the composer was absorbing Feuerbach's philosophy Marx was adapting it to the critique of capitalism. In the manuscripts written in 1844 and not published until a century later Marx reworked Feuer-bach's theory of religion to produce a philosophical condemnation of private property, arguing that man objectifies his will in property, endowing a mere object with his own subjectivity and thereby losing what is most precious to him, which is the freedom and integrity of the self. Property holds sway over human beings, by virtue of the power that it has appropriated from their own activity. In property, therefore, man endows objects with a human soul and becomes a mere object to himself. He is 'restored to himself' only by overcoming the institution of ownership, so that his relations with others are no longer mediated by the alienating world of things. Man returns from 'object' to 'subject' by rejoining at a higher, more self-conscious level the 'species-being' from which his ownership had sundered him.

That way of thinking, which has had a long subsequent history, can be discerned too in Wagner's portrait of Nibelheim, and in the story of the gold of the Rhine. And, like Marx, Wagner believed in the possibility of a revolutionary emancipation, that would free soci-ety from the grip of private ownership and put the free being in place of the captive slave. The most interesting aspect of Wagner's spiritual development is that the work of art in which he set out to express that idea matured into a conscious rejection of it.

The 1848 revolutions, which began in France, ending the July Mon-archy and bringing Louis Napoleon to power, were both nationalist and democratic. By the standards of the French or Russian revolutions they were fairly placid affairs – beginning, in their German manifest-ation, in Frankfurt, with a call for a constitutional monarchy to rule over a united German nation. An Assembly of the German states was put together by means of near-democratic elections, a constitution was adopted and in 1849 Friedrich Wilhelm IV of Prussia was offered the crown of a new and united Germany.

Friedrich Wilhelm declined the offer, recognizing that the Assembly did not have the endorsement of the many sovereigns whom it had by-passed and whose privileges he would effectively confiscate. The response of King Frederick Augustus of Saxony, where Wagner was Royal Saxon Court Conductor, was particularly severe. The King dissolved the Saxon assembly in the capital city of Dresden and, in the face of popular opposition, called on Prussian troops to enforce his will. Despite support from the city council, the 3000 or so revolutionaries, who had formed a provisional government, were no match for the 5000 disciplined troops from Saxony and Prussia, and the revolution collapsed.

Wagner had taken an active part in those events, writing in a revolutionary journal, the *Volksblätter*, passionate articles inciting people to revolt, making hand grenades and standing as a lookout at the top of the Frauenkirche. He was forced to flee and his friend and ally, the music director August Röckel, editor of the *Volksblätter*, was captured and imprisoned, his death sentence subsequently commuted to life imprisonment, of which he served thirteen years. Prominent in these events was the peripatetic Russian anarchist Mikhail Bakunin, whom George Bernard Shaw took to be the model for Siegfried – the artist hero who was to overthrow the old order of things and install a new realm of freedom.[24]

Whatever we think of Shaw's interpretation – I shall have more to say about it later – there is a deeper reason for seeing *The Ring* in the context of the 1849 events. Wagner's thinking at the time had been shaped by Feuerbach. He responded with heartfelt sympathy to the condition of the poor; he had a deep antipathy to the workings of industrial capitalism, and he half accepted Feuerbach's vision of a new political order, in which human beings would be liberated by scientific knowledge from the enslavement imposed by the old religion and the old forms of political authority.

Feuerbach inherited from Hegelian philosophy two critical ideas: first the idea of freedom, as a condition to be won through conflict and mutual recognition, and second the idea of history as the evolution of consciousness, and the steady overcoming of partial and illusory ways of seeing the world. And he attempted to incorporate the challenge posed by those positions into a fundamentally optimistic vision of the human future. Indeed Feuerbach was a future-fetishist, who presented a theory of religion, politics, art and philosophy in which all point towards the future realm of freedom and perfection. In that future realm our inherited illusions would finally dissolve, and the world would be seen and embraced for what it is. All this is spelled out in his *Principles for the Philosophy of the Future*, published in 1843. Feuerbach's book was the object of assiduous study by Wagner, who adapted, plagiarized and amplified its arguments in *The Art-Work of the Future* and *Art and Revolution*, both published in Dresden in 1849. It can fairly be said that when Wagner composed the poem of *Siegfrieds Tod*, his initial libretto for what was eventually to become the *Ring* cycle, he was a Feuerbachian, who saw the task of the artist as complementing that of the political revolutionary.[25]

The systematic way in which the characters and symbols of the tetralogy can be aligned with the themes and doctrines of Feuerbach's naively optimistic philosophy suggests that Wagner was indeed heavily indebted not only to Feuerbach but to the whole political vision of which Feuerbach was so lively an exponent. Many commentators have pointed out that Wagner's subsequent studies caused him to switch from Feuerbach's optimism to the pessimism of Schopenhauer, and that this switch is recorded in the printed poem of *The Ring*, which has two endings. The original ending, written when Wagner was still in thrall to Feuerbach, shows Brünnhilde announcing that the rule of the gods will give way to a human society of love. The more mystical, Schopenhauerian ending, has her declaring that she is 'redeemed from incarnation' and 'saw the world end'. In setting the poem to music, however, Wagner produced a third ending, reverting to the original, but leaving out the reference to a future society of love. In one of his best-known and most beautiful letters (to Röckel, 23 August 1856) Wagner wrote that 'while, as an artist, my intuitions had such compelling certainty that all my creations were moulded thereby, as a philosopher I was attempting to construct an entirely contrary explanation of the universe, an explanation which, though stoutly upheld, was always being dismissed out of hand by my instinctive, objective artistic perceptions, much to my own astonishment'. In effect, the third ending of *The Ring* rescues the work from philosophy – both the philosophy of Feuerbach and that of Schopenhauer which came to replace it – and hands the conclusion back to Wagner's 'instinctive, objective artistic perception'. The third, eviscerated version of the poem depends on the music to convey Brünnhilde's real meaning, and, as to what that meaning is, no commentator seems to be in entire agreement with any other. One thing is certain, however, which is that, musically speaking, the cycle ends in a spirit of resigned acceptance rather than visionary hope, and that the renunciatory outlook of the completed cycle is one to which Wagner was brought by his own artistic intuition, and not by philosophy. To put the matter simply, his admiration for Schopenhauer was the effect, not the cause, of the worldview to which he had been led by his art.

We should recognize, nevertheless, the debt that Wagner owed to the political thinking of writers like Feuerbach. At the time when Feuerbach produced his materialist version of the Hegelian view of history the industrial revolution was changing people's understanding of the social world. The 'labour theory of value', implicit in Adam Smith and made explicit by David Ricardo, presented labour as the source of economic value, the prime mover of the market and the part of man's nature that is inherently priced. By harnessing labour we replace the old relation between nature and need with the new relation between man and his products. The translation of use into exchange, of nature into commodities, of personal relations into the disguises assumed by human power – all these changes that mystify the world, placing a veil between human beings and their fulfilment, and surrounding them with the will-o'-the-wisps engendered by their own malleable appetites, had their origin in the trick, the deception, the 'forging' that had given one man the power to extract labour from another. To Feuerbach's contemporaries – to Wagner and Marx especially – Hegelianism promised a key to the greatest of mysteries, the mystery of our fall from nature into industrial enslavement. Labour, interest, accumulation, the sudden malleability and exchangeability of all that humans want and need and value – thinkers of Feuerbach's generation felt that they were on the verge of understanding these strange and alarming transformations.

Marx sought for the key in the science of political economy, since science, he believed, was the only real source of knowledge. Science, for Marx, would solve our mysteries by dissolving them – showing them to be ideological illusions. Wagner sought for the key in art, knowing, in his wisdom, that the real mysteries are those that must be repeated, since they cannot be solved. By repeating them in art, with their dramatic meaning amplified through their links to the other mysteries that trouble us, we do not dismiss them as illusions, but allow them to speak to us, to show us their inner truth. The 'forgery' that Marx exposes in his theory of ideology, becomes the 'forging' that Wagner discovers at the heart of all that we are.

There is one last aspect of Wagner's cultural and historical context that needs to be understood by the devotee of the *Ring* cycle, and that is the emergence of aesthetics as an intellectual discipline. Kant's *Critique of Judgement* had made the aesthetic experience central to the life of the mind, and also developed a conception of art that was to exert, through Schiller and Schelling, a far-reaching influence over philosophers, poets, painters and composers during the first decades of the nineteenth century. According to Kant there are two forms of aesthetic judgement. Taste, the aesthetic sense, can be awakened by the beautiful and by the sublime, and these represent two contrasting human interests. The sublime surpasses humanity in some way, awakening us to the fragility of our condition and challenging us to display our freedom in the face of it. The idea of the sublime, which Wagner identified in Greek tragedy, could not be realized merely by following rules or applying well-tried formulae. Always the artist must exercise the faculty that Kant called genius, which does not follow rules but invents them. Hence every true work of art is a departure from the natural order. Paradoxically, however, it can succeed as art only if it appears to be wholly natural, governed by an internal order that creates unity and harmony among its parts. Genius is the faculty through which 'nature gives a rule to art' – in other words, through which the original and rule-denying character of art is made to appear natural and rule-guided.

There was another suggestion that Kant made in his great work on aesthetics, and which was to have just as far-reaching an influence as his theories of genius and the sublime. This was the suggestion that there is a unique form of knowledge contained in, and obtained from, art, though a knowledge that cannot be expressed in words. A great poem presents its subject matter with a completeness that is never given in ordinary experience. Art deals in 'aesthetic Ideas', which penetrate the empirical veil to the transcendental core of things, so as to present, in sensory form, the wholeness and unity that cannot be grasped by the intellect.

Those suggestive theories inspired the attempt by Schiller, Schelling, Tieck and others to assign a kind of redemptive role to the arts. The sense of wholeness and harmony that had disappeared with the loss of the religious worldview can be recuperated, the idealists thought, through art, which presents our emotions and projects as they would be, could they achieve the completion and integrity to which they aspire. Hence the idealists connected aesthetic experience with the secret meaning of things, with the infinite, the absolute, the transcendental, the ineffable. Such we find in the writings of Schelling, Fichte, Hegel and Schopenhauer, the last of whom not only singled out art as a reliable respite from the 'wheel of Ixion', but also gave the highest place in the aesthetic pantheon to music. Music, Schopenhauer wrote, is not unconscious arithmetic, as Leibniz had claimed, but unconscious philosophy, since in music the inner essence of the world, which is will, is made directly present to the mind.

In Schelling, Hegel and Schopenhauer we also encounter a growing recognition that the subject–object relation explored by philosophical idealism has something to do with the power of music. They wrote at a time when music was coming newly into the cultural foreground with the Beethoven cult, with the rise in Germany of academic musicology and with the theory, which was later to dominate musical thinking, that 'absolute' music – music without a text or an explicit subject matter – is the true paradigm of the art. For E. T. A. Hoffmann (himself strongly influenced by Schelling and, through his fantastic tales, an indelible presence in the culture of Wagner's Germany) Beethoven's music unfolds a 'spirit realm', in which the subject is gripped by an infinite yearning.[26] For Hegel music claims as its own 'the depth of a person's inner life as such: it is the art of the soul and is directly addressed to the soul'. The chief task of music, he writes, 'consists in making resound, not the objective world itself, but, on the contrary, the manner in which the inmost self is moved to the depths of its personality and conscious soul'.[27]

Schopenhauer's importance for Wagner did not derive only from his intriguing metaphysics and his ethic of renunciation. Schopenhauer was the only post-Kantian who regarded music as a test-case for his philosophy, and his theories confirmed Wagner's conception of a drama that would unfold entirely through the inner feelings of the characters. These feelings, hinted at in words, would acquire their full reality and elaboration in music. Developing under its own intrinsic momentum, the music would guide the listener through subjective regions that were otherwise inaccessible to the outside observer, creating a drama of inner emotion framed by only the sparsest gestures on the stage – gestures which, for this very reason, would become so saturated with meaning as to reach the limits of their expressive power.

Unlike poetry or figurative painting, music employs no concepts, and presents no narrative of an imaginary world. Its meaning is contained within itself, inseparable from the ebb and flow of its abstract lines and harmonies. Yet listening to a great work of music we feel that we are gaining insight into the deepest mysteries of being – although an insight that lives in the music, and defies translation into words. Schopenhauer's theory offers both to explain and to vindicate this feeling, and at the same time to exalt music to a metaphysical position matched by no other art form. Music, Schopenhauer tells us, 'is the most powerful of all the arts, and therefore attains its ends entirely from its own resources'.[28]

Simply put, Schopenhauer's theory tells us that music acquaints us with the will, which is the Kantian 'thing-in-itself', the indescribable reality behind the veil of human perception, whose operations we know through our own self-awareness. The will cannot be known through concepts, since they provide us merely with representations, and never with the thing-in-itself. Our inner knowledge of the will is therefore non-conceptual, a direct and unsayable access to the metaphysical essence. This non-conceptual knowledge is offered also by music. Painting and poetry are narrative arts, which present the world of representation in the form of Ideas – the Platonic universals which are 'objectifications' of the will. Music, by contrast, exhibits the will directly. And this explains its power: for it also *acts* on the will directly, raising and altering the passions without the intermediary of conceptual thought. Through consonance and dissonance music shows, in objective form, the will as satisfied and obstructed; melodies offer the 'copy of the origination of new desires, and then of their satisfaction';[29] suspension is 'an analogue of the satisfaction of the will which is enhanced through delay',[30] and so on. At the same time, because music is a non-conceptual art, it does not provide the objects of our passions but instead shows the inner working of the will itself, released from the prison of appearances. In opera and song the words and action provide the subject matter of emotion; but the emotion itself is generated in the music. And 'in opera, music shows its heterogeneous nature and its superior intrinsic virtue by its complete indifference to everything material in the incidents'.[31]

Schopenhauer tells us that the non-conceptual awareness that we have of our own mental states is really an awareness of the will; he also tells us that the will is objectively presented to us without concepts in the work of music. In these two statements we can 'divide through' by the will, to use Wittgenstein's metaphor:[32] reference to the will is an unwarranted addition to another and more intelligible theory, which tells us that in self-knowledge we are acquainted with *the very same thing* that we hear in music. To put it in another way: music presents subjective awareness in objective form. In responding to expressive music, we are acquiring a 'first-person' perspective on a state of mind that is not our own – indeed which exists unowned and objectified, in the imaginary realm of musical movement.[33] In T. S. Eliot's suggestive words: ' . . . you are the music / While the music lasts'.[34]

So understood, Schopenhauer's argument can be detached from his metaphysics of the will, and reinterpreted as presenting the innate *subjectivity* of music. Music invites the listener to adopt its own subjective point of view, through a kind of empathy that shows the world from a perspective that is no one's and therefore everyone's. All this is true of music in part because it is an abstract, non-representational art, in part because it avails itself of temporal organization in a non-physical space.

Wagner likewise thought of music as an expression of the inner life, uniquely able to reach the otherwise ineffable motives from which our actions ultimately spring. Music is not just a language of the emotions but a forum in which emotional tensions could be put in play so as to work towards their resolution and quietus. Music is therefore both the expression and the fulfilment of our deepest longings. And Wagner followed the Beethoven cult in thinking that it is the purification of music by its purely instrumental use that has freed it to make a special contribution to the self-understanding of humanity. As he put the matter in his 1860 essay 'Zukunftsmusik' ('Music of the Future'), 'Beethoven matured the symphonic artwork to so engrossing a breadth of form, and filled that form with so manifold and enthralling a melodic content, that we stand today before the Beethovenian symphony as before the landmark of an entirely new period in the history of universal Art; for through it there came into the world a phenomenon not even remotely approached by anything the art of any age or any people has to show us.'[35]

It is in the context of that conception of music that we should see Wagner's adventurous claims on behalf of opera. *The Art-Work of the Future* (1849) already announces a new art-form, the *Gesamtkunstwerk*, in which all the resources of the arts – poetry, music, architecture, drama – will be combined in a unified presentation of a single intuitive idea, from which no parts may be sundered without losing their meaning. The suggestion is continued in *Opera and Drama*, 1851, which argues that opera has yet to attain the status of an art in its own right, being a muddled concoction out of music, drama and verse in which the action is constantly interrupted for the sake of some aria or ballet which forms no organic part of the whole. The role of music, Wagner argued, needs to be completely rethought, as does the nature of operatic dialogue and the versification that would permit the music to convey the deep subjective truths that are being symbolized in the drama.

This complete regeneration of opera, as an art-form in its own right, was now possible, Wagner argued, thanks to the revolution conducted by Beethoven. By purifying itself from the original encrustation of song and dance, music had conquered its own realm of expression. But, having taken its potential as an abstract art to the limits, it once again reaches out for language, not so as to accompany words in the manner of a song, but so as *itself* to 'burst into song', to find in words the answer to the 'why?' that it articulated in a way that had never been manifest before.[36] Words are no longer present at the beginning of music but emerge at the end of it, erupting in a new way from the demands that originate in the music itself.

This beautiful idea, so difficult to express with proper clarity, is fundamental to understanding the structure of *The Ring*. The poem, brilliant though it is as a piece of storytelling, is conceived in another way from traditional opera libretti. The words are not set to music: they are the foam on the musical surface, the bursting into light of the dark movements beneath them. The drama takes place in the music, which means that it exists in two distinct spheres, outer and inner, cosmic and psychic. Such, in the end, is the true meaning of *The Ring*. All that is most important in our lives occurs both outwardly in the realm of politics and law, and inwardly in the realm of love, need and resignation. And the two processes unfold in parallel, since they are ultimately one and the same.

All the influences that I have surveyed in this chapter – nationalist politics, the dawn of the new Germany, the post-Kantian theory of the self and its search for personality and freedom, the revolutionary philosophy of the Young Hegelians, the new vision of Greek tragedy and the classical ideal, the idea of myth as a form of implicit knowledge, the return to the ancient stories of the Teutonic people, the cult of Beethoven and the conception of music as an 'absolute' art-form – fed into Wagner's imagination in the white heat of his intellectual excitement during the years following 1849. Wagner was not a man to take shortcuts or to rest content with a second-hand view of the things that interested him. He was a dedicated scholar and man of letters, as well as a hard-working composer whose originality came as much through study and experiment as through the inspiration of the moment.[37] Not surprisingly, therefore, the *Gesamtkunstwerk* or 'total work of art' that was to bring all those influences together took shape only slowly, and was not completed until twenty-six years after its first conception.[38]

Wagner wrote the first plan for the drama in 1848, and then set about writing the poem of *Siegfrieds Tod*, which was to become *Götterdämmerung*, and for which he sketched the music (subsequently abandoned) in 1850. Realizing that the drama stood in need of a prologue, he wrote the poem for *The Young Siegfried*, which was to show how Siegfried had come to be singled out for his tragic fate. That poem also stood in need of an introduction, explaining the cosmic situation from which the young hero emerged, and by the time the whole thing had been thought through the poem consisted of four dramas, which Wagner referred to as a *Bühnenfestspiel* (stage festival play) over three days, with a *Vorabend* (introductory evening), in deference to the convention of the Greek tragic stage, of presenting three linked tragedies and a satyr play.

The poem was privately published in 1853, and Wagner began work on the music, composing in the order of the narrative and not, as with the poem, in the reverse order. On reaching the end of *Siegfried* Act 2 in 1857 he laid aside the score for twelve years, writing *Tristan und Isolde* and *Die Meistersinger von Nürnberg*. In those two works Wagner acquired new musical accomplishments – world-changing innovations in chromatic harmony and voice-leading and a new mastery of tonal counterpoint. Nevertheless, the material that he had assembled in the first three dramas proved perfectly adaptable to his new powers of expression, and the song of the Rhine-daughters, which leads us into the enchanted world of *Das Rheingold*, sounds in its original accents – to miraculous effect – at the end of *Götterdämmerung*.

3

The Story

Many commentators have told the story of the *Ring* cycle in their own words, sometimes at considerable length – for example, Ernest Newman in what is perhaps the most engaging example of the genre.[1] In following in their footsteps I shall anticipate the interpretation that I give in subsequent chapters, while covering as succinctly as possible all the salient turning points of the drama.

In *Tristan und Isolde* Wagner took an old story and told it as a tale of subjective emotion, in which the medieval setting is the ornamental frame around two very modern people. The opera follows the pattern set by *Tannhäuser* and *Lohengrin*, rewriting a legend as a symbolic exploration of sexual love. And thanks to the inspired music the long-drawn-out non-event on stage is experienced as a tumultuous inner calamity.

The Ring was conceived in quite another way. Although Wagner had a deep admiration for the old texts that inspired him, he recognized that they did not provide a unified narrative or a consistent theology. But he was intrigued by their intense moments of symbolism, in which some supremely important human experience finds outward form. He also admired the attempt, constantly renewed but always abandoned, to place these human moments in a cosmic perspective. I have remarked upon the serendipity with which Wagner found tension, meaning and climax in the ancient poems. But he had to invent the story as a whole for himself. At the same time he wanted his drama to have the mysteriousness and necessity of myth. The *Ring* cycle was to symbolize and reveal the deep spiritual truths that were once the property of religion but which art alone, he believed, can now communicate.

In Greek tragedy the human is placed side by side with the divine. The tragic heroes take their place in myths that spring from the communal religion, and the tragedy itself often has the aspect of a religious ritual, in which a victim is brought forth and sacrificed. This fact was noticed by Wagner, in *The Art-Work of the Future*, and later elaborated by Nietzsche in *The Birth of Tragedy*, a book written in response to *Tristan und Isolde*. Wagner composed the poem of the *Ring* cycle with Aeschylus in mind, and was therefore aware of the great difference between his projected work and the *Oresteia*. The Greek tragedian was setting his drama in the context of a shared public religion; but Wagner was treating religion as Feuerbach had treated it: as an elaborate fiction. The religion of the *Ring* cycle is the work of an anthropologist, not a priest. Wagner's gods are personified features of human psychology, and symbols of our spiritual need. In responding to them, we are, according to Wagner's conception, responding to what is deep in ourselves.

Moreover, the *Ring* cycle, as originally conceived, was to tell the story of man's *release* from religion and from thraldom to his own illusions. Siegfried, in destroying the rule of the gods, realizes himself as a free individual. And from this gesture the society of the future is born. Such, at least, was the Feuerbachian conception at the back of Wagner's mind when he first envisaged the story. The cycle was to evoke the old world of the German gods, and at the same time tell the story of modern life and its culmination. It would point the Germans simultaneously towards their noble past and their yet more noble future, in which a just society was to emerge from the destruction of the illusions that have shaped their language, their customs and their gods.

Already, in writing the poem, however, Wagner's feelings were moving in another direction. He was beginning to perceive the psychological and political reality beneath the veneer painted over it by Feuerbach's shallow optimism. Setting out to understand history as it is, and human beings as they are, Wagner could not fail to perceive that the socialist dreams were every bit as illusory as the religion they had set out to replace. In telling the story of the gods and their doom, therefore, Wagner found himself telling the deeper story of humanity – a story that is revealed in the evolution of the human race, in the history of human society, and in the destiny of the individual soul. And this deeper story is filled with meaning not so much by the words as by the music – music of an extraordinary originality and power, which tells us at every moment that what is happening on the stage before our eyes also happens in each of us, in psychic regions that are being explored and made known to us with an immediacy that mere words could never accomplish.

DAS RHEINGOLD

Described as the 'prelude' to a trilogy, *Das Rheingold* tells how Wotan's attempt to rule the world comes to depend upon Alberich's theft of the Rhinegold. The events of *Das Rheingold* are presented as occurring long after Wotan's original assumption of government. However, in mythical time, there is no true before or after and all is eternally present. In tracing things to a beginning we are exploring what is first in essence, not what is first in time. So it is with *Das Rheingold*. What we are shown in the opening of this opera is the emergence of the moral order. Each mythical beginning is a recurrence, always repeated, and always already there. This we understand from the music, and in particular from the extraordinary prelude with which *Das Rheingold* begins.

The tonal triad, the three-note chord that is the root of traditional harmony, here represents the natural order from which all that is and will be must emerge. The triad of E flat sounds throughout the three minutes of the prelude; but within the stationary harmony the voices move in counterpoint: nature is at rest, but also endlessly changing and endlessly expecting.

There are two families of nature motifs in *The Ring*: those, like the opening theme of the prelude (1), which spell out the triad, the source of natural harmony, and those derived from the pentatonic scale, which is the source of natural melody.* Thus, when the curtain rises to show the three Rhine-daughters playing in the waters of the Rhine,

---

* I have listed all the candidates for 'leitmotif' status that I have been able to identify in the Appendix, together with a few comments concerning their meaning and connectedness.

Woglinde is singing her lullaby of endearing nonsense to a pentatonic tune (4). Her sister Wellgunde interrupts with the question 'Are you keeping watch alone?' – for these playful creatures have been entrusted with a serious task and something important is at risk from their carefree manner.

The free-flowing radiant music is invaded by a stumbling motion in the depths. From a cleft in the riverbed emerges the dwarf Alberich, the Nibelung of the tetralogy's title, who lives in the dark underworld (Nibelheim) beneath the surface of the earth. Setting eyes on the nymphs, Alberich is seized by desire. Woglinde and Wellgunde exclaim at his ugliness, while Flosshilde, the most responsible of the three, urges them to protect the gold, adding 'Father warned us of such an enemy.' Nowhere else in the cycle is this father referred to. Presumably he is the Rhine, one of the demi-gods who, like Erda, Loge and the Norns, belong to the eternal order that precedes the reign of the gods. He is also elemental, standing to water as Erda to earth, Loge to fire and – perhaps – the gods to the air in which they reside (as the Icelandic Aesir).

The Rhine-daughters mock Alberich, whose lustful attentions flit between them in a manner that is almost as insulting as their taunts. The cruellest of these taunts (8) is shaped around a chord that will be reassembled later in Alberich's fearful curse on the Ring (45). The nymphs are evidently used to erotic games and are later condemned by the strait-laced Fricka, wife of Wotan, for their wanton habits. By playing such a game with Alberich they generate a slow crescendo of humiliation. At last, with a cry of 'Wehe! Ach Wehe! O Schmerz!', introducing the falling semitone that is henceforth to be his signature, Alberich gives vent to his deep distress (9). Taunted again by the suggestion that he has only to lay hold of one of the nymphs and she will be his (10) he announces that one of them *must* yield to him, and scrambles after them intent on rape, until stumbling with exhaustion, shaking his fist and crying 'Fing' eine diese Faust . . . ' – if this fist could catch one! (11)

It is at this moment that the rising sun, shining through the upper waters of the Rhine, causes a golden light to glow in the depths, the light of the Rhinegold. The motif of the Rhinegold (13), a major arpeggio belonging to the broad family of nature motifs, sounds on the horn, and the nymphs sing their two-chord chant in praise of the gold – a descending whole tone buoyed up by a luscious ninth chord (14). This chant will later undergo a remarkable change, as praise turns to hatred and revenge. But in its initial occurrence the leitmotif has a wonderful radiance, presenting the gold of the Rhine as a source of light, life and joy. In the Prose Edda the watery domains of the sea-giant Aegir are lit by gold, and gold is described by Icelandic poets as 'the fire of rivers'.[2] It is the mark of royalty, the aim of alchemy, the substance of treasure, the proof against corruption and the shield of the dead. It is the measure of all things worth less than their weight in it. To love gold without wanting to possess it is, in a sense, a mark of the highest bliss, and it is this bliss that is expressed in the radiant cry of the Rhine-daughters.

Alberich asks what it is that glistens and the nymphs, shocked at his ignorance of their treasure, mockingly invite him to swim and sport around it. He asks if the gold has a use that *he* could enjoy. Woglinde and Wellgunde tell him that the one who could fashion a ring from the gold would have unmeasured might; Flosshilde rebukes them for revealing their secret, but they scornfully remind her, to the music traditionally (but wrongly) known as the renunciation motif (17), that the Ring can be forged only by one who forswears love. (I explore the real meaning of this motif in the next chapter.) In their eyes a randy being like Alberich could never forswear love – a sign that they do not distinguish love from desire. They renew their cruel mockery, but the dwarf, with sudden resolve, splashes forward, seizes the gold and, in deepest need, renounces love, and also curses it (17). He then rushes away with the prize.

The audience comes away from this powerful scene with a sense that it was all fated to happen. The Rhine-daughters themselves provide the dwarf with the motive and the information that will rob them of their gold. And thanks to the theft things can move on: if Alberich had not stumbled into the river from his subterranean abode, if he had not disturbed the pristine rhythm and harmony with his syncopated and chromatic melody (7), if he had not been taunted at last into forswearing love, all would have remained in a condition of primal innocence, E flat major until the end of time. Who would want such a world?

And yet we do want it, and this fact is beautifully displayed in the music. That of the Rhine has a radiant and self-renewing beauty while that of the dwarf, with its crushed harmonies and jagged melodic lines, is constantly making angles against the musical flow. However much we deprecate the flippancy and cruelty of the Rhine-daughters, theirs is a world of enchantment and irresponsible joy. It is a place that we knew, a place of primal safety where our treasure once glowed in the amniotic twilight. The transcendently lovely music, which returns again and again in the tetralogy, never ceases to beckon from the place where it sounds. It tells of the amoral haven from which we set out, like Alberich, to forge a will and a world of our own.

The leitmotif attached to the Ring – a circular move around a keyless diminished chord (16B) – has been emerging in the orchestra, and following Alberich's theft this motif forms the substance of an interlude, in which it is magically transformed into the hymn-like theme of Valhalla (18), a theme with several parts, each capable of independent development, conveying the extent and majesty of Wotan's power. This interlude illustrates the musical chemistry that operates throughout the cycle. Motifs grow from each other, intertwine and reach across vast tracts of space and time for the phrases that continue or complete them. Only subsequently is the fact made plain that the serene promise of Valhalla depends on Alberich's theft. But by showing the one theme emerging from the other through a law-like musical process, the music implants the connection in our emotions, long before it is made explicit on the stage or in the text.

We find ourselves in a green valley, through which the Rhine flows peacefully, and above which, on a high mountain, stands the newly built castle of Valhalla. Wotan, the one-eyed sky-god, lies asleep in the grass, muttering his dream of the castle that is to bring him honour, might and fame. His wife, Fricka, awakens him to complain of the bargain that he made with the Giants, who built the castle in return for Fricka's sister, Freia, goddess of love, as their wage. Wotan scorns the idea that he will have to honour such a contract, but Fricka condemns him for his frivolous and loveless nature: had she known of the deal she would have prevented it, she says, remarking, however, that it is exactly the kind of deal that men, in their lust for power, will consent to, and the motif of the Ring (16B) sounds on cellos, as though echoing her words. But when Wotan points out that she too wanted the castle, she admits that she had longed for a fitting home, to put an end to her husband's wandering and philandering (21). Nevertheless she criticizes Wotan for placing the 'idle toys of power and dominion' above love and woman's worth – at which point we hear the motif (17) that accompanied Alberich's renunciation of love and his curse upon it.

Wotan governs the world by means of a spear, the motif of which – a descending diatonic scale played here softly on lower strings (19) – now accompanies him, as he protests that he risked an eye to woo Fricka: sure proof of the value he places on women. His wife should rest assured that he has no intention of yielding Freia to the Giants. (We later learn that the spear of government was fashioned from a branch of the World Ash Tree, and that Wotan paid for it with his missing eye: whether it is the eye he lost, or the eye he kept, that Wotan risked for Fricka is a contentious point to which I return.) Meanwhile Wotan has anxiously summoned Loge, the demi-god of fire, who had advised him to enter into the contract with the Giants, promising to find a way to wriggle out of it.

Freia now enters in flight, crying out to her brothers, Donner and Froh, for help. Her entry is accompanied by a theme from the orchestra (22) that was once known as the flight motif, but which is in fact an amalgam of two leitmotifs associated throughout the cycle with love – the first signifying love in its sensual aspect, the second love as longing and attachment. The Giants, Fasolt and Fafner, arrive with heavy steps, one brother, Fasolt, stamping forward to ask for the agreed fee. Wotan dismisses his request as pure folly, to which Fasolt replies (24) with significant words: 'Honour your treaties; what you are you are through treaties, which set limits to your power.' Wotan responds that the contract was made only in jest, which causes Fasolt to explode at the unjust privileges of the gods, who play with women and their beauty, while despising those who can obtain such things only through harsh and exacting labour.

There is a poignancy in this, as in most of Fasolt's utterances. For no amount of hard work will bring what the charmless Fasolt longs for, which is the love that he has witnessed in the enchanted world of the gods. Fafner reminds the company that Freia is not merely the goddess of love; she also tends the garden where grow the apples of eternal youth, to which idea Wagner attaches a motif of remarkable beauty (26), a variant of which is subsequently associated with Freia's brother Froh (28). Without Freia's apples the gods will lose the youth that makes immortality viable: the bargain with the Giants is one that a god could honour only by ceasing to be a god. Fafner then seizes Freia, Donner and Froh threaten violence, and Wotan thrusts his spear between the warring factions, persuaded by Fasolt's reminder that he who rules by treaties must also seem to obey them. The spear motif, sounded on four trombones, here takes on the character that is to attach to it throughout the cycle – the immovable authority of the downward moving diatonic scale, without charm or ornament, beginning nowhere in particular and also ending nowhere in particular, though never on the tonic since that would bring it to a conclusion, and Wotan's is a conclusion-less (though not inconclusive) will. The motif lays down a law that governs the space in which all this music, and therefore all this action, occurs. There follows an eloquent stroke of drama, foreshadowing much that is to come. For the first time Wotan stands by his treaties, and at once he is assailed by a plaintive woman's cry: 'Woe! Woe! Wotan abandons me!'

This lament from the lips of Freia is immediately backed up by her sister, Fricka, and we glimpse the deep conflict in Wotan's nature, between the desire for sovereignty and the need for home.

To the god's relief, Loge arrives, accompanied by a set of leitmotifs that are the first truly chromatic music we have heard (30, 31, 32), and which will later develop in subtle ways as the wily spirit of the fire-god penetrates further and further into the action. Loge evades accusations in the matter of the contract, since he undertook only to *try* to release Freia from the deal. He has searched the whole world for an acceptable substitute for woman's beauty and worth (associated here with the important motif 34), but only one being did he find who was prepared to forswear love for the sake of a substitute: the Nibelung Alberich, who had exchanged love for gold. The Rhine-daughters had pleaded with Loge to ask Wotan to bring the thief to justice, so as to return the gold to the Rhine.

During this scene Wagner presents us with one of his most original and compelling creations. Loge's melodic line runs smoothly from accent to accent like a lawyer's brief, bathing the situation in a stream of loquacious sarcasm, and foretelling already that the cosmos is moving beyond Wotan's control. In the remaining three operas Loge does not appear in personified form, but nor does he need to. His sinuous music is so brilliantly united to his artful personality that we are constantly aware hereafter of his presence in the drama. His wiles preceded Wotan's government, and were also conscripted to achieve it. Now they are flickering impatiently in anticipation of its end.

On hearing Loge's story the Giants, who have already suffered harm from the Nibelung, prick up their ears, wishing to know what value lies in the gold, and Loge tells them of the Ring that could be fashioned from it. Wotan too begins to covet the gold and Fricka, egged on by Loge, fancies that the trinkets fashioned from it would help to captivate her husband and ensure his fidelity. Too late, however, since the dwarf has already done the deed – he has renounced love and thereby been able to forge the Ring. But, adds Loge, it is now possible to obtain the Ring without paying such a heavy price – by theft. And in this way the original thief, Alberich, will be brought to justice and the gold returned to the Rhine.

Fafner suggests that the Giants would accept the Nibelung's gold as an adequate substitute for Freia. Wotan denounces the sinful idea that he should steal the gold and then give it to the Giants, though whether the sin attaches to the theft or the giving is a moot point neatly concealed by the alliterative verse. Fasolt seizes Freia and the two Giants stride away, retaining her as hostage until the evening, when they will return for the Nibelung's gold. As the fruit in Freia's garden loses its magic power, a mist invades the stage, and the gods begin to wither and weaken. Loge soliloquizes, teasing the gods in their sudden weakness. Freia, he reveals, had not shared her fruit with him, so that he could not enjoy the eternal youth bestowed on the gods. He notes how well the Giants have judged the situation, since without Freia the gods are nothing, and must therefore do whatever is needed to get her back. Fricka cries 'Wehe!' on a falling semitone, the clarinet echoing in Alberich's voice. The music winds the cosmos down in a masterly elaboration of the theme of the apples and the first part (22A) of Freia's leitmotif until at last Wotan, prompted by Fricka, starts up from his semi-coma, and commands Loge to follow him to Nibelheim.

Loge's suggestion that they pass through the Rhine is dismissed, since Wotan wishes to avoid an encounter with the Rhine-daughters. Instead they descend through the sulphurous cleft, to a stupendous musical interlude, beginning with the motif associated with the idea of woman's worth (34).* This theme is then mingled with Loge's music, Alberich's falling semitone, and the second part of Freia's love music – the part (22B) that signifies the grief and yearning which are the true price of love. This last motif sounds in augmented and diminished form, and frames the anvils of the factory where the unhappy Nibelungs are at work on the hoard. The 9/8 rhythm that accompanies their work is built into a simple smithing theme (37), which will henceforth represent the physical and mental servitude of Nibelheim, from which none of its denizens can escape, even if they make their way into the upper air.

In a subterranean cavern Alberich is dragging his brother, Mime, by the ear, commanding him in bullying tones to hand over the work that he has just completed. Mime tries to hide the newly forged Tarnhelm, but Alberich seizes it and places it on his own head, uttering the spell that causes him to disappear, to the eerie motif of *Verwandlung* or transformation (38). Invisible, he belabours Mime with blows for having wished to keep the Tarnhelm, and, reassuming his normal form, sings a blood-curdling song of triumph over the Nibelungs, who must now bow down to their invisible master. Exultant with malice, he departs from the scene.

Wotan and Loge now enter, to discover Mime nursing his bruises. Loge is known to Mime from the fire of the smithy, and he encourages the dwarf to recount his woes. Mime tells of the Nibelungs' once innocent life, destroyed by the pitiless tyranny of Alberich. Mime had made the Tarnhelm according to Alberich's instructions, hoping to use it in a bid for freedom. But he could not guess the spell with which to activate its magic. Alberich enters, driving a crowd of Nibelungs before him. He notices the visitors and orders Mime to join the

* Whether this association is right need not concern us here; but see the discussion of 34 in the Appendix.

other slaves before using the Ring to display his power. The Nibe-lungs cringe in fear as Alberich brandishes the Ring, to a leitmotif (the power of the Ring, 39) that first crams fragments of the Rhine-daughters' chorus into the falling semitone and then opens out onto a loud and strangely horrifying major chord. Like the motif of Valhalla as it emerged from that of the Ring, this theme shows Wag-ner's musical chemistry at work. We do not believe as a speculation so much as feel as a certainty, how joy in the gold has become anger and malice in the person who stole it, and also fear and annihilation in the realm that he now controls. As the motif throws itself onto that final chord it seems entirely right that the Nibelungs should rush in terror back to their work.

Alberich turns to Wotan and Loge, asking them abruptly what they want. Wotan replies that rumours of Alberich's wondrous work had reached him, and that he was eager to cast eyes on it. You were brought here by envy, says Alberich, at which Loge reminds the dwarf of all the good services he had already received from the god of fire, only to be rebuked by Alberich for his untrustworthiness.

But Alberich has the self-made man's need to talk big. He describes his ever-growing hoard and its purchasing power, and he sneers at the gods – the 'light-elves' (*Lichtalben*) – whose power he will over-come, seizing their heavenly abode and their pretty women along with it. In this sinister rant Alberich reveals that he is determined that no one else shall enjoy the thing that he has renounced. Love has been chased from his world, and hatred and exploitation put in its place – something we have already witnessed in his treatment of his brother. Wotan responds angrily to Alberich's blasphemous threats, but is restrained by Loge, who adopts the tone of the flatterer, encouraging Alberich to show his skills. How, for example, can he avoid being the victim of theft? Alberich, still talking big, shows off the Tarnhelm, turning himself first into a dragon and then, at Loge's suggestion, into a tiny toad – at which Wotan holds down the toad with his foot, Loge snatches the Tarnhelm, and the gods escape with the trussed-up dwarf towards the light, passing through the grim factory on their upward journey.

The three emerge in the realm of the gods. Loge addresses Alberich as his kinsman, and sarcastically shows him the world below, asking what bit of it the dwarf would allow to Loge as his dwelling place. Alberich bitterly agrees to surrender the hoard in exchange for his freedom, knowing that, if he keeps the Ring, he can easily make good his losses. The gods loosen his arm, so that he can summon the Nibelungs from the darkness. The dwarf holds the Ring to his lips and whispers the necessary command. He is then forced to watch in shame and humiliation as his slaves pile the treasure before him. Alberich commands the Nibelungs not to look at him, and in a sustained crescendo, the music (based on a motif, 40, associated throughout the cycle with the hoard), shows the hideously humiliated dwarf wrestling with his bonds in vain. Wotan then commands Loge to add the Tarnhelm to the pile, finally telling the dwarf that the golden ring on his finger also belongs with the treasure. 'My life, but not the Ring,' Alberich cries, to which the contemptuous riposte is 'I require the Ring; with your life do what you will.'

Alberich cries that hand and head, eye and ear, are not more his own than the Ring. Wotan responds that the gold of the Ring was stolen from the Rhine-daughters and that Alberich has never owned it. Alberich movingly summarizes the dreadful price paid for the Ring, which he alone was prepared to pay. He then looks up to Wotan and cries:

> Take heed, haughty god!
> If I sinned, I sinned only against myself:
> But you, immortal one,
> Seizing this ring, sin
> Against all that was,
> Is and shall be!

Unmoved, Wotan tears the ring from Alberich's finger and the dwarf utters a terrible cry of despair on his top F sharp, which is enharmonically changed to G flat in the orchestra for an eerie fragment of the Ring motif. Donington observes that 'this enharmonic transition is the slightest yet subtlest of hints that transformation of character is still the fundamental issue. It is not merely that the ring is changing hands; the ring is itself at work in bringing this change about, as we may infer from the very fact that it does not avail Alberich to prevent the theft.'[3]

After the dwarf has expressed his great grief, to motif 34 (here expressing the loss not only of love but also of its only substitute), Wotan tells Loge to release him. 'Am I free? Truly free?' the dwarf asks, with a despairing laugh. 'Then thus I give you my freedom's first greeting.' In a wonderful summary of all the evils that come from envying, coveting and possessing things, and with all his mortified and agonized soul, Alberich curses the Ring.[4] All henceforth will crave for it, he cries, all will covet what it promises, and to all will it bring neither joy nor true reward but only misery, servitude and death, until the day when I once again have it in my hand! Having delivered himself of this mighty utterance, which the orchestra echoes in a massive and threatening *tutti*, he scrambles away into the cleft and sinks from sight.

The motif of the curse (45) is introduced by Alberich with no initial accompaniment apart from a roll on the timpani. It rises through a half-diminished chord, and then falls through an octave to settle on a murky C major triad, with clarinets in their lowest register over a timpani pedal on F sharp. It is one of the most sinister musical ideas ever to have entered the operatic repertoire. And it succeeds in doing through music what Alberich does in the story – it transforms the Ring into an instrument of destruction, and spreads that destruction through the entire world of the drama. It is one of the most potent symbols in all music of the way in which things as we perceive them are transfigured by our need, so as to bear the imprint of our most urgent passions. Henceforth the curse is indelibly implanted in the world of *The Ring*.

The Giants approach from afar, and the gods assemble in the soft breeze that wafts from the captive Freia. Fasolt wishes to cling to Freia and will not let the gods touch her – not until the ransom is paid. If he is to let her go the gold must be piled so firmly and fully around her that she can no longer be seen. Donner and Froh stack the hoard between the two staffs planted by the Giants, Wotan and Fricka meanwhile giving voice to heartfelt feelings of shame. When the hoard is finally used up, Freia's hair still shines above it, and Fafner demands that it be hidden by the Tarnhelm. Fasolt, searching the pile, discovers a crack, through which Freia's glance shines on him, arousing all over again his yearning for her loveliness.

In this powerful scene we discover something important about the Giants, namely that they deal in quantities, not qualities. For Fafner the hoard is an inert and accumulated treasure. He notices the Ring, which is the active source of the hoard, only when Fasolt, in his touching desire for Freia, rediscovers the object of his love. For what can be exchanged for love, if not the thing obtained by forswearing it? Fafner now points to the ring that glistens on Wotan's finger. Loge cries that the Ring belongs to the Rhine-daughters; Wotan corrects him – it belongs now to me. Ask what you will, he says to Fafner, you cannot have this ring. Freia, Fricka and the other gods plead with Wotan in vain.

Suddenly, to a solemn minor-key variant of the original nature motif (47) a blue light begins to shine from a cleft in the mountainside. The goddess Erda appears, rising slowly from the depths. There is no earth goddess in the old Norse pantheon, and Wagner's goddess is derived from the Volva (German: Wala), the wise woman who appears to Odin in the Voluspo, the striking poem that heads the collection of Eddas in the *Codex Regius*.[5]

Erda utters mysterious and impressive words that contain the great truth that Wotan has yet to learn, and which he can learn only by renouncing his immortal ambitions.

> How things were, I know;
> How things are and will be,
> These too I see:
> The eternal world's first Ur-Wala,
> Erda, summons you.
> Three daughters, conceived before time began,
> Were born from my womb.
> What I see is told to you each night by the Norns.
> But the highest danger brings me
> Here myself today.
> Hear me! Hear me! Hear me!
> All that is must end.
> A dark day closes on the gods.
> I charge you, shun the Ring!

The motif introduced here, 48, will henceforth be associated with the doom of the gods, as Erda has foretold it. In a letter to Röckel of

25 January 1854 Wagner wrote that he had originally intended Erda to sing: 'A dark day dawns for the gods; your glorious race will end in shame, unless you give up the ring!' The passage as Wagner revised it no longer implies that Wotan can avoid the end, nor does the music offer any escape clause. Something else therefore hangs on Erda's prophecy, and it is a plausible suggestion that Erda is counselling Wotan not to avoid the end, but to avoid the wrong form of it.[6]

Erda's reference to the 'highest danger' is accompanied by the motive of resentment (44), with which Alberich had worked himself up to the tremendous curse on the Ring. The suggestion is that Erda has woken, not in order to take control of things, but to clarify the new disposition of forces in the world that Wotan seeks to govern. The god does not yet know that Alberich's resentment has entered the scheme of things, transforming itself from personal vengefulness to an impersonal force that troubles everything that the gods themselves might think, feel and do. Hence he imagines some specific evil against which the Wala is warning him. Wishing to know the meaning of her words, Wotan attempts to seize her; but the gods hold him back. The goddess disappears without explaining further. At the urging of the other gods Wotan at last surrenders the Ring, eliciting a sarcastic remark from Freia, whom he nevertheless embraces, singing 'kehr' uns die Jugend zurück!' – 'may youth return to us!' – to the motif of woman's worth (34).

Fafner begins packing away the hoard in a large sack, causing his brother to demand his share. Fafner dismisses Fasolt's plea on the grounds that the lovesick Fasolt wanted only Freia and not the treasure. Fasolt appeals to the gods to bear witness to his just claim, and Loge whispers that the treasure doesn't matter: just get hold of the Ring. Fasolt picks up the Ring, crying 'it is mine in exchange for Freia's glance!' Fafner then bludgeons his brother to death, seizes the Ring and packs the remaining treasure, before striding away from the scene. The gods look on in horror, Loge, to the motif of resentment (44), congratulating Wotan on his luck: you paid your debts with the treasure, and also passed it, curse included, to your enemies! But Wotan is gripped by dread, and resolves to go down to Erda so as to learn the meaning of her prophecy.

Fricka now begs to be admitted to the noble castle, while Wotan laments the unclean wages with which it was bought. A haze has settled over the scene, emanating from the actions we have witnessed. Donner swings his hammer to disperse it; there is a clap of thunder and Froh creates the shimmering rainbow bridge over which the gods are to proceed to their new home. At a certain point the relentless D flat major of Valhalla is interrupted by a C major arpeggio on the trumpet (51), a leitmotif that is later to be associated with the sword Nothung, bequeathed by Wotan to Siegmund, forged anew by Siegfried, and expressing the freely acting nature of the hero. As this motif sounds Wotan steps forward to sing: 'So do I greet the castle, safe from fear and dread!' And, turning to his wife, he invites her to dwell with him forthwith in Valhalla.

It is reported by Porges that Wagner, rehearsing the Ring, directed that Wotan should, as he greets the castle, pick up a sword, left amid the scattered debris of the hoard, and brandish it as the trumpet sounds. This instruction is not in the vocal or the orchestral score, and the leitmotif of the sword will become clear to the audience only in retrospect. For the moment Wotan's great thought is known only to himself. Yet the god has done what Alberich did when he cursed the Ring. He has implanted his will in the scheme of things, and he conveys this fact to his wife in mysterious words, when she asks for the meaning of the castle's name.

The gods make their way over the rainbow bridge and Loge turns from them, saying that he is almost ashamed to have anything to do with such beings, as they hasten blindly to their end. Should he change himself again into flames, so as to burn them who once tamed him? From the Rhine comes the beautiful lament of the Rhine-daughters (53), calling for their gold, and Wotan tells Loge to silence them. Loge calls out that Wotan has another future for them: without the gold of the Rhine they must take their radiance from the gods instead. This thought causes the gods to laugh aloud, while the Rhine-daughters retort that truth and trust now live only in the depths, and that falsehood and cowardice reign in the world above. Then, with a vast D flat major arpeggio from the whole orchestra, drawn out over all the available octaves in the now blazing but insubstantial theme of the rainbow (50), the gods march in empty triumph to their doom.

DIE WALKÜRE

The opening 'prelude' to the cycle has introduced the rich and adaptable musical material – the leitmotifs and their harmonic networks – from which the great edifice will be constructed. It has presented, with remarkable economy, a complete picture of the cosmos, and of the price that has been paid for Valhalla, the castle that is to secure Wotan's rule. It has introduced a large cast of believable and gripping characters, in whom are crystallized and immortalized the hopes and fears that govern us. It has shown that, in the world of the immortals, love is not necessarily the supreme value, and can sometimes be bartered for the good of government. It has shown that the serene world of the gods depends on an original sin of usurpation, and that the gods or 'light-elves' (*Lichtalben*) owe their blessed existence to the dark-elves, the *Schwarzalben*, and to Alberich's great 'crime against himself' in renouncing, and then cursing, love. And yet, ever sounding in the depths, is the lament of the Rhine-daughters, singing of a natural order that preceded the conscious will that has usurped it. This lament sounds in the unconscious of us all, as we pursue our paths to personality, sovereignty and freedom, while hearing faint echoes of a condition from which we departed in the irrecoverable prehistory of our kind.

There is another theme that runs through *Das Rheingold*, in addition to the cosmic story, and one more personal to Wagner. The narrative has shown the ruthlessness of the males, as they strive always to augment their power, and the plight of the females, objects of barter, enslavement and lust. All the women are victims: the Rhine-daughters of Alberich's theft, Freia of Wotan's heartless contract and of the Giants' determination to enforce it, Fricka of her husband's infidelity. Yet women, properly understood, harbour the wisdom that Wotan needs. Alberich too needs this wisdom, and might perhaps have obtained it had he not set out to steal what exists only if freely given, namely 'love and woman's worth'. This feminine wisdom is personified in the primeval mother, who speaks from the depths of unconscious nature, the only place, as the Rhine-daughters lament, where truth and trust still live. Erda does not belong to the world of the gods; the feminine has as yet a marginal existence in that world, and will be returned to us only if we can find our way back to it across the debris left by masculine ambition. This is the task that is assigned, in the next and equally imaginative drama, to a Valkyrie.

Wotan established his government before the crime of Alberich. But he has made himself dependent on that crime, by seizing the Ring and using it and its products to pay for Valhalla. Alberich, who rules his loveless domain by force and violence, has implanted in the cosmic order the curse that will henceforth infect it – the curse on the Ring, emblem of his lovelessness. Wotan has been warned by Erda to reject the Ring. But the curse poisons the world with Alberich's resentment, and the reign of the gods is threatened by the Nibelung's determination to repossess the Ring and to use it in a bid for revenge.

Prior to the opening scene of *Die Walküre* Wotan has visited Erda to find out the meaning of her prophecies, has made of her one of his habitual conquests, and has received from her womb Brünnhilde, one of nine Valkyrie daughters whom Wotan has one way or another acquired, and whom he employs to collect the fallen heroes from the battlefield. These heroes are to be assembled in Valhalla to serve as a Praetorian guard against the Nibelungs, when Alberich has amassed the forces necessary for his longed-for act of revenge – something that he will do, as soon as he can regain possession of the Ring. Meanwhile, however, Wotan, motivated by the obscure prophecies that he has obtained from Erda, has perceived the necessity to act in another way and in another sphere – the sphere of humans. Although mortal, human beings enjoy the freedom that Wotan, in assuming government of the world, was forced to relinquish. Among the many species, races and varieties of consciousness with which *The Ring* abounds, humans alone are capable of doing something without reward, and in furtherance of a cause that is not their own.

Wotan rules by treaties and by law. It is by a treaty that he lost the Ring to the Giant Fafner, who now, thanks to the Tarnhelm, has assumed the form of a fearful dragon and squats inert on the gold. Wotan is not free to rob Fafner of the Ring, nor would he, on possessing it, escape the curse. Only a mortal being, enjoying both a god-like freedom and the ability to forge his own life, without the burdens of cosmic government, could accomplish what Wotan lacks the power to do, which is to claim the Ring as his own, and to return it, consciously renouncing its power, to the Rhine. Wotan has therefore appeared in the world of mortals as Volsa (*Wälse*), and fathered the race of Volsungs, represented by the twins, Siegmund and Sieglinde, who are to live in defiance of the laws and treaties that bind the gods, acting freely on their own account. Only such beings could accomplish Wotan's desire, which is to gain the Ring by a free act, and without seeking the power that placed a curse on it. But how is this to be achieved? Wotan has shaped Siegmund to act freely, but in pursuit of a goal that he is not free to change, since the god himself imposes it. This is the paradox that governs the action of *Die Walküre*. And, as we shall see, it is a paradox that goes to the heart of what it is to be human.

Die Walküre opens with a storm, depicted by a truncated version of Wotan's spear, and a prolongation of Donner's hammer (54, 55). We are now looking up in consternation at tumults tearing the skies. Into a primitive dwelling, supported by the central pillar of a mighty ash tree, the exhausted Siegmund comes out of the storm. He looks around him, sees no one and, with a supreme effort, closes the door behind him to collapse unconscious on the hearth. The motif associated with Siegmund (56) is also taken from the descending scale of Wotan's spear, but turned round on itself, so as to become strangely vulnerable and lost, almost the opposite of the imperious decisiveness of the original. We are made simultaneously aware of Siegmund's ancestry, and of the enormous distance between the vast ambitions of the god and the vulnerable feelings of his human children. Sieglinde enters quietly, examines with sympathy the unknown man who lies before her, and responds to his sudden cry for a drink by hastily fetching a horn of water. Siegmund's eyes rest on Sieglinde as he asks who she is. She replies in words that illustrate her subdued and servile status: 'Dies Haus und dies Weib sind Hundings Eigen' – 'This house and this woman are Hunding's property' – to which she adds that Siegmund should await her husband's return as a guest. Siegmund, grasping the situation, says that he is unarmed and wounded, at which Sieglinde quickly starts forward to tend to him. He dismisses the wounds as slight, and although he had to flee from his enemies, his exhaustion has been dispelled, he tells her, by the sun of her presence.

Throughout this scene the orchestra has woven together Siegmund's theme with Sieglinde's rising motif on strings (58), and also with the second part of Freia's love idea – the melody representing tenderness and tragedy, here elaborated on solo cello in music of exquisite beauty (59). With the greatest economy of means Wagner shows the first two humans of his drama in all their vulnerable isolation, discovering each other in a world that has so far offered only comfortless suffering to them both. Drawing on a new theme, that of the Volsungs' sorrow (61), which will become increasingly important as the drama unfolds, the music weaves a web of love and distress around them; the audience, observing this, is entirely on their side. So necessary and right has Wagner made this love that the subsequent revelation that they are brother and sister will matter not a jot. If there is such a thing as an aesthetic refutation of a moral belief, this is it.

Sieglinde offers Siegmund mead, which he gratefully drinks after insisting that she drink it first. And then he makes to leave. She jumps to detain him, and he protests that he brings misfortune wherever he goes. Then stay, she says, since you cannot bring misfortune into a house where misfortune dwells. Profoundly moved he resolves to wait for Hunding, names himself as Wehwalt (Woeful), and looks long and rapturously into Sieglinde's eyes – a look that she now for the first time fully returns. Hunding, whose harsh, self-assured motif (62) has been barked out, first by horns and then by tubas, now stands in the doorway, eyeing the pair of them suspiciously. A terse, Ibsen-like, exchange ensues, in which Hunding offers hospitality as the law requires, and Siegmund accepts the same with a measure of rudeness. Hunding compares his wife's features to those of his guest, and sees the same serpent glistening in the eyes of both: as he soliloquizes on their likeness the motif of the spear (19) sounds softly on bass clarinet. What Hunding unconsciously guesses at, the orchestra knows.

Hunding begins to interrogate Siegmund on the events that have brought him exhausted to the house. Siegmund refers to his storm-tossed and fugitive condition, while Hunding boasts of his own settled, honoured and land-owning status. Urged on by Sieglinde, Siegmund describes his childhood, raised together with his twin sister by the father whom he calls 'Wolfe' (Wolf). Wolf and his son lived by hunting and scavenging, opposed in everything by a rival race, which we soon discover to be Hunding's kin, the Neidings. Returning one day to the lair Siegmund and Wolf found the place burned down, the mother dead, and the sister abducted. To further questioning from Sieglinde, Siegmund recounts that he and his father made war on the Neidings who had destroyed their home. But one day his father vanished, leaving only a wolf-skin in the forest, the first part of the Valhalla theme here sounding softly on trombones. Thereafter, though drawn to men and women (and women especially, the music suggests), Siegmund was in everything opposed and dogged by ill-luck. He recounts his misfortune without self-pity, and in full consciousness that it has set him outside society. What seemed right to him was wrong to others and everywhere he ran into feuds. Clearly, Hunding comments, the Norn who granted your fate did not love you, and no man enjoys offering you hospitality. Sieglinde boldly reproaches her husband, saying that only cowards fear the man who travels alone and unarmed.

Siegmund recounts the events that had brought him to Hunding's home. Called to rescue a girl who was being compelled against her will to marry, he found himself in a fight with her brothers; he slew them but their kinsmen rushed to the spot to take revenge. The girl was killed, Siegmund's weapons cut from him, and he was forced to flee. Now you know, he says to Sieglinde, why I am called Wehwalt, Woeful. The passage has introduced two noble motifs (64 and 64A), associated with the Volsungs' woe, and with their tragic race: motifs that reach forward to Siegfried's funeral march at the end of the drama, where they add a depth of tragedy to all that has gone before.

Hunding responds to Siegmund's narrative with the information that he too had been called to the fight and now finds the foe in his own home. 'My house shelters you, Wolfling, for this night. But tomorrow we fight. So arm yourself.' He orders Sieglinde to prepare his night drink. She bestows a longing glance on Siegmund, and then on the trunk of the ash tree, before being pushed from the room by Hunding. The motif of the sword, introduced here on bass trumpet, now begins to war with Hunding's tattoo, as Hunding picks up his weapons and mocks Siegmund for having none of his own.

Volsa had promised to his son a sword, which he will discover in his deepest distress. Siegmund recalls Sieglinde's sweetness and her beauty, and the mockery of his defenceless condition by Hunding. In a magnificent epitome of all the prayers that human beings have ever uttered from the depths of their sorrow and need, he calls out to Volsa for the promised sword (66). A light glimmers in the trunk of the ash tree, and he recalls the blaze that shone on him from Sieglinde's eyes. Then she enters on tiptoe, tells him that she has drugged Hunding's drink, and that he must now slip away and save himself. Siegmund responds that he is saved by her presence, and she tells him the story of her wedding night, when she, robbed from her home, was being forced against her will to marry Hunding. During the feast an old man entered, his hat pulled down over one eye, the other looking sweetly and sadly on Sieglinde. Then, taking a sword from beneath his cloak he plunged it up to the hilt in the ash tree, saying that it would belong to whoever can pull it out again. None of the guests succeeded. Sieglinde then understood the identity of the old man, and of the hero for whom he has left this sword – and the reference to Wotan, known to her as Volsa, is underlined by the music of Valhalla (18A, B). This is introduced with a sublime cadence into the major and orchestrated with supreme gentleness, with the choir of horns singing softly at the bottom of their register and the theme itself on strings. If she could find the friend for whom that sword was promised, Sieglinde declares, who came from far away to this most miserable of women, then she would be revenged for all that she has suffered.

Siegmund tells her that she has found that friend. She is all that he has longed for and lacked. They embrace and a gust of wind blows open the door, so that Sieglinde starts away, asking who came, who went? Siegmund responds that nobody went, but someone came – spring has entered the room. In defiance of the precepts laid down in *Opera and Drama*, which expressly forbids such things, Siegmund now holds up the action with a lyrical love-song (68), boldly claiming Sieglinde as his sister and bride, and she responds in kind: they knew already, she says, the moment they met, that they belonged to each other and had loved before. Their long, delicate exchange of memories goes as far as any artist has ever gone in celebrating incest, and when Sieglinde finally identifies him as Siegmund, son of her own father, Volsa, Siegmund jumps to his feet, seizes the sword, names it Nothung, the sword of his need, and claims it as a wedding gift. To the motif, 17, with which Alberich had pronounced his decisive curse on love, Siegmund, invoking 'holiest love', draws the sword from the tree and the twins run out to consummate their love, conscious that they do so not as lovers only, but as brother and sister, scions of a god-engendered race.

The first act of *Die Walküre* has shown the trajectory of erotic love, from the first encounter to the consummation, in a pair of uniquely sorrowful but un-self-pitying humans, and it has shown this through music that has captured the two lives and wound them together in a web of tenderness. In *Das Rheingold* Wagner had followed the precepts of *Opera and Drama*, adopting a melodious but declamatory style, in which the rhythm, metre, accent and period of the poem were aligned with equivalent qualities and quantities in the music. The cold contests of immortal forces, and the often forbidding characters that embody them, were thereby endowed with their precise musical weight. In Act 1 of *Die Walküre*, however, we are in the world of human feeling, and Wagner has perforce strayed from his written precepts, allowing the music to work on its own. From the outset it is the melodic line that weaves the two hearts together. It is the incomparable softness of the harmony that removes all hesitation from their feelings. And when Siegmund bursts at last into song, and Sieglinde pours out her heart in response, it is because the music, by that point, is so burdened with the weight of their emotion that nothing else will do. It is not a routine love-song that we hear, but the climax of a long emotional crescendo, and the music tells us what the words merely hint at, that this love is a destiny long prepared by suffering, and one that makes the suffering worthwhile, by showing that just *this* is what it has meant from the beginning. Only in music can such a complex thought be given the immediacy, the emotional validity, that Wagner's drama provides for it.

The second act derives from the composer's inspired re-creation of the story of the Victory Bringer (Sigrdrifa), from the hint in the Poetic Edda. It begins with a prelude, introduced by a variant of the sword motif, in which the love music of Act 1 and the theme of longing

(70B) sound in rapid diminished form over rhythmic figures associated with the Valkyries (72), suggesting a god's-eye view of the events
that we have just witnessed in the grief-filled world below. Wotan has
summoned Brünnhilde, his daughter and his favourite among the
Valkyries, who comes leaping from rock to rock towards him, with
the exultant cry that is to be the signature of these fierce virgins to
whom the call of love is unknown (73C). He charges her to ensure
victory for the Volsung in the forthcoming battle. As for Hunding, he
is not wanted in Valhalla, and she can dispose of him as she wishes.
After expressing her excitement Brünnhilde warns Wotan of the
approach of Fricka in her ram-drawn chariot. Much as she enjoys the
battles of bold men, she says, these domestic skirmishes are not to her
taste, and she will slip away. 'The old storm, the old trouble!' Wotan
sighs, as his wife enters. Fricka looks coldly on Brünnhilde, one of
many unwanted products of her husband's philandering, and the
Valkyrie retires from the scene.

Fricka begins by saying, to music expressing a pained haughtiness
(74), that Hunding has prayed that she punish the blasphemous pair.
But what wrong have they done, asks Wotan, in ceding to the magic
of love? Fricka is amazed by this response, since for her the moral
law, the sanctity of marriage and the ban on incest are all fundamental to the rule of the gods. Relinquish these things, and what remains
of Valhalla? Since when has it been known for brother and sister to
make love? Wotan responds that now she has witnessed it: sometimes
things happen for the first time, and he warmly implies, as the orchestra recalls the love duet of Act 1, that law without love is an empty
shell. In saying this Wotan is not merely rehearsing the 'law-versus-love'
theme that exerted such a pull over Wagner throughout his creative
life. He is suggesting that after all law, the establishment of which has
been his aim in seizing control of the world, is not in itself sufficient,
but must give way to something higher, something which he as yet
has not fully grasped, but which is present in the Volsungs' love
despite its illegality.

At this Fricka explodes with rage, recalling Wotan's amorous
exploits and their insult to his lawful wife. 'At least you made the
Valkyries – even your favourite Brünnhilde – obey me as their sovereign. But now, roaming the world as Volsa, you have debased yourself

so far as to embrace a common human. And you would sacrifice me to a she-wolf's litter – so do it, and trample on the wife you have betrayed!' Fricka agrees that law is not enough – not because it is cancelled by love, but because there is something else at stake in our moral conduct. Already in *Das Rheingold* Fricka has referred to this other thing: the household and the hearth, that which was promised to her in the form of Valhalla, the shield of her honour and the vindication of domestic life (21). It is precisely this that has been desecrated by the Volsungs in their incestuous union.

Wotan responds that Fricka understands only convention, whereas the crisis of the gods requires a new kind of deed – the deed of a hero who, free from divine protection, acts outside the law, in order to accomplish what the god himself cannot. But heroes can act only with the favour of the gods, says Fricka. The Volsung was shaped by Wotan to be bold and free; but he is so only because he trusts the god to defend him. Wotan protests that the Volsung grew up by himself, unprotected; in which case, Fricka rejoins, don't protect him now: take away the sword. Wotan protests that Siegmund won the sword himself, in his hour of need. You created the need, says Fricka, just as you left him the sword. Then she adds a penetrating thought. Against you, the god, I might go to war, but I cannot fight with Siegmund. By giving him victory you make me, your immortal wife, obedient to a slave! My husband surely cannot in this way profane a goddess!

Throughout this dialogue the music has conveyed the deep dejection of Wotan, as he recognizes the impossibility of meeting Fricka's arguments. A new leitmotif weaves this dejection into the narrative. Sometimes known as the motif of Wotan's frustration, it is built from another broken fragment of the spear (76). As the opera proceeds we will find the spear broken again and again to be reassembled, now as something wounded, now as an icon of despair, and finally, as a symbol of hope, but hope composed of fragments. The symbolism here is not something mechanical, but worked into the movement of the music, to create a far-reaching transformation of Wotan's will. We respond to this transformation with unconscious but immediate understanding, being carried by the music into the god's state of mind. Seldom have the dilemmas of sovereignty been expressed with such direct sympathy, and in the character of Wotan we discover something about the nature of government that shows its deep and uneasy place in the psyche of us all.

Wotan reluctantly agrees that the Volsung will go his own way, deprived of divine protection. Fricka urges the point: the Valkyrie too must be prevented from helping him. They wrangle a little longer before Fricka, seeing Brünnhilde return, gives a triumphant summary of the marital council. 'Men will laugh at us, our power will be lost and we gods will disappear, if today my rights are not upheld by that bold girl. The Volsung shall die for my honour. Do I have Wotan's oath?'

'Take my oath!' Wotan bitterly replies, and the orchestra rises chromatically, through a series of unresolved cadences, to a striking dissonance, as Fricka unfolds from her prey and turns a piercing eye on the Valkyrie, haughtily instructing her to go to the father of hosts: 'let him tell you how the lot shall fall'. And Fricka departs quickly from the scene.

Writing to Liszt on 3 October 1855 Wagner described the scene between father and daughter that follows as 'the most important scene in the whole tetralogy'. It is the metaphysical heart of the story and surely the greatest piece of recitative in all opera. As Fricka strides away the curse motif (45) is followed by the motif of Wotan's frustration (76). The quarrel must have gone badly, Brünnhilde remarks, seeing that Fricka went away laughing. And she asks her father what is troubling him.

Wotan responds with an outburst of anger and despair, the music beginning from a motif sometimes known as Wotan's revolt, taking in Alberich's curse, and blending them with the dissonant chord of Fricka's departure (78) to form a dissonance in which six pitch-classes are packed together, crying for a resolution that does not come. 'Endless anger! Endless grief! I am the most miserable of all!' he cries, and Brünnhilde in distress, and with moving candour, begs him to confide in her. In speaking to her, she says, he addresses his will, which is what she is. Wotan acknowledges this, and therefore allows himself to reveal his troubles, holding her close, stroking her hair but uttering his inner thoughts as though to himself in secret. In the long narrative that follows the god makes clear that he has not always ruled the world, and indeed that his aspiration for sovereignty emerged from a completely different way of being – an immersion in sensuous delights perhaps not unlike the thoughtless sporting of the Rhine-daughters. Sovereignty, we learn, is a departure from the natural order, and not given in the normal run of things even to a god.

When the delight of young love waned in me, Wotan sings, I began to long for power, and by tricks I gained it, tempted by Loge, who has now fluttered away. I wanted power, but I also wanted love, which I could not forego. Wotan does not explicitly say so, but it is presumably for this reason that he wished to impose his sovereignty through law, so as to guarantee the freedom without which love is no more than a fleeting pleasure of the kind that he no longer relishes. He summarizes the events witnessed in *Das Rheingold*, saying that, on hearing Erda's prophecy, he lost his peace of mind and longed for knowledge. He therefore descended into the womb of the earth, over-powered the Wala with love's magic and learned her secrets. In return Erda demanded a price, in the form of their offspring Brünnhilde, whom he was to raise as his daughter. (We know that Brünnhilde is Wotan's daughter, and it is surely hard to imagine who could have been father of the other eight Valkyries, if not Wotan, who goes on to mention them in the same breath. Nevertheless, it might still be doubted whether the others were born from Erda. Brünnhilde's distinctive attributes of wisdom, intelligence and will suggest that she is of more distinguished parentage than her sisters.) And he found a use for Brünnhilde, along with her eight Valkyrie sisters: they were to stir up the men whom the gods had subjected to their laws through deceitful treaties, and set them violently against each other. The Valkyries were then to cull from the battlefields the best of the fallen, for the eventual defence of Valhalla.

In this way, Wotan says, Valhalla has been secured against Alberich's army of darkness. However, should Alberich regain the Ring then all is lost: only Alberich, unique in his forswearing of love, can use the spell forged into the Ring, and he would use this spell to turn Wotan's heroes against him. The motif sometimes called the need of the gods (79) begins to animate the music in the bass. 'Fafner now has the Ring,' Wotan goes on, 'the Ring that I gave to him in payment. Because I covenanted with him I may not attack him. I became ruler through treaties and by my treaties am I now enslaved. Only one person could do what I cannot, a hero whom I have never helped, stranger to the god and free from his favours, one who, from his own need and with his own weapons, will do what I avoid. But how can I find this Other, this friendly foe, who by defying me will be most dear to me, the opponent of my will who does my will? The free man for whom I long must create himself, whereas I can only create subjects to myself.'

There is an acute dramatic irony here, since, although Wotan, in his self-centredness, cannot guess it, the free being, rescuer of the gods, whom he despairs of finding and whom he cannot create, is in fact staring him in the face, and listening in rapt sympathy to his words. 'In everything I do I find only myself!' Wotan cries, and we sense both the poignant loneliness of the supreme god, and the solution to that loneliness – the Other who is also the god's inner Self. In the relation between Wotan and Brünnhilde we see emerging, in magical dramatic form, a version of the relation between God and Christ in Christian doctrine: and it is clear from Wagner's draft for the play *Jesus of Nazareth*, which he worked on in 1848–9, at the time when he was conceiving the poem of *The Ring*, that he saw the God–Christ theme as the heart of a far-reaching human drama.

Wotan goes on to reflect that his attempt to create a hero who would defy the gods with a weapon fit for the purpose was bound to fail, and he acknowledges that Fricka saw through the trick at once. The curse of the Ring still lies on him, and this is the sign of it, that he must forsake the man he loves, betray the one who trusts him: and the two motifs of renunciation (17) and woman's worth (34) are here woven together in a manner that suggests that they are, deep down, one and the same.*

At this point Wotan gives vent to his deep despair, saying 'only one thing I want now: the end!' He recounts a prophecy of Erda's, that 'when Love's dark enemy begets a son in anger, then the end of the blessed ones is nigh'. Wotan has heard a rumour that, through force and money, Alberich has impregnated a mortal woman. Her child will be the dwarf's avenger. The god, however, who wooed by love, cannot beget the free man he is seeking. 'So take my blessing, Nibelung's son, what deeply revolts me I bequeath to you: the empty glory

---

* See the discussion of the two motifs in the Appendix.

of divinity – greedily feed your hate on it!' This, the first of two bequests of the world, is made to music of catastrophic force, in which the theme of revolt invades that of Valhalla, thrusts it upwards like a great wave and then sends it crashing down in fragments (80). It is not a gift of the world, but a bitter rejection of it. Wotan's second bequest, to Siegfried, will be of an altogether different kind.

Wotan tells Brünnhilde to fight for Fricka and for marriage – two items hitherto at the bottom of the girl's agenda. Since he cannot will a free man into existence, the Valkyrie must take the side of Fricka's subjects, not the side of Siegmund. 'But you love the Volsung,' Brünnhilde protests, 'and out of love for you I must protect him.'

Wotan repeats the order and she retorts that Wotan himself has taught her to love the Volsung. 'I will never be turned against him by your two-faced orders,' she says defiantly, and he explodes in anger, saying 'when I confided in you did I sink so low as to receive abuse from my own creation?' He threatens her with destruction should she defy him, and repeats his command, before striding angrily away to motiv 82.

Brünnhilde's armour lies for the first time heavily on her, as she sings 'Weh, mein Wälsung', and laments that she, the Volsung's friend, must now forsake him. In a poignant soliloquy the orchestra takes up the sentiment, and weaves it canonically into the musical texture as the Valkyrie disappears from the stage, giving way to the twins in their flight.[7]

As the Volsungs enter, Siegmund is begging Sieglinde to rest, but 'Further! Further!' she cries. 'Although I found bliss with the man I love, and although I belonged to a man who took me without love, I am cursed, disgraced, a source of shame to you.' Siegmund instinctively recognizes the real source of her shame. She is reliving the sexual slavery of her marriage, and the sense of pollution that it has planted in her. He assures her that her disgrace will be paid for by Hunding's blood. In her delirium Sieglinde hears Hunding calling his hounds to the hunt, and their wild baying for vengeance against the broken marriage vows, the music climaxing on eight fierce horn chords with appogiaturas in an epitome of primal terror. She describes the scene in vivid detail, their teeth tearing Siegmund without respect for his noble features. Finally she faints away in Siegmund's arms, and he addresses her in tenderness and pity.

Brünnhilde enters, leading her horse, and there follows one of the most inspired scenes in all Wagner, a stichomythic dialogue in which the Valkyrie announces death to the hero, only to be overcome by compassion for his fate. Here the verse, derived in part from a Norwegian skaldic poem, makes its own special contribution to the *Legendenton*, to borrow Schumann's apt expression: the sequence of pregnant questions, and the slow, magnificent unfolding of Siegmund's destiny like a great curtain being drawn back from the icy stars – these things recall the mystery of the Eddas, and also the Greek tragic stage.

The scene begins with the solemn fate motif (84), sounding on tubas and muffled timpani, followed, after a heart-stopping silence, by the *Todesverkündigung* (85), the announcement of death, on trumpets and trombones. These two overwhelming dramatic ideas, heard here for the first time, will cast their shadow over all that follows in the cycle. The sense of the fate motif is of an infinitely sorrowful 'why?' to which there is no answer, but only another question, as the motif is prolonged into the *Todesverkündigung*. This, through its constantly evolving harmony and melodic drive – its restless search for an answering phrase – repeats and amplifies the question.

By giving the melody of 85 to Siegmund, and repeating it always with softer orchestration, Wagner illustrates the structure of man's relation to God, in which yearning and interrogation are such crucial ingredients; he also shows the evolution over time of our predicament, the working of the great question into the heart of what is most personal – into love itself. At the same time the question never loses its cosmic character, suggesting always that in death we face the mystery of creation, the illuminated edge between being and nothingness. This is the first point in the drama in which the world of the gods and the world of humans coincide – it is the 'point of intersection of the timeless with time'. And the fate motif announces as a necessity in one world what has been freely willed in another.

'Siegmund, look at me. I am the one whom you soon must follow.' So Brünnhilde begins. In solemn verse she tells him that only those destined to die can set eyes on her, and that she is leading him from the battlefield to Valhalla, where he will be welcomed by Walvater, lord of hosts, by the dead heroes and by Volsa, his father. (The name

'Walvater' is a title assumed by Odin in the Eddas, meaning 'father who chooses' – i.e. who chooses who should fall in battle.) Siegmund anxiously asks whether there are women in Valhalla, and Brünnhilde describes, to the first part of Freia's love motif, 22A, the 'wish-maidens' who abound there, saying that Wotan's daughter herself will serve his drink. He recognizes her as that very person and asks urgently whether he can bring his sister and bride to Valhalla. The answer is no, and Siegmund says that in that case he will not follow. But you must, she says, now you have seen the Valkyrie's blazing glance. Undaunted, he declares that he will remain always with Sieglinde – nothing will force them apart. Death will force you apart she responds, but he laughs at the suggestion that his death will come from Hunding. He raises the sword and tells her that he who made it has promised him victory, at which she reveals the truth: he who made the sword has taken away its power.

At this Siegmund pours out his grief over Sieglinde, to a tragic prolongation of the second part of Freia's love motif (22B). He laments that he must, by dying, betray this woman who loves and depends on him, and calls down shame on the one who made the sword, saying he will not go to Valhalla but to Hell instead. Brünnhilde is stunned that he should value this weak woman more than everlasting bliss, prompting him to turn on her, reproaching her coldness and the heartlessness of the realm from which she comes. Brünnhilde, no doubt for the first time judged adversely to her face by a human, and in consequence deeply moved, promises to protect Sieglinde after Siegmund's death, but he spurns her offer, saying that only he shall protect Sieglinde. Brünnhilde, expressing the intuitive knowledge that she has inherited from her mother, Erda, announces that Sieglinde is with child, but even this fails to deter him as he raises the sword with the intention of killing both his sister and himself. The music has now worked itself to a climax, which is also the turning point of the entire cycle. Brünnhilde, overcome with compassion, discards her Valkyrie identity, throws in her lot with Siegmund and promises victory in the battle to come.

Siegmund looks down on the now sleeping Sieglinde, relieved that her sorrow seems to have been soothed by a smiling dream. And on hearing Hunding's horn he rouses himself and goes in search of the foe. We now discover that Sieglinde's dream was not a pleasant one at all, but a nightmare recalling the terrible moment when her home was sacked, her mother killed and she herself taken away into forced marriage. The music for this dream (beginning from 87, and elaborating 55 in dissonant harmony) has an extraordinary primordial quality, as though the millennia of suffering stored in our collective memory were calling through the mist of Sieglinde's semi-consciousness. She awakens to the sound of Hunding and Siegmund challenging each other in the mist, Siegmund boasting of the sword that he pulled from Hunding's ash tree, Hunding invoking Fricka in revenge. Sieglinde cries out for them to stop, while Brünnhilde, appearing above Siegmund, urges him to trust the sword. Wotan is suddenly visible, holding out his spear, and commanding the sword to break on it. Siegmund falls, pierced by Hunding's weapon.

Brünnhilde quickly gathers up the pieces of the sword, takes Sieglinde onto the saddle of her horse, and escapes into the sky, while Wotan stares at the dead body of his son. The motif of Wotan's grief (88) gives way to that of fate as Wotan turns slowly to Hunding, commanding him to kneel before Fricka, and to tell her that Wotan's spear has avenged what caused her shame. He fiercely repeats the command, at which Hunding falls dead to the ground. Wotan then bursts out in anger at Brünnhilde and mounts his horse in pursuit of her.

The fight between Hunding and Siegmund returns us with utmost vividness to the ancient idea that when we mortals fight over what truly matters to us, the immortals fight beside us, and for goals of their own. Wagner adds a new twist to this idea, central to the Eddas, and also to Homer. He shows the supreme god shattered by a human grief – a grief that beckons from the world of mortals since it is here, not there in Valhalla, that the meaning of these conflicts lies. Wotan has been instrumental in producing the death of his son at the hands of a moral slave. Siegmund's life of sorrow and his final cruel destruction have been to no avail, and Wotan's own part in this has been both unavoidable and, in his own growing awareness, criminal. If properly produced this scene cannot be witnessed without the most profound desolation: total silence should follow that final D minor chord.

We have learned that Wotan's power depends just as deeply on upholding treaties as the Giant Fasolt had said it did. Wotan is the supreme god, brought into being by our prayers, the god on whom we place our burdens, whom we trust because he rules by law and who promises justice, not now perhaps, but in the end. But this god also confronts what one might call 'the paradox of sovereignty'. To rule by treaties you must have the power to enforce them, and no treaty would confer that power, since it is a power that would remove sovereignty from all the signatories save one. Hence it is a power that can be obtained only by a trick, by an act of usurpation. And this is what we have seen in *Das Rheingold*. Wotan has understood that his rule of law depends upon actions that his law could never justify, and that as a result there is another power at work in the world besides the law by which he rules it, namely Alberich's resentment, and the army that he is recruiting to give vent to it.

The consequences are these: first, Wotan can see no immediate solution to the problem of maintaining the rule of the gods other than the extraordinary one of spreading strife among mortals, and planting in the minds of men the idea of the hero, for whom salvation awaits in the afterlife, but who meanwhile must die a victim to the very god to whom he prays for safety. This troubles Wotan's conscience, but it is a stroke of genius on Wagner's part to have included in his portrait of the supreme god the aspect of religion that is most puzzling to the outside observer – namely its capacity for violence. The promise of a blessed safety that is the gift of all religions, makes sense because life among humans is supremely dangerous, and it is God himself who has made it so.

Second, Wotan has become aware, in the failure of his attempt to save himself through Siegmund, that Erda's prophecy of the end of the gods cannot be evaded merely by passing the problem to a human being shaped expressly to confront it. Wotan is coming to see that the end of his rule is inevitable. Having seen this, he bequeaths the thankless task of sovereignty to the son of Alberich. But this bequest is a gesture of despair, and not an expression of Wotan's will.

Third, Wotan's burst of despair is not the end of the matter. Wotan senses obscurely that there might be another way out – another way beside the maintenance of the rule of law on the one hand and the triumph of resentment on the other. And he is feeling towards the conclusion that this way involves a free being acting out of love alone.

This free being, as yet only a glimmer in Wotan's eye, will be able to renounce power for love – just as Alberich renounced love for power, while Wotan precariously clung to both love and power, having avoided paying the true price for either.

All these paradoxes and conundrums have their reality in political life, and also in the life of each of us as moral beings. And all are instinctively understood by Brünnhilde in the intuitive choice that she has made, and which she goes on to translate into a conscious policy. For the moment things are as she said, in her first outrush of daughterly love for her troubled father. It is she who is Wotan's will, and not Wotan himself.

Act 3 begins with the celebrated ride of the Valkyries, in which Brünnhilde's eight sisters arrive one by one on their mounts from the battlefields, each with a dead hero slung across her saddle. This evocation of Viking demi-goddesses inspires mixed reactions among Wagnerites, some decrying what they hear as the crowd-pleasing bombast of the music, and the raucous cries of upper-class schoolgirls on the rampage. Properly conducted, however, with the rhythmic figures standing clear of the melodic line, this music is every bit as exciting as the scene depicted, capturing both the exhilaration and the bloodthirsty savagery of those ancient combats with sword and spear. The scene is a fitting sequel to the desolation that we have just witnessed. It returns us to the amoral pagan world, in which storms in the sky are not happenings but actions – a world in which we mortals, surrounded everywhere by gods brimful of interest in our doings, strive in vain to comprehend the powers that govern us. The scene is also remarkable for the bantering dialogue, in which the girls discuss the dead heroes as though the horses beneath them were speaking for their human cargo. (Anybody who has spent time in the hunting field in England will know this kind of conversation, which is both profoundly feminine and also full of aggression of a kind that is shocking to men, since they are, obliquely, the target. It amazes me that Wagner imagined so completely something that he surely never had occasion to witness.)

The Valkyries notice after a while that one of their number is missing. They see her and call out. The rhythm changes from the 9/8 gallop to a subtle cross rhythm, in which dotted crotchets in three-four time, to the motif (79) associated also with Wotan's need, represent Grane, Brünnhilde's horse, in the last stages of exhaustion. The Valkyries are astonished to see that it is not a man but a woman on Brünnhilde's saddle. To their anxious questions she tells them that, for the first time in her life, she is running away – and from Walvater himself. She asks her sisters to watch for him and they confirm that indeed a thunderstorm approaches from the north. Brünnhilde begs them to save her, and to save the woman too. She explains who Sieglinde is, and the sisters are astonished and appalled at Brünnhilde's desire to protect her from Wotan's anger. None of them will lend the horse that Brünnhilde needs.

Sieglinde now breaks her silence. 'Don't trouble yourself for my sake,' she says. 'Who asked you to rescue me from the fight, where I might have been struck down by the same weapon that killed Siegmund, so as to die at his side? If I am not to curse you, maiden, then plunge your sword into my heart.'

Brünnhilde tells Sieglinde that she must live for the sake of love, so as to save the child – the Volsung – whom she carries in her womb. Rising at once from her despair, and showing thereby the noble generosity of her soul, Sieglinde begs Brünnhilde and her sisters for protection. The sisters refuse, but Brünnhilde offers to stay and face Wotan's vengeance, thus allowing Sieglinde to escape. In a singularly evocative recitative the Valkyries give directions to the part of the dark forest where Fafner the dragon has his lair – not a safe place for a lonely woman, but a place that Wotan shuns. So hurry there, says Brünnhilde, be brave and defiant, laugh at your sufferings and always remember that in your womb you carry the bravest of heroes. Take these fragments of the sword that he will forge anew, and take his name from me: 'Siegfried, rejoicing in victories!'

The music, having introduced the motif of Siegfried as hero (89), now moves on to a passionate climax with the motif of Sieglinde's blessing (90, sometimes called 'redemption'), which we do not hear again until the very end of the cycle. Shaw dismissed this motif as 'the most trumpery phrase in the entire tetralogy', a judgement repeated in other terms by Adorno.[8] Both were hostile to transcendence in whatever form, and especially in the form of a melody that so self-consciously pulls at the heart-strings. Whatever we think of their opinion, this moment, and the motif associated with it, raises the great question that all interpreters must confront – which is what is he offering us? Is it (to use Wagner's much abused word) redemption? And if so, redemption from what, to what? Or is it all a trick, as Nietzsche insisted?

'For him whom we loved,' Sieglinde sings, 'I will save the dear child. May the reward of my thanks one day smile on you.' And so she departs – narrowly avoiding Wotan, who is descending from his horse off stage, with the cry of 'Stay, Brünnhilde!'

Brünnhilde, with sinking heart, begs her sisters to protect her, and for a while they succeed in hiding her, attempting to defuse the raging anger of her father. He threatens them with a like punishment if they do not give her up and they implore him to show mercy. Wotan reproaches them for their un-warrior-like behaviour and tells them, over an emphatic repetition of motif 76, why he is angry. 'No one knew my inner thoughts as she did – she who was the fount of my will and the fertile womb of my desires. Now she has defied my will, she whom my will created. Do you hear this Brünnhilde, to whom I gave life and weapons, and do you flee like a coward?'

She steps forward from behind the screen of her sisters, and with lowered eyes says: 'Here I am father. Pronounce your punishment.' 'It is not I who punish you,' Wotan responds, 'but you yourself,' and in an extended description of her defiance he explores the idea that she, whom he created as the agent of his will, has made herself anew, as his opponent. Hence she is no longer a Valkyrie: what she is now, she herself has made.

He goes on to describe all that Brünnhilde has lost, to a new melody (92) formed from 76 (frustration) and 85, the announcement of death, implying that death is indeed what he is pronouncing. She will no longer ride out from Valhalla to fetch heroes from the wars; she will no longer attend the solemn banquets of the gods or hand the drinking horn to her father, so as to receive his kisses. She will be banished from the realm of the gods. 'So do you take from me all that you gave?' Brünnhilde asks, as her sisters cry out in horror. 'He who overpowers you will take it,' Wotan replies, 'since I shall lock you here on the mountain in defenceless sleep, prey for whichever man should pass by and awaken you.' In a magnificent fugato passage (93) the Valkyries cry out in protest at this punishment, the shame of which would besmirch them all. Wotan turns on them, describing his decree in more detail, invoking the image of Brünnhilde as victim of a domineering man, withering to old age in domestic subordination, the butt of malicious jokes – an invocation all the more vivid, given the picture that Sieglinde has painted of her married life. Whichever of them lingers further, Wotan adds, will share Brünnhilde's fate – and with that they fly shrieking into the sky.

Alone with her father, Brünnhilde addresses him in solemn and moving words, to a new motif (95, 95A) expressive of Brünnhilde's purity of mind and selfless compassion. This motif is in fact the spear broken in two, transposed up by an octave at the break, so as to leap through a seventh before descending again. I call it the purity motif: it is both an expression of Brünnhilde's selflessness, and also a purification of the will that she shares with Wotan by once again breaking it on the reef of suffering. Donington compares the spear and the purity motifs in illuminating words:

> Wotan is trying to shut himself off from human feeling. He is trying to shut himself off from life itself in the attempt to shut himself off from the pain of it. He is trying to be uninvolved. Brynhilde will not let him spare himself the pain and will not let him be uninvolved. Brynhilde is his own warmth of feeling personified; and it is uncommonly interesting to find the music telling us that this warmth of feeling is nothing but the other side of his hard, cold will ... Cold-hearted or warm-hearted, it is still Wotan's heart. Harsh as at 19, or compassionate as at 95, it is still the same sequence of notes. Yet the difference between life and death is not wider than the difference between these motives.[9]

Brünnhilde asks Wotan to set his anger aside, and to explain instead why what she did was so dishonourable that she must herself be robbed of all honour as a punishment. In a quick exchange she makes clear to him that, while she disobeyed his orders, she obeyed his real intentions. Fricka had made those intentions foreign to him, causing him to act as his own enemy. Throughout this, the first presentation of the case for the defence, the purity motif is wound into the narrative by the ancillary motif, 96, with the most delicate counterpoint on the woodwind, like the weaving of fingers in a pair of beseeching hands.

Wotan acknowledges that Brünnhilde understood him well, but that her behaviour was treasonable in another way, because she was judging him to be a feeble coward. She retorts that she knew only that Wotan loved the Volsung, and that he was forced to turn against this love and therefore against himself. 'When Wotan is at war,' she adds, 'I guard his back. So I went to warn Siegmund of his death. I saw his eyes, heard his words, and beheld the sorrow of his boundless love. I stood ashamed before him, resolved to serve him and knew that this was the lot I must choose. For the one who breathed this feeling into my heart; for the will that allied me with the Volsung – faithful to *that* one, I disobeyed your order.' Those thoughts are expressed to a reprise and enhancement of the *Todesverkündigung* (85), which sounds on the woodwind while the strings repeat the accompanying figure 97A, another fragment of the spear that here serves to animate the melodic line. The passage culminates in the glorious statement of the purity motive by the whole orchestra, in Brünnhilde's key of E major.

In response, instead of reproaching Brünnhilde for what she did, Wotan condemns her for what she felt. At the moment when he, in self-torment, had turned against himself, taking the dread decision to end his sadness in the ruin of his world – at that very moment she was smiling, as she drank the sweet draught of love. For that reason, Wotan adds, our ways must part forever. Brünnhilde confronts him with the thought that, in separating from her, he is separating also from half of himself. Dishonour inflicted on her is therefore a dishonour to Wotan.

He tells her that she has followed the power of love, and therefore must follow the one whom she is obliged to love. 'But let it be no cowardly boaster who wins me as a prize,' she implores, and lets slip that the greatest hero will be born to the Volsung race. Wotan commands her not to speak of the Volsungs, whom he has vowed to destruction. But she insists on telling him of Sieglinde's escape, pregnant with a hero and carrying the pieces of the sword. In a crisis of despair Wotan strives to dismiss the reference to the sword, which he smashed to pieces. But even as he brushes Brünnhilde's words aside, Wotan takes in their meaning. When he has told her that she will be locked fast in sleep she beseeches him so to surround her with terrors that only a fearless and freely acting hero will finally awaken her. 'You ask too much,' he responds, but, clasping his knees, she begs that the rock on which she sleeps be surrounded by fire.

Overcome, Wotan gives way to an outpouring of love, recognizing that what she wills, he wills also, and that once again their wills coincide, though now the initiative is hers. To the motif of Siegfried the hero (89) he declares that 'only one shall win the bride, one freer than I, the god!' The act ends with Wotan's sublime farewell, in which, in beautiful verse set to yet more beautiful music, Wotan recalls the part that his daughter had played in those times when Valhalla was a place of festive triumph. To a chromatic melody (100), fitting symbol of the fact that his will, hitherto locked in the diatonic scale, has at last bent in the softer direction already taken by his daughter, he kisses the eyes that he had so much loved, so that they close in sleep. 'May their star shine for the happier man who will awaken you.' The motif to which Brünnhilde falls asleep (98) is a descending chromatic scale, harmonized to convey the complete extinction of Brünnhilde's agency. The motif is later given to Erda, to express the goddess's normal state of dormant wisdom. In falling asleep, therefore, Brünnhilde is also returning to the mother who bore her, to reconnect with the primordial source of moral knowledge.

Wotan summons Loge to create the ring of fire, declaring, to the Siegfried as hero motif, that 'Whosoever fears the tip of my spear shall never pass through the fire.' The opera ends with the magic fire music (101), incorporating a figure (99) that has been accompanying the vocal line throughout this scene, and which is sometimes called the 'sleeping Brünnhilde' motif, while the chromatic melody of Wotan's farewell sounds again on the strings. The god retires from the scene, leaving the world to the free hero who is to replace him as its sovereign.

SIEGFRIED

Die Walküre has effected an enormous transition, from the world of gods to the world of men. Metaphysically speaking these are the *same* world, viewed from two separate perspectives. But they are distinguished in the drama as they are in the imagination of religious people. Wotan has entered the realm of mortals, believing that it is only there that the free being can be created. Only such a being, whose power is acquired neither by theft nor by the loss of love, could be free from the curse, and so able to return the Ring to the Rhine-daughters. In entering the world of mortals, however, gods become subject to the moral law that they impose on it. Hence they acquire a conscience. Wotan is troubled by the trick that underpins his legal authority – the trick whereby he paid for Valhalla with twice-stolen goods – and by the constant deception practised on humans, so as to encourage them to fight and die. Moreover, his own need for love diverts him from his divine purpose.

His children are expressions of his will, so that his search among them for the Other who will act independently is always frustrated. Yet he loves his children too, as creatures that look back at him with his own freedom-revealing eye. He creates Siegmund as a lawless outsider, hoping in this way to withdraw from his creation so that the hero acts for himself alone.[10] But the trick doesn't work, and no one, least of all Fricka, is deceived by it. And when, finally, one of his children, creature of his will, acts against his will, he responds in anger, taking her godhead away. But what she has done out of love is exactly what had to be done if the wound in the cosmos is to heal. Wotan does not yet fully understand this, but he is on the way to doing so, and has already begun the work of forgiveness. It is beginning to dawn on him that she is the Other for whom he has been seeking – the one who is prepared to renounce divine love for its sadder, shorter but completer human version.

Although, as in *Das Rheingold*, the women who appear in *Die Walküre* are victims, they are beginning nevertheless to assert themselves against their abusers. The enslaved and brutalized Sieglinde is prepared to defy Hunding and all the weight of his conventional morality in order to express her love for Siegmund. Fricka, humiliated yet again by her husband's sexual predations, is able to triumph over his arguments, and in doing so rises to a new grandeur as the guardian of honour in a world of tricks. And the wild, pure, intelligent Valkyrie is able to extract from her father the action that she needs, in the very moment of her punishment. Now she can look forward to the kind of love that she had witnessed in Siegmund – love that heals the cosmic wound.

From this point onwards attention shifts to the human sphere, where Nibelungs still strive for dominion, but where, asleep somewhere on the heights, is the woman who bears the secret of the future. The prelude, derived from the motifs of smithing, the hoard and brooding (33, 37, 40), expresses the obsessive mind and heartless ambition of Mime. The sparse melodic motifs from Nibelheim are repeatedly hammered out over bare, static harmonies as though on an anvil. After frenzied repetition of the 'world's mastery' motif (16A) the curtain rises to reveal Mime working at a natural farrier's hearth in a cave. He has escaped from Alberich's dominion, and is trying to forge a sword for the young Siegfried; but the music tells us that his escape from Alberich's objective prison has not altered the subjective prison within.

Mime exclaims that the boy snaps every sword that he produces. Yet there is one sword that Siegfried would not be able to snap, if only Mime knew how to forge it, the sword made from the fragments of Nothung. With such a sword Siegfried, with his youthful strength, would kill Fafner the dragon, and so win the Nibelung's Ring for Mime. But alas, the dwarf cannot weld the pieces together: he goes on tapping and hammering at these toy swords, only because the boy insists; but the task is fruitless.

Thus we learn how things are for Siegfried, issue of the doomed siblings. Somehow he has been brought up by Mime, who wishes to use him to obtain the Ring, the object of an all-consuming obsession. With such a start in life, Siegfried is inevitably an uncouth creature. He is also deeply hostile to the dwarf who houses him, and wishes only for the opportunity to win his place in the world with a sword of his own. This we discover at his first appearance, when he comes in driving a bear before him and laughingly egging on the animal to eat the dwarf. 'Go on, Bruin,' he urges, 'ask for the sword.' The trembling Mime produces the sword and Siegfried, with a slap to its back, releases the bear into the forest.

During the ensuing dialogue it becomes clear that Siegfried patrols the forest alone, playing the silver horn that Mime made for him, in the hope that it will summon a friend. He takes the sword that Mime has forged and breaks it with one blow over the anvil. Then he pours out insults while the dwarf, in insinuating tones, tries to convince the boy of his fatherly concern. Siegfried will have none of it, refusing the broth that Mime offers and listening with revulsion to Mime's wheedling protestations of love, and to his catalogue of reasons why Siegfried should be grateful for all that he has received at the dwarf's hands. 'Much you have taught me,' Siegfried concedes, 'but you have not taught me how to bear the sight of you. Every beast is dearer to me than you are. So why is it that I constantly return?'

'Because you love me really,' is Mime's response, and he elaborates with a tale of the beasts and the birds that return to their parents' nest, proof that Siegfried, in the same way, *must* love Mime. Siegfried here, showing the first spark of natural feeling, recounts how he has observed the love between the birds and beasts of the field, as they pair off in spring time and nurture their young. 'Where, Mime,' he therefore asks, 'is your loving wife, that I may call her mother?'

The music of this passage, based on two new motifs (108 and 109), effects a radical change in atmosphere. Heartless antagonism gives way to warm yearning, as the voice of nature sounds in Siegfried's soul. The chromatic motif, touching on Wotan's farewell (100) at the beginning and Freia's love theme (22B) at the end, moves the drama in a new direction, and we are made aware that Siegfried will one day fill this cold world with the warm emotions that were not extinguished at the end of *Die Walküre*, but merely put to sleep there.

Mime tries to persuade Siegfried that he is both father and mother, but Siegfried rebuts the suggestion. He has seen his own face in the sparkling stream, and knows that he and Mime are as alike as a toad and a fish, and never did a fish have a toad for a father. But that, he suddenly realizes, is why he always returns from the forest – in order to learn from Mime who his father and mother were. Mime ducks out of the question, but Siegfried, grabbing him by the throat and larding him with insults, eventually brings the dwarf to tell the story of his birth, which he does to music associated with the sorrow and love of the Volsung twins. (58, 59 and 61.)

A woman lay whimpering in the wild wood, and the dwarf brought her into the warmth of the cave where, wretchedly, she gave birth. Great was her distress but, though she died, Siegfried lived. 'So my mother died through me?' Siegfried asks, again showing the un-explored realm of sympathy that he bears within. Not answering the question Mime here introduces a habitual litany of self-praise and self-pity – the 'starling song' (107), which Siegfried always shrugs off with disgust. (The starling mimics the songs of other birds, but has no song of its own: likewise Mime, who mimics the soft emotions that he cannot share, has no real love of his own.) Siegfried asks how he got his name and learns that his mother commanded Mime to call him Siegfried. 'And what was my mother called?' Siegfried asks. Mime goes back to self-pity until again forced to the point by Siegfried, revealing that the mother's name was Sieglinde. As for the father she said only that he was killed – and Mime resumes his starling song. 'Stop that squawking!' Siegfried cries, 'and give me some proof of this story!'

Here Mime produces the fragments of the sword, saying that Sieglinde left these in paltry payment for all the great cost of Siegfried's nurture: they are the pieces of the sword that was shattered in his father's last fight. Joyfully Siegfried springs to his feet and commands the dwarf to forge the pieces together, threatening him with a real drubbing if the weapon is not ready today. 'But why do you want it today?' Mime asks. 'In order to leave here forever,' returns Siegfried, expressing in song his joy that Mime is not his father, that this cave is not his home, that he can fly away free of guilt into the forest and never see the dwarf again. Siegfried's exuberant song, which contains a wealth of new material, and in particular motif 111, which is to assume great importance in *Götterdämmerung*, foretells the free and self-created Siegfried who is soon to be launched upon the world. Mime calls after Siegfried as the boy storms off into the forest and then gives voice to his anxiety that Siegfried will leave before obtaining the Ring. Besides, he reflects, how can he possibly forge Nothung from these pieces that no dwarf's hammer could dent? The resentment and toil of a Nibelung will not knit such a sword.

As the dwarf mutters to himself Wotan enters in the guise of the Wanderer, greeting Mime as 'wise smith', and asking hospitality for a way-worn guest. The first motif associated with the Wanderer (113A) consists of whole tone steps arranged on a descending chromatic scale – a striking and original idea that beautifully expresses the transformation in Wotan's character, from the wilful god who imposed law on the world, to the wanderer who now stands back from it. Like the sleep motif at the end of *Die Walküre* (98), which it spells out more circumspectly, the theme suggests a mystery that lies in the heart of being. It is like a trapdoor into nothingness that might at any moment give way and on which meanwhile the world is remade. Wotan, the music urges, has become passive and, in his second motif (113B), almost serene, though what he observes so calmly came about as a result of his will. The world that he witnesses is a determined world, but also the result of his own determination.

To Mime's suspicious rebuffs the Wanderer declares that good people grant him haven and gifts, and that only the ungenerous fear evil from him. Mime's response to this recalls that of Sieglinde to Siegmund in Act 1 of *Die Walküre*: misfortune is my constant companion; would you bring more on a poor man? (Sieglinde, by contrast, had said: you cannot bring misfortune to this house where misfortune reigns. Hers was an invitation, not a rebuff.) The Wanderer tells Mime that he has explored much and has useful advice to offer to those with heavy hearts, to which Mime replies: 'I have no need of spies and loiterers, my own wits suffice for my needs', and endeavours to show the Wanderer the door.

Here begins Wagner's version of the Icelandic 'wisdom contest'. The Wanderer sits by the hearth and stakes his head in a war of wits. 'My head is yours if you do not hear from me what will help you.' Mime sees no way out of the situation save to accept the challenge, and proposes three questions as the test. He asks, first, which race dwells in the depths of the earth? The question is not asking for factual knowledge, but for the sign of inward acquaintance – the familiarity that comes from intimate dealings. So the Wanderer's answer, describing the Nibelungs and their enslavement by Alberich, and the subsequent loss of the Ring, is a shock to Mime. Just who can this be, who is intimate with that cosmic mystery? He then asks which race dwells on the Earth's back, eliciting a description of the Giants and their erstwhile chieftains, Fasolt and Fafner, who won for themselves the Nibelung's gold. The Wanderer recounts the slaying of Fasolt and the metamorphosis of Fafner into a dragon, who now guards the gold.

Mime, yet more troubled, asks which race dwells in the cloudy heights, enabling the Wanderer to give us the first clear description of how he, as Wotan, Lord of Light, gained government of the earth. He cut a branch from the World Ash Tree, the trunk of which then withered, although the spear that he made from it will never decay. With its point he governs the world. Solemn treaties are carved in runes on its shaft, and before the one who holds the spear the Nibelungs bow down, and the Giants too are quelled. This summary of Wotan's relation to the world is expressed in musical rather than conceptual connections. In the brief course of it the god refers to himself as *Licht-Alberich,* and the summary ends on a new motif (114) associated with the power of the gods, but which, in its final appearance, will accompany Brünnhilde's incendiary suicide, with which she sets fire to Valhalla. This *summa theologica* in two and a half pages of vocal score is an instance of Wagner's ability to build huge arcs of narrative in the smallest physical time, relying on the music to give force and clarity to the story. And in the course of summarizing his position Wotan is also feeling his way towards a new self-knowledge, recognizing that he and Alberich form two sides of a single bid for domination.

As he draws to the end of his narrative the Wanderer lets his spear strike the ground as though by accident, causing a clap of thunder which strikes fear into Mime. The dwarf, collecting himself, tells the Wanderer to go on his way, but is reproached for his inhospitable behaviour and for asking questions in order to gain power rather than knowledge. So by the rules of contest his head is forfeit if he does not answer the Wanderer's three questions in his turn. Mime has by now recognized his guest as Wotan, and gathers his wits for the trial. While Mime's questions had concerned the cosmic order and the powers that have striven for mastery over it, the Wanderer's questions are directed towards the world of practical affairs, reminding the dwarf that he ought to have asked for needed advice, and not striven for an unobtainable mastery. They also have another and more metaphysical function, which is to ensure that Siegfried obtains a sword without Wotan doing anything directly to provide it.

First the Wanderer asks which is the race that Wotan oppresses even though its life is dearest to him. Mime answers with an account of the Volsungs, fathered by Wotan, of Siegmund and Sieglinde and of their offspring Siegfried, revealing incidentally, that he *did* know the name of Siegfried's father. Wotan feigns amazement at the dwarf's knowledge, and goes on to say that a wise Nibelung now watches over Siegfried, who must slay the dragon for him and obtain the Ring. What sword must Siegfried use, if he is to achieve this purpose?

Mime exultantly responds with a description of Nothung and its history, from the time Wotan plunged it into Hunding's ash tree, to the time when it broke upon Wotan's spear. Wotan interrupts Mime's triumphant giggles, reproaches him for exploiting the youthful hero, and poses a third question: who will forge the sword from the splinters? Mime now curses the fragments of the sword, regrets that he stole them,* rails against the task that he cannot accomplish and causes the Wanderer to remind him of the rules of the game. You asked about idle and distant things, the Wanderer says, but not about what was closest to you and what you needed to know. And now, when I point it out, you go berserk (*verrückt*)! And the Wanderer concludes with a prophecy: 'Only one who has never learned fear shall forge Nothung anew.' He departs, leaving Mime's head forfeit to the one who has never learned fear.

Mime, now on the verge of delirium, peers out beyond the mouth of the cave. The trees rustle in the breeze and the sun's light shimmers in their branches. In his terror Mime imagines Fafner to be approaching through the forest. A distorted version of the magic fire music invokes the crazed fantasies of the dwarf, who doubles up with terror and hides behind the anvil, crying 'Fafner! Fafner!' The sword motif sounds in the minor and then, to the sound of the freedom motif (110), Siegfried bursts in from the forest, again demanding the sword and looking around for Mime, whom he discovers cowering behind the anvil. Mime, in fear and trembling, repeats the Wanderer's prophecy: 'Only one who has never learned fear shall forge Nothung anew.'

Siegfried is bewildered by this, and by Mime's confused references to his forfeited head. Eventually, however, the dwarf incorporates the idea of fear into his self-vaunting litany, saying 'in my anxious care for you alone, I forgot to teach you something important. I was down on the ground learning fear, in order to teach you.' And he delivers his lesson concerning the nature of fear. To the distorted magic fire music

* The idea that he stole the fragments played no part in Mime's story to Siegfried, and suggests another prehistory than the one that Siegfried has learned. Should we make anything of this? I think not.

he describes the gloomy forest, the rustling and humming, the bluster-
ing and roaring, the whirling and swirling, the flickering of flames.
'Do you not feel a trembling in your limbs and a beating of the heart
when you encounter these things?' The 'sleeping Brünnhilde' motif
(99) has emerged from the shimmering music of the orchestra, and
sounds in a sweet C major as Siegfried remarks how very strange that
feeling must be. The music (which I discuss at more length in the next
chapter) is telling us not only that Siegfried will learn fear from Brünnhilde, but that the hero's existential invulnerability is also a mark of
sexual innocence. He has not yet been tried in the encounter with
what is wholly Other. 'How can I learn this thing?' he asks, and Mime
promises to lead him to the evil dragon that will teach him. 'Where is
the dragon's lair?' asks Siegfried, and Mime names the place as Neidhöhle, to the east, on the edge of the forest. 'So not far from the world?'
Siegfried asks. He orders Mime to take him there, and asks again for
the sword. 'Accursed steel!' cries Mime, 'which I cannot mend.' And
he again repeats the Wanderer's prophecy.

Siegfried treats Mime to some more verbal abuse and orders him to
produce the pieces of the sword. 'My father's steel must obey me: I'll
forge the sword myself.' Mime reminds him that he was lazy at his
lessons in smithing, but so what, replies Siegfried, since your knowledge of smithing got you nowhere with this sword? Mime first offers
solder, which Siegfried pushes dismissively away, and then watches in
amazement as the boy files the steel to shreds. It is clear that Siegfried
is succeeding with the sword, and Mime soliloquizes again about the
Wanderer's prophecy. He recognizes his dilemma: Siegfried will not
slay the dragon if he learns fear; nor will he forge the sword. But only
if he learns fear will Mime keep his head.

Siegfried asks for the name of the sword, and sings his eulogy to
Nothung, blowing on the embers of the forge with the bellows. Four
ideas are here woven into a contrapuntal tapestry (120), over truncated fragments of the spear motif (19) in the bass. As the song fills
the cave with uncouth jubilation Mime mutters of the sleeping
draught that he will brew so that, the fight over, Siegfried will lose his
head to the very sword with which he has killed the dragon. The boy
comments on Mime's new calling as a cook, and then returns to the
work of the forge.

The long-drawn-out scene of the forging, in which Siegfried files, smelts, casts and hardens the steel, crying 'Hoho! Hoho! Hohei! Hohei!' and similar, while Mime exults in the background over his future as lord of the Ring, is uncomfortably near the bone for those sensitive to the 'blond beast' interpretation of Wagner. It is, for all that, a musical and dramatic triumph, and a scene of sustained comedy, as the two actions of the boy hero and the malicious dwarf move incongruously in parallel to their conclusions, sword in the one case, poison in the other. The action is as accurate a portrayal of forging as is the ride of the Valkyries of horsey women, and also has an important place in the philosophy of the *Ring* cycle, by showing labour in its joyous, unalienated form – the form of which Nibelheim is the perversion and negation. Siegfried's labour is will and self-expression, the labour of Nibelheim submission and enslavement.

In the prelude to this act we had seen the trace of Nibelheim in the joyless mind of Mime. The relentless smithing theme was there like an imprint, a constantly returning and imprisoning addiction, from which the dwarf cannot escape. By contrast the music of Siegfried's forging is as though exhaled from his very being – as yet an unformed, callow and hardly socialized being, but one that has found its own voice, its own rhythm, and its own way of impressing itself on the world. This is the musical expression of the first step in the process of *Selbstbestimmung*, which, in the philosophy of Fichte and Hegel, leads to freedom and self-knowledge. The next, and critical, step, the encounter with the Other, is yet to come. The third and final step, the achievement of self-knowledge, is never taken. That, we will discover, is the tragic destiny of the self-created hero.

With the prelude to Act 2 we are back in the world of alienation. We hear the motifs of the dragon (124), the Ring, the curse and Alberich's resentment (44), as the curtain rises to reveal Alberich keeping watch in the night outside the cave of Neidhöhle. From this moment on the music will bring us constantly into contact with the reality of resentment, with the effect of the curse on all human projects, however well intentioned, and with the machinations of evil. All this is foreshadowed in the prelude, which is the first of three remarkable attempts to present the sound of malice.

Dawn seems to glimmer in the distance, but as the light approaches

Alberich describes it as a shining horse, breaking through the wood. Perhaps the dragon's slayer is at hand? But the glow disappears and a figure approaches through the shadows. It is Wotan in the form of the Wanderer again, who comes questioningly forward. Alberich recognizes him and cries: 'How dare you show yourself here, shameless thief!' The Wanderer replies that he has come to watch, not to act, and Alberich informs Wotan that he is well aware of the god's wiles, and of his vulnerable points. He will not let himself be tricked again of the Ring. 'With my treasure you paid your debt to the Giants. But what you once promised them remains inscribed on your spear, so that you dare not snatch back from the Giants what you paid them as quittance. If you did so, your spear would shatter and your reign would be at an end.'

The Wanderer reminds him that no treaty bound him to Alberich, who was subjected by the power of the spear, not the runes inscribed on its shaft. The point here is significant: the rule of law through which contracts are upheld is not itself bestowed by another contract, but only by an act of usurpation buried in the mists of time. It is this usurpation, the stripping of the branch from the World Ash Tree (for which Wotan paid, somehow, with the loss of an eye), that bestowed on him the power to govern Alberich, not a contract between them. Faced with this fact Alberich then releases one of his blood-curdling threats, to music that recalls the original encounter with Wotan in Nibelheim. 'Doomed to death through my curse is he who guards the treasure. Unlike the stupid Giants I will use the power of the Ring to storm Valhalla's heights with Hella's host – then I shall rule the world!'

'Yes,' says the Wanderer, 'but it doesn't worry me. Let him who wins the Ring be its master.'

'How darkly you speak,' Alberich responds. 'Is it because you have reared a hero who will pluck the fruit you dare not touch?'

'Quarrel with Mime, not with me,' the Wanderer replies. 'Your brother brings a lad here who must kill Fafner for him. The boy knows nothing of the Ring, but Mime will tell him. So do as you think fit, my friend.'

This show of divine graciousness astounds Alberich, who asks if the Wanderer will keep his hands off the hoard. The Wanderer replies that he avails himself only of heroes, who act for themselves and are their own masters. He who seizes the Ring will therefore win it. The new leitmotif that accompanies this declaration (126), sometimes called the motif of the free hero, has an expansive, generous character, suggesting that Wotan has decided already to make a gift of the world to Siegfried. 'Would you know more?' he asks of Alberich. 'Then why not warn the dragon of death – maybe he will give up his toy.' And with that he calls out to Fafner to wake up. 'What is the madman doing?' Alberich asks aloud, and 'Will he really let me have the Ring?'

The voice of Fafner is heard, asking who disturbs his sleep. The Wanderer tells him of approaching danger. Fafner's life will be saved if he surrenders the treasure to the person who comes in search of it. Alberich adds his own warning of the approaching hero, saying 'he wants nothing except the golden ring: give it to me and I will prevent the fight.' To this Fafner replies: 'Here I lie and here I hold; let me sleep'.

The Wanderer laughs and says 'Well, Alberich, that didn't work. But call me a rogue no longer. This place I cede to you, contend with your brother Mime, you may fare better with his kind. More than that you soon will learn.' To the music associated with Erda (47), he adds that 'everything follows its own nature, and nothing can alter it' – again an expression of resignation, as though he has already relinquished the world to the hero who is to succeed him. So saying he mounts his horse and speeds away into the sky, to the poignant sound of the farewell sung to Brünnhilde at the end of Die Walküre (100). Looking after him Alberich repeats his habitual threat to overthrow the frivolous pleasure-seeking gods, and then withdraws into the shadows.

In this encounter between the two Alberichs, light and dark, a deep contrast is drawn, between the god who can renounce the world, and the dwarf whose only thought is to regain it as its sole possessor. In the original version of Der junge Siegfried the dialogue was very much longer, since Wagner had to fill gaps in the story that he later covered in Die Walküre and Das Rheingold.[11] The comparison of the two texts shows Wagner retaining only what is essential, in order to reveal the continuing growth of Wotan's character, and the static condition of his stunted opposite.

Mime and Siegfried arrive, Mime saying that this is the spot where Siegfried will learn fear. The boy expresses his distrust, asking Mime to leave him alone. Mime points to the dark mouth of the dragon's cave and says that, when Siegfried's heart quakes and the earth sways beneath him, then he will remember how Mime loves him. 'You must not love me,' Siegfried cries. 'Out of my sight with your nauseating nodding and blinking', at which Mime says that he will wait for Siegfried by the stream nearby. If you do that, Siegfried replies, I will make sure the dragon goes to the stream, so that he can eat you before he is killed. Mime describes the dragon's venom and its dangerous tail, and adds, to Siegfried's enquiry, that its heart lies in the breast, where other beasts have theirs. Siegfried sends Mime away, the dwarf offering to be on hand when needed, before uttering beneath his breath the hope that Siegfried and the dragon will kill each other.

Alone now Siegfried expresses his relief that Mime is not his father, and reflects on the dwarf's ugly appearance, which surely would be shared by his son. Forest murmurs sound from the orchestra and there begins one of the most moving scenes in the entire cycle, in which the character of Siegfried is again filled by music that speaks to the heart. Siegfried begins to meditate on his mother: 'what did she look like . . . and why did she die? Do all human mothers die of their sons? How sad that would be. If only I could see her!' As Siegfried is filled with yearning for his mother, motif 108 sounds in the orchestra, soon giving way to the first half of Freia's love music (22A) – love in its natural, universal, form, not yet attached, with whatever tragic consequences, to the particular object of desire. A wood-bird begins to sing, a pentatonic melody related to the Rhine-daughters' lullaby (128). We have been suddenly returned to the state of nature from which the cycle began, Siegfried's mother-longing reflected all around him in the sounds and sights of the forest.

If he could understand the bird's song, Siegfried speculates, he might learn from it about his mother. Maybe, by attending to the tune he can come to understand the bird's language. In a comic scene that outlines his innocent sympathy for the natural world, Siegfried cuts a reed and fashions it into a pipe, striving to make the notes of the wood-bird's song, but failing dismally. He then takes his horn, which he has often played in the hope that it might bring him a

companion, but which has hitherto produced only wolves and bears.
It is thus that he awakens the dragon.

After an exchange of taunts they fight and Siegfried plunges his
sword into the dragon's heart. As he lies dying Fafner summarizes his
history, to a musical narrative that winds together Alberich's resentment, fragments of Siegfried's horn call and Fafner's own tritone
distortion of the original Giants' motif (124). There is a remarkable
pathos to this scene, as the dragon, in dying, recalls a former and
better life. 'For the accursed gold got from the gods I did Fasolt to
death. I, last of the Giants, have now fallen to a fresh-faced hero. Be
warned, bright boy: he who prompted this deed is surely plotting
your death. Mark how it will end! Heed my words!' 'You seem wise
in dying,' says Siegfried. 'So tell me where I came from; you will
surely know from my name. Siegfried I am called.' 'Siegfried!' repeats
the dragon as he dies.

Siegfried pulls the sword from the dragon's body and a spot of
blood splashes on his hand. It burns like fire and he sucks the place to
cool it. At once he can understand the song of the wood-bird. The
bird tells him that he will find the hoard in the cave, that the Tarnhelm will help him to perform wondrous deeds, and that the Ring
would make him ruler of the world. Siegfried thanks the bird for its
counsel and enters the cave.

Mime now returns, eager for the booty, only to encounter Alberich
hastening from the opposite direction. There follows a vicious alter-
cation as each lays claim to the treasure, Mime as Siegfried's guardian,
Alberich as the one who paid the price of it. Eventually Mime offers
the Ring to Alberich in exchange for the Tarnhelm. 'Be the master,'
he concedes, 'but call me brother. Share the spoils with me!' 'Share
with you?' Alberich cries, 'and the Tarnhelm too? I would never be
safe from your snares!' 'So nothing for me?' asks Mime, 'Not a jot!'
Mime responds that he will call Siegfried to his aid and so take all for
himself.

Siegfried enters and they see, to Alberich's especial dismay, that he
holds the Tarnhelm and the Ring. The two dwarfs retire in opposite
directions. As Siegfried studies the Ring, the lament of the
Rhine-daughters sounds in the orchestra, a sign that for Siegfried this
trinket, whose use he cannot fathom and which he will keep, he says,

as a reminder of the day's events, has as yet no power for him, and no power over him either. The beautiful music returns us to the beginning of the story. This ring on Siegfried's finger reassumes its original identity as the Rhine-daughters' treasure. From this moment on, indeed, the power of the Ring lies dormant, though not the power of the curse that Alberich has placed on it.

The wood-bird sings again, warning Siegfried against the treacherous Mime, and telling him that, thanks to the dragon's blood, he will now understand what Mime is concealing behind his lying words. Mime advances with unctuous flattery, asking whether the valiant boy has now learnt fear. 'I have not yet found a teacher,' Siegfried replies. 'Not the dragon?' asks Mime, to which Siegfried replies that, grim and spiteful though the dragon was, its death grieves Siegfried sorely, given that more evil villains still live unpunished. 'More than the dragon do I hate the one who bade me kill it!' There follows a waltz-like serenade from Mime, in which, to a bundle of sing-song cantillations, the dwarf outlines his deep hatred for the boy, the pentatonic melody of the wood-bird interrupting to remind us that what Siegfried hears, and what Mime intends him to hear, are opposites. This brilliant scene, in which the dwarf dancingly reveals his malicious nature through the very musical syntax that is intended to disguise it, represents the world of the 'Kitschmensch', as Hermann Broch was to describe him: the world of fake emotion, in which language, music, art and everyday life are all devoted to the cause of disguising cynical exploitation behind a candyfloss of simulated love.[12]

Mime offers the drink that he has brewed for Siegfried, revealing his intention to drug the boy and then hack off his head. Eventually, after the dwarf has (through the bird's translation) made all his malicious thoughts so clear that there is no choice but to respond to them, Siegfried takes his sword and cuts Mime's head from his shoulders. We hear the voice of Alberich off stage, laughing to the smithing motif.

Siegfried drags the body of Mime to the cave and throws it on the treasure, saying 'now you can be lord of the thing you longed for'. And he drags the body of the dragon across the mouth of the cave, as an obstacle to thieves. His blood is on fire, his head burns, and he seeks rest under a linden tree. To a plaintive version of the longing motif, 108, he asks the wood-bird to sing to him again, lamenting that he is alone, his mother dead, his father slain, and his sole companion a detestable dwarf whom he was forced at last to kill. 'Can you, friendly bird, grant me a good companion?'

The bird responds with the description of a wonderful wife for Siegfried, asleep on a rocky height and surrounded by fire. Whoever can break through the fire can possess her. Siegfried leaps up for joy, singing of the flames that have started in his heart. He asks the bird to tell him the meaning of this new sensation, and the bird replies with mystical words:

> Lustig im Leid sing' ich von Liebe;
> wonnig aus Weh web' ich mein Lied:
> nur Sehnende kennen den Sinn!

'Gaily in suffering I sing of love; blissful from woe I weave my song: only those who yearn know its meaning!'

Siegfried responds with questions: can he break through the fire? Can he waken the bride? And the bird tells him that only the one who does not know fear can waken Brünnhilde, and Siegfried cries 'why, that is me! The day that I failed to learn fear from Fafner I long to learn it from Brünnhilde! Dear bird show me the way!' And the bird, after a few circles, sets off for the mountain, with Siegfried in eager pursuit.

This is the point at which Wagner laid the composition of the music aside for twelve years, writing *Tristan und Isolde* and *Die Meistersinger von Nürnberg* together with a plethora of essays on cultural and political themes. There is a recognizable increase in symphonic complexity in the music of *Siegfried* Act 3 and *Götterdämmerung*: the chromatic harmony and voice-leading of *Tristan* and the contrapuntal mastery of *Die Meistersinger* have all left their marks on Wagner's score. But the material introduced in *Das Rheingold* is still deployed in its original meaning, has lost none of its freshness and melodic grace, and adapts to the intensified polyphony entirely without strain. It is as though the idiom of *Siegfried* Act 3 had been implicit all along and, emphasizing this, Wagner begins the act with a prelude incorporating and reaffirming motifs associated with

Wotan, and also with Erda and her prophecy of the doom of the gods, but in a new and agitated idiom expressive of a once-orderly world thrown into disorder, as though by the impact of an asteroid.

Wotan, still in the guise of the Wanderer, stands before a crypt-like cave, urgently summoning Erda to arise from her brooding sleep. We hear the sleep motif – the chromatic sequence of chords (98) with which Brünnhilde had been put to sleep at the end of *Die Walküre* – as the immortal Wala emerges, asking who has disturbed her slumber. Wotan identifies himself as the awakener, saying that he has wandered the world, awakening with spells whatever sleeps, roaming in search of knowledge. 'Thus I have come to you, who know all things. Where there are beings, your breath stirs; where brains brood, your wisdom works.'

Erda acknowledges that while she sleeps she accumulates wisdom; the Norns, however, are awake, and zealously spin the rope of destiny, which records what Erda knows. Why not ask the Norns? Wotan answers that the Norns are subservient to the world, and can alter nothing. From Erda, however, he would gladly learn how to arrest a rolling wheel. Erda responds that she is bewildered by the deeds of men. 'Even I, with all my wisdom, was once overcome by a conqueror. To Wotan I bore a wish-maiden who is brave and wise. Why not seek wisdom from Erda and Wotan's child?'

Wotan briefly recounts Brünnhilde's transgression and punishment, adding that it would help nothing to question her now. This sends Erda into a paroxysm of bewilderment. 'Does he who taught defiance punish defiance?' she asks. 'Does he who ignites the deed, hate the deed when done? Does he who defends the right and protects the oath banish the right and rule by perjury?' Having thus summarized Wotan's predicament she begs to be allowed to seal up her wisdom again in sleep. He declares that he will not let her go, since with her prophecies she has filled him with fear. 'So tell me now: how can the god conquer his care?'

To this question Erda gives an astonishing reply. 'You are not what you call yourself.' Does she mean that he is not a god? Is this her way of foretelling the end of the gods? Wotan replies in kind, saying 'You are not what you believe yourself!' He adds that the Earth-mother's wisdom is drawing to an end, since it will wither before Wotan's will.

And what does Wotan will? He wills the end! What once in fury and loathing he flung to the Nibelung's resentment, he now bequeaths freely to the valiant Volsung. 'He whom I chose, though he knows me not, has gained the Nibelung's Ring, and will awaken Brünnhilde. On waking she, the child of your wisdom, will do the deed that will redeem the world – *die erlösende Weltentat*.' As Wotan sings those last words the orchestra gives voice to the broad motif of the world's inheritance (134), which inverts the motif of the spear and which should sound, Wagner said, like the announcement of a new religion,[13] though just how confident Wotan is in Brünnhilde's mission is rendered immediately unclear when the melody peters out onto an unsettled diminished seventh chord. But the music recovers strength, and the motif is repeated more confidently, to the words 'Whatever now befalls, to the eternally young the god joyfully yields!' With this, his second great bequest, he dismisses the Wala to her endless sleep.

This mystical scene (the music of which I discuss in the next chapter) must be understood as mysteries generally are understood: it is the representation in a single moment of a long process of discovery. Wotan has wandered the world, awakening its sleeping wisdom, discovering everywhere that the gods are doomed, and that he must choose between resisting the end and willing it. He has hoped to resist, but now knows that the only choice is to will as a gift what he must otherwise suffer as a doom. By willing the end he continues to assert his sovereignty, makes destiny irrelevant, and plants in the mortal who is to replace him the seeds of his own immortality. The divine is to take on human flesh, and to set out in the form of a mortal woman to attempt what Wotan can no longer accomplish.

This air of mystery survives into the succeeding scene. The Wanderer descries Siegfried, still following the wood-bird. At the sight of Wotan's ravens the bird flutters quickly away, and Siegfried looks around in doubt. The Wanderer asks him where he is going. 'To a rock surrounded by fire, where sleeps a woman whom I wish to awaken.' 'Who told you to seek the rock? What made you yearn for the woman?' asks the Wanderer. Siegfried describes his encounter with the wood-bird, his slaying of the dragon, and the effect of tasting the dragon's blood. 'Who made you fight the dragon?' 'A deceitful dwarf led me to the dragon, though the dragon itself incited the sword-stroke from which it died.' 'Who made the sword so sharp and strong?' 'I myself.' 'But who made the splinters from which you forged the sword?' Siegfried responds impatiently that he doesn't know, but that the fragments would have been useless if he had not reforged them. 'I think so too!' says the Wanderer, laughing (though to the motif, 61, in its revised form 61A, associated with the sorrow of the Volsungs, suggesting that Wotan's laughter is the expression of a deep inner conflict).

Siegfried is irritated by all these futile questions and, addressing the Wanderer as an old forbidder, tells him either to show the way or hold his tongue. 'If you think that I am old, then you should show me respect,' the Wanderer replies. 'All my life an old man has stood in my way,' Siegfried responds. 'Watch out you don't meet the same fate as Mime. But why do you wear such a big hat and why does it cover your face?' Siegfried looks closer and discovers that an eye is missing. 'Doubtless someone struck it out because you barred his way,' the boy says. 'Take yourself off or you might lose the other one!' To this the Wanderer reproaches Siegfried's ignorant behaviour and his determination to get his way, adding that 'with the eye that is missing you yourself are looking at me'. Siegfried laughs and repeats his request that the old man give him directions or else get out of the way.

Wounded, the Wanderer says 'If you knew me, insolent youth, you would spare your insults.' To music woven from the motif of Wotan's frustration (76) he adds that he has always loved Siegfried even if he has also made the hero suffer. Siegfried now becomes belligerent as the Wanderer tries to stop his advance. The Wanderer identifies himself as the guardian of the rock, points the way to it and describes its terrors. 'Go back, rash boy!' he commands as the flames begin to flicker on the heights. 'Go back yourself,' Siegfried retorts. The Wanderer now bars his way with the spear, saying that Siegfried's sword once shattered on its shaft and will now be shattered again. Jubilant to have discovered his father's enemy Siegfried rushes forward and smashes the spear. The stage directions tell us that a flash of lightning springs from the broken spear and strikes the top of the mountain, which begins to shine from this moment with ever-brighter flames. The lightning is accompanied by a clap of thunder, which quickly dwindles. 'Forward then,' says the Wanderer, calmly picking up the pieces of the spear, 'I cannot stop you.' In the orchestra Erda's motif is followed by its inversion (48, the motif of the doom of the gods), as the Wanderer suddenly disappears into the darkness.

As in his encounter with Erda, Wotan has made as if to avert the outcome that he also intends. He is in a state of conflict, and in the metaphor of the eye he expresses his identity with the boy who stands opposed to him. Siegfried is the true inheritor of the world for which Wotan paid the original price, and the need for Siegfried arose at the very moment when the spear of government was stripped from the Ash Tree. Wotan now knows that governance of the world, however lawful, confers mortality on the one who claims it. His only choice is to will his own end, or else to be overtaken by it. But to will the end is to will the end of his will, so how can he really will it? Only if his spear – the instrument of his will – is broken by someone other than himself who is yet the god's own will, can the god will his own demise. And surely it is thus with all wilful people, that their acts of renunciation are also affirmations, and that they can give things up at last only by provoking others to seize them. Their love is never without an admixture of anger at the otherness of the one they love. Wagner himself was like this.

Siegfried looks around in vain for the Wanderer, and now turns delightedly in the direction of the flames, where the road lies shining and open before him. An orchestral interlude, combining Siegfried's horn call, the sleeping Brünnhilde motif and the magic fire music, leads to the final scene. Siegfried emerges above the fire, clouds clearing around him. A long unison passage on the violins, interrupted at a certain point by the fate motif, creates an extraordinary atmosphere of isolation. Siegfried is at the top of the world; all ordinary concerns have been left beneath him, cut off by the fire, and clear sunlight is dispelling the clouds. He sees a horse, standing asleep amid the pine trees. And then he discerns a warrior in armour, lying beneath a shield, and Wotan's farewell (100) sounds softly on violins and cellos. This moment – the discovery of Brünnhilde by Siegfried – is the final parting, the music tells us, the ontological parting, so to speak, of father and daughter. Henceforth they, who were one, are two.

Siegfried is stunned by the warrior's beauty as he removes the helmet. He cuts through the breastplate, to make it easier for the sleeping figure to breathe, and starts back with the cry 'that is no man!' This much derided outburst is surely appropriate to the situation in which Siegfried finds himself – not just encountering Woman for the first time, but also sensing his own manhood. He is now aflame with anxiety, his senses swimming, and calling out to his mother for help. At a certain point he cries 'O mother, mother, this is your valiant child: a woman lies asleep and has taught him fear!' He calls to Brünnhilde to awaken, but she does not respond until at last he resolves to suck life from her sweet lips, though he should die in doing so. As Wagner put the point to Cosima, using Schopenhauerian language: 'the kiss of love is the first intimation of death, the cessation of individuality – that is why Siegfried is so frightened.'[14]

Brünnhilde awakens to two chords on full orchestra (138) that seem to echo through the bars that follow, and which sound again twice, and to extraordinary and mystical effect, in *Götterdämmerung*. She sings her great hymn to the sun and the gods, adapted from the *Sigrdrífamál*, and asks who is the hero who has woken her? Siegfried tells her and praises the mother who bore him. Brünnhilde too praises Siegfried's mother, telling Siegfried that he was always her care, even before he was born. 'So did my mother not die?' he asks, which provokes an outburst of tenderness from Brünnhilde, who explains how she always loved Siegfried, having divined Wotan's idea, though she only felt it, did not think it, did not dare to think it, for the idea was her love for Siegfried.

Throughout this scene Wagner provides an abundance of new material, expressive of the grandeur and purity of Brünnhilde's feeling, and also of its idealized nature, and consequent remoteness from the carnal union that Siegfried desires with increasing urgency. Wagner has touched here on a profound psychological truth, which is that the moment of falling in love has been prepared long before it happens. The person who appears to us as a destiny is a person whom we ourselves have invented from the raw material of our need. This need is not an animal need. It is not a need for that primordial warmth from which the process of growing up so painfully severed us. It is a spiritual need – so Wagner insists, even if Freud had much to say to the contrary. In the moment of falling in love we project onto the face and form of another human being an ideal nurtured in our sympathies, as Brünnhilde projects onto Siegfried the complex emotions that were nurtured when her father made himself vulnerable and troubled before her, when she encountered Siegmund's devotion, and when Sieglinde blessed her from the depths of her sorrow and loss. In the scene of Brünnhilde's encounter with Siegfried, Wagner shows how the sacred error of religion – the error of projecting our hopes and fears onto imagined objects, and then worshipping them as visitors from another realm – is repeated when we fall in love.

Wagner has therefore undertaken one of the hardest tasks that an artist can confront – which is to show how the highest ideal of love can seek and find expression in physical desire, and a desire that acknowledges and builds upon the male–female divide: not just to say it, but to *show* it. Probably it could not be shown in words, which would become clumsy and confused when bent to the moment of touching (though Shakespeare comes near to showing it in *The Tempest* and *The Winter's Tale*). But it can be shown in music, and this is what makes this scene into the great artistic triumph that it is. The motifs that Wagner uses (139–144) have a mutual magnetism, each leading the music inexorably forward, so that the process whereby Brünnhilde's resistance is overcome is shown to be not merely inevitable, but also a tribute to her purity, rather than an assault on it. She has come down from the world of the immortals, but her incarnation needs to be completed, and the music shows us how this happens, and why it must happen, for her sake and for the sake of the world.

Brünnhilde casts her eyes about her, seeing Grane, now awoken and grazing happily, and the scattered pieces of her armour, while Siegfried gives voice to his desire. Noticing her severed breastplate, she becomes conscious of being exposed and unprotected. To Siegfried's importuning she responds with troubled shame, crying that no god had ever come so close to her and heroes, in the past, would bow to her virginity. Siegfried begs her to awaken again – to be a woman to him. Brünnhilde sinks into doubt and dread. The curse motif sounds in the orchestra, together with the motifs of Wotan's revolt and Fricka's moral judgment (78 and 74) – suggesting that Brünnhilde's trouble now, on the verge of giving herself to a mortal, originated in the cosmic dilemma of Wotan, when in despair he bequeathed the world to Alberich's son. It is because she is, or was,

Wotan's will, that Brünnhilde has been flung down into the world of mortals; to rise again and be herself she must accept what is now being thrust upon her, which means accepting the root cause of Wotan's trouble, namely the world, whose fallen nature she already knows from her father's bleak description.

'Emerge from the darkness,' Siegfried pleads, and she sings her mystical invocation, 'Ewig war ich' (143), urging him to remain pure, to reflect on his own image in the clear stream, to love himself and to let her be. This theme, which originally came to Wagner as an idea for an instrumental work and which is prominent in the *Siegfried Idyll*,[15] has a god-like serenity. It is as though, for a brief moment, Brünnhilde stands calm and majestic at the edge of the cliff from which she is about to throw herself. Too calm, perhaps: certainly some listeners hear this sublime passage as out of place and detached from the drama.

Siegfried develops the metaphor of the stream, urging her to be lost with him in the flood and gradually she responds until, in a heart-stopping moment, Brünnhilde acknowledges the truth, singing 'O, Siegfried! Dein war ich von je!' – I was always yours! – to the motif of love's greeting (140), the latest version of Freia's second love-theme (22B). Then, in an ecstatic duet, Brünnhilde says farewell at last to Valhalla's glittering world. 'You Norns, snap your rope of runes; twilight of the gods, let your dusk descend; night of annihilation, let your mist fall!' Together they invoke 'radiant love, laughing death', eagerly embracing a love that belongs nowhere else but here, on the unapproachable mountaintops, defying the immortals, but with only the sketchiest knowledge of the real world. The love music is seamlessly entwined with the theme of the world's inheritance (134), reminding us of the real price of their 'radiant love'. Death, yes; but not a laughing one.

GÖTTERDÄMMERUNG

Siegfried has shown a god-haunted but human world, where the contest that began among the immortals has been bequeathed to an ignorant hero and his sleeping bride. The drama is built from a series of awakenings. Siegfried is awakened to the knowledge of his origins by Mime, who is awakened to his dire situation by the Wanderer, who then goes on to awaken Alberich to the new divine plan, and the dragon to his fate. Finally, after awakening everything and everyone in his search for knowledge, the Wanderer rouses Erda from her slumbers and tells her that she is superfluous, since he is ready to will as an action what she merely predicts as a fact.

Meanwhile Siegfried has awoken and slain the dragon, and has been awoken by the wood-bird to the reality of Mime and to the existence of an ideal companion. He has been awoken again by the sight of Brünnhilde, the climax of his many awakenings, and she in turn wakes to her new condition only to need waking again from her shame. In the course of all this Wotan has also finally awoken to *his* condition, as a superannuated god, and retires from the scene, carrying his shattered spear, his inheritance bequeathed, half willingly, half grudgingly, to his uncouth grandson.

Because he possesses the Ring, Siegfried is ostensibly master of the world. But he has no knowledge of the Ring's power, and in any case no desire to exert it. Apart from Erda, who is a natural principle rather than a woman, only one woman appears in *Siegfried*, and that is Brünnhilde, whose former life as a Valkyrie has not prepared her for what she must suffer as a mortal. Yet it is in her that the future is vested, since Siegfried lacks the wisdom to protect himself from the dire contrivances of the Nibelung. Henceforth the world is in the hands of mortal beings, the gods have lost their hold over it, and religion is no more than lip service offered to powerless gods in their doomed and distant refuge.

Götterdämmerung therefore brings us fully into the human world, the world bequeathed to Siegfried by Wotan, which Siegfried must explore and discover for himself. And it is a world thoroughly penetrated by the forces that have erupted and grown in the previous dramas, and whose presence is revealed in music of a redoubled intensity. Perhaps there is no great drama, certainly nothing in the world of opera, so telescoped as *Götterdämmerung*, into the taut action of which the whole cosmos is crammed like the burnished souvenirs in a Pharaoh's tomb. The leitmotifs, with their huge burdens of memory, mingle and overlap in surprising and disconcerting ways. And all are absorbed into a symphonic narrative that is immediately intelligible to the ear, even if hard to transcribe in words – and harder still as the drama unfolds towards its enigmatic ending.

This new complexity is made immediately apparent in the opening prologue, which sets the action in its mythical context. This highly poetic and arresting scene gives us a long look backwards across the reign of the gods, as seen by the three Norns. These are the Scandinavian equivalent of the three Fates of Greek mythology, and Wagner represents them as primeval daughters of the Ur-mother, Erda. The work opens with the two chords of Brünnhilde's awakening (138), a semitone lower than they originally sounded, followed by a variant of the original nature motif (1). Why does this opening sound so exactly right? In some way the moment of Brünnhilde's awakening is echoing through the cosmos, but with a darker resonance, as though the joy of that cosmic rebirth is about to be put in question.

The fate motif sounds in the orchestra and then, to a slowed-down version of the magic fire music, we find the three Norns, sitting outside the cave occupied by Siegfried and Brünnhilde, in a pre-dawn mist and darkness. As in the poem of *Helgi Hundingsbani* in the Eddas they are weaving the rope of destiny, throwing it to each other from north to east to west, but hampered, as they soon reveal, by the events recounted in the previous dramas. They comment on the light from Loge's minions, ringing the rock with fire. As they pass the rope, they take turns to spin the fate of the world into its threads.*

The first Norn laments the time when they spun beside the World Ash Tree, where the well of wisdom bubbled and a primeval holiness lay undisturbed. A god came to drink at the spring, and gave one of his eyes as forfeit for an ash branch, from which he made a spear. Over a long time the tree died from its wound, the well began to dry up and the rope could no longer be attached to the World Ash Tree. A fir must now suffice to fasten her end of it. The motif of the doom of the gods (48) sounds as she relates these events, implying that Wotan's presumption in assuming sovereignty must be paid for.

She throws the rope to the second Norn, and as she does so the announcement of death (*Todesverkündigung*, 85) sounds in the

---

* The idea of spinning the fate of a child occurs elsewhere in ancient literature – for example, *Iliad*, 20, line 127.

orchestra, with its original harmonic network, but now in 3/2 time, a kind of sarabande foretelling a far greater death than that announced to Siegmund. Over motif 114 (the power of the gods) in the bass, the second Norn continues the story, describing the treaties carved in the spear's shaft, and the hero who has shattered the spear, so that the sacred register of contracts has fallen in pieces. Wotan, she says, bade Valhalla's heroes fell the Ash Tree and the well has dried up forever. She must fasten the rope to a jagged rock. She throws it to the third Norn, asking her to say what will happen, and again we hear the *Todesverkündigung* in the orchestra.

The third Norn, to fragments of motif 114, describes Wotan waiting in Valhalla, the logs of the Ash Tree heaped against its walls. When the wood is ignited the hall will burn and the gods will meet their end. Her narrative is rounded off by the orchestra, not with the *Todesverkündigung* but with the motif of fate (84). The end of the gods has now been foretold, and will be foretold again by the Valkyrie Waltraute. It might be objected that it spoils the drama to go on rehearsing the plot in this way, revisiting it again and again from some new but foreseeable viewpoint. But Wagner was wiser. Like the Greeks he recognized that the greatest tragic emotions focus on what is necessary, and known to be necessary, even if the human will wrestles with the necessity and is overcome by it. The very same sense of mystery that attaches to the fate motif and the announcement of death haunts this scene with the Norns: the sense that freedom and necessity come together in a single event, and that what is willed from one perspective is suffered from the other. We cannot, in the end, resolve this contradiction, because it is a contradiction that we live.

The third Norn throws the rope back to the first, who sings that her eyes grow dim, and that she cannot recall the holy ancient times, when Loge burned so brightly – 'what happened to him?' she asks. The second Norn, taking the rope, describes how Wotan tamed Loge. To regain his freedom, the fire-god gnawed with his teeth at the runes in the shaft of the spear. Then, with the spear's point, Wotan commanded him to burn around Brünnhilde's rock. She asks what will happen to Loge.

The third Norn answers that one day Wotan will plunge the splintered spear into the fire-god's breast and throw the flaming torch in the piled up logs of the Ash Tree. As the sleep motif sounds in the orchestra, the third Norn asks 'Do you want to know when that will be? Then weave the rope, sisters.' The first Norn, weaving again, but ever more confused, now refers to Alberich and his theft of the Rhinegold. What happened to him? The second Norn warns that the rope is tangled and chafing against the rock. From need and greed the Nibelung's Ring rises: an avenging curse gnaws at the strands. The third Norn complains that the rope is too slack, and then, as first the sword motif (51) and then Siegfried's horn call (104) sound loudly in the orchestra, she cries out 'Es riß', it snaps! The three sing in unison: to end with our ageless wisdom, the world will hear us no more, and, to the motifs of the curse, the doom of the gods, and sleep, they sink down to the primeval mother.

This scene, the text of which was added before Wagner recognized that he needed three dramas rather than a mere prologue to clarify the plot of *Siegfrieds Tod*, is in one sense unnecessary, since it rehearses events of which we are already for the most part aware. But it serves a deeper purpose, reminding us that the story of the Ring is the story of the world, which must be told again and again, each of the characters finding his place in it, by making the story his own. The repetitions in the narrative are not redundancies, but ways of emphasizing the mythic nature of the action, constantly drawing the outer limits of the cosmos, like a searchlight scanning the heavens.

The scene of the Norns gives another glimpse into the hidden origin of things, showing that nature has been twice turned from her dreaming course – by Wotan when he took the branch from the World Ash Tree, and by Alberich, when he stole the gold of the Rhine. The attempt to rule the world by law is as destructive of the natural order as the attempt to enslave it. The Norns show us that the human freedom that is about to burst forth from Brünnhilde's cave is part of a larger cosmic order. This order is threatened precisely by our existential choices, by our fatal need as free beings, to become what we are – the need that has led to Alberich's forging of the Ring, to Brünnhilde's defiance of her father, to Siegfried's forging of the sword and to the shattering of Wotan's spear.

As the Norns disappear the fate motif sounds twice in the orchestra, followed by a beautiful orchestral interlude depicting the dawn, and drawing on two new themes (149 and 150) representing the mature personalities that the lovers have acquired: resolute and manly in Siegfried's case, replete with fulfilled love in Brünnhilde's. The two come forth from the cave, Brünnhilde urging Siegfried 'to new deeds' – for how would she love him, if she did not wish him to enhance his wisdom and power? As I noted earlier, the great transitions in *The Ring* are often condensations of long processes, and this is one instance. Brünnhilde's gesture represents what has grown between the two on their mountaintop, symbol of the apartness from the world that is the first gift of love, and of the maturation that this apartness brings, as each lover assumes full responsibility for the other. Brünnhilde's first words on emerging express the completeness of her trust in him. And just how long it has taken to achieve this trust is not a question that we need ask, since time on the mountain-top flows in another way and at another speed – the speed symbolized by the broad and flowing music.

The two renew their vows with words that express, in Brünnhilde's case, the singular purity of her nature, desiring what the other needs, and ignoring all needs of her own. She has bestowed on Siegfried her godly knowledge, but feels unworthy nonetheless. Siegfried reassures her. He concurs in her plan to send him out into the world, perhaps too readily, but in any case with no *arrière pensée*, and convinced of the need for it – after all, ignorance of the world has so far been the cause of all his failings. Brünnhilde embraces Siegfried, as the motif of the world's inheritance (134) underscores the great gift that they have each received – the gift of each other, which is all that the world, here on the mountaintop, amounts to. He takes the Ring from his finger and hands it to her as a pledge of love. Brünnhilde gives her horse, Grane, in exchange. They entwine their hopes and intentions in ecstatic music, the motif of love's delight (151) pressing the emotion to the very boundary of the possible, as Brünnhilde summons the gods to feast their eyes on this sacred couple, who can never be separated, even when apart – an act of *hubris* for which she will in due course be punished.

Siegfried departs on his Rhine journey, to music that wonderfully accomplishes the transition from the pure air of the mountaintop to the sullied world below. Moving from the theme of Siegfried's manhood, via the freedom motif (111) to that of Brünnhilde's love

(151), the interlude takes up Siegfried's horn call in a symphonic meditation, wrapping the fire music around it before plunging into the waters of the Rhine. Gradually the pure music of the water nymphs gives way to their lament, then to material associated with the Ring. The motif of woman's worth, 34, emerges as a cadence, suggesting grief over all that was lost when Alberich placed his curse on love. The interlude ends on the hollowed-out version of the Rhine-daughters' call, the first part of 39, the power of the Ring, which will hereafter be associated with the machinations of evil. This cry *de profundis* leads straight into the music of Act 1, as the curtain rises on the interior of a hall beside the Rhine, the feudal seat of the Gibichungs, children of Gibich, whose eldest son, Gunther, has inherited the power, wealth and status attached to his father's sovereign domains.

The world that we have entered is a threatened world, in which the resentment of the Nibelung is no longer countered by the law of the gods, but flows through all things. The cosmic conflict that has been portrayed in the first three parts of the cycle is now percolating everywhere through the human world, which we are shown in its normal, comfortable and fully domesticated version for the first time.

Gunther, chief of the Gibichung clan, with his sister, Gutrune, in attendance, is asking his half-brother, Hagen, about the family's social standing. Status and reputation are written all over the motifs assigned to Gunther (152), while the timid ambitiousness of Gutrune is scarcely disguised by the cloying sweetness of her music (154, 155). The contrast with the poignant inwardness of the music assigned to Siegmund and Sieglinde in *Die Walküre* is eloquent, and a sign of how far the world of *The Ring* has moved on.

Grimhilde, mother of Gunther and Gutrune, no longer lives; but it was she who, overcome by force and gold, yielded to Alberich's embrace, and gave birth to a son. We therefore encounter in Hagen Alberich's resentment in its new, human, and manipulative form. The connection and contrast between the two half-brothers is expressed by assigning to Gunther, as a motto, the falling fifth, and to Hagen the falling tritone, the two intervals being played against each other in such a way as to convey a vivid sense of the poisoned nature of all that the Gibichungs undertake.

Hagen responds to his half-brother's enquiry that Gunther's legitimate title fills him with envy, and Gunther replies by praising the cunning and know-how that Hagen has brought into the family. Hagen shows these qualities at once by reminding Gunther that, unmarried, he cannot possibly lay claim to the status that he desires. And Gutrune likewise stands in need of a husband. 'So whom do you advise us to wed,' Gunther asks, 'to add to our renown?' Union between man and woman in the Gibichung world is not for love, but for power and status. That said, the Gibichungs clearly maintain a friendly establishment – a 'nice family', Wagner said to Cosima, 'who are greeted by their vassals with love and respect'.[16] Were it not for the presence in their midst of Hagen, they would have put their naïve fixation on social status to a largely beneficent use. As it is, domination, exploitation, manipulation; lying, faking and cheating; coldness, sentimentality and the pursuit of power – all these contend with love, which is regarded by Hagen as a weakness to be exploited rather than a home to be reached.

Hagen, we now understand, has the kind of cosmic knowledge that sets him apart from the human world. The Nibelungs belong with the gods, in the world of spiritual forces and contending principles. He has therefore learned from his father about the Ring, and the story of Siegfried's ownership. 'A woman I know,' he says, 'the finest in the world; high on a rock she dwells, and a fire burns around her home. Only he who breaks through the fire can be Brünnhilde's suitor.' As he recounts this information the voice of the wood-bird is heard in the orchestra – utterly beautiful and appropriate, since Hagen is revealing his inwardness with a mystery, but hard to explain in words.

Resentment is a source of penetrating knowledge. All that is fine, superior, generous, all that enjoys the sunlight of happiness, is like a sword in its heart. Resentful people become experts in distinction, through the obsessive desire to destroy it. This too is symbolized in Hagen's knowledge of Brünnhilde.

Hagen responds to Gunther's enquiry: only one man has the courage to pass through the fire, and he is Siegfried the Volsung, son of the twins Siegmund and Sieglinde. He grew up strong in the forest, and slew the dragon that guarded the hoard of the Nibelung. He would make a good husband for Gutrune, Hagen slyly adds. To Gunther's enquiry Hagen says that he who knows how to use the

Nibelung's wealth would be master of the world, and that the Nibelungs are Siegfried's slaves. This is of course not literally true, since Siegfried has never exercised the power of the Ring. Nevertheless Gunther's appetite is whetted by what he hears, and we recall the terms of Alberich's curse: those who learn of the Ring will not rest until they possess it, when it will bring to them only destruction and death. But Gunther is at once overcome by what we soon discover to be a habitual sense of inadequacy, the inadequacy of the aristocrat who has never done anything for himself. 'Why do you rouse my desire for what I cannot obtain?' he asks.

At this Hagen unfolds his plot. Siegfried is to bring Brünnhilde as bride to Gunther, and Gutrune will be Siegfried's reward. A truncated appearance of the Tarnhelm (*Verwandlung*) motif, leading into the motif of forgetting, 156, shows the nature of Hagen's plot, and the kind of forces that he will call upon to execute it. Little by little we discover that the power of the Tarnhelm has evolved: *Verwandlung* is no longer just a matter of changing shape – in the offing now is the possibility that a whole life might be changed by the spell that Alberich wound into Mime's work. Gutrune protests that she cannot possibly win the heart of such a hero, who must already have enjoyed all the most beautiful women on earth. Here Hagen reminds her of a potion that they possess, which will cause the one who drinks it to forget all previous loves and to fix his heart on the one before him. Reminded of this useful inheritance Gunther says 'Praised be Grimhilde, who gave us such a brother!'

Hagen tells them that Siegfried hunts the world joyously for new adventures, and is likely to turn up on the Rhine before long. Sure enough, because mythic events call each other up from the womb of time, there is a horn call from the Rhine, and Hagen cries out 'A warrior and a horse in a boat. It is he who blows the horn and now he is rowing fast against the current: it is surely Siegfried!' Siegfried's rowing music combines the 'Rhinegold!' motif (14) with Siegfried's horn, stretching the horn call from 6/8 to 9/8 so that we hear the rising of the oar towards its stroke, and the constant drag of the current against it. This is one of those places where Wagner steps back from the drama to give us the background scenery, and as always with an infallible sense of the sounds and rhythms of the real world.

The music is both exciting and frightening, showing us that the untried Siegfried is already a vital instrument in the plans of three socially accomplished people. When Hagen calls across the water, asking where the rower is going, we feel the shared anticipation of the household in his cry, and Hagen is briefly humanized by this. Siegfried replies 'To Gibich's powerful son.' Hagen invites Siegfried ashore, and as the hero springs with his horse onto the beach, greets him as Siegfried, singing the name to the melody of the curse motif (45), which simultaneously sounds in the orchestra. We know now that Siegfried is doomed, having descended into this poisoned world without the wisdom needed to understand its machinations. The wisdom given to him by Brünnhilde is the wisdom of the ideal, not the real. And the wisdom absorbed from the forest was absorbed without the love that would make sense of it. It has remained embryonic, so that the hero is unequipped for the trial that he now confronts. He is entering a world in which friendship and treachery are inextricably entwined, in which marriage is not so much a vow as a deal, in which loyalties can be dissolved in forgetfulness, and in which the lust for power and the power of lust can both triumph over love and honour. It is the world we all know and in which, nevertheless, we seek for meaning. But how does meaning come? This is the question that Wagner puts before us and, whatever we think of Siegfried as a vehicle through which to explore it, we must concede that the question has seldom been so comprehensively presented.

Siegfried enters, asks for Gibich's son, and addresses him in his charmless manner: 'fight with me or be my friend!' Assured of friendship Siegfried turns to Hagen and says 'you called me Siegfried: have we met before?' Hagen replies 'I knew you by your strength alone', and takes Grane from him. Siegfried commends Grane for special care, telling Hagen that he never held the bridle of a nobler horse while, in the orchestra, there sounds the motif of Brünnhilde's love (150). With a warm outpouring of friendship (157, 158) Gunther invites his guest to treat all that he sees, hall, land and people, as his own, and Siegfried responds that he can offer nothing in exchange save himself and the sword that he forged.

'But rumour has it that you are lord of the Nibelung's hoard,' says Hagen.

'I almost forgot it,' Siegfried replies. 'I left it in a cave where a dragon once kept it.'

'And you took nothing from it?' Hagen asks.

'This chainmail,' Siegfried replies, 'though I don't know its purpose.'

Hagen recognizes the Tarnhelm and, to the accompaniment of the smithing motif, describes its powers, which now include the power to transport its wearer instantly from place to place. (This power, required by the subsequent action of the drama, belongs to the Tarnhelm as the primary instrument of mutation: the power of the helm is never still, but always increasing, so as to subject new areas of the moral life to the rule of *Verwandlung*.) And then he questions Siegfried as to what else he took. 'A ring.' 'And you keep it safe?' 'A noble woman keeps it.' So now Hagen knows that the Ring is with Brünnhilde, while Gunther, remarking that the Tarnhelm is worth more than all that he possesses, offers to serve Siegfried without reward.

Here Gutrune enters to offer the drink of forgetting. As he raises it to his lips Siegfried sings, over the motif of love's greeting (140), and presumably entirely to himself and unheard by the Gibichung household, 'Were I to forget all that you gave me, one lesson will I never lose. Brünnhilde, to you I offer this first drink to faithful love!' He drinks a draught while the violins settle on a long trill, which changes eerily into whole-tone harmony before settling on the motif of forgetting (156). Siegfried lowers the horn, which he then hands back to an embarrassed Gutrune while fixing his gaze on her. 'Why do you lower your eyes before me?' he asks, and she raises them, blushing, to his. With inflamed emotion he asks Gunther his sister's name, and then addresses her with the offer to serve her as a suitor. She involuntarily meets Hagen's gaze before giving a gesture of unworthiness and leaving the hall.

This is clearly another of those transitions in which a long process is presented as though it takes place in a moment. The inevitable corruption of Siegfried by a world in which resentment and the lust for power have made love negotiable is here represented in a symbol. Siegfried is a victim of something that works inwardly and without his intention or knowledge, as drinks do. And because his education in the ways of the world is, to say the least, deficient, he cannot

understand that the force that has taken hold of him comes from elsewhere, and should be resisted, not adopted, by his will.

Siegfried asks if Gunther has a wife and Gunther replies that he has
set his heart on one whom it is impossible to obtain. 'What could be
denied you, with me at your side?' says Siegfried. Gunther describes
Brünnhilde's rock and the surrounding fire, Siegfried repeating the
words as though striving to attach a meaning to them, the voice of
the wood-bird crying out in vain from the orchestra. At the mention
of Brünnhilde's name, Siegfried stands silently in a dream-like state,
revealing that his most poignant memories have been wiped away.
And then, in a burst of passion, he promises to bring Brünnhilde to
Gunther so as to win Gutrune as a bride, adding, to Gunther's
enquiry, that he will use the Tarnhelm to change his shape, so as to
appear on the mountaintop in the guise of Gunther. At this the two
swear an oath of blood-brotherhood, pricking their arms with their
swords and collecting the blood in a drinking horn that Hagen has
filled with new wine.

The oath that they swear (161, 162, 163) is not a contract but
belongs, like marriage, in the world of existential ties. 'Should either
betray his trust,' they sing, 'then the blood we have solemnly drunk
in drops today will flow in torrents, in full atonement to a friend'
(163). The motifs of the oath are combined with those of the sword,
the spear and the curse, in a demonic cry of reckless resolve. Seldom
has the sound of two people rushing to mutual destruction been so
thrillingly presented, and the orchestra leaves us in no doubt that all
bonds of obligation, this one of blood-brotherhood included, have
been severed, and the fragments eaten to nothing by the curse. When
finally Siegfried takes the horn from Gunther and drinks it to the
dregs the orchestra gives out a long-held C minor triad, which the
violins fill out with a trill in thirds – a sudden recall of the sound-
world of Brünnhilde's awakening, and the last sign before Siegfried's
final destruction that he is bound to her by the most solemn of ties.

Siegfried asks why Hagen did not join in the oath, and Hagen
replies (to a muted reminiscence of Freia's apples, 26) that his blood
would taint the drink: it does not flow pure and noble like Siegfried's
but lies stagnant in his veins. Gunther shrugs off Hagen's habitual
moroseness, and Siegfried hastens to proceed to Brünnhilde's rock,

refusing rest, saying that they will go in the boat, and Gunther will wait during the night on the Rhine while he ascends to capture the woman. Gunther entrusts the hall to Hagen, Gutrune enters to ask where the men are going and Hagen explains to her that Siegfried has gone to woo Brünnhilde in order to gain Gutrune as his bride. 'Siegfried – mine!' Gutrune cries, and she returns to her room in great agitation. Hagen sits brooding, looking out across the Rhine, anticipating the return of Siegfried who brings a bride for Gunther but for Hagen the Ring. 'You sons of freedom, happy spirits, take sail: though you despise him, you will yet serve the Nibelung's son!'

'Hagen's Watch', as this scene is known, is accompanied by music of matchless brooding evil. Siegfried's horn call sounds in the bass, rearranged around Hagen's tritone, and under the syncopated chords of Alberich's resentment (44). A new theme is introduced, associated with Hagen's envy (165), and ending with a strange ascending scale on solo trumpet, in which it is as though all joy and contentment is emptied out, so that only the shell of ambition remains. From time to time the flow of baleful hatred is interrupted by the final degraded form of the Rhine-daughters' lament. The joyous salute to the gold (14) has passed through Alberich's abuse of it (39) and the Rhine-daughters' lament for it (53), to become a semitone wail of desolation (164), in which the pure triadic harmony of the original has been corrupted to eerie dissonances that cannot rest in any key. The threat to subdue the 'sons of freedom' is again accompanied by Wotan's original bequest of the world to the then unknown Hagen (80), and rounded off with the wrenching chords of desolation, the motif of the gold sounding in the minor. The state of mind invoked is one of total destructiveness: envy that abolishes its object, and lust without hope of joy. One way or another we have all known this state of mind, have all turned away from it in revulsion, and are all now faced with the truth, that it is not just a feeling but a motive to action, and one planted in the depths of what we are.

An extraordinary orchestral interlude moves from the darkest malice to the bright realm of womanly love, and we discover Brünnhilde on her rock, looking with fond memories on the ring that she wears, and kissing it. The motif of forgetting rises like a mist from a long trill on the violins, and fragments of Valkyrie music erupt in the orchestra as Brünnhilde notices a winged horse approaching, sweeping on the clouds like a storm. From afar comes the voice of Waltraute, calling 'Brünnhilde, sister! Are you asleep or awake?' The Valkyrie's horse comes to earth with eight astounding thuds on the timpani, beginning off the beat and shattering the peace of this nest above the world.

Brünnhilde is overjoyed by the visit, praising her sister's courage in seeking out the banished favourite of the god. 'My haste,' Waltraute responds, 'was for your sake alone.' 'Then you broke Walvater's ban for love of me?' Brünnhilde asks. 'Or has Wotan relented? I know that his anger ceased, when he granted me the ring of fire, for I have won thereby the greatest hero. Have you perhaps come to share in my fate and my joy?' All this pours from Brünnhilde in a rush of joy, the purity motif rising to the top of the melodic line, together with a new theme (167), expressing her longing to be reconciled again with her father. But Waltraute interrupts her, saying 'do you want me to share the frenzy that has crazed you?' And Brünnhilde notices that her sister is seized by fear, not by love or joy. Waltraute tells her to listen carefully as she explains the trouble that has taken hold of the gods.

Since parting from Brünnhilde Wotan has ceased to send the Valkyries into war, and has shunned Valhalla's heroes, roaming the world as the Wanderer instead. Recently he returned, holding the splinters of his spear, shattered by a hero, and we hear again the echo of his first bequest of the world (80). He ordered the nobles of Valhalla to fell the World Ash Tree and to pile its logs around the hall. (This to motif 168, already heard during the scene with the Norns, expressing the changed situation of the gods.) Wotan then summoned the council of the gods who sit, with the heroes, in fearful rings around his throne. There he presides in silence, holding the shattered spear, refusing to touch Freia's apples. He has sent his two ravens on their travels: if ever they return with good tidings then, for the last time, the god will smile into eternity. 'He remains blind to our tearful glances and when I pressed myself to his breast learned that he was thinking of you, Brünnhilde. He closed his eyes and as if in a dream whispered these words: "If she would return the Ring to the Rhine-daughters, the curse would be lifted and gods and world would be freed."' At this point in Waltraute's narrative the violins, playing on the G string, trace with Mahlerian intensity the melody of Wotan's farewell (100), so emphasizing the separation of father and daughter that cannot be repaired, however much the god may wish for it. This gives way to the curse motif, and then to an elaboration of 18C, the third section of the Valhalla motif. 'So I crept away from Valhalla,' the Valkyrie continues, 'to beg you to accomplish this deed, and to end the eternal torment.'

Brünnhilde is bewildered by this strange story, which belongs to another world from the one she now inhabits, and which comes wrapped in music associated with Wotan and the realm of the gods. Brünnhilde herself will make use of this music, in magnificent enhancement, when she finally does what Wotan wishes at the end of the opera (186). But at this juncture the whole story seems to her unutterably bizarre, having no relation to the feelings that inhabit her mountaintop. So what does Waltraute want? The answer, that she should throw the Ring to the Rhine-daughters, causes amazement. 'Siegfried's pledge of love? Are you out of your mind?' Waltraute begs her to take the world seriously, and to see her love as a mere part of it. But in fact, since Wotan's bequest, it has all been the other way round: the world is now a mere part of Brünnhilde's love. To a motif expressing anger (169) Brünnhilde berates her sister, saying that one flash of the Ring's sacred lustre is more to her than the eternal joy of the gods, for it shines with the blessing of Siegfried's love, and the music conveys the substance of this blessing, with the theme of Wotan's second bequest, that of 'World Inheritance' (134). 'So tell the gods that they shall never wrest love from me, though Valhalla collapse in ruins!' This she announces to the motif (17) that marked Alberich's renunciation of love, Siegmund's need for the sword and Wotan's farewell to his daughter – the motif that announces the irreversible commitment of the person who makes use of it.

Brünnhilde drives away the Valkyrie as the curse sounds in the orchestra, and Waltraute leaves, crying 'Woe to you sister, and woe to the gods!' Brünnhilde expresses the hope that this raging storm-cloud will never come her way again. And then she notices that the fire around her rock is blazing more brightly: surely a hero must be approaching through the flames; Siegfried must be returning. 'Up to meet him,' she cries, 'into the arms of my god!' Rushing to the edge of the flames, she is confronted by Siegfried in Gunther's shape, wearing the Tarnhelm, which covers half his face, leaving only the eyes free. 'Betrayed!' she cries, and backs away. Siegfried, disguising his voice, announces that he has won her for a wife and that she must follow him. 'Who are you, fearful one: are you a mortal, or from Hella's hordes?'

The motif of forgetting sounds in the orchestra and Siegfried identifies himself as the Gibichung, Gunther. Brünnhilde cries out against Wotan, pitiless god, who has devised so terrible a punishment for her. As Siegfried approaches she endeavours to repel him, holding out the Ring and crying 'fear this token!' But Siegfried, declaring that the Ring belongs to Gunther as his wedding ring, comes forward, seizes her and, in the course of the struggle tears the Ring from her finger. As she sinks into his arms, her eyes unconsciously meet those of Siegfried, and their love-music in the orchestra suggests that she has half recognized her assailant. Cosima's diary for 4 June 1870 has the following words: 'R. shows me in the sketch the theme from the love scene between Brünnhilde and Siegfried, which appears like a mirage as Siegfried overpowers Brünnhilde and she subconsciously recognizes him. R. says "when the Ring was snatched from her I thought of Alberich; the noblest character suffers the same as the ignoble, in every creature the will is identical." '

Siegfried drives Brünnhilde before him into the cave as Gunther's bride, the motif of forgetting now wound into that of Alberich's resentment and Hagen's tritone, to create a horrible reminiscence of the destructive state of mind portrayed in Hagen's Watch. It is as Erda foretold in her original appearance in *Das Rheingold* – not in words, but in the music that swelled beneath them: Alberich's resentment has been planted in the scheme of things. This cosmic truth will be brought home again in the next act, when Brünnhilde's need for vengeance will take the musical shape of Alberich's biting syncopations. Drawing his sword, Siegfried calls out in his normal voice to Nothung to bear witness on behalf of his blood brother to his chaste wooing, and the motifs of blood-brotherhood wrap Siegfried's naïve sentiments in a warm cocoon. The act then ends with a brief elaboration of the motifs of forgetting and *Verwandlung* which are as though crushed together in the final B minor chord.

*

Act 2 opens with Hagen, sitting by the shore of the Rhine before the hall of the Gibichungs. It is night, Hagen's Watch continues, and the prelude draws again on the earlier material, developing the motif of resentment and the desolate remains of the Rhine-daughters' lament (164), until emptying itself in the trumpet's eerie ladder into nothingness. The syncopations of the resentment motif have now been intensified, fracturing each bar in many places, and creating a grim sluggishness, like blood congealing in the veins.

Alberich appears, as though dreamed by Hagen, saying 'Are you asleep, my son?' Hagen replies 'I hear you, evil gnome. What have you to say to my sleep?' Alberich, whose life is a kind of negative imprint of Wotan's, is now the passive observer of actions that originate in Hagen, just as Wotan, as Wanderer, had been the passive observer of Siegfried. Alberich tells Hagen, to the motif of woman's worth (34), to remember his mother's spirit, but Hagen responds that he has no reason to thank her, since he is prematurely old and wan, hating the happy and never glad. His father tells Hagen to hate the happy but to love Alberich, who is weighed down with sorrows. He recounts that Wotan, the robber, has been overthrown by one of his offspring and in anguish awaits his end. 'I fear him no longer,' Alberich says.

'So who inherits the might of the immortals?' Hagen asks.

'You and I,' Alberich replies, 'if you are true to me.' And he explains that the curse on the Ring has no effect on Siegfried since he does not know the Ring's value and makes no use of its power. He is laughing in carefree flow of love, and must now be destroyed. Hagen indicates that he has understood as much and has set the matter in motion. Alberich expresses his fear that Brünnhilde might persuade Siegfried to return the Ring to the Rhine-daughters. 'I bred you to inexorable hate,' he adds, 'so now avenge me and obtain the Ring. Do you swear it?'

'I will obtain the Ring,' Hagen replies, and 'Do you swear it?' Alberich repeats.

'To myself have I sworn it,' Hagen says, and the scene ends as Alberich fades away, muttering 'Be true! True!' to the two-chord sequence that expresses the world's desolation.

Throughout this scene Alberich has sung in the speech-rhythm idiom of *Das Rheingold* – though to music far more complex than was heard in the earlier drama. He leaps with gnome-like agility across the peaks and chasms created by the orchestra, nimbly adjusting to the syncopated rhythms and flashing his darts of malice into every pungent discord. His vocal line is the perfect illustration of the ideas set forth in *Opera and Drama* and Hagen's brooding responses make this episode into a dramatic triumph equal to Wotan's confession to his daughter in Act 2 of *Die Walküre*.

A beautiful transition evokes dawn over the Rhine, introducing a four-note motif (172B) that summarizes the social power that Hagen will soon display, as he leads the Gibichung vassals in a kind of initiation dance for the newly-weds. Siegfried bounces in, boisterously greeting Hagen, and telling him that he comes from Brünnhilde's rock. He asks whether Gutrune is awake, and Hagen calls for her.

Siegfried recounts his success in wooing Brünnhilde, and how the Tarnhelm worked to perfection in disguising him. In response to Gutrune's anxious questions he reassures her that during their night in the cave his sword lay between him and Gunther's bride. He tells Gutrune that he quickly and unnoticeably changed places with Gunther after leading the bride down from the mountain in the morning light. Thanks to the Tarnhelm he transported himself in a flash to the hall in search of Gutrune, who cries 'Wie faßt mich Furcht vor dir!' – 'How I am in awe of you!'

The boat bringing Gunther and Brünnhilde appears in the distance. 'Let us give her a gracious welcome,' Gutrune good-naturedly adds, 'so that she will gladly stay with us', revealing thereby how carelessly she had joined in the plan to capture Brünnhilde, as though it had been simply a matter of purchasing a household pet. She asks Hagen to call the vassals to the hall for the wedding, while she goes to assemble the women.

Hagen summons the vassals with the call to war, on massive steer-horns sounding neighbouring semitones. Bring weapons, he cries, and 'Woe, danger, woe!' A hefty chorus develops around a fragment of the dawn music (172B) over an exhilarating bass line (176), as the vassals assemble with anxious questions concerning Gunther's safety. Hagen replies that Gunther has taken a wife. 'So are her family in pursuit?' the vassals ask. No? Then why has Hagen summoned the Gibichung army? He replies that they must slaughter steers on Wotan's altar, kill a boar for Froh, a goat for Donner, and sheep that Fricka might bless the marriage. Then take your drinking horns, fill them with mead and wine, and get drunk in honour of the gods! This striking way of introducing the gods emphasizes both their distance and the fact that they are, from the perspective of these comfortable but ordinary mortals, powerless formulae with a merely liturgical use.

The vassals burst into laughter at the unusual event of a joke from Hagen, who tells them to attend to their lady and avenge her if ever she is wronged. He retreats to the back of the crowd to watch events while, to a chorus of greeting, and a solemn wedding march (177), Gunther leads Brünnhilde forward. She walks with downturned eyes in silence. Siegfried now enters with Gutrune, and Gunther greets them affectionately, rejoicing in the happiness of the two couples, Brünnhilde and Gunther, Gutrune and Siegfried. At the sound of Siegfried's name Brünnhilde starts up in astonishment. Soft pulses on the timpani introduce the fate motif, miraculously resolved onto the open fifth of the *Verwandlung* (Tarnhelm) theme. Gunther lets go of Brünnhilde's trembling hand and all look on in consternation, wondering whether she is demented.

'Siegfried? Here?' she utters. 'Gutrune?'

'Gunther's gentle sister,' Siegfried replies, 'married to me, as you to Gunther.'

'You lie!' she cries. 'My eyes grow dim' and, to the music of her mature love (150), poignantly delivered on solo clarinet, she adds 'Does Siegfried not know me?'

Siegfried tells Gunther that his wife is not well, and urges her to rouse herself. She sees the Ring on Siegfried's finger, and cries out with terrible vehemence: 'The Ring . . . on his hand!' and, as the vassals respond with alarm, Hagen urges them to mark carefully the woman's complaint. Brünnhilde points to Gunther, saying 'This man snatched the Ring from me, so how come you [Siegfried] got it from him?' The music here, based again on the resentment motif, 44, which had sounded in the background as the transfigured Siegfried had overcome her, shows Brünnhilde in the grip of a cosmic force. In the new world of the broken spear even she, the vessel of purity, has been emptied of the exalted emotion that was to bring fulfilment to her and Siegfried. This moment is one of the most disturbing in the whole cycle. It is as though Brünnhilde has been voided of moral resources, even replaced by a zombie-like replica. Wagner pushes us through to the next stage of the drama, relying on two devices: the conundrum of the Ring on Siegfried's finger, and the by now fully established harmonic language of *Götterdämmerung*, which compels us to stumble forward like Brünnhilde, in search of a resolution that lies always out of reach.

Brünnhilde commands Gunther to claim back the thing that he took from her as his wedding ring. 'But I did not give it to him,' Gunther says, and as the confusion mounts Siegfried interrupts them, saying 'I won the Ring for myself, from a dragon at Neidhöhle.' For he too is transfigured: a whole area of his psyche has been blocked out by the drink of forgetting.

Hagen steps forward to say to Brünnhilde that, if this is the ring that she gave to Gunther, Siegfried must have obtained it by a trick, for which the traitor must atone. And she cries, to a hair-raising motif (178) that exerts a commanding influence over all that follows, 'Treachery, to be revenged as never before!' She invokes the gods, crying 'If you shaped me to suffer as no one has suffered before, then aid me to a revenge such as never raged! May Brünnhilde break her heart, if only it will destroy her betrayer!'

Gunther tries to calm her but she brushes him away, saying to the company that it is not to Gunther but to the man over there that she is married, since he 'wrung from me pleasure and love'. Siegfried is astonished, asking 'have you no regard for your own honour?' adding that Nothung lay between him and Gunther's bride. But she persists, saying well she knows the sword and knows its blade, as she knows the scabbard in which it reposed when its lord won his beloved. This sexual reference leaves Siegfried with no choice but to silence her accusations, and he calls for a weapon on which to swear an oath. Hagen steps forward with his spear and first Siegfried, and then Brünnhilde, place a hand on it, the one inviting the spear to pierce him where death can strike, if the woman's accusation is true, the other blessing the blade and conjuring it to pierce the traitor who has perjured himself. The vassals, distraught, call on Donner for a storm that will silence this shameful display.

Siegfried advises Gunther to control his wife and abate her ravings. Then, privately, he suggests that perhaps the Tarnhelm did not work quite as well as it should have done. He adds that woman's anger is soon appeased (suggesting that there have been flirtations, even before the fateful drink of forgetting). And then, with habitual ebullience, he turns from the scene and invites the company to join him in the feast.

Left behind with Gunther and Hagen, Brünnhilde gives vent to her distress, describing herself as Siegfried's prey which, wealthy now, he gaily gives away. And she calls out for a sword to sever her bonds. Hagen comes forward, offering to take revenge, but she dismisses him as a nonentity, who would fade away at a single glance from Siegfried's flashing eye, such as lighted on her from his lying face. With a few probing questions he discovers that, while with her magic she protected his body from wounds, she did not protect his back, knowing he would never turn it to his enemy. The resentment motif is again prominent, showing that it is indeed the desire to destroy Siegfried, and not just mortification at his infidelity, that has entered her soul. 'There my spear shall strike,' says Hagen, and now he turns to Gunther, saying 'why do you sit there so sadly?'

Gunther groans against the disgrace that has fallen on him, and Hagen confirms that he has indeed been disgraced, Brünnhilde making her own contemptuous attack on the coward who hid behind Siegfried in order to obtain the prize. 'Your noble race sank deep indeed,' she adds, 'when it produced such a coward!' 'I was a fraud, and I was defrauded, a cheat who was cheated,' cries Gunther. 'Help Hagen, help my honour! Help your mother who bore me too!'

Nothing will help, Hagen says, save Siegfried's death, and to Gunther's anxious questions Brünnhilde replies that yes, Siegfried did betray Gunther as you have all betrayed me. But one death will suffice, Siegfried's death. Hagen adds secretly to Gunther that Siegfried can be parted from the Ring only by death and that the Ring is the Ring of the Nibelung, which brings immense power. This decides Gunther, who nevertheless remains in awe of Siegfried and troubled by the oath of blood-brotherhood; he also has qualms about Gutrune, whom Brünnhilde identifies now as the sorceress who has lured her husband away. Hagen proposes that, in order to conceal the deed from Gutrune, they should kill Siegfried on the following day, when hunting together.

The three of them take a vow of vengeance, to an extended version of 163, the oath of atonement. Brünnhilde and Gunther call on Wotan to uphold the vow, while Hagen, expressing his determination to have the gold of the Nibelung in his hands, calls on the 'Guardian of night and lord of the Nibelungs, Alberich'. As they end their oath, the music changes abruptly from C minor to C major, and the wedding fanfare of the Gibichungs intrudes in 'a stroke of dramatic pathos which has no superior in opera', as Donington puts it. Siegfried and Gutrune enter with the marriage procession, Siegfried playing his horn and carried high on a shield, Gutrune on a chair. Gutrune's friendly smile calls forth a fierce stare from Brünnhilde, who turns away from the ceremony. But Hagen steps forward and pulls Brünnhilde to the side of Gunther, who takes her hand before being hoisted onto a shield by the laughing company. The falling semitone of the Nibelung's woe, the tritone of Hagen's mischief, and the boiling anger of Brünnhilde (179A) all compete for prominence in the bass, beneath massive C major triads, until the curtain falls on a jubilant catastrophe.

The prelude to Act 3 consists of horn calls and Rhine music, including some inspired new material that captures the directionless melancholy of the Rhine-daughters (181). The curtain rises to reveal the three nymphs swimming near the bank of the Rhine, and lamenting the loss of the Sun's light in the depths, as it shone once when the gold was gleaming there. They pray to the sun to send the hero who will give back the gold.

Siegfried's horn sounds offstage, and they dive under the water to take counsel. Siegfried enters, complaining that an elf has led him astray, and that he has lost his quarry. The three nymphs rise from the water and tease him, asking what he would give if they grant him his quarry. He has nothing, he says. But a golden ring gleams on your finger, Wellgunde replies, and 'Give it to us!' they all cry. Siegfried explains that he slew a giant dragon for the Ring, and that his wife would scold him if he wasted it on a mere bearskin in exchange. The nymphs tease him, suggesting that his wife bullies him, and then praise his strength and his looks before dismissing him as a miser.

They disappear and, stung by their taunts, Siegfried takes the Ring from his finger and calls out to them to come. 'I have changed my mind. Take it!' They surface in solemn mood.

'Keep it, hero, until the calamity contained in it overtakes you,' they sing. He coolly replaces the Ring on his finger and asks them, to the motif of the Ring, to tell what they know. They sing of the theft of the gold, the loss of the Ring and the curse that clings to it, which only the Rhine can wash away. 'As you slew the dragon, so shall you be slain, and this very day.' Siegfried brushes off their warnings, but they repeat them, saying that nightly the Norns have woven the curse into the rope of primeval law (in des Urgesetzes Seil). Siegfried responds by saying that his sword once shattered a spear and can sever the Norns' rope just as well. He knows about the curse, since a dragon warned him against it. 'For the gift of love I would gladly relinquish this Ring; but your threats have the opposite effect. As for life and limb, here is how I care for them.' And he takes a clod of earth, holds it above his head and then throws it behind him.

The behaviour of the Rhine-daughters in this scene implies that they want something more than the return of the gold to the Rhine. They want the Ring to be returned by someone fully conscious of its power and history, so that the gesture will be the equivalent of the act of renunciation by which the gold was originally stolen. The return of the gold must be a *reversal* of its theft. And Siegfried cannot understand this. The nymphs now urge each other to leave him, saying 'He swore oaths and does not keep them; he knows secrets and does not heed them'. To the music of Brünnhilde's womanhood (150), Woglinde sings that a glorious gift was granted him, and, they all add, he does not realize that he threw it away. 'Only the Ring, the Ring that condemns him to death, does he wish to keep. Farewell Siegfried, stubborn man. A proud woman will inherit your treasure today: she will give us a better hearing.' And they swim away, singing 'Weialala leia, wallala leialala'.

Siegfried meditates on the ways of women, about which he is learning much, and especially about their empty threats and their scolding. 'But if I hadn't given my promise to Gutrune I would gladly have taken one of those pretty women.' After a series of horn calls the rest of the hunting party arrive, Hagen leading, and Siegfried calls them down to the shore where it is fresh and cool. Hagen orders rest and a meal, and asks Siegfried to give an account of his hunt. 'I caught nothing,' Siegfried replies, 'though had I been rightly forewarned I would have caught three wild water-birds who sang that I should be slain on this very day.' Hagen darkly remarks that it would be a sorry hunt in which the hunter is killed by his quarry.

Siegfried calls for a drink and a meditative motif on three notes, marked '*weich und ausdrucksvoll*', is introduced by the strings (183). This motif, associated with the recovery of Siegfried's memory, slowly seeps into the narrative that follows, lifting us out of present events to create an arc of memory spanning the entire drama of Siegfried. Taking the horn from Hagen, Siegfried offers it to Gunther, saying 'Your brother offers you drink.' But Gunther shuns it saying, to the theme of anger, 179B, 'your blood alone was mixed in it'; at which Siegfried takes Gunther's horn and pours the contents into his own so that it overflows, crying, let it be a refreshment for Mother Earth! Interestingly Erda gets no mention here in the music, which is a joyful expression of high spirits, based on Loge's motif 30.

Gunther rebukes Siegfried for his unstoppable good humour, and fragments of the magic fire music sound in the orchestra, as Siegfried asks Hagen apart whether Brünnhilde is causing Gunther problems. To this Hagen replies, as the motif of memory (183) holds up the musical flow, 'If only he understood her as well as you understand birdsong.' Siegfried says that, since hearing women's voices, he has forgotten the birds completely. And then, prompted by Hagen, he turns vivaciously to Gunther and offers to cheer him up with stories of his boyhood days.

Gunther agrees, and there begins a beautifully shaped narrative, in which Siegfried describes his days with Mime, his forging of the sword, his killing of Fafner, and the strange effect of the dragon's blood. Woven into the music is the theme of the Volsungs' sorrow, in Siegfried's version (61A), as well as the motifs that relate the original context of the narrative. He sings again the song of the wood-bird, as it tells him of the hoard, the Tarnhelm and the Ring. He recounts the bird's warning against Mime, who came to him with a deadly draught. Frightened and stuttering, the dwarf confessed what he intended, so that Siegfried felled him with his sword. This elicits a malicious laugh from Hagen, which, like the laugh of his father, has the rhythmic and melodic contour of the smithing motif.

The vassals ask for more about the wood-bird and Hagen, having prepared another drink into which he squeezes the juice of a herb, hands it to Siegfried, saying that it will help to waken his memory. Siegfried gazes thoughtfully into the horn and then drinks slowly as the motif of forgetting sounds on clarinets and bass clarinet, slowing down and leading, pianissimo and dolcissimo, to a long-held dissonance. He sings again the song of the bird, as it told him of a wonderful wife, sleeping on a rock and surrounded by fire. He describes his journey through the fire, and the discovery of a woman asleep in armour, how he awakened her with a kiss, and how he was enfolded in Brünnhilde's arms.

'What do I hear?' cries Gunther, and two ravens fly up out of a bush, circle Siegfried's head and then fly off towards the Rhine.

'Can you also understand the cry of those ravens?' Hagen asks, as Siegfried jumps to his feet and gazes after the birds, the curse motif sounding in the orchestra. 'To me they cry revenge!' And he plunges his spear into Siegfried's back. To the new motif of death (184), the onlookers cry out against Hagen, but he marches away saying 'I have revenged perjury'. Siegfried, supported by Gunther and the vassals, revisits his love for Brünnhilde, in a narrative that begins with the two chords of her awakening, constantly rises and falls, his love surging towards her remembered form, reaching out for it, and then losing its grip as his body weakens.

This consummate passage, built from motifs that represent all that is heroic in Siegfried's past, shows a Siegfried reborn in death, his innocence restored, and all the criminal schemes in which he has been embroiled washed away by his blood. In some way the music both rescues Siegfried's character in our eyes, and also casts a new light on the entire story.

Siegfried's death leads into a famous interlude (the 'funeral march'), built from poignant reminiscences of the Volsung siblings and their now destroyed offspring, summarizing the hopes and sufferings of their race and establishing a unity of being between Siegfried and his sorrowful parents. The music grieves with almost unbearable intensity, not over Siegfried only, but over the entire human condition, reminding us of the supreme price we pay for our snatched moments of enchantment. The death of each of us, the music says, is the death of a world. Freedom, individuality, ambition and law must run their course and nothing will sound thereafter save the distant lullaby of nature.

This return to nature, if it is not to be mere destruction, must also be an act of will, a peace-giving renunciation in which compassion triumphs over resentment. That is what the final scene both attempts and, to the astonishment of almost everyone who has studied it, also achieves. The funeral music dies away, introducing as it does so, first the motif of Brünnhilde's love (150) and then that of Gutrune (159), whom we find wandering distraught in the hall of the Gibichungs. Gutrune's music is throughout expressive of her vulnerable character, and although once again the women in *Götterdämmerung* are victims, Gutrune is a special case, having wandered in from another realm of the psyche than that occupied by the fate-governed characters around her. She is not cut out for any heroic or cosmic role, nor is she the initiator of any of the events in which she is embroiled. She is an ordinary, spoiled, affectionate person, with a somewhat saccharine manner and modest, largely well-meaning ambitions, who is dragged down by terrible events that she precipitates more by accident than design. In this highly atmospheric passage, wonderfully expressive of Gutrune's isolation from the drama into which she has stumbled, she listens out for Siegfried's horn. She has been disturbed by bad dreams, and timorously attends to the ambiguous sounds from the distance as she gropes her way in the dawn around the castle. She recounts that suddenly, in the night, Siegfried's horse Grane had neighed. A woman had been walking by the Rhine. Brünnhilde frightens her, she says, and she tries Brünnhilde's door to discover that the room is empty. So it was Brünnhilde going to the Rhine. Why?

All these disturbed meditations are driven out by the triumphant cry of Hagen, as he storms into the hall crying for torches to light the spoils being brought from the hunt. 'Up, Gutrune,' he says, 'Greet Siegfried! The mighty hero is coming!' Her anxious questions fall away as the funeral procession enters with Siegfried's body, and Hagen gleefully rejoices that the pallid hero will no longer go off hunting, fighting or wooing. He points to 'a wild boar's prey,

Siegfried, your dead husband!' Gutrune shrieks and falls on the body. Gunther tries in vain to comfort her as she accuses him of murder. Gunther tells her to accuse Hagen, not him, and Hagen says 'Do you revile me for it?', causing Gunther to wish anguish and misfortune on Hagen forever.

'So then,' Hagen defiantly responds, 'I, Hagen, struck him dead, since he was forfeit to my spear on which he falsely swore. I now demand the sacred right of booty, this Ring.'

Gunther claims the Ring as Gutrune's inheritance, and Hagen falls on him with his sword. In the ensuing melee Hagen kills Gunther and reaches out to seize the Ring. To the sound of the sword motif Siegfried's dead hand rises menacingly; all freeze in horror, the orchestra sinks to a whisper, and the motif of the doom of the gods, followed by that of Erda, accompanies Brünnhilde's emergence from the background, commanding silence. 'All of you,' she says, 'betrayed his wife, who comes now for vengeance. I have heard children crying over spilt milk, but no lament fit for this supreme hero.' Gutrune reproaches her for having brought disaster on their house, but 'I was Siegfried's wife,' Brünnhilde says, 'before ever you set eyes on him.' Understanding at last, Gutrune curses Hagen for suggesting the drink of forgetting that began all their woes.

Brünnhilde stands for a long time in shock and grief, gazing at the dead face of Siegfried. The fate motif sounds, opening the way for the motif (168) that summarizes Brünnhilde's assumption of control, and which had been introduced by the Norns and Waltraute as they each described Wotan's preparations for the burning of Valhalla. She orders a pyre of logs to be stacked by the Rhine, and his horse to be brought so that Grane and Brünnhilde may together join the dead hero. She sings an encomium to Siegfried, saying that no man more honest ever took an oath, none more true made a treaty and none was more pure in love, yet none so betrayed his oaths, his treaties and his truest love (185). Why was this? She looks upwards and addresses Wotan as guardian of oaths. 'Through his bravest deed that you rightly desired, you sacrificed him to the curse that had fallen on you. This innocent had to betray me, so that I should become a woman of wisdom. All is clear to me: I send your ravens home now, with the tidings you dread and desire. Rest, rest now, o god!' (186)

Those words, so mysterious when standing alone, are clarified by the music, which from this point onwards leads the drama. As she turns to address the distant god, the *Todesverkündigung* sounds in the orchestra. This is her second announcement of death, the death that her father had at first sought to avert, and then to postpone but which, she now understands, he has willed on himself and his world. The purity motif (95) now pushes its way into the bass line, harmonizing the fate motif above it, in a combination already heard in the first scene of Act 3 of *Siegfried*. The music reminds us that Brünnhilde has unfinished business with her father. She has returned from the condition of autistic destructiveness that we witnessed in her last appearance, and has learned wisdom. She now knows that, in the world of humans, ideals will always be tarnished by the need for power, and betrayed by the pervasive spirit of *Verwandlung*. All is clear to her, she says, as the fate motif generates the curse out of its own harmonic structure, and then resolves it magically with a reminder of what Wotan had wanted from Valhalla, namely peace (18C). The orchestration takes in the Rhine-daughters' original joyous call of 'Rheingold!' and, with the motif of Wotan's agitation (79) in the bass, inserts a beautiful plagal cadence before ending on the final section of the Valhalla motif (18D and E) over perhaps the most piercing suspension in all music. This matchless setting of 'Ruhe, ruhe, du Gott!' offers so poignant an enactment of the words, that we are in no doubt that this really is the end, that the perturbation and conflict, in both Brünnhilde and Wotan, have now been resolved, that father and daughter are once again united in an act of renunciation that will give meaning to their suffering, and that the business of consciousness, freedom and law has been accomplished in the only thing that has really mattered – the love and compassion that emerged 'by an invisible hand', so to speak, from Wotan's pursuit of a law-governed order. All this is embodied in the music that transfers the destiny of the cosmos from Wotan to his daughter. She now commands what he recoiled from, since this is the end.

She signals to the vassals to place Siegfried's body on the pyre, taking the Ring from his finger and gazing at it. Addressing the Rhine-daughters she tells them that she is giving them now the thing that they crave. 'The fire that consumes me shall purge the Ring of the curse. You in the water, wash it away and keep now what was stolen from you.' She puts the Ring on her finger, tells the waiting ravens to fly home to recount what has happened, but first to pass by Brünnhilde's rock and direct Loge, who still blazes there, to Valhalla. 'Thus do I throw this torch at Valhalla's vaunting towers!'

She throws the torch, the flames leap up, and catching sight of Grane she runs to him, as he neighs to join his master in the flames. First embracing the horse and then mounting him, she leaps with him onto the pyre. The flames flare high and the vassals retreat in terror. When the fire dies down, leaving only a cloud of smoke that lingers on the horizon, the waters of the Rhine rise up to swamp the stage. Hagen, who has waded in to snatch the Ring from the ashes, is then dragged to his death by the Rhine-daughters, as the first half of the curse motif sounds in its original key. Flosshilde holds the Ring high above her head and then plunges joyfully beside her sisters into the depths. In the distance Valhalla appears as Waltraute had earlier described it, Wotan motionless on his throne as the castle curls like a scrap of paper in the flames. And on that paper is written the story of the world.

Throughout this cosmic coda the orchestra takes the various motifs associated with the end of the gods, with the Rhine, with Loge and Valhalla and resolves them first in the motif of Siegfried as hero, and then in the melody of Sieglinde's blessing, recalling the holiest moment in the cycle, when a god sacrificed herself for a mortal, and the mortal understood. That, we now recognize, was the moment when all the machinations were forgotten, when the feminine triumphed, and the world was turned towards its end.

Götterdämmerung presents problems of interpretation that I shall address in what follows. But the action is clarified if we remember two observations. The first, already made, is that significant transitions often represent long processes of change and decay. Musical time moves differently from physical time, and can, in the right hands, represent huge arcs of activity in a few well-hewn bars – Siegfried's Rhine journey and his final narrative being two spectacular, but very different, examples of this. Throughout *Götterdämmerung* we encounter vast movements presented through telescoped episodes, since that is the clearest way to show that we humans cast shadows in the cosmos, and that those shadows are what we mean.

The second observation is this: that the action of the opera takes place entirely after the defeat, or capitulation, of Wotan, and the splintering of his spear. Wagner is telling us to take seriously what happens when the twilight really comes. No longer does the guardian of oaths and treaties preside over the world. However urgently we swear fidelity, bind ourselves with vows and oaths and contracts, there is no power beyond ourselves that can enforce these things, and all trust is jeopardized by our own enlightened consciousness. Already this was bound to happen, the Norns tell us, when the curse was placed on the Ring – for it is then that the rope of destiny began to fray – the moment when untruth and manipulation gained an equal footing with truth and trust. But Siegfried's second great act of *Selbstbestimmung*, which was the smashing of Wotan's spear, has brought into being a world in which Siegfried, the truest of heroes, as Brünnhilde ultimately describes him, will be false to all his vows.

Hence, just as *Siegfried* unfolds as a series of awakenings, *Götterdämmerung* unfolds as a series of betrayals. The rope of destiny snaps at the very outset, betraying the order of the world. Siegfried and Brünnhilde then swear true love, committing themselves totally and existentially to each other. But in the course of the drama he captures, enslaves and barters her, and she instigates the plot to kill him. Siegfried and Gunther swear blood-brotherhood, and this, the second most solemn of all bonds, is broken by Gunther when he too joins in the plot to kill Siegfried. The ties of family piety have already been snipped through by Hagen, as are the bonds of feudal allegiance, when Hagen misuses the call to war in order to gather the vassals for the double wedding. Brother then betrays sister when Gunther sacrifices Gutrune's husband to his own honour. Honour itself is put at nought by Gunther, in gaining his wife by human trafficking.

Hagen, implored by his father to swear an oath, swears it only to himself, and his father's pleading to stay 'true' is so orchestrated as to remind us that there is no such possibility, and that true means false in any case. To establish his innocence Siegfried swears an oath, but this oath too is without lasting effect and is promptly cancelled by a counter-oath from Brünnhilde. And the crucial oaths are sworn on

Hagen's spear, the spear that represents lawless resentment, rather than the lawful authority of the spear that Siegfried splintered. Hagen's spear is therefore the instrument of vengeance when the oaths are broken. So it goes on, to the very end of the drama, when Brünnhilde, having learned the truth from the Rhine-daughters, recognizes that in some sense all is as it had to be, and the one moment of truth from which the opera began can still be recuperated, by an act that burns all this corruption away. In this her will coincides again with Wotan's, and what he suffers passively she, in a magnificent gesture, wills on them all.

4

How the Music Works

Wagner's artistic intention, as explained in his theoretical writings, was to make music into the vehicle of the drama. In other words, the music was not to be an accompaniment to the words, but the channel through which the emotions of the drama flow – both the motives of the characters, and the responses of the audience. We all know that this is possible. But it raises a philosophical question of general import: the question of what music means and how that meaning is conveyed. As an abstract art-form, which makes no statements, deploys no concepts, and presents no image other than the images of sound, music is debarred from the normal channels of representation. It has structure and syntax of a sort, but no formal semantics. When we speak of the meaning of music we do not, as a rule, assume that we can translate that meaning into words, or give any paraphrase that even approximates to the sense of what we hear. Music is meaningful, in something like the way that a gesture, a face or a sigh is meaningful – not because it embodies some truth-directed proposition but because we sense the peculiar flow of human life that is expressed in it. Exactly how we account for this connection that we hear, between music and life, is a matter of intense philosophical dispute; but that the connection exists is assumed on every side, and was assumed long before the arrival of Wagner. What Wagner added was the attempt to synthesize the expressive power of music with a drama, in such a way that the drama would be presented *through* the music. The music was no longer to be subservient to the words: if anything, the roles of words and music were to be reversed, with the first explained by the second. The music was to import into the drama all those deeper levels of meaning, symbolism and primordial emotion that the words alone could merely hint at.

Three innovations promoted this aim. The first, which Wagner advocated at length in *Opera and Drama*, was the development of verse-forms that would unite the movement of the music with the emotional rhythm of the words. Strophic verse, end rhymes, regular feet – all the normal devices of German verse, which Wagner had used memorably and effectively in his earlier operas – stood in the way of the dramatic immediacy that he was seeking in *The Ring*. The extraordinary characters in *Das Rheingold* are not *accompanied* by music: they are *realized* in music, and realized because the words and the music are inseparable. The audience hears the musical accents as though they were verbal accents: the music speaks, just as the words sing. The use of *Stabreim* gives a kind of epic dignity to utterances that are both integrated into the melodic line and entirely governed by the action on stage. One consummate example of this is the narrative with which Loge first announces himself – a story necessary to the plot, which perfectly expresses the demi-god's wily and ironical character. Another example is the great declamation with which Alberich pronounces his curse on the Ring.[1]

The second innovation was Wagner's reinvention of the orchestra. Connected with the composer's search for unity between words and music was his desire for the *exact sound* of the sentiments portrayed. Seldom since Bach's inspired use of the obbligato parts in his cantatas have the instruments of the orchestra been so meticulously and lovingly adapted to their expressive role as by Wagner in his later operas. In *The Ring* it is as though he takes the orchestra completely apart and thoroughly cleans each component, before reassembling it as something new. As well as inventing the Wagner tuba, and finding new uses for marginal instruments like the bass trumpet, the alto oboe and the steer-horn, Wagner was able to match instruments with impeccable judgement, so as to create the sound of every emotion presented on the stage. Never has the sound of terror been better captured than by the orchestration of Hunding's pursuit (83), using bassoons, bass clarinet and violas in unison – an unforgettable timbre that presses the knife to the bone. Equally striking, and also sublime in its effect, is the instrumentation of 'Ruhe, ruhe, du Gott!' (186): a choir of tubas suddenly displacing the horns, softly accompanied by trombones and contrabass tuba, and in the background the rising and falling motion of the agitation motif (79) on cellos, basses and bass clarinet – all this leading to the Valhalla cadence (18E) sounding clear but subdued on bass trumpet. Never has something so mighty been laid so gently to rest.

The third and most remarked-on innovation was the leitmotif – the short, pregnant phrase that would arise out of the drama, gathering to itself the emotion associated with some event, idea or character, and thereafter woven into the musical fabric, so as to carry the memory of its original appearance. Wagner did not invent the device, nor did he use the term 'Leitmotif', preferring 'Hauptthema', 'Grundthema' and similar idioms. (The term was already current in 1860, when it appeared, describing the compositional techniques of Wagner and Liszt, in August Wilhelm Ambros's Culturhistorische Bilder aus dem Musikleben der Gegenwart.) Nevertheless it is to Wagner that we should turn in order to understand just what can be achieved by the use of such motifs, and how they function in the musical totality.

The Wagnerian leitmotif is an intelligible and emotionally charged musical idea, memorable in itself and replete with musical possibilities. Consider that with which the whole work begins, the nature motif associated with the depths of the Rhine (1). Wagner's first sketch for this idea was simply an ascending arpeggiation of the E flat triad.[2] As a pure symbol of watery depths and a cue to the listener to think back to the origins of the story that might do perfectly well. But it is musically inert, ending on a note (the tonic) from which all potential has flowed away, and prompting no emotional uplift in the listener. In the final version Wagner recrafted the arpeggio as a melodic idea, beginning with the leap of a fifth, suggesting the deep and elemental laws of cosmic harmony, and ending on the mediant, with all its restlessness and leading-note potential activated. The result is still an arpeggiated triad, but one that stays in the memory, and also permits interesting musical development of the kind that it receives in the prelude to Das Rheingold, and much later in the parallel motif of Erda, in the scene of the Norns and in Siegfried's Rhine Journey. Moreover, in this form, the triad spells out the overtone series of the first E flat in the basses. It is drawing our attention in another way to the natural order of things – the order that sounds in the musical tone itself.

The Wagnerian leitmotif is always recognizable, but it is also an integrated feature of the musical argument. The music does not come to a sudden halt in order to allow the leitmotif to be stated, Debussy's jibe about 'visiting cards' notwithstanding.[3] The leitmotif appears in the course of things, a natural outgrowth of the musical development, in just the way that a thought is sparked off in the flow of ordinary experience and then submerged by it. In almost all the important cases, the leitmotif is *precipitated out* of the musical movement, of which it forms a natural and often culminating part. A brilliant instance of this occurs with the first appearance of the theme associated with Siegfried as hero (89), which grows naturally from the escalating excitement with which Brünnhilde announces Siegfried's existence to Sieglinde, and which leads in turn seamlessly to Sieglinde's ecstatic blessing of the Valkyrie who has resolved to save her.

When such motifs recur, woven into the musical fabric, they recur as memories, burdened however with an accretion of thoughts and emotions, so that with each recurrence the meaning of the motifs is changed and enhanced. Words in a language retain a constant meaning from use to use – that is their function. The reason for this is that meaning is attached to them by convention, and is, in an important sense, arbitrary – there is nothing in the sound 'dog' that attaches it by nature to the species denoted by 'hund', 'chien', 'kalb' and 'pes'. By contrast the meaning of the leitmotifs arises from the events, emotions and actions to which they are attached, and each recurrence adds something more to the accumulated association of ideas. A leitmotif is a musical idea with a memory. It brings to mind objects, events and people that are absent from the stage – which perhaps had never been entirely present there.

The Wagnerian leitmotif is able to accumulate meaning in this way in part because of its architectonic potential. Like the theme of a fugue or a symphonic movement, it is susceptible to countless musical uses – it can often be augmented, diminished, varied, hinted at, combined in contrapuntal sequences in ways that owe nothing to the words or action on stage but everything to the intrinsic dynamical qualities of the musical material. Hence the process whereby the leit-motifs accumulate meaning is to a great extent independent of the action, even if carefully coordinated with it. It is more like the process by which a symphonic theme gains in meaning as the movement unfolds. To put it another way: it is as though the dramatic emotion from which the leitmotif first emerges is then entrusted to it, and carried by it through a purely musical development, to be returned in transfigured form to the action on the stage.

This is the process that we witness in the transformation of the Rhinegold praise motif (14), as it passes through the poisonous harmonic cloud thrown up by the music of Alberich's resentment, to become the two-chord sequence that we hear in the prelude to *Götter-dämmerung* Act 2 (164). The subtle musical transformation here conveys the vast distance in emotion, between joy in the gold and the hate-filled need to repossess it after many thefts. Yet the thing itself, the music implies, is the unaltered object of these mutating states of mind.[4] The two-chord phrase is the symbol, or rather the musical enactment, of *where we have got to*, since Alberich's original transgression – a transgression on which we all depend, just as the gods depend upon Alberich's theft to pay for their own usurpation. The phrase has this meaning on account of its musical history. A continuous dramatic development has enfolded this cadence, sucked out its innocent life, and filled it with poison. Such examples show the way in which Wagner's drama is embodied in the music. The themes and motifs do not simply remind us of original situations: they make connections; they analyse, synthesize and also render transparent the emotional realities that are being shaped into myth.

Ernest Newman made an apt comparison between the leitmotif and a face. The leitmotifs have a distinct physiognomy, which makes the same kind of impact on the ear as a face on the eye – the unmistakeable and re-identifiable other, with his inner life revealed. Just as a face reveals what it is like to be another and to see the world as he sees it, so does the leitmotif present the 'what it is like', the 'subjective reality' of an event, a passion or a character. Like a face, the leitmotif is hard to unpack: it is a unified whole, an outward summary of inner complexities; but at the same time it has the immediacy and simplicity of the face, and we understand it with the same directness with which we grasp another's expression. And, as with the example just given, a face can change, grow old and weary, and yet be instantly recognizable as the person it was.

Musical connection takes place behind the action, so to speak, hidden in the depth of things. Hence it becomes a potent symbol and artistic realization of the cosmic order and of the intertwining of individual and cosmic destiny. The musical connectedness of Wagner's leitmotifs already accomplishes one of his principal aesthetic tasks, which is to make each event of the drama resound through mythical space, so as to evoke and to symbolize the unchanging and unconscious order of things. The most important examples of this musical connectedness are the nature motifs, among which we should count the arpeggio motifs of the Rhine, Erda's minor-key version of the same, and the various voices of nature – the song of the Rhine-daughters, that of the wood-bird and the beautiful phrase representing Freia's apples.

These motifs are not merely connected with each other; they are also connected with the founding principles of music in our tradition, the principles of tonal harmony and pentatonic melody. The harmonic motifs are prolongations or elaborations of the triad, each pointing in its own highly individual way to the common musical substance from which they are composed. Somewhere in the depths, preceding all our efforts at individual existence and personality, these motifs tell us, is the primal matter of life, matter from which individuality is forged and to which it returns. And these nature motifs saturate the musical texture of *The Ring*, which constantly calls us back to the *Urerlebnis* – the timeless experience of natural harmony, and therefore of life at its origins.

One of the most remarkable features of the music of *The Ring*, therefore, is the fact that the diatonic language of Western music is not just used but *reflected* upon. The syntax of music has become the semantics – what the music is about. Music, Wagner is suggesting, has its primordial forms, from which the song of the free individual emerges and into which it lapses when the struggle is over. The diatonic and pentatonic scales, the arpeggiated triad, the octave and fifth – all these are singled out by Wagner to become not just motifs but objects of musical attention. In the music of Alberich and Hagen they are eaten away by tritones, just as they are softened and melted into chromatic melodies by the search for love. The high point of this process – the melody of Wotan's farewell – shows the god, whose spear has assumed command of tonal space through the diatonic scale, finding his identity in that space through a chromatic melody on neighbouring semitones. He has been reduced from sovereign to subject; but has also emerged as a free individual, a being capable of renunciation and love.

At the very moment when Wagner, in *Tristan*, was remaking the language of tonality, therefore, so as to make full use of all twelve tones of the chromatic scale, he was reflecting in this highly original way on the traditional syntax. He was remaking tonality as a symbol of the primordial flux from which the free individual emerges, in order to fight the short but glorious battle for existence. The move from natural harmony to chromatic tension is a symbol of the entire story of the Ring, both of what we lose and what we gain when species-being becomes self-conscious life.

The same framework, in which the individual emerges from the primordial, can be witnessed in the melodic motifs. Modern ethno-musicology tells us that the pentatonic scale is the scale most widely used in folk music, as well as the one that can be slotted most easily into the diatonic grammar of Western art-music.[5] Wagner anticipated this observation, using the pentatonic scale to represent the original birth of language out of song. The 'Wallalalalala' of the Rhine-daughters is like the lisping of a child on the threshold of speech. And in the song of the wood-bird we hear the pre-conscious voice of nature – the voice that knows what it does not tell but which bursts into speech in Siegfried's ear, when the dragon's blood awakens the hero's yearnings. (Why does it do this? See Chapter 6.)

One of the leitmotifs in particular should be mentioned here: that traditionally associated with 'sleeping Brünnhilde', which becomes prominent when the Valkyrie is put to sleep, and remains thereafter as a reminder of her presence on the mountaintop. This motif (99) has a distinctive rhythmic contour, which enables it to retain its identity through every kind of melodic and harmonic variation. It begins life as a simple nature image: the descending pentatonic scale, but despite this pure beginning it is used to spell out the complete range of tonal harmonies. Finally it melts into an accompanying figure, supporting the most chromatic of all the melodies in the cycle. This magical transition (which I discuss later in this chapter) is again a vivid symbol of the emergence of the free individual (in this case Brünnhilde) from the primordial nature that we share.

The invocation of natural music takes on a greater significance as the drama unfolds. Wagner's style, following *Tristan*, incorporates chromatic harmonies and semitone progressions in a way that revolutionized music, his own included. Hence when he returned to work on *Siegfried* Act 3 it was with a new and more plastic conception of tonal relations. Despite this – and also because of it – he was able to rescue the nature motifs of the earlier sections of the drama by giving them a new and enhanced significance, as emblematic of a long-postponed return to the primeval order.

Thus Wagner provides leitmotifs at the beginning of his drama that endure with amplified meaning and musical conviction until the very end. Among the factors that contribute to this achievement we should place special emphasis on the order in which the tetralogy was conceived. In writing the poem of *The Ring* Wagner began at the end and worked back, step by step, to the beginning. He was acutely aware, in composing the drama, of where he had to get to, and the same was surely true of his first ideas for the music that would take him there. Consider the motif of Wotan's spear, so simple in its original form (19), yet with an entirely *musical* authority – the descending diatonic scale asserting its mastery over musical space, but restless too, never ending on the tonic. Curtailed, turned on itself and sorrowful, it becomes the résumé of Siegmund's suffering (56); broken and hesitant it is the theme of Wotan's frustration (76); reassembled through octave transposition, it is the glorious tribute to Brünnhilde's purity (95); buoyed up by shifting key-centres and the themes of frustration and wandering, it thrashes in helpless self-doubt through the prelude to *Siegfried* Act 3. And its broken remnants still form the bass line at the end, as the world is gathered into the consciousness of Brünnhilde, and there extinguished. Even as the drama fades into eternity, contracts call out from the void.

All the leitmotifs announced in *Das Rheingold* are similar: clear and gripping musical ideas, which magnetize the surrounding drama, attracting its deposits of meaning so as to carry them forward to the next appearance. In his many published references to Beethoven, and in his study of the Ninth Symphony, Wagner showed a deep appreciation of the motivic structure of Beethoven's symphonic works. The structural motifs of Beethoven's movements rarely take the form of lyrical tunes, great though Beethoven was as a melodist. However attractive to the ear, they are also building blocks, often composed of independent parts, like the magnificent first subject of the Ninth Symphony, first movement, which can be taken apart and developed in many contrasting directions.[6] The theme of Valhalla (18) is like this, with parts that develop separately in the narrative and acquire distinct characters as the drama proceeds – the last part (18E) sometimes attaching itself as a cadential ending to the sword motif, the third part remembering the two-chord sequence of 'Rheingold!', and preparing itself throughout the drama as the final answer to the Curse, in 'Ruhe, ruhe, du Gott!'

Adorno's no-holds-barred assault on Wagner is written in prose infested by Marxist jargon and by overblown claims to expertise. Often barely intelligible in its layer upon layer of abstractions, it is nevertheless the product of a musically sensitive intellect, capable of making profound criticisms of musical grammar. Among the more reasonable of his criticisms are these: first, that Wagner's motivic structure is a sham, since the motifs never really develop as Beethoven's do, but remain static, lying inert on the surface of the music like dead things cast off by some hidden struggle. Second, Wagner's material does not form consecutive paragraphs from its own inner dynamic, but is simply assembled in sequences, which defy the logic of traditional chord grammar without achieving a new logic of their own.

I return to the second criticism below, but the first must be answered here. It is true that the Wagnerian motifs are not developed as Beethoven would develop them. To subject them to a purely symphonic elaboration would be to deny their dramatic meaning, and to destroy their most important feature, which is their memory. Of course, the Beethoven theme has a memory too – a purely musical memory, as when the opening theme of the Eroica, first movement, remembers the C sharp to which it leads, constantly moving the tonality sideways towards D flat. But the Wagnerian leitmotif remembers other things, besides music. It remembers events, emotions, ideas, encounters and characters. It is freighted with a precious dramatic cargo that it cannot risk spilling into the kind of oceanic polyphony of a Beethoven sonata movement. Only at the end of *Götterdämmerung* does Wagner free his motifs sufficiently to allow them a purely symphonic development. In other places the motifs are contained within carefully shaped dramatic paragraphs. Nevertheless, they are connected to each other, and move into each other, by purely musical means. This particular criticism of Wagner, therefore, seems to me to be an *ignoratio elenchi*: criticizing Wagner for not doing something that would completely destroy his artistic aims.

In an essay describing the composition of *The Ring* Wagner remarked that the motifs of the cycle had all evolved from a few 'malleable nature motifs'.[7] And Deryck Cooke has shown, in the introduction to *The Ring* that accompanied the original Decca recording of Solti's performance, that the leitmotifs belong to distinct families.[8] This is true not only of the nature motifs, but also of themes that arise in separate contexts and reach for each other across the intervening narrative. Alberich's threat of rape in the first scene of *Das Rheingold* is set to material that is later, quietened down and re-harmonized, the theme of Freia's golden apples – an indication that Alberich was reaching for the unreachable. The agitated 9/8 smithing theme of Nibelheim, in which all the machine-like enslavement of the Nibelungs is contained, is later reworked in 6/8 tempo and with lilting melodic contours, to become the vehicle of Mime's faked affection for the hero whom he seeks to use and then destroy.

In the tetralogy we witness two spectacular attempts at self-creation, in which a person puts his whole being and individuality into an object that he uses to assert his will: Alberich's forging of the Ring, and Siegfried's forging of the sword from its broken fragments. The huge distance between these two actions, the one poisoned with resentment and the denial of love, the other a joyful opening to a world of freedom, is revealed in the two leitmotifs associated with Ring and sword respectively, that of the Ring a keyless diminished chord, that of the sword the purest arpeggiation of the major triad. (Though it should be noted that the sword motif can be translated into minor mode without loss of musical direction, and therefore frequently appears in that guise.) The sword motif unequivocally aligns Siegfried with the natural order, and even if his bid for individuality is destined to destroy him, and to destroy the order of law that Wotan had for so long upheld, it is heard as a more natural thing than the use of the Ring by Alberich. To forge the Ring Alberich had to *renounce* what is most essential to human life; to forge the sword Siegfried had only to affirm it.

There is a distinction among leitmotifs between the saturated and the unsaturated – those, like the curse and the Tarnhelm (*Verwandlung*) that stand alone and resist completion, and those like the sword and the *Todesverkündigung* (the announcement of death) that constantly nudge the music onwards to some kind of answering phrase – whether a perfect cadence, in the case of the sword, or a prolongation, in the case of the *Todesverkündigung*. In the later Wagnerian style motifs have a tendency to become ever more unsaturated, like the Wanderer motifs in *Siegfried*, or the look motif in *Tristan*, which constantly repeat themselves or attract to themselves answering phrases, so as to work their way through long passages of musical narrative.

Many of the motifs are engagingly melodic, but we should never regard a Wagnerian motif as simply a melodic fragment. Always the melody is replete with harmonic meanings, some of which may be implied, as in the nature themes, but others of which may be explicitly given in other voices of the orchestra, as in the curse motif (45), in which a jarring C major triad on chalumeau clarinets bites into the B minor harmony before releasing it, replete with venom, onto the dominant seventh plus minor ninth of B minor.[9]

Rhythmical ideas might also be just as much a part of the motif, and able to stand alone in suggesting it. Thus Hunding's aggressive motif, which announces his appearance, standing suspiciously in the door of his hut, reappears as a purely rhythmical call on one note throughout Act 1 of *Die Walküre*, notably as he summons Siegmund to battle. Likewise the wood-bird's song, reduced to a single note, is recognizable as a rhythmical structure when Siegfried advances to the foot of Brünnhilde's mountain in *Siegfried* Act 3. Most memorable of all is the smithing motif, which is present as a rhythmical tattoo in the anvils of Nibelheim, in the futile work of Mime at his forge, and in the malicious laughter of Alberich and Hagen.

That said, the motif must always be understood in its entirety, as a complete musical organism, capable of linking to others and developing in all dimensions, melodic, harmonic and rhythmical. It is the unit of musical meaning, and Wagner's great achievement – not matched by any other composer – was to discover motifs that would be memorable in themselves, but also plastic, capable of combining into a unified musical surface and prolonged tonal argument, so as to carry the rich associations of the drama as they accumulate.

In this connection we should recognize again the influence of Beethoven. Wagner, like Beethoven, was a master of musical form, whose themes seem to develop from musical seeds that become fully apparent only in their elaboration. An obvious example is *Die Walküre* Act 2, Scene 4, in which Brünnhilde announces death to Siegmund and is gradually won over by his emotion, the announcement motif pushing towards its own prolongation, burdened with the feelings of the characters, until finding the phrase that completes it, and which conquers Brünnhilde's heart (Ex (viii)). Several early commentators were so struck by this organic growth of the musical line that they tried to give general accounts of the Wagnerian 'method', so as to represent it as a triumph of form comparable to the symphonic architecture of Beethoven or the contrapuntal tapestries of Bach. The most striking of these attempts was that of Alfred Lorenz, whose four-volume *Das Geheimnis der Form bei Richard Wagner* attempts to explain, as the title indicates, the 'secret' of these works that, because of their complex dramatic structure and extreme length, seem at first sight to be collections of episodes rather than organic unities. Lorenz was writing in opposition to Hans von Wolzogen and his followers, who had sought to interpret Wagner's works by giving lists of the leitmotifs and their interrelations, and who, Lorenz thought, overlooked their formal unity and perfection.

It is fair to say that musicologists have not been convinced by Lorenz's account of the Wagner operas.[10] Lorenz was far too concerned to show the unity in Wagner's works by finding formal principles other than those evident in the drama. He tried to break the music down, melodically and harmonically, into prosodic structures, such as the ABA and Bar forms of lyrical poetry, while looking always for tonal centres that would enable him to identify this region as a 'subdominant' episode, that as 'dominant', this as working *towards* the tonic, that as moving away from it, the whole reconciled and brought to closure in accordance with the rules of functional harmony.[11] The result, for all its musical insights, has an obsessive and factitious air to it, and the reader cannot avoid feeling that Lorenz has forgotten the most important point, that Wagner's music is organized according to the demands of a drama. Unity is achieved in part by providing every dramatic question with a musical answer, and every musical question with an answer that is also a deed.

That is not to say that Wagner ignored musical form or that formal relations play no part in establishing the movement and meaning of the work. Several recent commentators have emphasized the subtle and powerful use of key relations in the dramas, and in particular the device of tonal progression, whereby particular keys, associated with particular episodes, characters or ideas, modulate towards dramatic climaxes and away from them, so as to weave the action into a tonal argument. This device has been studied by Robert Bailey and Patrick McCreless, and remains a fruitful, if somewhat controversial, topic in the literature.[12] We can see it at work in the relation between Siegfried and Brünnhilde, which is dramatized in the keys associated with each of them – C major for Siegfried, E major for Brünnhilde. And I give an example below of the way in which such tonal relations are woven into the memory of the music, so as to add another dimension to its dramatic force.

This returns me to the philosophical question, of how music means. Music does not refer to the world in the way that language refers to it – by virtue of semantic rules established by convention. Nor does it work as figurative painting works, through detailed pictorial resemblances. There are such resemblances, of course, between musical and extra-musical objects, and these can be given a representational significance – as in the song of the wood-bird and the sound of Siegfried's horn. But to depend on them for the entire meaning of the leitmotifs would limit the field of reference to the sound-world alone.

Hence far more usually the reference to extra-musical reality is established by a kind of metaphor, in which a musical element is attached to its object by a leap of the imagination. Here are some simple examples: the 'flowing' music of the Rhine, the 'sparkling' music of the magic fire, the 'hammering' music of the smithing theme. But the metaphors extend beyond the reach of synaesthesia. For example we hear the music of the Ring motif as though wrapped around a tight diminished chord. Harmonically and melodically it makes a closed circle in the music, disconnected from the material to either side. In the horn-chord harmonies of Freia's apple motif we hear the rejuvenating freshness of the fruit. The thrust of the warrior's arm sounds in the sword motif, while the bitterness of Alberich is instilled in the harmonies of the curse. The idea of *Verwandlung* is captured by the Tarnhelm motif, which alternates unrelated triads – A flat minor and E minor – before settling on an open fifth that could belong to either key, the note C flat having sounded throughout, magically transformed from C flat to B and back again while remaining the same.

In that way Wagner exploits our imaginative capacity to hear one thing in another, and whether we call the result 'representation', 'imitation' or 'expression' is of less importance than the wider significance attached to it in the drama.[13] The leitmotifs are absorbed into a musical narrative, which associates them with the things that they symbolize, and imbues them with the memory of their origins and history. They can be attached to things of any category: objects (the sword, the Tarnhelm), people (Wotan, Siegfried), actions (smithing), races (the Volsungs), states of mind (forgetting), moments (awakening), ideas (redemption), spiritual conditions (the curse), existential predicaments (dragon); and so on. While it is sometimes useful to give them names, we should never forget that they are not assigned a meaning as a semaphore symbol is assigned a meaning, but *acquire* a meaning, in the course of a drama in which they are the principal dynamic elements.

Precisely because they do not have meaning assigned to them by convention, the leitmotifs can make connections that could not be made on the stage or by the words pronounced there, since these connections lie deeper than the conscious knowledge and purpose of the characters. Hence always, in *The Ring*, the orchestra knows more than the characters on the stage, since it has kept in its memory the critical episodes that they have either not noticed or forgotten or never had the chance to observe. In this way Wagner re-creates the effect of the Greek tragedy, in which the chorus (the orchestra), and therefore the audience, knows more than any of the principal characters.

A good example of this is the motif that accompanies Alberich's original forswearing of love (17), and which was called by Hans von Wolzogen (the first to attempt a catalogue of the leitmotifs in *The Ring*) the '*Entsagungsmotiv*' or motif of renunciation. Wagner himself wrote '*Entsagung*' beside this theme in his sketch for the score. But the motif reappears with all the force of its first occurrence on other equally pregnant occasions. Thus it appears, in the original key of C minor, to the words 'Heiligster Minne höchste Noth' – the highest need of most holy love – as Siegmund draws the sword promised to him by his father, Volsa, from the ash tree in Hunding's hut. It appears as Wotan kisses away Brünnhilde's divinity, and lays her to sleep on the rock, without the faintest suggestion on Wotan's part that Frau Minne has anything to do with what is going on. (Though, deep down, Brünnhilde's 'mortalization' is Minne's work.)

The theme appears elsewhere too, and is a paradigm example of an unsaturated motif, reaching out for the phrase that will complete it. In these three occurrences, however, it would be plausible to say only of the first of them that it has something to do with renunciation. Better to say that the theme is replete with the huge resolve that is being enacted on the stage – the sense of an existential turning point, which the three characters experience in their contrasting ways. And by gathering into it the emotions first of Alberich, then of Siegmund and finally of Wotan it makes a connection – a connection that the listener hears in the very notes, but which lies deeper than anything said or revealed in the drama – between the three actions depicted. Each of the characters is staking his being on something outside himself – on the gold that will substitute for love, on the sword that will win safety for love, and on the daughter who will find love in the human world, and bring its healing power to the gods. The idea of each life, even the life of the gods, as shaped by its crisis point, which may also be a moment of existential choice – this idea is presented to the listener as a truth not about the individual only, but about the whole cosmic order. And a connection is being made in feeling, which is not yet a connection in conscious thought, between Alberich's sin against himself in forswearing love and the intensest loves in the upper world – the love of Siegmund for his sister and bride, the love of Wotan for the daughter who is to accomplish his semi-conscious designs and later (in the meeting between Brünnhilde and Waltraute) the love of that daughter for Siegfried.

To put the point another way: the leitmotif is not describing things but subjecting them to a process of musical development. If, in retrospect, we can summarize this process in a word or phrase, all well and good, and of course names, in these circumstances, are extremely useful. However, the knowledge enshrined in the motif is not 'knowledge by description' but 'knowledge by acquaintance'. It forges a connection between episodes by responding to them in a similar way and bringing the memory of one to bear on the reality of the other.

This is how we should understand the motif associated with Freia (22), which first appears when Freia comes on stage, in flight from the Giants. Hans von Wolzogen's description of this as the flight motif has been exploded by Deryck Cooke, who points out that its two parts develop independently in the cycle, and that the real burden of meaning is borne by the second component, 22B.[14] The theme, derived from a four-note cell that occurs so widely in Wagner (for example in the grail theme from *Lohengrin*) that Ernest Newman has described it as a Wagnerian tic,[15] is associated almost everywhere in the cycle with love and the sufferings of love. It is the leading device of *Die Walküre* Act 1, where it persuasively humanizes what is, from the standpoint of traditional morality, a criminal sexual union. The theme is noteworthy not only for its poignant beauty, but also for its harmonic versatility, both of which it acquires, however, only when detached from the cold realm of the gods and released into the world of humans. Thus it can effortlessly modulate from C sharp minor to C minor in the space of a bar (Ex (i)); it can go on falling for bar after bar, or even, though rarely, find completion in a great rising arch (Ex (ii)). In all this it conveys some of the abandon of erotic love, and also the acceptance of suffering that comes through love.

There is one place where the occurrence of the theme has seemed mysterious – which is the descent into Nibelheim, where Wagner first evokes the bondage that has entered the world with the forging of the Ring. The theme does not merely occur here: it binds everything

together, first in an agitated diminished form (36A), which anticipates the hammers of the factory below, and then, introduced by the
Rhinegold motif, in an augmented version that takes the music down
in trepidation to the underworld (36B). All this occurs before the
theme has acquired its subsequent, human, identity, as the theme of
love and the sufferings of love. Until now we have heard it only in
association with Freia, who represents not love in its human form but
the plastic material from which love between humans is composed.
However, nothing could be more gripping or dramatically right than
this descent into Nibelheim: why is this?

The answer goes to the heart of the drama. Erotic love, in *The
Ring*, means two different things: there is the need implanted by the
species – the natural force that spreads its attentions far and wide –
and the longing which is also an existential choice, an assumption of
responsibility for another life. Erotic love grows from the invisible
root of sexual need, and the pre-personal voice of the species sounds
through this, our most free and individual endeavour. Alberich is
susceptible to this first kind of love – the need that flits from object to
object, as he flits from one Rhine-daughter to another in his vain
efforts to seduce them. But he cannot attain to love of the second
kind, love that wins the heart of an individual and overcomes the
fleeting temptations of impersonal desire. Therefore he renounces it,
and with it every hope of personal fulfilment: now there is nothing
for him to strive for, save power. Hence, for Alberich, even love of the
first kind is a cause of suffering, and launches him on the loveless
path that he thereafter follows.

The first half of Freia's theme, 22A, is a 'nature' theme in *The
Ring*, sounding always with the voice of the species. It is ethereal,
impersonal, conveying the primordial delight of sensual love. But
when Freia comes onto the stage in *Das Rheingold* she has been precipitated into another and more passionate love – that of Fasolt,
before which she trembles. A force greater than Freia's divinity now
threatens to overwhelm her, and she flees before this force in terror.
The two parts of her leitmotif point in two different directions. The
first is eternal, immutable, the Ur-principle of carnal love. The second
is agitated, variable, pursued and fulfilled by circumstance: in other
words, it has a history. The character of this second motif is not

given, but acquired, so that by the end of the cycle it has an enormous accumulation of meaning. By then it is overborne by personal tragedy and by the catastrophe of erotic love – a catastrophe that cannot be avoided, since the attempt to avoid it, as Alberich shows, is simply catastrophe of another kind.

Freia's double theme therefore captures a metaphysical truth about the erotic: that it is a synthesis of a primeval, pre-personal force with that which is most intensely personal and most deeply compromised by time and change. While the first is pure delight, the second, which grows from it, is fraught with shame, fear and tragedy, and is fatally exposed to the threat of *Verwandlung*. Hence the first part of Freia's theme, 22A, innocently soars, while the second part sinks constantly lower, borne up from time to time by a forlorn yet renewing hope, but ineluctably dropping nevertheless under the weight of its emotional burden. When 22B reappears during the descent into Nibelheim the context is again one of suffering, the ultimate cause of which is the first kind of love – Alberich's desire for the Rhine-daughters. The suffering is amplified by Alberich's inability to transcend the first kind of love, and by his forswearing of the attempt. The music consequently curses love and its suffering, takes hold of the motif and hammers at it in order to annihilate its power. 36A is beaten flat by the relentless 9/8 rhythm, losing all trace of organic emotion and transforming itself at last into the mechanical smithing theme of Nibelheim (37). Only then does the augmented version, 36B, sound through the orchestra, now in tones of helpless lamentation for a world deprived of love in its personal form.

Return now to the motif as it appears in *Die Walküre*. Here it conveys not lamentation but a kind of grieving gentleness. Love has passed from the general to the particular; two individuals are in the grip of that anguished concern for each other that admits no substitutes, and in which the vocabulary of love – glance, caress, kiss, silence – has taken on another and higher meaning. Siegmund and Sieglinde are face to face, and the music outlines them with erotic tenderness. At this new, personal, level, the suffering of love is a premonition of bereavement, a recognition of the irreplaceability of another life, in which the self and its glance have become the focus of an existential tie. At this higher level, the suffering of love is also a vindication: a sign that the lovers have risen above the natural order and possessed themselves of the individuality and the freedom that justify the trouble of existence, and of which bereavement is the price.

Looking back now to *Das Rheingold*, we can appreciate the pathos of Fasolt's claim for the Ring – 'mir blieb er für Freias Blick', it is due to me for Freia's glance. For the Ring is the only thing that can be exchanged against love, the only thing that can dissolve even the object of love in the stream of substitutes. Of all the treaties and bargains struck in *Das Rheingold* it is only that between Wotan and the Giants that has a genuine moral basis. Freia is promised in reward for a creative act, whereby something of value is brought into the world: Freia is the price of labour. Fasolt's touching description of the need of 'uns Armen' for woman's beauty and worth, which the gods enjoy in abundance, makes it clear that the Giants worked so hard precisely because love was to be their wage. (See the passage appended to 22B in the table of leitmotifs.) Freia is not promised in exchange for an object, but in exchange for labour, and this labour embodies the soul of the Giant, all that is 'properly his'. The Ring, therefore, is no mere trinket, but the means to transfer the goal of labour from use to exchange – from the intrinsic value of love, to the instrumental value of power. A creature whose essence is labour can accept this transfer only by losing his soul – for he has wasted his self on a thing with no intrinsic use.

Even when used to call some specific object or person to mind, the real meaning of the leitmotif lies not in any conventional or referential function, but in its expressive power as music. A clear instance of this occurs in Sieglinde's narrative to Siegmund, describing the wedding feast through which she sat as a forced and humiliated bride. Sadly I sat as they drank, she says, when a stranger entered – an old man in a grey robe. It doesn't require much knowledge of *The Ring* to know who this stranger is. The rightness of Wagner's allusion here lies, however, not in the reference to Wotan – Sieglinde later shows that she too recognized the stranger's identity – but in the way that his motif captures Sieglinde's heartbeat, as she raises her eyes from despair and glimpses hope, sensing all at once those intimations of another and higher order that hope can bring to us. Her E minor recitative cadences here in the major and on the mediant, magically lightening her grief, and summoning of its own accord the theme that refers back to the realm of the gods. The musical transition is what counts, and it is a transition in Sieglinde's soul.

The tonal 'argument' of *The Ring* is well illustrated by an example to which I have already referred – the sleeping Brünnhilde motif. At the end of *Die Walküre* Brünnhilde, having been condemned to become mortal, entreats Wotan to surround her with protecting fire, so that only a hero might finally awaken her. This is the point at which the divine chooses to incarnate itself in the human, out of sympathy for human love and for the free being who enjoys it. Wotan is persuaded to grant his daughter's wish, and the orchestra announces the sleeping Brünnhilde motif – a pentatonic scale, which can also be understood, from the surrounding syntax, as a descending triad with added sixth (99). At first this seems merely to round off the statement in the bass of the Valkyrie's ride which had preceded it. But the motif recurs at the climax, as Brünnhilde and Wotan embrace, and their unconscious complicity becomes apparent.

This massive statement in Brünnhilde's key of E major at once assumes enormous musical significance, as the motif is repeated, suitably stretched, at each inversion of the triad, so as to erect a great pillar of triadic harmony. We begin to hear the motif's musical potential. It can be expanded and compressed so as to encompass different arpeggiations of the same harmony; it can be adapted, as we discover at once, to form an accompanying figure, and a figure, moreover, capable of moving effortlessly between keys. Above the motif, sounding softly on violas and cellos, Wotan now sings his farewell, which shifts back and forth between C major and E (minor and major), taking in neighbouring keys along the way, and climaxing on that breath-taking chromatic sequence in which the harmonic and melodic flexibility of the original motif, sounding in the bass, is shown to fullest advantage, as the tonal centre slips from E to C and back again. (Ex (iii).) Here is Wotan's godhead, 'subdued to what it works in, like the dyer's hand' (Shakespeare, Sonnet CXI), and Wotan himself reduced by Brünnhilde's purity to a subject in his own sovereign space, both of them outlined by the chromatic melody against the shifting tonal background, in which the destinies of Siegfried and Brünnhilde are subtly and pre-consciously entwined, as the tonic shifts from E to C and back to E.

After Wotan's kiss, and Brünnhilde's lapse into sleep, the music sinks at last to a quietus on the fate motif. This is harmonized in two ways, first as a cadence from a flattened sub-mediant triad in F sharp minor onto the dominant seventh of the key, secondly as a progression from a D minor to an E major triad. (Ex (iv).) The first harmonization is the one that Wagner had used until this point, for dramatic reasons that I explore below. The second harmonization is far more significant here. For it enables Wagner to imbue the final bars of the opera with a serene foreboding – a premonition of a tragedy that will also be an acceptance, and a renunciation of life that will also affirm it.

Wotan summons Loge, the fire-god, whose music at once flares up through the orchestra, exchanging minor and major sixth against the dominant. After an extraordinary chromatic passage that sets the whole orchestra ablaze, the fire-music moves towards E major, and the major sixth to dominant, C sharp to B, emerges as the recurring element in the high sparkle on harp and strings. Just as the audience begins to hear the melodic potential, the downward-turned glance of these two notes, they are taken up by the woodwind to become the first two notes of the original sleeping Brünnhilde motif. The motif is therefore completely integrated into the fire-music, and imbues it with its own affirmative atmosphere. (Ex (v).) The pentatonic melody sparkles above the chromatic harmony, symbol of Brünnhilde's unspoiled and protected purity.

Wagner now exploits the figurative potential of the motif, which, haloed with flame, accompanies first the hero theme, then Wotan's farewell, and finally, in the most magical transformation of all, the fate motif, in the second harmonization mentioned above, causing the music to sink down twice into D minor before resolving in E. This whole passage is cadential, the original movement from C to E occurring several times before that newer and stranger cadence, introduced by the fate motif, which interpolates a D minor triad into music to which the key of D minor is entirely foreign. (D minor has been the key of tragedy in *Die Walküre*, setting the tone at the outset of Act 1, and bringing Act 2 to its devastating conclusion.)

The sleeping Brünnhilde motif, we see, is wholly misrepresented by its usual title. The motif effects a transformation, and forever afterwards bears the memory of this transformation, applying it in new and surprising contexts, welding together our responses to disparate situations, and making us subliminally aware that they are not disparate at all but deeply connected.

In its original form the motif is quintessentially affirmative, and in its first appearance cadential, advancing to an internal full stop. It reminds us that Brünnhilde, for all her imaginative defiance, has not defied nature, forsworn love or in any other way embarked on the path marked out by calculation and the pursuit of power. But the motif is also moving of its own accord away from the natural order, towards the world of individuality, freedom and love. Its intervals can be expanded and compressed, it can become chromatic and even keyless without losing its musical shape, and it can shift between keys without distortion.

The triumphant 'yes' with which it begins at once collapses to a tender and mutating figure, one whose mutability suggests the inconstancy of earthly things. Wotan's chromatic farewell emphasizes this, and the effect of the accompanying figure is to bring the god's love for Brünnhilde down to earth, to make it real and tender and mortal, imbued with the renunciation which he has yet openly to embrace. We might say that the affirmative, cadential character of the theme *normalizes* Wotan's love, just as it normalizes Brünnhilde's extraordinary project, both god-like and god-defying, to become mortal and to take a human lover. For the 'yes' was made possible only when the lover too was normalized, as a husband, one that would awaken Brünnhilde to a life worthy of her divine nature, a life of faithful attachment to another who is able to live up to the ideal that she embodies.

Brünnhilde's project can be fulfilled only if she is saved for the hero – and this means protected from the rest of humankind. Wotan summons fire, the destructive primeval force that outlasts even the gods, and to which everything must succumb. But the destroyer is also a protector. Brünnhilde's self-sacrifice has humanized the fire, just as she has humanized herself. And you feel this at once, when the fire-music moves through its chromatic orbit and settles in E major, and the purely musical process has the effect of bringing C sharp and B to the fore, and inviting the sleeping Brünnhilde motif to complete them. The fire acquires the restful and cadential aspect of the theme, and is also transformed into a constantly mutating accompaniment.

The cadence that follows is constructed from two ideas: the theme associated with the unborn hero Siegfried, and the chromatic climax of Wotan's farewell. These two elements are fused by the fire that sparkles above them, and are heard as a moral unity. The heroic is foretold in the same affirmative cadence that says farewell to the divine. That which is being put to rest at the end of the opera is a complex gift to the future: love, renunciation, death and redemption, fused in a musical unity.

The musical process that I have described is not a piece of anthropology – it does not explain the myth or relate it to universal features of the human psyche. On the contrary, it creates the myth – and creates it as myth, as something more deeply grounded in the 'as if' than any fiction. It does this by forging connections in our feelings. The attentive listener is aware not merely that Brünnhilde is asleep on a mountaintop surrounded by forbidding flames, but that love, renunciation and destruction have been fused, made normal, and buried in the heart of things. This awareness, being induced without concepts and through music alone, remains too deep for words. It has the inscrutability of ritual, and comes about, indeed, through the ritual sacrifice of a god, destined to be reborn as a mortal – a sacrifice accomplished in music.

In *Siegfried* Act 1, Mime endeavours to explain fear to the hero by invoking the primitive terror of night, storm and forest shadows. The music, having begun from low trills suggestive of the fire of Mime's forge, rises during the course of the evocation to a version of the fire-music, but wondrously distorted, using augmented triads that drift keylessly through the upper register, as though beyond Mime's control. Thanks to the musical synthesis accomplished in *Die Walküre*, the listener hears without the least surprise as the sleeping Brünnhilde motif, in distorted form, sounds through the flames, with keyless augmented and diminished harmonies. And, in a moment of supreme magic, a D minor triad gives way to a cadence that ought to be resolved in E, but which slips sideways at the last minute to C – a brief résumé of the original tonal argument in *Die Walküre*. The beautiful setting of Siegfried's words – 'Sonderlich seltsam muss das sein!' (Strange indeed must that be) – transmutes Mime's evocation of fear to an innocent wonder. And then, through the innate logic of the motif as it sets off, together with the fire-music, on a chromatic journey in search of its home key of E, wonder turns to a premonition of love – love that will be prefaced, when it comes, by fear. For it is from the sleeping Brünnhilde that Siegfried is to learn the emotion that Mime is vainly trying to arouse in him. Siegfried will learn fear as a part of love and not, as it is for Mime, a denial of love.

This passage cost Wagner a great deal of work. Patrick McCreless argues that this was because inspiration had, by the time it was written, worn thin, and that the composer was trying to find new uses for exhausted material.[16] That seems to me to be the opposite of the truth. Wagner was in fact finding new meaning and new connectivity in material that carried with it the musical memory that he needed – music that, far from being exhausted, was imbued with remembered life. A connection that has already been forged is now being exploited. The mystery that sleeps in the heart of things has suddenly made itself known, through Mime's uncomprehending fear of it. Death and destruction – the objects of Mime's fear – are united to love and renunciation, and excite wonder in the soul of the hero. Mime, in whose soul there is no love, and therefore no renunciation, can understand the mystery only as something fearful. He is the creature of superstition, for whom nothing is beautiful and nothing worthy of worship. In the hero, by contrast, we see the equivalent of the religious spirit – the spirit that embraces the mystery as the occasion for love. This contrast between two familiar spiritual kinds is drawn without any reference to the gods. The heroic soul, we understand, is the one open to love. And he is of a different moral kind from the mean and superstitious Mime. This difference is expressed as a different relation to the world – a different understanding of the mystery that sleeps in the heart of things.

It is perhaps worth mentioning two later appearances of the sleeping Brünnhilde motif. First, at the climax of Siegfried's journey through the fire, when again we hear the original vacillation between E major and C major, and secondly, encrypted in Brünnhilde's brief attempt to reaffirm her divinity, and to withdraw from the world of mortal love: 'Ewig war ich, ewig bin ich', the music of which forms the central strand of the 'Siegfried Idyll' (142). Here the famous melody, now in E minor, reassembles the notes of the original triad with the added sixth, although in an ascending rather than a descending pattern, while the bass recalls the original, although without the dotted eighth-note which caused it to wander from key to key. Passion is being held at a distance, so that the fire-music is no longer heard. But the music acts as a denial of Brünnhilde's denial – a reminder of the project that drives her towards Siegfried and which can culminate only in love and death-through-love. And when the music again loses its bearings and slips sideways from E major to C major, as Brünnhilde enjoins the hero to love not her but himself, the motif is suddenly explicit, making it clear that she cannot mean what she says (Ex (vi)). A vacillating cadence back to E is contaminated by the C, which returns in the bass, as Siegfried gives vent to his passion.

Wagner gives the intricate emotional connections that enable us to make sense of the heroic soul. And he gives them without asking us to deny our sceptical modern outlook. The story is a realistic presentation of one of the few human ideals that remain available – the ideal of heroic love. This ideal cannot be assessed merely from an acquaintance with the text, any more than the ideal of moral integrity that Shakespeare sets before us in Cordelia could be assessed from a prose translation of the play. Just as the great poet forges through words and imagery the moral links that sustain his ideal, so does the great composer forge those links through music. And the Wagnerian ideal of the hero would be shown to be a sham, as Nietzsche thought it to be,[17] only if we could demonstrate that the music fails to raise the hero to the level that the drama requires. This elevation of the passions is what the music attempts to achieve.

This is not the place to discuss the leitmotifs in detail, or to show the way in which they grow into and away from each other.[18] However, certain leitmotifs are connected with turning points in my argument, and an examination of them here will help to substantiate the claim I have made, that the full meaning of the drama resides in the music, and not merely in the words. This is illustrated by the motif of the Ring itself, which comes into being, first, in the form of the 'world mastery' theme (16A), with which Woglinde sings of the power that the gold might confer, and which gives way to an intermediate form that continues the lilt of the Rhine-daughters' song of joy. The Ring then enters the picture, in the form of 16B, in which a descending half-diminished chord leads to an ascending diminished chord. The tightness of the melody here interrupts the flow of the music, and is also understood by the ear harmonically, through the lingering diminished harmony that will henceforth be associated with Alberich.

The first part of the Ring motif – the half-diminished chord consisting of an A minor triad with F sharp, over a pedal on F sharp – forms the first part of the curse motif (45), while the second part of the Ring motif, reassembled as a syncopated chord, forms the second part of the resentment motif (44). Both of those motifs have a large role to play until the very end of the drama, and always a harmonic aura radiates from them, causing an instant change in the surrounding musical context. Alberich exchanged love for the Ring and did so by means of a curse. That he is robbed of the Ring, with which his soul is mingled, is the worst thing that could happen to him. So he says, in effect, to Wotan. Hence he must transfer the burden of the curse (which is the loss of love) to all who try to exploit his property. In the new world of exchange and mutation the curse becomes transferable. It haunts the cycle thereafter, reminding us that nature has been deflected from its course, that all is unsettled and at odds with itself, that the cry from the deep must be answered, if the world's equilibrium is to be regained. Hence, even when we are not hearing the motifs of the curse and of resentment, they can linger in the harmonic air, instilling an atmosphere of evil. The Ring motif is contained by implication in the motif of scheming (33), while the half-diminished chord of the curse is a critical component in Hagen's form (164) of the power of the Ring motif (39), itself an imprisoned version of the 'Rheingold!' call (14). In this way the music is able to show the slow steady pollution of the world from which the cycle begins.

Curses have a particular importance in myths, for they attach the will of absent people to present objects – they symbolize the traps that are everywhere laid for the unwary, the inexplicable danger by which we are always surrounded, as we encroach on what has been fought for and died for by people whom we shall never know. A curse activates and makes present some part of the immeasurable suffering that precedes us. Although curses feature in this way in literature they are never present in verbal narratives in the way Alberich's curse is present in the Ring cycle. For the music can bring the curse to mind in the course of other things, can make surreptitious reference to it, even when the characters on stage are completely indifferent to its existence.[19]

The curse motif has this power not only by virtue of the striking melody, but also through its harmonic structure, derived, as already mentioned, from the Ring motif, but given a special character of its own. Over a prolonged but muffled F sharp pedal on the timpani the melody rises from F sharp through the triad of A minor to E, those four notes forming a half-diminished seventh. The melody drops an octave to spell out the triad of C major, the F sharp still sounding in the bass. All three notes of the C major triad are then sounded in the orchestra, using clarinets in their lowest register and bass clarinet. The resulting contaminated sound is poisoned still further by the F sharp pedal below. This, the murkiest C major triad in all music, sets up a bitter conflict in the ear of the listener, which continues as the triad is 'resolved' onto a discord – the dominant minor ninth on F sharp – so enabling the music to settle on B minor for Alberich's blood-curdling prophecy. The motif divides into two parts, the half diminished chord and the C major triad, both over a pedal on F sharp. The first chord acts thereafter as a condensation of the curse, often resolving, as in 164, onto a dominant seventh.

As it occurs in *Götterdämmerung*, the curse chord, as I shall call it (the first chord of 164), is a perfect vehicle for the techniques of chromatic voice-leading developed in *Tristan und Isolde*. That opera opens with a famous half-diminished chord, 'resolved' onto a dominant seventh, which is left unresolved. In just this way the half-diminished chord of the curse appears in *Götterdämmerung*, differently spaced and 'resolved' onto a different dominant seventh, its bitterness increased by the suspension in the bass. This strange half-cadence, carrying with it a weight of memory, from the first cry of 'Rheingold' to Hagen's hate-filled oath that he will have the Ring, permeates the narrative, unsettling harmonic expectations in the manner of *Tristan*, though to opposite effect – not amplifying the yearning for a resolution, but emphasizing the dead-end to which we have come.

Another as-it-were-cadence, however, has entered the music from quite another source, and works in another direction: the fate motif.

Melodically speaking this is no more than the old 'question cliché' of operatic recitative, the three-note phrase over an imperfect cadence, as in Ex (vii). (It was under just such a three-note phrase in the Op. 135 Quartet that Beethoven wrote 'Muss es sein?')[20] Thanks to Wagner's revolutionary harmonization, however, the motif is used to slip out of the traditional tonal syntax, and at the same time and for the same reason to give a wholly new and metaphysical meaning to the question. It is as though the earth opens beneath us and we glimpse far down into the darkness where Erda sleeps.

The effect is readily appreciated by attending to the fifth scene of *Götterdämmerung* Act 2, in which the music expresses the emotional turmoil in Brünnhilde's breast, following Siegfried's oath that he never touched her. Hagen's version of the power of the Ring motif is here combined with that of resentment, followed by the atonal motif associated with murder (171, here on the same half-diminished harmony). Brünnhilde gives vent to a series of anguished questions. 'What devil's cunning lies hidden here? What magic is working? How can my wisdom unravel it? What power are my runes against this mystery?' Each question is accompanied by the fate motif, not resolving the dominant seventh on which it ends, but lifting the vocal line constantly upwards by whole-tone steps until the great cry of 'Ach Jammer!', when the motif (landing on the dominant seventh of C) suddenly and unexpectedly resolves onto the triad of F major. The melody of the world's inheritance (134) then sweeps through the orchestra as Brünnhilde declares that she passed all her wisdom to Siegfried, and that he has held her in his grip, only to throw her away.

Wagner's use here of the rootless half-diminished chord and the shifting half-cadence of the fate motif is immensely effective. You sense from within the disorder of Brünnhilde's feelings, which can rest nowhere among this bundle of inexplicable facts, making all the more poignant that sudden reaching, in memory, for a home key, with a melody that expresses the gift once brought to her by Siegfried, and now taken away.

A similar use of the fate motif, this time not to pose a question without an answer, but to provide both question and answer together, occurs in the passage leading to 'Ruhe, ruhe, du Gott!' The musical logic of this passage, and the inevitability with which that final

double cadence is prepared, is one of the miracles of musical organization that no technical analysis will ever explain. Feelings captured
from the drama lie dormant in the notes, and are here released in a
new order, in which ancient tensions are confessed to and resolved.
Without their dramatic and emotional cargo the notes in this passage
would drift past each other, with no hooks to grapple with. Quite
unrelated chords stand side by side, as Hagen's Rhinegold cadence (164)
and the fate motif bring each other to a stop in A flat minor, the curse
motif rising up only to be soothed into nothingness by the sublime
return to the 'Rheingold!' in its original form, now wound together
with the peace once longed for by the gods.

This returns me to the second of Adorno's criticisms of Wagner's
musical grammar: the criticism that Wagner's paragraphs do not
develop musically, but simply repeat sequences which are tied together
in blocks by strings of melody.[21] If I understand the criticism correctly
(and it is more hissed than explained), Adorno accuses Wagner of
denying all grammatical relation between neighbouring harmonies,
piling them up against each other until they begin to soften at the
edges and stick together. But what is the contrast here? Obviously
Wagner does not follow the chord grammar that we find in Mozart,
according to which the triads of the key stand in intrinsic grammatical relations to each other. So what? Old-fashioned chord grammar
based on root progressions is as likely to degenerate into mechanical
repetition as any sequence built by melodic voice-leading – just think
of the concerti of Vivaldi. Already in Schubert third progressions
were beginning to displace the circle of fifths as the motor of harmonic development, and in Wagner these progressions have become
routine.[22] This facilitated Wagner's way of building harmonic
sequences: not through the roots of chords, but through the voices
that compose them. This is, indeed, Wagner's true 'secret', illustrated
perfectly by the opening harmony of *Tristan*: Wagner uses
voice-leading by whole-tone and semitone steps to move from one
harmony to another, creating half-diminished chords that could be
resolved in a variety of keys. The effect is of a seamless web of musical movement, which magnetizes the words and feelings of the
characters, so that they are carried from one place to the next, never
resting, but pressing always towards a dramatic conclusion.

It is worth revisiting here the first occurrence of the fate motif, which illustrates the way in which the most striking psychological transition is accomplished by purely musical means. Brünnhilde, having made her announcement of death to Siegmund, is prompted by Siegmund's resistance to enunciate the immutable law of the gods, knowing it to be a sham: 'You saw the Valkyrie's withering glance: with her you now must go!' This is set to the *Todesverkündigung* (85), so that the great metaphysical question is now passed from Siegmund to Brünnhilde. When, a moment later, Siegmund turns on her with the cry 'Shame on him who bestowed the sword, if he gives me disgrace, not victory!' you sense her recoil before him, since she is the very person whose will is being so acutely criticized. The *Todesverkündigung* is then reshaped as a beautiful melody (Ex (viii)), with which Siegmund hurls his denunciation at Brünnhilde and by implication at all the gods. Because the *Todesverkündigung* is always elaborated, but never answered, the music, which becomes ever more excited, with a wholly credible sympathy for Siegmund's predicament, passes the hero's defiance into the soul of Brünnhilde. From this moment the forces are in place that will lead to her own mortality.

The *Todesverkündigung* is later varied, to form the subject of the fugato chorus sung by the Valkyries in their vain attempt to protect their sister (93). In this ironed-out and re-harmonized version the motif at last finds an answering phrase (94), foreshadowing Brünnhilde's pleading to Wotan, and the purity motif (95), which in a mystical way will work the reconciliation with Wotan that will set her on the path to enjoying the kind of love that she had observed with wonder in Siegmund. The completed melody sounds softly on bass clarinet, as Brünnhilde steps forward to receive what is at first a punishment, in retrospect a redeeming gift. The very fact that the passage is wordless reminds us that we have been brought to this wholly convincing turn of events by the musical elaboration of Siegmund's defiance.* (The use of the bass clarinet here is a striking illustration of Wagner's ability to find the exact sound of a soundless feeling.)

Many of the difficulties that commentators have experienced with the turning points in Wagner's drama reflect a failure to attend to

---

* See also Porges's description of this theme, quoted in the Appendix.

what the music is saying, at those moments when it is clear that the words offer only a sketch of what is at stake. This is especially true of the passages in which Brünnhilde's nature as the mediator between god and man carries the weight of the story. In the mysterious meeting of the Wanderer and Erda in the first scene of *Siegfried* Act 3 the Wanderer asks the goddess how to arrest a rolling wheel, and she, in response, tells him to consult her wise daughter. The Wanderer tells her of Brünnhilde's fate, asleep on the mountaintop, awaiting the man who will waken her, and asks 'How would it help to question her?' The fate motif sounds, transferring this question from the Wanderer to Erda, who then, after a moment of sleepy confusion, asks her own questions: does he who taught defiance punish defiance? Is he who he incites the deed inflamed when the deed is done? Does he who guards the right and shields the oath, banish right and rule by perjury?

Those questions are not answered by the Wanderer, who proceeds to harangue the goddess until she declares 'You are not what you call yourself!' But the questions *are* answered by the music, which brings together the fate motif and the purity motif in a vivid synthesis, the first constantly repeating its 'why?' in the treble, the second buoying it up in the bass. We are taken back to the two decisive moments in Brünnhilde's life as a goddess – the announcement of death to Siegmund, who incited her defiance, and the pleading with Wotan, to whom she justified her defiance while taking on the future of Wotan's world. The music is telling Wotan that the future is no longer his, and that all that Wotan stands for has been transferred to his daughter. Erda's declaration that 'you are not what you call yourself' summarizes the far more complex thought already present in the music.

The music of that passage is repeated with only slight alterations, at the end of *Götterdämmerung*, when Brünnhilde accuses Wotan of sacrificing Siegfried to the curse, before acknowledging that 'this purest of beings had to betray me, so that I should become wise'. What exactly is she saying to Wotan? Is she accusing or forgiving? Is she accepting or rejecting? The music gives the answer. We are again returned to the two decisive moments in Brünnhilde's previous life, the moments when she lost her godhead, and in doing so became accountable for Wotan's world. It is *she herself* whom she condemns, and she herself whom she forgives. And as the passage works its way forward, through the repeated 'why' of the fate motif, to the acknowledgement that the curse lay in the scheme of things, and therefore in her own soul, we feel that the great question placed in the heart of being at the moment of Brünnhilde's encounter with Siegmund has now found an answer. And the answer is the sublime music of 'Ruhe, ruhe, du Gott!' which marks the restoration of love between father and daughter, but which also, while ostensibly addressed to Wotan, is addressed in fact to us all.

Such passages raise the question of the overall unity of the cycle. The sequences of half-diminished chords and chromatic voice-leading point *Götterdämmerung* towards a different musical space from that occupied by *Das Rheingold*. And yet the music that follows Brünnhilde's mystical gesture of acceptance is undeniably intended as a resolution of all that has gone before, a releasing of a hundred subsidiary tensions, and a knitting together of loose ends that have been left hanging for scene after scene. Does it work? *Can* it work? It can and it does, and it does so because Wagner never loses sight of diatonic harmony, and its symbolic meaning in the story of the *Ring*. Diatonicism is a symbol of the primeval order, of that which remains through all our acts of defiance. That is why the nature motifs involve a deliberating cleansing of the triad and the diatonic scale. The horn call, its harmonics and its natural chords are present throughout. And all the revolutionary material that follows does not replace the diatonic order but marks out localities within it, places of tension, crisis and suffering.*

We witness this not only in the survival of all the original material throughout the cycle, but also in the way in which the complex language of *Götterdämmerung* is taken apart before our ears, shown to be derived by invention and degeneration from the basic elements of tonal harmony. Throughout this opera the open fifth, symbol of natural music, is a melodic motif, associated with the Gibichungs, but reached for at moments of crisis by other characters – and in particular by Siegfried and Brünnhilde in their confrontational oaths, 'Helle Wehr, heilige Waffe!' (180). As though to drive the point home Hagen's diminished fifth sounds at this moment, as in so many places,

---

* Surely we must acknowledge the influence of Schubert here, and in particular the horn-call harmonies and sun-lit melodies of the songs.

in the bass. (It should be noted that the fifth and the diminished fifth, added together in the right way, make the chord of the curse, which is in this scene used to harmonize the melodic line – another example of the curse making its presence felt, even when it is not overtly spelled out.) The oaths are marked by emphatic octaves, and in the background we hear the forces of nature, corrupted by the machinations of humans who have 'forged' them into alien shapes. It is thus with the melody of the Dawn on the Rhine (172), when from the pure tonality of the horns the motif of Hagen's manipulation (172B) is snatched as though by force. It is thus in the reminiscence of the Rhine-daughters who distantly wail, as though from the depths, behind the dissonant corruption of their song (164). And when, at the end, we hear again their song in its natural purity, we recognize that the journey through chromatic regions and shifting dissonances has been no more than a pool of turbulence in an unending tonal flow.

5

Understanding the Story

Der Ring des Nibelungen is in a certain measure elusive, since no character is the centre of the drama, enabling us to say that the story is his or hers, and no standard account is consistent enough to displace its competitors. In this chapter I give an interpretation of what the story is about. It is only one of many possible interpretations. But it will serve as a framework within which to place the philosophical and moral themes that I go on to address.

The story is of course about Wotan, Alberich, Siegfried, Brünnhilde and the other leading characters. But it is also about the human world, the *Lebenswelt*, the world as we humans experience and construct it. We do not understand the *Lebenswelt* merely by giving a scientific explanation of our experience – an explanation in terms of cause and effect – relevant though that explanation might be.[1] We understand it through our own experience, and by exploring the concepts and categories that arise from experience and which order experience in an intelligible way. These concepts and categories may have no place in science – not even in the science of what we are.

Take the concept of the person – the free and accountable being who acts for reasons and who faces other persons eye to eye and I to I. This is the concept that occupied German philosophy in the generations after Kant, and which is expounded in all the most influential arguments of the German idealists, touched on in Chapter 2 of this book. What place for that concept in human biology, which treats of organisms and brains, finds nothing in the physical world that could conceivably correspond to freedom, and regards the I as no different from the here and the now: the vanishing point in a space-time continuum that makes no objective place for it? Yet for us self-conscious beings the concept of the person is indispensable; we cannot relate to our world without it, and the distinctions between person and thing, subject and object, action and movement, reason and cause, understanding and explaining, are distinctions that we must make if we are to live with each other in a world of shared meanings.

In their efforts to understand the *Lebenswelt* our ancestors elaborated myths and tales expressive of the deep intuitions that informed their daily conduct. They told stories of gods and heroes, of sublime actions, and of the forces that opposed them. They distinguished, in their experience, between good and evil, free and unfree, duty and right, sacred and profane, permitted and forbidden. In a thousand ways they painted the world in the colours of their own emotions, not in order to hide the truth, but in order to make the truth – the truth about themselves – perceivable.

In the *Ring* cycle Wagner is doing something similar. But he is not merely telling another story; he is telling *the story of our stories*. He is expressing the deep truths that inform the myths and tales of human communities, showing, in personified form, the many aspects of the human psyche that compose the *Lebenswelt*, and which are represented in the religious and moral legacies of mankind. Wagner is recuperating what religion means, in a world without religion. And in doing so he aims to restore the immediate truth of what we are, in the face of the scientific worldview that sees the *Lebenswelt* as a mere superficial film, to be peeled away from the raw facts of our biology.

In the life of our first ancestors, we may suppose, human beings lived as part of nature, and their world was an endless cycle of reproduction, whose principles were only obscurely known to those who hunted and gathered for their survival. It was a harsh but innocent world, which paid no special respect to what we would now think of as human needs, and in which man and beast contended for their share of the earth's resources. Earth and its fruits, the water that flowed on it and the air above, were the world's enduring attributes, as was fire, the magic source of all transformation, which turned cold to hot, raw to cooked, earth to metal, and metal into the weapons that gave mastery over other species and other tribes. The memory of our need for those primal things and of the fears and hopes that surrounded them survives, so that they still haunt our imaginings. We find them personified as demi-gods in Wagner's drama, where they represent the enduring presence of the *Urwelt*, the world before the free individual, before personhood, will and law. Freedom and person-hood belong to a new world, which has emerged from the *Urwelt* of species-being into the light of consciousness.

The drama tells the story of this new world and of the original sin (or rather sins) that secured it. Men have become conscious of their situation, and begun to take control of the natural order. Now they must live by law and treaties. Law requires power to enforce it. Whence comes that power? What is it that enables human beings to obey a law that runs counter to their interests, or to honour a treaty when breaking it would be a gain? In the first instance, unaided by a tradition of reflection and self-understanding, human beings imagine a power that enforces the law, and which rewards those who submit to it. The need for law, therefore, is also – initially at least – a need for gods. But gods can attract our obedience only if they exist in another way from the mortals who worship them. They must be immortal, endowed with the happiness and peace for which we yearn in all our conflicts, and able to confer those gifts on their followers. From the need for the gods, therefore, is born the belief in immortality, and in the heavenly realm where all is as it should be and nothing decays.

But what maintains that belief? What enchants our world with the 'real presence' of supernatural beings and the signs of their immortal happiness? Somehow the natural needs of human beings must be turned in a new direction, so as to create culture, and a vision of the rewards that our labour will one day enjoy. We must accumulate things for the future, create temples and castles, and endow our frail human status with the dignity of office and the grace of inherited ties. Our most generous and self-sacrificing feelings must be channelled into maintaining the great edifice of law. Men must submit to cus-toms and institutions that offer 'love and woman's worth' only at the end of their endeavours, and never as ripe fruit to be plucked without thought for the longer term. It is only thus, by making sexual love into the gift of the gods, to be bestowed on mortals from the sphere of immortality – in other words, as a 'sacrament' – that we can per-suade people to build a temple to their own idealized emotions, and not to enjoy sexual love as the birds and beasts enjoy their version of it, for the moment alone. But all this requires surplus and the leisure that attends it. Who is to create that surplus, how, and at what cost to himself?

In the enchanted world of civilized man love granted depends on love withheld. The transferable lust for the human form becomes a violation. (The transferability of lust is made plain from the very outset of the tetralogy, since its object, the Rhine-daughters, is plural.) Once the moral law is in place, therefore, love is supposedly confined within the bounds of marriage, maintained by Fricka's vigilant eye. But real love cannot be so confined. For erotic love, at its highest, is neither sensual delight nor domestic harmony, even if both are in some way implied in it. At its heart lies sympathy, and the sense of the absolute value of the individual, to whose being the lover is attached and whose sufferings he suffers in turn. Such is love between mortals, the love between Siegmund and Sieglinde, and it is a higher and nobler thing than the love enjoyed by the gods or the conventional tyranny of the hearth, since it involves a gift of the self, and a readiness to sacrifice self for other. Moreover the capacity for this kind of love is the greatest gift of personality, and without it our journey into freedom will be incomplete.

On the other hand, the fruits of love are distributed unequally and those who are ugly or unlovable, and who want to snatch love nevertheless, will always be frustrated, as Alberich was. Out of resentment such people may then replace the longing for love with the pursuit of power, treating others as objects to be used, rather than as subjects to be cherished. And it is on this resentment, buried in the heart of things, that the world of our postponed desires now rests. For this bruised sense of absolute rejection contains a new and disruptive motive – namely the urge to compete, to use others as instruments, and to see everything, love and personhood included, as a means to domination. By instrumentalizing the world in that way the humiliated Alberich can force others to respect him – such is the meaning of his great tirade against the gods in Nibelheim. He also generates something that the blessed gods need but never get round to creating – the surplus that can be used to pay for their castles in the air.

The world of religious man is therefore precarious. The enchantment on which it depends is also the object of the resentment that seeks to destroy it. All kinds of tricks maintain it in being – in particular the imaginary rewards offered to heroes, and the competition for territory and spouses that fills the world with conflicts, and therefore with the endless prayers to the gods. At a certain point, however, it becomes clear that the gods are no longer able to govern, and that the ideal of which they were the guardians has become dependent on the human will to renew it.

The ideal is therefore returned to the human world where it belongs, to lie dormant in the scheme of things, protected from desecration only by the residue of primitive belief that surrounds it with a fire of prohibitions. The human world moves on from the rigidly structured system of laws, offices and powers, and gives way to a post-religious order, in which it is for us humans to maintain our values, with no obvious help from the gods. At the same time the resentment on which this all depends – the resentment of those who pay the price of civilization without receiving its reward – remains. All that we esteem and value depends upon our ability to keep resentment at bay. But in the end resentment will surely win, since religion, becoming conscious of itself, can only retire from the scene, unable to justify its rule or to conceal the trick on which it is founded.

This is the precarious situation that we moderns have inherited and which is portrayed in the action of *Siegfried*. We have retained our longing for the ideal, but not acquired the ability to sustain it. Our efforts in this direction have all been frustrated, depending as they did on the belief in a divine power which in fact has always let us down. Yet our world is haunted by the memory of sacred things; the ideal lies dormant in the heights, and by a free gesture, by taking full responsibility for our condition, we may open a path to it. By forging his identity, Siegfried awakens the world. He too is awakened, and the gods in turn awakened to their doom. Wotan then wills his own end, and bequeaths the world to Siegfried, who is now free to discover the ideal in its human form – the form of 'love and woman's worth'.

Siegfried has acted freely, as a self-created being. He has defied the laws and conventions that stood in his way, and acted from a pure longing for the ideal woman that the voice of nature had aroused in him. In taking full possession of this sacred thing, Siegfried inherits Wotan's bequest. But he also destroys Wotan's authority and the rule of law – the law in the soul – that was sustained by it. As he comes down from the heights of his heroic love, therefore, he enters a world where, thanks to his own defiance of the god, all vows and oaths have become negotiable, and even what is most dear to him can be forgotten, overridden or traded for something better. The gods, who existed outside time and change, escaped the terrible force of *Verwandlung*. We mortals, however, are subject to the rule of time; what we are is inconstant and temporary, and even the most absolute of our values risks being discarded if it stands in the way of our momentary urges.

The world of substitution and 'Mutabilitie', as Spenser called it – the world brought into being by the Ring – is no longer opposed by the divine rule of law. Siegfried falls, his integrity undermined by the machinations of those whose goal is not love but status. In the last act of *Götterdämmerung* we encounter Siegfried looking on the three Rhine-daughters with feelings that echo those of Alberich at the outset of the drama. He is prevented from pursuing the nymphs only by a fragile promise made to the woman who replaced his true love and who, should he live, will one day be replaced in her turn.

There is one thing that can rectify this spiritual disorder, which is the feminine ability to recover love from beneath its abuse and degradation. In an act of supreme understanding Brünnhilde, having connected with the Rhine-daughters and seen into the primeval heart of things, comes to believe that Siegfried's true nature was revealed in the moment when he gave himself to her. All the rest has been imposed on him by the corrupt world of power and substitution, the world to which he does not in his heart belong, even if it was his own free gesture that destroyed his capacity to stay out of it. Understanding this, she knits together the threads of her life and his in a final triumph of forgiveness. In the sacrifice of Brünnhilde – immolated once in sleep and then in death – lies the meaning not only of her life but also of the human world, as it emerged into consciousness from the order of nature and created its great castle in the air. But the music tells us that the castle is as important as it ever was, and that Brünnhilde's gesture of renunciation and forgiveness is directed as much to her father among the gods as to her mortal husband.

As the gods disappear they receive the blessing once bestowed on the Valkyrie. It was bestowed by a mortal woman, from whom everything had been taken away, save love. And Wagner leaves us with a mystery: why does this blessing save the world?

When he first began work on the *Ring* cycle Wagner was persuaded of a particular view of this mystery, which is that the humans can take the world from the gods, and make a better show of running it – not ruling, but sharing. Like Feuerbach, the Wagner of the 1849 revolution saw the future of humanity as one of emancipation from servitude. Human beings, according to the Feuerbachian conception, are living organisms, and in their original state were a part of the order of nature, subject to the laws that govern all things in a condition of mutuality and equilibrium. But in the course of time man acquired language, and with it consciousness of himself and his condition. This birth of consciousness was the original sin, the departure from the natural order, which must be paid for.

With consciousness came freedom, personhood and the lust for power. Science and technology enable human beings to turn the natural order in their own direction, to manufacture goods and materials through which to satisfy their needs. Their appetite for power brings about the money economy and the trade in labour. The original equilibrium gives way to a competitive world in which people strive for possessions. Order can no longer be maintained by the laws of nature, since organic life, acted on by the new forms of envy and covetousness, is riven by conflict. Only through law can men now live in harmony, and law demands sovereignty. Through sovereignty, humans can guarantee their agreements; but they also create a dominating power. This power must inculcate the belief in its legitimacy, and is aided in this by religion, through which we accept illusory rewards in return for earthly obedience.

Wagner's writings of this period, and his deep study of the old mythologies, added a new twist to the Feuerbachian story. Religion, Wagner argued, is not a tissue of illusions: concealed within the myths are deep truths about the human condition, and religion owes its power to these truths, some of which I spell out in Chapter 7. In religion truth enters our consciousness through the back door, and we are thereby guided through life to our advantage. However, consciousness works always against the religious doctrines, sowing the seeds of doubt and undermining the divine authority. In these circumstances it is given to art to rescue the deep truths about our condition, to present them in symbolic form, and so to bring about a new order in the human soul, free from illusion but true to the distinctiveness and sacredness of the human condition.

There is strong evidence that Wagner originally conceived the story of Siegfried in this way and, as Paul Heise shows, it is possible to develop a far-reaching interpretation of the cycle in its finished form from Feuerbachian premises. In a world turned away from its original order by personhood and the consciousness of self, subjected to the tyranny of property and exchange, kept in order nevertheless by the law maintained by religion, there is a fatal flaw. Resentment broods in the heart of things: life, governed by the rule of property, is increasingly loveless, and the blissful vision of immortality on which our acquiescence depends is eaten away by the worm of science. Meanwhile our true freedom, promised by that original sin of consciousness, has been stolen from us by the powers that maintain things in being. Only the free hero, who forges his own future, can cast off the chains that bind humanity – the chains of religious illusion, of property and the money economy.

This hero, who begins from nothing, must also be an artist. He is the spirit of poetry itself, producing a new form of consciousness in which freedom prevails over law and truth over illusion. This artist-hero cannot create a new world by his own efforts, however, any more than the poet can carry the whole burden of the new work of art that is to tell the hero's story. Only through the free union between man and woman, between hero and heroine, in a love in which self-giving is the ruling principle, can the new world be born. Just as poetry stands in need of music to create the art-work of the future, so does the hero stand in need of the loving bride, who has come down from the world of religious illusion into the sphere of mortals, there to unite with him in the action that will liberate the world.

However, that story is moving in a direction that Feuerbach would not have countenanced. Feuerbach saw the liberation of mankind as a political event, a total transformation of the social and economic order, in which we would win through to freedom as the scales of religious illusion fall from our eyes. Wagner was already seeing that liberation occurs, if at all, only in the individual soul, and that it is not achieved alone but through loving union with another. Moreover, the liberation that comes from love also threatens the love that causes it. This is the sorry lesson of Siegfried's fall – his journey down from the exalted height where he and Brünnhilde enjoyed their eternal moment, into the world of machinations and deals symbolized by the drink of forgetting.

The act of liberation brings together the separate spheres of the masculine and the feminine, and of poetry and music, in a mystic act of sacrifice. But even if the result is liberation, it is liberation *from* the old enslavement, but not liberation *to* the free order that will replace it. Gradually, as the message of his own music sank in, Wagner recognized that liberation is not a political but a spiritual process, and that what is being asked from us is not the self-affirmation of the sword-wielding Siegfried, but the self-sacrifice of his suffering wife. Redemption does not mean entry into another and better life, but a rearrangement of this one. Neither Brünnhilde nor Siegfried understands this at first. She cheerfully waves him on to 'new deeds' and then calmly awaits his return as though the world below the mountaintops could never be a threat to her. And when he returns it is in an altered form, repeating his first encounter with her not as love but as power. You might say that, in composing *The Ring*, Wagner put the optimistic philosophy of the Young Hegelians to the test of drama, and the drama refuted it.

Wagner's original conception constantly appears beneath the surface of the story, and has been meticulously spelled out by Paul Heise, who assumes that individual characters, objects and actions represent other, more general features of the human condition – motives, interests and processes which are of broadly cosmic or political significance. Sometimes this allegorical interpretation seems plausible, at other times less so. But there is a real question of what allegory is and when it is part of the meaning of a work of art. An allegorical meaning can be assigned to just about any story, by correlating characters and events one-to-one with another story about more general things. But to say that this second story gives the *meaning* of the first is to go beyond giving a one-to-one correlation. In a truly allegorical work of art the allegorical meaning is *embodied* in the primary action and characters. That is to say, it becomes part of what you respond to, in responding to the primary story. Thus both Heise and Nattiez[2] tell us that, in the union of Siegfried and Brünnhilde, the first represents poetry and the second music. But do we hear things in that way? Are we responding to Siegfried as the voice of poetry, when he starts away from the sleeping female whose armour he has opened? Do we hear Brünnhilde's declaration of love as the voice of music, as well as the voice of an individual woman awoken by her lover? It seems to me that this particular 'allegory' adds nothing to our experience of the drama, and is more like an academic curiosity, inspired, of course, by Wagner's own theory of the art-work of the future, but for all that not much more than a theory that lies dormant alongside the work of art without becoming a part of it. A character can mean something other than himself only when the meaning enhances his presence in the drama and gives a richer content to his motivation. And the enhancement should be mutual. The drama should illustrate the allegorical meaning, which in turn should amplify the drama.

In an allegory two stories are told, one the explicit story, involving character, action, place and time, the other the implicit or esoteric story, concerning abstract ideas, cosmic forces and moral doctrines. Sometimes there is a one-to-one correspondence between elements in the two stories, as in Spenser's *Faerie Queene*. Sometimes the allegory is not hidden but explicitly stated, as in *The Pilgrim's Progress*, where we encounter Christian, Obstinate, Hopeful, the Slough of Despond and Giant Despair, as well as the obscure Apollyon, who is more symbol than allegory, since what he means is not clearly distinct from what he is. *The Ring*, I suggest, is not an allegory in either of those senses, but a work of symbolism.

Symbolism is distinguished from allegory in that the symbol both expresses a meaning and also adds to it, so that meaning and symbol are to a measure inseparable. Although the money economy is in one plausible interpretation the meaning of Alberich's Ring, the Ring is also the meaning of the money economy: its story tells us something about the money economy that we might not otherwise have understood or known. A symbol, if it is effective, is a condensation of many ways of thinking, and this is what the etymology of the word implies, Greek *symballein* meaning to throw together. Thus the Ring is also a symbol of the human disposition to see all things as means and nothing as an end in itself; it is a symbol of power and the lust for it, of exploitation, of the desire to possess, of consciousness, the original sin that separated humankind from the work of nature and conferred on us a shared *Lebenswelt* in which we contend for recognition and status. The Ring means all of those things and they in turn mean the Ring, which is the thing that shows us what they really are. By condensing many meanings into a single symbol, art enables each meaning to cast light on all the others, so that the symbol shows us the moral reality that unites them.

From the artistic point of view allegory presents a twofold danger: on the one hand the allegorical meaning risks breaking away entirely from the dramatic vehicle, so as to become irrelevant to the aesthetic experience, a mere intellectual commentary which has no status in our emotional response. On the other hand, if the allegory is too obviously necessary to the response, the drama takes on a didactic character, like a religious parable or a cautionary tale for children. That observation warns us, I think, against giving a straightforwardly allegorical interpretation of the *Ring* cycle. Nevertheless several such interpretations have been ably defended, including one in Marxist terms by George Bernard Shaw, besides the Feuerbachian one by Paul Heise.

Shaw's interpretation benefits from the exuberant style of its author, and includes his celebrated account of the Tarnhelm – the top hat of the capitalist class, which represents the many guises of capital, its ability to disappear into stocks and shares and interest rates, to hide from every call for liability and to work in secret for those who deny all knowledge of its whereabouts:

> This helmet is a very common article in our streets, where it generally takes the form of a tall hat. It makes a man invisible as a shareholder, and changes him into various shapes, such as a pious Christian, a subscriber to hospitals, a benefactor of the poor, a model husband and father, a shrewd, practical, independent Englishman, and what not, when he is really a pitiful parasite on the commonwealth, consuming a great deal and producing nothing, feeling nothing, knowing nothing, believing nothing, and doing nothing except what all the rest do, and that only because he is afraid not to do it, or at least to pretend to do it.[3]

Clever stuff, which engages with one of the themes that very obviously influenced Wagner in his initial ideas for the cycle, and reflects on truths about the human condition with which we can all largely concur. As the cycle proceeds, however, the drama fits less and less to the Shavian allegory, and the identification of Siegfried with the revolutionary Bakunin begins to appear more and more irrelevant to Wagner's intention.

Shaw, becoming aware of this, resorted to the expedient of dismissing *Götterdämmerung* as a lapse into 'grand opera', a departure from the *Gesamtkunstwerk* idea in which the music and the drama develop together. He is prompted to this position by his view that Siegfried's revolutionary work is accomplished with the smashing of Wotan's spear. Yes, he deserves the reward of Brünnhilde, since 'Brynhild is the inner thought and will of Godhead, the aspiration from the high life to the higher that is its divine element, and only becomes separated from it when its resort to kingship and priestcraft for the sake of temporal power has made it false to itself.'[4] But the work that Siegfried has begun must be completed in another way, not through passionate love, which is 'an experience which it is much better, like the vast majority of us, never to have passed through, than to allow it to play more than a recreative holiday part in our lives'.[5]

The 'love panacea' idea, in Shaw's view, is a survival from Wagner's original conception, and also the trap that leads him into Grand Opera. What is required of Siegfried is not that he should lie ecstatic in his beloved's arms, but that he should set about creating the post-capitalist order. This order cannot be achieved with the available human material. Instead of setting off to 'new deeds' in the polluted world of capitalist production, Siegfried should sign up to Shaw's favourite programme of eugenics, and begin breeding the 'new man' who will free the world of the existing oligarchies. Whatever appeal that way of thinking may have possessed for Shaw and his socialist contemporaries, we must surely be glad that Wagner's cycle is at odds with it.

Even from the outset, it is a vast diminution of Wagner's drama to pin such a thin Marxist allegory to its extraordinary and believable characters. To see Wotan as 'Godhead and Kingship' – i.e. as the leisured monarch, in league with the priesthood in maintaining the church (Valhalla) on which both depend – is to ignore all the ideas about man's religious need and dependence on legal order embodied in this stupendous creation. To reduce Alberich to the factory-owning capitalist is to misrepresent entirely his 'sin against himself', a sin that we all commit, and which leads us to sympathize with Alberich even in his extremes of helpless resentment. Alberich, as Cooke points out, is no hypocrite, no fake-Christian shareholder, no frequenter of city streets. And the Tarnhelm stands for something deeper than the money illusions of the capitalist economy, being a symbol of *Verwandlung* – the mysterious way in which one thing becomes another, in which what is most trusted betrays us, in which the real and the unreal may coincide in a single personality and a single state of mind. This kind of transformation, which does not happen in nature, is the crucial flaw in the *Lebenswelt*, the hole in the scheme of things, through which the moral being can fall.

Heise's Feuerbachian allegory is more plausible. It is surely true that, at one level, the tetralogy concerns the eruption of consciousness into the world and the departure from the natural order that ensued from this. It concerns the birth of the gods out of fear and aggression, and dramatizes the illusions of religion on which we depend for the rule of law and political order. It concerns the erosion of those illusions by thought, and our need for some other source of hope in the face of the bleak vision offered by scientific knowledge. And in some way Siegfried was to embody that hope as well as inviting all the things that conspire to defeat it. All those ideas are developed in Heise's narrative, which repays detailed study.

On the other hand, illuminating though Heise's account is, the allegorical method frequently leads to the eclipse of the characters by the ideas that Heise pins to them. Here, for example, is a passage describing aspects of Siegfried's encounter with the dragon:

> Brünnhilde, representing the unconscious mind and its special language, music (in which the music-dramatist Siegfried – i.e. Wagner – will instinctively attempt to repress dangerous knowledge which is rising to consciousness within us, and particularly within him), will be the secular artist's substitute for lost religious faith. As such, it will be the artist's substitute for the fear of knowledge, the basis of faith, which

protected the faithful from examining the religious mysteries which, as Feuerbach expressed so well, they had involuntarily and unconsciously invented in the first place. Since the music-dramatist Siegfried is going to unwittingly deliver the death blow to religious faith (Fafner), in taking responsibility for guarding the Ring, Tarnhelm, and Hoard which Siegfried will soon inherit, he must also take responsibility for keeping Wotan's unspoken secret.[6]

There is truth in that account, which decodes some of the hidden messages that have been buried in the drama. But it prompts the response that Siegfried is *not* a music dramatist, but an orphaned hero, that Fafner is something more, and also something less, than a symbol of religious faith, being a relict of an ancient deal that went wrong, a résumé of all the accumulated obstacles that lie in any hero's path and a symbol of the inertia that lies at the heart of human affairs. It reminds us too that Brünnhilde, even if she was, for Wagner, an epitome of the spirit of music, is also a Valkyrie, one who has surrendered her godhead out of pity for a mortal, and who has arranged her own future with breathtaking intelligence before sleeping on the plan. To put the point in a somewhat Leavisite way, Heise's reading of the cycle, full of insights though it is, puts cabbalistic *decipherment* in place of a critical *response*.

Feuerbach's philosophy is at the centre, too, of Mark Berry's allegorical vision of the cycle.[7] On Berry's reading, the *Ring* contains a denunciation of property, of political order, and of civil law equal to the fiercest diatribes of the Young Hegelians. The radical political vision that had compelled Wagner onto the barricades with Bakunin survives, according to Berry, in the mordant deconstruction of Wotan, representing law, and of Alberich, representing capitalist accumulation. Feuerbach's debunking of religion animates the drama, which shows the gods as human dreams, worthless shadows of the live human passions that conjure them. It was indeed the Young Hegelians, and not Nietzsche, who first proclaimed the death of God, and on Berry's reading *The Ring* is an exploration of what this momentous death means – both personally and politically – for us who have survived it.

Berry leaves the reader in no doubt that there are abundant insights into both music and drama to be obtained by wearing Young

Hegelian spectacles. He points to the way in which Hegel's dialectic of master and slave is repeatedly dramatized in the power-relations among the principal characters, and he emphasizes the enduring dichotomy – love or power – which can be overcome only in the recognition of death as a part of love. He describes the gradual conquest of *eros* (sexual love) by *agape* (Christian charity) as the cycle proceeds, and seems to recognize that, by the end of *Götterdämmerung*, the Young Hegelian who had begun work on the cycle a quarter of a century before no longer exists. But what has come to replace him? Berry's allegory, like Shaw's and Heise's, peters out at this point, offering only an enigmatic stare into the void.

Any interpretation that respects the dramatic pressure of the narrative must acknowledge the sympathy which the music conjures for Wotan, and the very real attempt to present the rule of law – established though it is by an 'original usurpation' – as the necessary background to enduring love. Wagner's initial conception, which saw Siegfried as the emancipating hero who was to break the bonds of an old and moribund authority, gave way to another and quite incompatible vision, in which Siegfried is the true transgressor, the one who, by failing to understand the meaning of promises, contracts and laws, brings about his own and others' destruction. No matter that the god who upholds these contracts and laws is a projection of our human need for him; no matter that he is imbued with all our human imperfections; no matter that he, like us, must die. The point is that, in destroying the gods, we destroy a large part of ourselves. In liberating ourselves from religion, therefore, we expose ourselves to another kind of spiritual disorder.

The *Ring* cycle therefore warns us of a deep and ineradicable fault in the scheme of things, a fault that lies concealed in freedom itself, and which we must confront not in the realm of power politics but in our own hearts, where love battles with selfishness, and renunciation with biological need. *The Ring* is not simply about power or money or even love; it is also about original sin, what Schopenhauer called 'the crime of existence itself'. Heise grasps this point, and tries to embed it in his complex allegorical reading of the drama. But it is not through allegory that we understand such deep features of the human condition. We understand them through the symbolism inherent in the drama, and not by looking behind the characters and actions to the abstract ideas and arguments that they supposedly represent.

A further word of caution is necessary here. Wagner adopted and elaborated the view of myths as forms of pre-scientific knowledge, ways of approaching deep truths about the human condition that resist translation into ordinary literal prose. Myths are already turned towards the kind of symbolism that his art was designed to exhibit. And this view of myth persisted into the twentieth century, by which time it had become wound together first with Freud's theory, that the deep meaning of myth lies in our unconscious desires, and subsequently with Jung's idea of myth as an expression of the 'collective unconscious', the residue of emotions that we share, but which can be easily acknowledged only through symbols. For Jung these symbols, the 'archetypes', recur in the myths and deities of many nations, and immediately elicit from us those pre-conscious nods of recognition, as we attach them to the unconscious processes whereby we live. On this view certain objects – dragon, ring, fire – already conjure universal psychic material, and stories of ordeals overcome and heroines won appeal to us because they are parables of the process whereby the masculine and the feminine seek each other out in the unconscious of us all. Such is the approach adopted by Robert Donington, in his Jungian interpretation of Wagner's tetralogy. Donington rewrites the story of *The Ring* as that of the universal ego (Siegfried) in search of the anima (Brünnhilde) that completes it, battling the demons of the unconscious along the way, and under the dominion of the libido (the Ring), whose power comes not from the forswearing of love, but from the renunciation of 'escapist, childish fantasies', which is apparently what is achieved in the opening scene of *Das Rheingold*.[8]

The problem with all such interpretations is that, if they are true, they absorb the individual characters of the drama into abstract categories that apply to us all. The Jungians believe of every male ego that it pursues the anima that will complete it, that it is in contest with the terrible mother, that it goes through life accompanied by its dark shadow, and so on. Hence we are told nothing special or revealing about Siegfried's journey when we learn that the dragon Fafner is 'really' the terrible mother, who had previously appeared in the guise of a bear captured in the forest, or when we read that Brünnhilde is

Siegfried's anima (having been Wotan's anima in *Die Walküre*) and that Hagen is Siegfried's shadow. And when, at the end of *Götter-dämmerung*, we discover that Gutrune too is Siegfried's anima, that the role of shadow is shared by Gunther and Hagen, and that all the destruction visited on the world at the end of the drama is merely the work of the 'transforming fire' that is to lead to the rebirth of the ego from the arcane womb of Self – when, in this way, the great drama is reduced to a piece of clumsy theorizing, we are surely entitled to wonder whether anything very much has been proved in the course of it. Surely it is unhelpful to be offered such conclusions as this one:

> The implication of the *Ring* is that every heedless over-indulgence in unconscious mother-longings and every wilful obstruction to the underlying purpose of our lives will be paid for by disasters until we either go under or are shaken out of our mother-bound and wilful state into going on.[9]

I do not mean to disparage Donington's dramatic insights, upon some of which I have drawn in my own telling of the story. I wish rather to suggest that the Jungian approach to works of art, which looks for universal symbols in their local manifestation, leaves the real matter of artistic symbolism untouched. Deryck Cooke puts the matter well:

> The fatal defect of Jungian interpretation is that it simply imposes its own categories on the work interpreted. Sieglinde and Brünnhilde have to be anima-figures, Hunding and Hagen have to be representations of the shadow, the dragon has to be the Terrible Mother, because these are the only categories available. Just so, in *Hamlet*, say, Ophelia would have to be Hamlet's anima, Claudius his shadow, and Gertrude the Terrible Mother, and the whole work would have to be treated as a therapeutic development of the psyche; likewise, the last stage would have to be nobody's actual death, but a general rebirth, except for the shadow, which would disappear, leaving the psyche in one final healthful state of transformation – and the peculiar quality of the masterpiece *Hamlet* unilluminated.[10]

Having picked Donington's interpretation apart, Cooke rightly concludes that the 'fairest thing to say about [it] is that it is a "Jungian interpretation of *The Ring*" – just as there can be a Jungian interpretation of any other dramatic work – which nevertheless does not explain what *The Ring* is actually about'.[11]

This leads me to a general point in response to all psychoanalytic readings, which is that they risk replacing the particular by the general, the deep meaning that resides in the specific drama by the general theory of what we humans are. No interpretation can be valid, or have any real claim on the listener's attention, if it does not illuminate *The Ring* as a drama. No work of dramatic art can be an effective symbol of some general meaning if it does not work as a drama. And it is by understanding *The Ring* as drama that we can approach, in Wagner's words, the 'concealed deep truth' within it.[12] If we use psychoanalytic categories, therefore, it should be as Jean Shinoda Bolen uses them, in the study of the characters, and not, as Donington uses them, in order to rewrite the plot.[13]

For Bolen *The Ring* should be seen as the portrait of a succession of dysfunctional families – Wotan and Fricka, Sieglinde and Hunding, Wotan and Brünnhilde, Mime and Siegfried, the Gibichungs, Alberich and Hagen, and so on – in which attachment, abuse and patriarchal denial of the feminine are played out and dramatized. And there is truth in her interpretation, which finds in Wagner's characters the residues of conflicts and trials that are familiar to Bolen from her psychotherapeutic practice. As symbols, however, Wagner's characters contain far more significance than Bolen allows to them, and if we do not see the cosmic character of their every deed and feeling, we miss the essential meaning of the cycle.

Wagner lived before the rise of psychoanalysis. But it does not follow that he lived before the insights on which people like Freud and Jung built their theories. On the contrary, many of the insights were his. Moreover his mind was both more poetic and more scientific (in the broadest sense of the term) than those who have made use of his findings. Like the Freudians he believed that our emotional lives are built on unconscious residues. But he believed these residues to be inherited from the prehistory of our species, rather than deposited in childhood. He understood that the law against incest does not exist because we wish, unconsciously, to defy it, but because domestic order, symbolized by Fricka, depends on obeying it. (As it would now be expressed: the incest taboo is an adaptation.) Nothing could be further from Wagner's thinking than the Freudian theory of the infantile libido. He saw human sexual desire as a *telos* of the personality, something that matures, and which flourishes only through the existential tie that leads people to take full responsibility for each other's being. Sexual union might be foreshadowed in childhood, as in the forest murmurs that speak to Siegfried. But desire becomes what it essentially is only in the encounter with the free being who returns it. Wagner did not see dreams as exercises in wish-fulfilment but as psychic deposits, full of the primeval inheritance of the hunter-gatherer as well as the traumas of the individual life. In all those ways he differed from, and was nearer to the truth than, Freud.

Like Freud he recognized that the Greek tragedians had grasped profound facts about the unconscious forces that govern us. However, unlike Freud, he saw those forces as rooted in the wider life of the species, and not merely in the life of the family. While Freud saw the unconscious as filled with material deposited in the lifetime of its owner, Wagner saw it as a shared foundation, where the earliest impulses of *Homo sapiens* lie dormant. While our path through life is marked by successive 'awakenings', these occur on two planes – that of the individual, in his search for self-knowledge and freedom, and that of the species, which is indifferent to any such aim. No experience displays this more clearly than sexual attraction, and that is why Siegfried's awakening of Brünnhilde is key to the drama, and so richly prefigured in all that leads to it.

All those points should lead us to treat Freudian and Jungian treatments of the cycle with reserve. It is not as though Wagner were unaware of the importance of the Mother in shaping the psyche of the child, or in prefiguring the sexual ambitions of the adult – virtually no artist in history has put the matter as explicitly as Wagner puts it in *Siegfried*. It is rather that, because of his far-reaching and cosmic vision, he was able to *make use* of this psychical material in building the entirely individual personalities of his story. Consider, as one important instance, the question of incest. The Freudian (and by default Jungian) view is that we are repelled by incest because we have acquired, from the discipline of family life and the internalized commands of the superego, a prohibition against it. The desire to do it is natural; the prohibition cultural.

As we now know, and ought to have known since Edward Wester-marck's researches at the end of the nineteenth century, that is the opposite of the truth.[14] The prohibition is natural; the desire to defy it cultural. And it is precisely this fact that Wagner uses to such artistic advantage. In Siegmund and Sieglinde he is symbolizing the search for freedom through sexual desire. It is because their desire is forbidden by the natural law that he can show the two lovers triumphing over their condition, breaking the bonds that constrain them, and taking possession of a freedom that is also inseparable from commitment, and which leads therefore inevitably to their downfall. As Wagner remarked, in the course of discussing the tragedy of Oedipus, sexual desire is precisely opposed to familial love: it is the force that draws the individual out of the family into communion with human society as a whole.[15] Hence desire is for the *stranger*, the one who splinters the home. But it is precisely the *natural* opposition to incest that gives dramatic sense to Siegmund and Sieglinde's love. Their passion is a reaffirmation of their shared nature as outsiders, a defiance of the unreal home that Hunding has made, and an attempt to re-kindle, in imagination, the only comfort that they have ever known.

All the dramatic beauty of this relationship depends, in the end, on rejecting the Freudian vision, and perceiving instead the 'concealed deep truth' that the Freudians deny – the truth that desire is an inter-personal relation, towards which we grow, and not a residue from early childhood. Wagner returns to the matter in the beautiful transition from Siegfried's mother-longing to the awakening of Brünn-hilde. And the emphasis throughout is that sexual feeling comes to fruition as an existential choice. The prehistory of our species feeds into this experience, but only because it presents us with that which we must overcome.

To return to the point already made in response to Donington, no interpretation of *The Ring* can illuminate the work if it does not acknowledge that the cycle is, in the first instance, not an allegory or a mystery but a drama. Philip Kitcher and Richard Schacht, who are distinguished philosophers in their own right, conceive *The Ring* entirely in dramatic terms, and identify Wotan and Brünnhilde as the central characters.[16] For Kitcher and Schacht the drama begins long before the opening of *Das Rheingold*. Wotan has seized control of the world with a view to improving it. His aim is to impose law on a shallow, cruel and conflict-burdened universe, so as to uphold agreements and administer justice. But this noble goal requires him not only to maintain the law but also, in the emergencies of government, to by-pass it – as we see in his treatment of the Giants and in his snatching of the Ring from Alberich.

In this latter episode Wotan disturbs the cosmos so deeply that the Ur-Wala herself rises from the depths to put paid to the god's current plan. Erda informs Wotan of the truth that is henceforth to haunt him – the truth that everything ends. Wotan can postpone the end, but he cannot escape it; the drama explores Wotan's search, in the wake of this prophecy, for an ending that will make his government retrospectively worthwhile. Here is how Kitcher and Schacht express the point, contrasting their interpretation with the obvious one:

> In *Walküre*, Wotan's immediate goal has been to promote the success of Siegmund. He appears to have pursued that goal as a means to regaining the Ring. In its turn, regaining the Ring would enable him to consolidate his power, and that would allow him not only to establish but also to secure a new kind of order in the world. But there is a different way of placing Project Siegmund within a hierarchy of goals. We might view Wotan as having recognized already in *Rheingold* that his overt larger end – the consolidation and perpetuation of his system of law and order, which would make the world an enduringly better and more admirable place – is beyond even his power and contrivance, and thus that what he has striven for from a time in the distant past (well before the opening of the *Ring*) is unattainable. His revised task, therefore, from late *Rheingold* on, has been that of *finding an ending.* Knowing that his fledgling order must pass, he wants a conclusion that does not simply make a mockery of all he has stood for.[17]

Kitcher and Schacht explore all the stages of Wotan's growing self-awareness: his despair, which causes him to toy with the idea of bequeathing the future to Alberich; his recuperation, as he understands and adopts the new project that has grown in the pure heart and unconscious mind of Brünnhilde; his self-transformation from ruler to Wanderer, and his ambivalent renunciation in the face of Siegfried's insolence. In all this, they argue, Wotan is not trying to refute Erda's prophecy. He is 'groping towards a tragic ending', one that will dignify his doomed government, endow it with a meaning, show it to be deeply worthwhile and not just a random intrusion into a world that has no design unless and until we impose one. At length, thanks to Brünnhilde, who ensures that by losing everything, she ends everything for the gods, Wotan finds the tragic consummation that he has unconsciously sought, but consciously so often evaded. *The Ring* is the story of these two central characters, and of their search for meaning in a world where meaning exists only if we ourselves provide it.

Kitcher and Schacht's approach unlocks many of the secrets of *The Ring*. They are surely right to emphasize the relation between Wotan and his daughter. But their interpretation also raises questions concerning the nature of tragedy, and why it is that tragic conclusions exert what Wagner would call a 'redeeming' force over the events that lead to them (though the 'redemption' concept is one that Kitcher and Schacht explicitly avoid, as they avoid the idea of the sacred). In what follows I take note of their conclusions, sometimes qualifying them, sometimes supplementing them. But I see the drama as centrally focused on the emergence of the free individual from the natural order, and on the puzzle planted in the heart of things by the accountability of persons. Such is the framework on which Wagner mounts a vision of what is at stake in human life – a vision that, for its philosophical depth and poetic richness, is surely supreme in the world of opera.

6

Character and Symbol

Any account of *The Ring* must begin with Wotan, not only an inspired creation and a supremely imposing character, but on one understanding the central character in the cycle, the one who is most consistently put to the test by events, and who shows the greatest capacity to change and develop in response to them. (Such is the interpretation of Kitcher and Schacht to which I referred at the close of the last chapter.) One thing is surely very evident, which is that Wotan has a long-term vision, and an ability to project his will forward into events so that nothing that happens to him should be wholly accidental. It is this very ability to see forward that enables him to do what no other character save his daughter Brünnhilde is able to do, which is to *will* the end, his own end included.

The raw material for Wotan is taken from many sources. First among them is Homer's Zeus, the 'father of the gods', who maintains the cosmic order in equilibrium, who takes full advantage of his position to indulge his desires for mortal women, but who is often thwarted in this by his vigilant wife, Hera, the model for Fricka. Second there is the God of the Hebrew Old Testament, the God who rules through law, and who is bound to his chosen people by a 'covenant'. Finally there is Wotan's Scandinavian original, the god Odin, who, though at the summit of the Viking hierarchy, is not notably superior in status to his son, Thor, Wagner's Donner, the god of thunder and wielder of the hammer that is such a prominent votive symbol on the Old Norse archaeological sites. In the primary sources – the Seeress's Prophecy (Voluspa), the Sayings of the High One and Grimnir's Sayings – Odin is characterized by his obsessive quest for wisdom, particularly for information about Rognarök. His power is supreme but qualified, since the ultimate truth about his own fate is hidden from him.

In Wotan, in effect, Wagner achieves a synthesis of the god idea, as we Europeans have shaped and been shaped by it. He is the imperious father-figure, who rules by law but who also has a consuming interest in us, which we sense in those sacred moments when love or death waylays us. He is the being to whom we pray in our greatest need, who has imbued our world with the tantalizing symbols of his power and the hopes that spring from it, but who always lets us down in the end, since he is subject to the very same conflicts and foibles as the mortals who created him.

Wagner also takes a hint from those three sources as to the dual nature of Wotan. Although he has his home in Valhalla, Wotan is also a wanderer on the face of the earth, as is Odin in the Poetic Edda. To put it in Judaeo-Christian terms, Wotan is a 'real presence' among his mortal subjects, and the music of the Wanderer shows a person who is nowhere and everywhere, as its keyless whole-tone steps descend a chromatic ladder like glimpses of sunlight on a darkened stair. It is as though the imperious diatonic scale of the spear motif, which cuts through all our projects like a final judgement, has been replaced by the careful steps of the curious observer, who is leaving space for us to reveal our will and our mortal failings.

In every religion we find, projected onto the person of the Supreme Being, all the deepest needs of humanity. The theological problem of reconciling these conflicting needs in a single deity is duplicated, for Wagner, in the problem of creating a unified character who can plausibly represent them. Wagner's solution is an unqualified success. Unlike Alberich, Wotan has power from the outset, so that we do not ask about his origins. It is only *as taken apart by the narrative* that we understand this power as a thing acquired, rather than self-created. The narrative parallels the 'peeling away' of divine attributes that is the inevitable result of scientific knowledge. Moreover, the power that Wotan possesses is the power of law. In his meetings with the Giants, those rude beings who do not understand that justice is a weapon and not just a restraint, Wagner wonderfully reveals the way in which justice and law are woven into the practice of government, and also bent to its hidden purposes. Wotan is both law-giver and law-enforcer and, like the God of the Torah, he is bound in a covenant, which is the covenant to uphold our deals, that one included. And like the God of the Torah, who on Mount Sinai gave to Moses not only the tablets of the law but also the design for his temple, he can maintain his authority only if he also has a home, a sanctuary, from which his sovereignty can be serenely exercised. In order to achieve this, however, he has had to make a promise that he is determined not to honour.

This promise of Wotan's to the Giants encapsulates the promise made from the beginning of time by the gods that we mortals conjure from our deepest longings. Wotan promises them the goddess of love, Freia, who is also the purveyor of the apples of immortality. But if we really possessed the gifts of Freia – if we were immortal and swimming forever in a bath of love – what need would we have of the gods? And if we no longer need them, the gods must die. Hence, Freia cannot be *shared* by us and the gods: either we have her, or they do. Yet it is only because the gods promise such things that we are prepared to erect in their honour the temples from which they govern us. What the gods promise, therefore, they must also withhold. A trick is needed, and on that trick depends the rule of law whereby all such tricks are forbidden. Such is the paradox of justice: that it depends upon the arts that it forbids. And this paradox is built into the personality of Wotan at every level, as it is built into all forms of historical legitimacy.

Here we see a curious similarity between Wotan and Alberich, which is also, and again paradoxically, the greatest difference. If Wotan's promise to the Giants had been honoured then Wotan would have done exactly what Alberich did – he would have exchanged love for domination. He only avoids Alberich's 'sin against himself' by adding another sin on top of it, the sin of a dishonoured promise. And yet, as the Giant Fasolt reminds Wotan, 'what you are, you are through treaties' – it is only because Wotan avoids this additional sin that he has any power at all. But somehow it is all understandable: justice requires law, which needs power, and power needs legitimacy, the throne of Valhalla, which is exactly what Wotan has striven to achieve. If a trick is necessary to gain this result, so be it. For it is only through lawful government that we mortals are able to protect ourselves from tricks at all.

Trickery, therefore, is an essential part of Wotan's capabilities. But, as ruler of the world, he cannot initiate the tricks on which he depends. Instead he relies on Loge, the demi-god, whom Wagner based on the Icelandic Lokke or Loki, the spirit of fire, the outsider at the feast of the gods.[1] Wotan's rise to world-government, we understand, has been made possible by an alliance with a demi-god who, like Erda and the Rhine-daughters, belongs to a more durable and more inscrutable order than the gods who have emerged into consciousness.

Through his trickery Wotan narrowly avoids the crime of Alberich, and this must lead us to ask what exactly he has retained, in the person of Freia. Since Freia has so few words of her own, and is witnessed largely as the reluctant booty of the Giants, her whole character is given by the music – the music that is hers, and the music that is given to Fafner as he describes the golden apples that grow in her garden. Both are among the most beautiful of Wagner's melodic ideas, the first being not only decisive for an understanding of the drama, but also famously misunderstood by the early commentators, who associated it with 'flight', since it first appears as Freia runs onto the scene in flight from the Giants who have come to claim her as their wages.

Deryck Cooke sees this theme as illustrating the way in which leit-motifs *accumulate* meaning, through expanding and fulfilling their musical potential. As I pointed out in Chapter 4, the two halves of the theme develop independently in the narrative, the one spelling out the enchantment of erotic love, the other the suffering tenderness, the burden of tragic dependence and longing, that is the price we mortals pay for our attachments. In Valhalla and the world of the gods, we discover, it is only the first part of the theme that accompanies the invocation of love – rising, weaving, wafting around the branches of an arpeggiated triad, reminding us that the gods know only the blissful half of an experience the real meaning of which is not delight but passion – and therefore the suffering to which our mortality condemns us.

Like many an authority figure, Wotan views his children as the natural extension of himself. And he regards his erotic potency more as a way to exert and amplify his power, than as a source of sexual pleasure. In Siegmund and Sieglinde he sees the instruments of his own and the world's salvation – so that his love for them, real though it is, also has a calculating side: they are needed if the rule of law is to be maintained. But, as it turns out, they are needed as sacrifices too. Wotan's calculating love, founded on elaborate self-deception, is easily demolished by the sarcastic observer, and Fricka has no difficulty in persuading Wotan to sacrifice Siegmund to her outrage. At the same time she brings him face to face with the true cost of his sovereignty, and the fact that he has inflicted this cost on his children, who have no one to depend upon but him.

Only through sublimating his grief over Siegmund's death in anger against Brünnhilde can Wotan move on from his love for the Volsung twins, so as to resume control – though now a faltering control – over the cosmos. In the case of Brünnhilde, however, Wotan displays an attachment that, while in a sense equally calculating, is qualified by a poignant sense of identity with its object. Brünnhilde is Wotan's will: she is intimate with Wotan in the special way that girls can be intimate with their fathers. For daughters often take pride in manliness and adopt it as their own, while allowing, as wives seldom allow, the revelations of vulnerability and the hunger for understanding that Wotan displays in his memorable confession in *Die Walküre* Act 2. When Brünnhilde does what she thinks Wotan *really* wants, his anger with her is also anger at himself, and at the frustration of a scheme that could never have worked in any case. And when, glimpsing in her the new vehicle for his own and the world's rescue, he allows his love to be reborn, his anger is overcome in a flow of tenderness as moving as anything in the cycle.

The scene of Wotan's confession to his daughter is remarkable in another way. Gods, in their natural state, as recipients of unquestioning worship, don't have much of an inner life. They have character, will and emotions. But they are not prone to self-doubt, anguish or despair; they do not wrestle with half-conscious longings, or confide their anxieties to other gods. A god with a developed inner life, who is prepared to confide in a loving daughter, is surely already on the way to being something other than a god – something less than a god, might once have been said, something more than a god for Wagner. At one level *The Ring* is the story of Wotan's search for self-knowledge, including the knowledge that law without self-sacrificing love brings only an illusory freedom, and only an empty joy. But Wotan's self-knowledge is also man's knowledge of his own predicament, projected onto the screen of Valhalla. Wotan's anxiety for the future is *our* anxiety, and peace can be bestowed on the gods only when *we* find peace, through accepting our mortality, renouncing the will to power, and devoting ourselves to those whose love we have consciously or unconsciously counted on. This is, in one reading of this multiply ambiguous moment, the meaning of Brünnhilde's 'Ruhe, ruhe, du Gott!', which puts not only the gods but the world to rest, before the great musical résumé that imposes order on all that we have seen and heard. This musical culmination resolves the dissonance caused by the intervention of will in the flow of nature with the theme of Sieglinde's blessing – a blessing conferred by a mortal on a god.

The story of Wotan shows a wilful and dominant personality whose acts are constrained by justice, the source of his power. Gradually Wotan is overcome by the weariness of living within this constraint, with the knowledge that the price of his original sin has not been paid, and with the recognition that the joys of immortality are more illusory than the tender love of mortals. The portrait of Wotan's spiritual wrestling on the way to renunciation and defeat is one of Wagner's masterstrokes, and it is only through the music that it can be fully understood.

At the end of *Die Walküre*, when his divided will has been beautifully knitted into a single but sleeping premonition by his imaginative daughter, we are given the melody of Wotan's farewell, cushioned by the sleeping Brünnhilde motif that I discussed in Chapter 4. This melody shows the extent of Wotan's transformation. A new serenity has entered his soul: not the serenity of power, triumph and blessedness captured in the empty D flat arpeggios of the rainbow bridge, but the good-night kiss in which a parent feels with a melting tenderness the absolute value of the mortal being who is escaping into sleep and who will one day escape into nothingness. The melody of Wotan's farewell is the first entry of chromaticism into the hitherto blatantly diatonic language of Valhalla – the only other example, the second half of Freia's leitmotif, being no more than an embryo until taken up by Siegmund and Sieglinde in the course of their tragic love. It is as though Wotan has stepped down from the immortal throne of natural music, leaving behind him both the diatonic scale (the spear) and the tonal triad (Valhalla), and losing himself in the chromatic flow of mortal emotions, shaping his own mortality as he confers the same on his daughter.

The music of this scene shows, with Wagner's characteristic psychological penetration, the *existential* change that occurs in Wotan, confronted by his daughter's purity of spirit and by her decision to act for another's good. Wotan falls beside her – not into sleep, but into the love-filled mortal attitude to the future. Henceforth he will not try to trick his way to security, using his mortal progeny as instruments. He will bequeath to mortals the business of maintaining the sacred order. This existential transition in the character of Wotan explains the appearance, as he kisses Brünnhilde's godhead away, of the 'renunciation' theme (17). Just as Alberich, in cursing love, became what he henceforth would be; just as Siegmund, in drawing the sword from the tree, put all that he was into the love that was to lead him to his death, so Wotan, in his kiss of farewell, adopts his new character, as wanderer and observer in a world from which his will is now withdrawn.

Thus, when Wotan, in his new guise as the Wanderer, precedes Siegfried to Fafner's lair in the forest, there to encounter Alberich lingering obsessively beside his stolen treasure, the god looks serenely on his enemy. Wotan has put behind him the pursuit of power and in doing so discovered true freedom – which is the ability to look on the world in a spirit of acceptance. This 'renunciation of the will', which Schopenhauer advocated as the highest morality, is also an affirmation of the will – a conscious tracing of the boundaries within which lesser beings are trapped. And when Wotan, making way for Siegfried, mounts his winged horse, we hear again the serene chromatic melody with which Brünnhilde was put to sleep, the voice of the love that Wotan has discovered, to his surprise, in the heart of all his futile scheming. It says much about Alberich that the dwarf senses, at this moment, only a mocking laughter directed at himself. For he who cursed love will inevitably be humiliated by the sight and the sound of it.

True, Wotan's previous life as ruler of the world has left its traces, and can still erupt through the crust of his renunciation with the imperious gesture of the spear. We understand this from the opening of Act 3 of *Siegfried*, which begins with that astonishing prelude. Here Wagner reveals the full extent of his symphonic mastery, combining themes associated with Wotan the Wanderer, and with the birth and death of the world, in a striding and urgent counterpoint. The whole-tone steps of the Wanderer take us now through constant changes of key, veering from path to path and goal to goal in a kind of transcendental restlessness – a compulsive search for nowhere which is all that remains of the god's desire to be everywhere.

Wotan summons Erda, seeming to berate her for her merely passive knowledge of destiny, while contrasting his own knowledge, won through ambition and suffering, and through the active attempt at government. Yet, he concedes, his knowledge amounts to no more than hers – namely, knowledge that things must come to an end. On the other hand, there is a difference between knowing this and willing it, and will it he does, having summoned her to bear confused and somnolent witness to his gesture. And, from the mingled anxiety and weariness, he extracts the great affirmative theme, with which he bequeaths the world again – not to the son of Alberich this time, but to Siegfried, the free being who will act for himself alone.

It is worth remarking that this scene between Erda and Wotan is one of the many that recalls the themes of Greek tragedy. At the end of the *Oresteia* Athene, representing the new race of Olympian gods, who have wrested their governance from the old gods of darkness and instinct, settles the case of *Orestes v The Furies* with a trial in which she has the casting vote. The jury is tied, half demanding retribution, half acquittal. By casting her vote Athene both rescues Orestes, and at the same time affirms the rule of law over the rule of vengeance, the settlement of disputes over their perpetuation. But the tied vote is a recognition of the Furies' right and accordingly she invites them to take a place, albeit a subservient one, among the Olympian gods, and to be renamed 'the kindly ones' (*eumenides*). They agree to this, and the rule of law is thereby finally established. In a similar way, when Wotan summons Erda in *Siegfried* Act 3 the new order of the rule of law is confronting the older, darker and more mysterious order of instinct. But the confrontation is an anxious one. Wotan is not defeated, but nor is he intent on affirming his reign. Rather he wishes to trump the goddess of instinct by showing that he is consciously willing what she can merely predict. He does this, but not before she has told him that he is not what he seems, that his pretensions to legal authority are in fact founded on nothing. Set the scenes from Aeschylus and Wagner side by side, and you will find that each illuminates the other. In Aeschylus the gods are free; in Wagner all freedom has been confined to the precarious world of mortal love, and its price is suffering.

Wotan knows he must renounce his realm, and that all must end, but he can also bequeath the world to the free being, and in doing so express all that he knows by way of love. He can do this, however, only by a show of opposition: to give the world openly to Siegfried would be to bequeath not a sphere of action but an age-old burden of guilt. Hence it would be to deprive Siegfried of his freedom. Only by obstructing Siegfried's will can Wotan liberate Siegfried from the original sin that has poisoned his inheritance. The scene that follows is a masterly portrayal of the conflict in Wotan's soul, between the love that would gladly give the world to Siegfried and the anger of the father who cannot accept being parted from his power. In such scenes, seemingly so riddled with contradiction, we encounter a moment of transition between the universal myth, in which human destiny is figured, and the individual soul, indifferent to destiny and living by will alone. The cosmic drama shows the unchangeable struggle between law and bondage, between freedom and resentment, and between authority and power. The end point of this struggle is in all of us the same – death, which is the loss of everything. But it matters how we die. Serenity comes with renunciation, and renunciation is the gift of love. And so Wotan, holding his shattered spear, finally departs from the drama, leaving Siegfried to reap the reward of his unwitting impiety.

For Kitcher and Schacht, Wotan is a god with a project. Wotan seeks to improve the world – the shallow, unstable, thoughtless world that we see depicted at the beginning of *Das Rheingold* – by establishing justice and a rule of law. This project has required constant trickery – of which the contract with the Giants and the seizure of Alberich's Ring are merely the latest instances – in order to maintain the power without which laws and deals are not enforceable. In this Wotan is aided by Loge, who represents (among other things) the constant amendment and creative interpretation of the law that reasoning makes available. But Wotan's project pushes the cosmic order to the brink of instability, so that Erda rises to warn him of the end. Little by little he comes to see what she means, recognizing that while his rule must end, he still has the question whether to end it himself, and if so how. His search for an ending that will in some way vindicate what he has done is, for Kitcher and Schacht, the principal story of the Ring. Wotan does not provide that ending, but he learns how to pass the search for it to his daughter, who is capable of the feeling without which the world can be neither truly owned nor finally relinquished.

All that is beautifully worked out by Kitcher and Schacht, and it is worth quoting their final judgement on Wotan, since it contains truths that every interpretation must acknowledge:

> Long ago, at the World-Ash, Wotan's knowledge grew with the sacrifice of a part of himself. And the sacrifices continue. In tapping Erda's intuitive wisdom, he diminishes it, weakening and eventually losing her and her guidance. In exhausting Loge's instrumental rationality, he reduces Loge to a more primitive state, and so deprives himself of valuable counsel. In fathoming the intricacies of the relations among his goals and strategies, he must give up first Siegmund and then Brünnhilde. In finding his way to a new goal, the goal of achieving his own ending in a meaningful manner, he must forsake the active role he has played in the world. At each stage, Wotan mutilates himself; parts of him drop away, leaving a god ever more crippled and forlorn. Yet even at the end of his quest, even after all the struggles and sacrifices, he does not know enough. He cannot resolve the question of how his world is to end. A part of his tragedy is that he has abandoned love in the service of law; another is that along the way to the end of *Walküre*, he relinquishes everything that is most precious to him. At its centre is his commitment to a grand task, which he pursues with ferocious determination – and yet he ultimately realizes that not only has he failed to achieve it, but he has also contributed to the failure by the ways in which he has attempted it.[2]

That portrait leaves us with the question of why Wotan should be this way. Might a rival god have stopped by the World Ash Tree, stripped from it the branch of government, and used it to some other purpose than the imposition of law? Surely not: Wotan rules freely, but his freedom is the 'consciousness of necessity' – only by being as he is, with the dilemmas imposed by both love and law, does he embody the human need for his existence. At some level the tetralogy is addressing the question of what remains, when this being with 'necessary existence' slips from the actual to the possible before fading away. That is the real question that troubled Wagner, the question of life in a post-religious world.

Wotan's spear symbolizes law in its public aspect. But law in its public aspect depends, in the last analysis, on law in its private aspect – on the acceptance of moral constraints. This is the meaning of Fricka, an essential adjunct to Wotan's rule, without whom he could not be what he is in the eyes of mortals. Here and there the story suggests that, having given an eye for the spear of government, Wotan risked his second eye for Fricka. Alternatively – and this seems to be Cooke's view – the spear and Fricka were acquired simultaneously, and the eye that Wotan risked was the price of both. Either way, the lost eye symbolizes the spontaneous freedom that is later to stare at Wotan from the eye of Siegfried, and which he exchanged for law, piety and the home, since nothing else endures. It was only through marriage to the goddess of domestic piety and honour that Wotan could acquire lasting sovereignty. Moreover, only the being whose freedom is limited by moral customs and a sense of honour can be truly free, since only he will be bound by his self-imposed obligations. That, in brief, is the cause of Siegfried's downfall.

To put it in another way: our ability to order our lives by free agreements depends on our obedience to obligations that arose in another way and without reference to our consent. These obligations are the 'blind spot' in the law, since they are not subject to legislative amendment and lie outside the bounds of the sovereign's decrees. Fricka is the guardian of these obligations and, as she rightly points out to Wotan during his great crisis, the rule of the gods would vanish if mortals should ever regard themselves as free to disobey them. In the marriage of Wotan and Fricka, therefore, we see the mutual dependence of morality and law. And in the character of Hunding, Wagner shows us just why piety and honour are necessary in the world of humans: without them such brutes would live by violence alone. As it is, even Hunding must offer hospitality to his unwelcome guest, and

Hunding's arrogance is limited by the claims of kinship, marriage and the hearth.

In considering the characters of Wagner's story we should bear in mind that their mythical status invites us to understand them both as complete individuals, and as parts of what we are. In all of us there is the need for sovereignty – the need to live as free, accountable beings, able to impose and obey the laws that guarantee our authenticity. All of us are entangled in the bargains and promises that we have made in order to preserve this sovereignty, and in all of us freedom and self-fashioning are tied to the unchosen obligations of honour and family life.

Wotan's predicament is our predicament, writ large, and the same is true for Alberich, an equally compelling creation, extracted by strokes of genius from the dark residues within us all. Like Wotan, Alberich realizes himself through renunciation – but not the slow renunciation born of self-knowledge that is Wotan's great achievement, but the impetuous renunciation of the thing that he cannot possess, and without which mortal life is in any case nothing – namely love. In fact Alberich does not merely renounce love: he curses it. And because the thing for which he curses love is also taken from him, he curses that too. Alberich's being is suspended from these two curses as from a gallows. The contrast between true and false renunciation is one of the themes of *Parsifal*, embodied in the characters of Parsifal and Klingsor. And at the time of composing *Parsifal* Wagner confessed to feeling 'total sympathy' for Alberich, whose fate is that of the person forced into consciousness of his ugliness by the cruel mockery of those who move in the world of easy conquests.[3] But he also portrayed Alberich as someone who is devoted to a single-minded work of destruction: for his crime against himself the whole world must pay! And in this too his feelings coincide with those of Klingsor.

In Christianity and Islam we are presented with a God who is all good, presented with an adversary whose antagonism stems from spiritual pride, for which there is no justification. In *The Ring* we encounter a similar contest, but not one between good and evil: it is a contest between two forms of domination – a contest between the free being whose power is conferred by agreements, and the self-imprisoned being whose power is elicited by violence, beginning with the violence against himself that expels love from his psyche. Satan, in the Abrahamic story, is not wronged by God, even if Milton sometimes suggests the contrary, whereas Alberich *is* wronged by Wotan, and to that extent suffers from a justified resentment. At the same time the world of *The Ring* is riven by the cosmic conflict between the two principles of light and dark, associated in Wagner's original speculative essay on the historical origins of the Scandinavian stories with the religious vision underlying the Eddas:

> In the religious myths of the Scandinavians the term Nifelheim, i.e. Nibel = Nebelheim (the Home of Haze), comes down to us as designation of the (subterranean) sojourn of the Night spirits, 'Schwarzalben', in opposition to the heavenly dwelling of the 'Asen' and 'Lichtalben' ('Light-Elves'). These Black-elves, 'Niflungar', children of Night and Death, burrow the earth, find out its inner treasures, smelt and smith its ore; gold gear and keen-edged weapons are their work . . . [4]

Although Wagner abandoned the vision of that original essay, he retained in altered form the Manichaean contest between light and dark, between free sovereignty and relentless coercion, epitomized in the antagonism and mutual dependence that unite Wotan and Alberich. And he uses the character and situation of Alberich to explore the nature of resentment as a comprehensive worldview. It is this feature that is so striking in Wagner's portrait.

Two features of resentment are highlighted in the character of Alberich: its *existential* nature, and its ability to transfer itself from object to object, restlessly policing the world in search of the happiness that should not be. These features were later noticed by Nietzsche, who built them into the accusation that he levelled against the Christian religion – an accusation that was rebutted by Max Scheler in his study of the topic.[5] Alberich's resentment is not just an emotion – not even an emotion. It is *what he is*. Having cursed love nothing remains in him that would permit others to exist for him as persons. All his encounters are with objects to be used, and we see this not only in his remorseless exploitation of the Nibelungs, but also in his relations with Mime, his brother, and Hagen, his son.

Although Alberich lost the hoard to Wotan, who lost it to Fafner, he retained sufficient power to satisfy his sexual urges. In recounting the rumour of this fact to Brünnhilde in Act 2 of *Die Walküre*, Wotan reports that a woman is carrying in her womb the fruits of Alberich's hatred and the strength of his envy. Alberich, it seems, 'overpowered' a woman, and also seduced her with gold:

> . . . ein Weib der Zwerg bewältigt,
> des Gunst Gold ihm erzwang:
> das Hasses Frucht hegt eine Frau,
> des Neides Kraft kreisst ihr im Schoss . . .

'The dwarf subdued a woman and seduced her with gold; a woman bears the fruit of his hatred; his envy's strength stirs in her womb . . . ' The image recalls the hideous Beria, Stalin's head of secret police, scouring the streets of Moscow in his black limousine and sending his thugs to arrest whatever young woman might attract his dwarf-eyed gaze, sometimes offering compensation, such as the release of a beloved husband, father or brother from the Gulag, sometimes merely threatening his victim with the same terrible fate.

There is desire born of resentment, which has no relation to love, since it aims to dominate, to humiliate and to enslave. It might purchase the body on which to practise its games, or it might, by force or trickery, ignore the other's will entirely. Wagner leaves it unclear exactly how Alberich accomplished his purpose, though in the great prelude to Act 2 of *Götterdämmerung* Alberich and Hagen refer to Hagen's mother who 'fell victim to [Alberich's] guile' ('[s]einer List sie erlag'). Following this encounter Grimhilde gave birth to a twisted being, old before his time and never glad.

In the worldview of *The Ring* the purpose and value of sexual feeling lies in the love that lifts us above the other animals. Sexual desire can remain in the realm of lust, power and manipulation. But sexual *love* rescues us from that sinful condition; true lovers meet as free individuals, each affirming the other's freedom. This meeting in the realm of freedom cancels all the conventions that stand in its way – even the laws against adultery and incest, cast peremptorily aside by Siegmund and Sieglinde. But those who drag sexual relations into the realm of calculation and trickery commit the primary moral offence – their sin against the other is a sin against the self, the sin of Alberich.

It is important to understand that Alberich's resentment begins before the Ring is stolen from him. Having cursed love, he finds hateful to him the very spectacle of others who enjoy its blessings, and the sight of happiness arouses the fervent desire to destroy it. When Loge and Wotan visit Nibelheim and Alberich discovers them, Wotan questions the value of the hoard, saying 'What help is the hoard to you, since Nibelheim is joyless and nothing can be obtained here for treasure?' Alberich responds with a sneering description of the gods, who 'live, laugh and love' in the soft breezes above, but whom he will one day grip in his 'golden fist'. 'As I renounced love,' he says, 'so all living things shall renounce it', so as to hunger instead for gold. And he follows this with a blood-curdling threat replete with fantasies of rape:

> Beware! Beware!
> For when you men serve my might
> The dwarf will take his pleasure
> On your pretty women who scorn his wooing,
> Though love does not smile on him.

Alberich then foretells the day when he will lead his 'nocturnal host' from the depths into the daylight. The leitmotif of the hoard leads to the falling semitone that began as Alberich's cry of 'Wehe' in the face of his humiliation by the Rhine-daughters, and which then became the first part of the spell with which he commands obedience to the Ring. (Early commentators described this (39) as the servitude motif.) It now resolves on a version of the original Rhinegold motif, but in the key of B flat minor (which is Alberich's home key throughout the cycle, being also the relative minor of Wotan's key of D flat major), leading onwards in malicious jubilation to a caricature of the motif of Valhalla.

This musical representation of a primordial desire for revenge against all that is sacred calls forth the understandable cry of 'Cease, blasphemous wretch!' from Wotan. Alberich seeks to desecrate the object of desire, and with it all that speaks of the blessedness that only love can bring. This, the music implies, is the origin of blasphemy, the desire to pull down the gods from their pedestal and to trample them underfoot, since they represent what the blasphemer cannot possess. And blasphemy against the gods is associated in this crucial passage with the spoiling of sexual love, which is the great good that Alberich sacrificed for the sake of the Ring.

The gods, Loge included, blithely dismiss Alberich's claim over the gold of the Rhine, repeatedly saying that he stole it, and implying that it is therefore no crime to take it away. But that is not Alberich's view of the matter. In his eyes he paid the proper price for the gold: by forswearing love he gave for the gold the only thing that could be exchanged against it, as Loge makes clear in narrating these events. That is why Alberich warns Wotan that, in taking the Ring, he sins against all that was, is and shall be. He is taking the thing for which nobody can pay the price except the one who originally paid it, and who gave up himself – his *Eigen* – for the sake of it. Wotan is therefore sinning against what is most sacred, trampling on a deal for which someone gave his freedom, his hopes and his self.[6]

Alberich's resentment is conveyed by the syncopated chords following a slithering up-beat in the bass, which precede the first pronouncement of the curse laid on the Ring. This leitmotif (44) reappears in *Die Walküre* when Wotan recounts Erda's prophecy: 'When love's dark enemy begets a son in anger, the end of the blessed ones will not be delayed.' It accompanies Alberich's subsequent appearances, first during his vigil at Fafner's cave, and then in his night-time visit to the sleeping Hagen in *Götterdämmerung*. In this latter scene – Alberich's final appearance – the syncopation is reinforced by subdivisions and ties within the bar-line, and Alberich's falling semitone is harmonized and orchestrated so as to become the wailing remainder of the cry of 'Rheingold!' that accompanied his original humiliation (164). This constantly repeated cadence has an obsessive character, as though intruding from a remembered calamity that cannot be put out of mind. The whole scene displays the feature of resentment that most clearly distinguishes it from love, namely that it is transferable. It is not that resentment has no specific object; rather, it flows like slime from object to object, contaminating whatever it touches. Resentment of the existential kind – the kind that inhabits the soul of Alberich – is incapable of forgiveness since it is unable to understand either self or other as truly needing it.

In bequeathing his resentment to his son Alberich issues the following imperative:

Hagen, my son, hate the happy
And love me, burdened with sorrows,
As you should.

Alberich treats love as something that he can order – an instrument to be used for his ends. Hagen is the same, and shows in his brooding responses that he can obey the first part of this command, to hate, but not the second part, to love, and certainly not the command to love his father, with whom he is now in competition for the Ring. The operative emotion throughout this scene is one shared by father and son – the transferable hatred that is called forth by the very sight of a person who is free from it. Love must be willingly bestowed or not bestowed at all; it is the sign of freedom – of the deep freedom that arouses Alberich's spite. And from behind this spite comes the obsessive call of the Rhinegold, the call of the thing that, claimed, possessed and 'forged' (i.e. subjected to the regime of substitution and exchange), renders our ventures empty and provisional. The resentment of Alberich is also the grief of the Rhine-daughters, the grief of a world whose primordial oneness has been fatally disturbed.

Alberich knows that love cannot be commanded, and he ends his intrusion into his son's unconscious with the vain attempt to command an oath of loyalty instead, fading away at last on the repeated call to be true. The motif of the curse here sounds in the orchestra, soon followed by the anguished reminiscence of the gold, and the scene ends on the word 'Treu' sung by Alberich, to be immediately negated by the two-chord sequence, 164, associated with lust for the gold and the pain of losing it, and harmonizing the descending semitone from G flat to F that is Alberich's signature. This wonderfully desolate passage conveys a deep truth about truth, which is that it vanishes from a world in which power alone arranges human dealings.

Much of the literature of totalitarianism is devoted to this singular fact. Solzhenitsyn and Havel argued that truth is the first casualty of totalitarian government, which requires us to 'live within the lie', to treat truth and falsehood as interchangeable, and to acknowledge that all our communications are to be judged as warnings issued by power. Orwell too noticed this, making the Ministry of Truth central to the government of his totalitarian dystopia. To displace truth by power is to rearrange the entire language through which people relate to each other. Hence there arises the idiom that Orwell called 'Newspeak', in which words are dropped or introduced according to the needs of the ruling power. Wagner had a premonition of this in the way in which words like 'love' and 'truth' appear on the lips of Alberich and Mime, as when Alberich exhorts Hagen to be true (meaning, to do Alberich's bidding) or Mime insists that Siegfried *must* love him (in other words, become his slave). The lust for domination saturates the designs, the consciousness, and the words of Nibelheim, removing the very idea of truth from the thoughts of those imprisoned there.

We might on one interpretation see the revolutions of the twentieth century – communist, fascist, national socialist – as beginning in resentment and perpetuating resentment as their moral core. And for this reason they regarded truth as their enemy, since through the pursuit of truth people express their freedom, the very same freedom that issues in trust between them and, if they are lucky, love. It was essential to the totalitarian governments of the twentieth century, and to communism in particular, that people should *not* trust each other, that society should be atomized by mutual suspicion. Without trust love too is jeopardized, and with the loss of truth the rule of resentment is perfected – now nothing can stand in its way. All this, I think, is contained in that last 'Treu' of Alberich, whispered on F, and negated at once by the G flat riding on its poisoned half-diminished harmony.

In the character of Alberich, then, Wagner tells us much about resentment. But there is an interesting question raised by his account of it, which is this: why is Wotan free from resentment, despite knowing that he must lose the power that he has gained to Siegfried, who must himself lose it in his turn? This brings us to one of the deepest themes of the *Ring* cycle, which is the theme that centres on Fichte's philosophy of self-realization and Hegel's dialectic of the master and the slave. In his long confession to Brünnhilde in Act 2 of *Die Walküre* Wotan reveals his dilemma in founding the race of the Volsungs: only a free being can release him from the curse placed on the Ring, only someone who is wholly *other* can fulfil the god's will. 'The other for whom I long, that other I never find: for the free one must create himself, while I create only subjects to myself.' Yet it is clear that precisely in creating Siegmund as the instrument of his will, by putting his will *into* Siegmund, he has created someone whom he can love, and who is not *merely* a subject of Wotan. Indeed he does love Siegmund, and grieves that he must now betray him.

It is inconceivable that Alberich should ever find himself in such a dilemma. He does not put his will *into* the other, so as to see the other as a free being like himself: he exerts his will *over* the other, whom he treats merely as a tool, as he treats Mime and Hagen. And in denying freedom in the other he denies it in himself: that is the source of his resentment. Wotan is attempting to *realize* himself through Siegmund, but has not yet understood that he can realize his own freedom only if he is recognized on equal terms by the other whom he seeks to use. Only when relations of domination have been entirely transcended, so that his will *confronts* him from the other, as a face in the mirror, will he have found the free being who will liberate him from his bondage. And he finds this opposing will, first in Brünnhilde, and then in Siegfried. Thus it is that Brünnhilde, whom both she and Wotan describe as Wotan's will, confronts and deflects Wotan's will, and at the same time elicits from him the reconciled and tender love that has no place in the world of Alberich. Wotan's frustration arises from willing the existence of the other whom he can love and respect as his own. Hence it causes not resentment but grief. What we experience in the music (and also in the beautiful words) of Wotan's farewell to Brünnhilde is the quietus that comes when the will is recognized by the one whom it recognizes, and is accepted by the one it accepts.

Here Wagner portrays the process that Fichte and Hegel had in mind when, in their dark ways, they argued that we achieve freedom only through confrontation with the other, and only when the other is finally recognized as an equal, with an autonomy and will of his own. To this Wagner adds the deep thought that the other will is what *I* will in the search for freedom, so it is in a sense my own will that confronts me, when love of the other is born. Thus it is that Wotan comes to see, at last, that his goal of perpetual sovereignty cannot be realized, that all relations must be continually renegotiated, and that the respect for freedom means the loss of control. And in that loss there is also gain, which is the love that he feels, first for Siegmund, and then for Brünnhilde, the love that only free beings can feel, and only when they acknowledge the freedom of the other. But love of that kind means mortality, and Wotan must die.

All hierarchies breed envy. The sight of judges in their robes, of bishops in their processions, of nobles around the throne and Gatsby in his swimming pool – such sights are daggers in the flesh of those who envy them. Envy, however, is not the same as resentment. The envious person wishes to possess what the other has. The resentful person wishes to destroy the other's possession, whether or not he can possess it himself. There are defences against envy – 'envy-avoiding stratagems' as Helmut Schoeck describes them[7] – through which we gain permission for our goods. Ceremonies, robes of office, anointings and titles; duties, public appearances, works of charity and humility – all have a part to play in making distinction legitimate in the eyes of those who do not possess it.

Against resentment, however, there is no such defence. The resentful person does not want to share your good fortune but to destroy it, whether or not there is any benefit to himself. He is locked in a kind of 'zero-sum' mentality, believing that the gains of the fortunate are losses to the rest. Every distinction, he believes, is paid for by someone who does not enjoy it, he himself being the principal victim. Until distinction is destroyed, therefore, the world is out of joint.

The Marxist theory of society is an extension of this zero-sum way of thinking, made explicit in the labour theory of value, which describes all profit in the hands of the capitalist as a loss to the one who works for him. It is fair to say that a similar thought was at the back of Wagner's mind in creating the mutual dependence of Wotan and Alberich. The dwarf pays the cost for the god's dominion, and his resentment feeds on the injustice. But Wagner digs deeper into the psyche than Marx, since he recognizes the extent to which Alberich's resentment precedes his loss. Alberich is already humiliated by a world that makes no place for him, and he sets out to remove the aura of the gods because they enjoy what he can never enjoy. Against that kind of resentment there is no defence.

But the dialectic of distinction and resentment is not merely to be witnessed in the political sphere. In each of us the incessant war exists, between our high ideals and our resentment at the cost of them. In the high summer of religion the ideals prevail, and we bear the sacrifices cheerfully. But as the star of religion declines so does the lust for desecration grow; and this, in brief, is the twilight – the inner twilight of the modern psyche – into which Wagner leads us.

There are several other characters, and a few important objects, whose symbolic significance needs to be grasped. Most important is Brünnhilde, who embodies an ideal of womanhood that is to a certain extent strange to modern audiences, and whose plausibility is missed by those who look solely to the text and not to the music. In *Tristan und Isolde* Wagner dramatizes the first look of love – the meeting of eyes in which lovers appear to each other as though haloed by their subjective life. That moment of falling in love, which is the central episode in all lyric treatments of the erotic, gives rise to the strange thought that this person before me is a visitor from another sphere, a being who comes to me as a destiny, like an angel. That emotion is extremely difficult to present in dramatic form – which is why the motif of the look in *Tristan* is so important, since it endeavours to present through music what cannot be said in words.[8]

In *The Ring*, however, Wagner dramatizes the first look of love in another way. Brünnhilde really *has* descended from a heavenly realm. And she has prepared herself as an offering precisely for this man, the one who finally awakens her. Brünnhilde is not an idealized woman, but an *ideal* woman. She is the incarnation of a femininity prepared in the realm of pure ideals – the realm that we ourselves create through our belief in it. She is what the woman transfigured in that first look of love *would* have been, if her prehistory corresponded exactly to her lover's fantasies.

Wagner's portrait is derived from moments of transition, in each of which some element of Brünnhilde's feminine sensibility is put to the test. She appears first as a wild but devoted daughter, able to elicit from her father confessions that his wife would never hear. She identifies herself as Wotan's will, and Wotan responds with the remark 'I talk only to myself when I talk to you', making it clear, however, that he can love only those beings through whom he has exerted his will, so as to love them as realizations of himself. It is thus that he loves Siegmund, whom he has willed to be free, and who therefore is not free but bound by Wotan's will. Brünnhilde, absorbing this paradox, finds the way to be both identical with Wotan's will, and also free from it – something that she can achieve by renouncing her godhead and entering the world of mortals, where it is not will but fate that determines what occurs.

We next encounter Brünnhilde at one of the great turning points of the cycle: her announcement of death to Siegmund. The music here, which develops out of the fate motif, accompanies a dialogue that arouses for the first time in Brünnhilde's soul the emotion that is fatal to her Valkyrie nature, the emotion of pity. It is not necessary for a Valkyrie to announce death to her quarry, rather than to snatch him mortally wounded from the field; evidently, however, Brünnhilde's interest has been fired by Wotan's confession, and she comes as her father's unacknowledged will, to study this hero who is also her half-brother, born of a mortal woman. The monumental half-cadence of the fate motif, expressing the implacable will of the gods, is prolonged into the announcement of death, which Siegmund shapes as a repeated interrogation, until the melody sweeps everything before it and Brünnhilde is overcome. Her compassion is god-like, more decision than suffering, and this lends plausibility to her subsequent life as a mortal woman, whose feminine emotions are the sheath around a blade of will, a blade capable of murder.

German intellectuals of Wagner's youth were profoundly affected by the controversial *Life of Jesus* by David Strauss (1835–6), in which the miracle stories of the gospels were described as myths, and the Christian religion placed on a par with its pagan competitors. Wagner shared the enthusiasm for Strauss's work, and regarded Jesus' attempt to found a religion of compassion, in defiance of the religion of law, as the real meaning of Christianity. His sketch for the drama *Jesus of Nazareth* (1848/9) is devoted to the clash between law and love, and he gives a central place to the gospel story of the woman taken in adultery. In the religion of Jesus, on Wagner's interpretation, we glimpse the divided will of God. The God of the law stands against the God of love, and defies his own edicts in the name of the son with whom he is identical. Whether or not the Christian doctrine of the Trinity can resolve this paradox, Wagner saw it as fundamental to the religious consciousness. The God who rules by law cannot bend the law for love's sake; but his law is empty unless renewed through love.

The paradox is dramatized in the great scene of Brünnhilde's trial and punishment. She has defied the god's command and entered the world of human suffering. And she speaks from that world to the god on behalf of his mortal creations. 'My counsel told me one thing,' she says, 'which was to love what you love.' In other words she points out that the conflict between what she did and what Wotan commanded was a conflict within Wotan himself, between the law-giving aspect of the godhead and the love-involving need that stems from it. True, Wotan's love for the Volsungs originates in a calculating project: but it is a project required by the upkeep of law. What Brünnhilde adds to the conflict is a new motive entirely, one hitherto unknown in the realm of the gods – compassion. The emotion begins in sympathy for her father. But already it is moving in a more human direction as she stands, troubled and alone after her father's confession, singing 'Weh, mein Wälsung!' – 'Woe, my Volsung!'.

And it is to compassion that Brünnhilde appeals in her vindication at the opera's end. The music of the final scene of *Die Walküre* conveys in an inimitable way the god-like tone of her beseeching, and when Brünnhilde produces in her father the transformation that she has already suffered, you hear it as both a free gift and a musical necessity. The adamantine god is softened at last, and in feeling compassion for his daughter he prepares the way for the mortal who is to replace him as her lord. (All this is contained in the treatment of motif 95, Brünnhilde's purity.)

Thus ends Brünnhilde's apprenticeship among the gods. From now on she is to represent the *Ewig-weibliche* in the realm of mortals. She is there sleeping on the heights in the first two acts of *Siegfried*, a kind of mystical absence during his growing up, an unconscious longing dormant within his orphaned loneliness. And then he awakens Brünnhilde, and awakens to her awakening. The Fichtean philosophy of freedom, self-determination and the *Entäusserung* – the making objective – of the self is again suggested by the narrative. But something else is at issue too, the theme that Wagner can fairly claim to have made his own and to have illuminated through music as it can be illuminated in no comparable way: the theme of erotic love as self-discovery.

This theme had been explored in the love between Siegmund and

Sieglinde in the first act of *Die Walküre*. But it acquires a new dimension in Act 3 of *Siegfried*, as Brünnhilde, awakening to her mortal state, reinterprets her previous life among the gods as no more than a prelude to her love for Siegfried. This love existed in that former life *in potentia*, outside the reach of her conscious self:

> O Siegfried, Siegfried! Conquering light!
> I have loved you always;
> For I alone divined Wotan's thought –
> The thought I never dared to name,
> That I could not think but merely felt,
> For which I fought and struggled,
> For which I defied him who conceived it,
> For which I paid penance in punishment
> Because I did not think it, merely felt it!
> For that thought – you can fathom it! –
> Was in my mind only love for you!

Contained within the paradox of divinity, as the solution to its contradictions, is love in its erotic, predestined and self-awakening form. *This* is how the sacred is bequeathed to us, and how we guard it through the death of our gods. Until her encounter with Siegfried, however, Brünnhilde is not aware that love is many things, or that erotic love is dangerous in the way that care, compassion, parental love and neighbour-love are not. This is something that she has to learn the hard way.

Wagner's view of erotic love coincides neither with traditional family-based morality nor with modern liberal openness. He saw sexual difference as fundamental, and the idealization of woman as a necessary prelude to any advances that would be worthy of a man. But marriage, children, family and the veil of respectability that maintains them were, for Wagner, inessential to the deal. What mattered, for him, was the encounter between man and woman, in which both come to experience the fatal dawning of an existential need: the need of one sex for the other, which has become *my* need for *you*.

Animals feel sexual urges, and may form lifelong partnerships in the manner of geese or wolves. But what raises humanity infinitely above the other species, and what opens erotic love to yearning, tenderness and tragedy, is the role of the 'I' in desire. From that first look of love to the union that completes it, lovers are I to I, seeing each other not simply as physical bodies, but as windows thrown open, so that soul meets soul. The object of erotic love is not the abstract man or woman, nor even the attractive instance: it is that thing we address as 'you' and know as 'I' – the individual self, which confronts the other from that strange horizon where no other can go. Wagner's *Tristan und Isolde* turns upon this familiar but extraordinary fact, and it is dramatized also in Brünnhilde's awakening, as she opens her eyes to the light and, after her great hymn to the Sun, turns her eyes to Siegfried, to ponder the fact, which has just dawned on her, that this is the man she has always loved, even though she never loved a man before.

The problem that Wagner confronts at this point of the drama, and not only at this point, is how to make Brünnhilde *credible* in her symbolic meaning. The brilliant artifice, whereby he has isolated Siegfried and Brünnhilde on a mountaintop, dramatized the moment of sexual awakening in both of them, and condensed into that first kiss an entire philosophy of sexual desire and its significance in the life of self-conscious beings, prompts the thought that these two characters are merely ciphers, cartoon representations of purely philosophical ideas. And if that is so, of course, the drama falls apart at the most important point in the cycle, the point when the world of mortals awakens to its own sacred character, and inherits the redemptive task of the gods.

At this point in the narrative the symbolism has indeed become precarious – not because it is obscure, simple or predictable, but because it risks voiding the two characters of their humanity. They meet on this mountaintop in the realm of pure ideas, as much Platonic universals as human particulars. And for those commentators who study only the words there is little else to the scene than the philosophy of love that inspires it. That is why the music is, at this point, supremely important, since it is the vehicle for Wagner's dramatic intention. Wagner seeks to show the transformation of Brünnhilde from warrior maiden to loving woman, and in doing so to reveal what consent really means in sexual relations.

The removal of Brünnhilde's breast plate, cut away by Siegfried's sword, has left her defenceless, and manifestly female, quarry for a warrior as warriors had once been quarry for her. Bodily shame overcomes her, and is gradually eclipsed by Siegfried's importuning, but not before she has tried to redirect his love towards himself.

In all that happens to Brünnhilde in her mortal state long processes are telescoped into rapid transitions, which are not rapid at all, because the music, which creates a time of its own, spreads them out in our feelings, and enables us to understand the slow steady emergence of the woman from the maiden, and the flesh from its shell. It is partly for this reason that Wagner imports into this scene such a wealth of new material, including the arresting melody of 'Ewig war ich, ewig bin ich' ('Eternal I was, eternal I am') (142), which moves in another time from the action on stage, cushioned by an adaptation of the sleeping Brünnhilde motif (99) in the bass. (See my remarks about this melody in Chapter 4.) The purpose of this music is to idealize the moment of surrender, to show that what is given by Brünnhilde in desire is her whole being, her 'immortality', made mortal in the moment of gift. Her passion is not a sweeping away of inhibitions by the power of physical desire; it is the gift of herself. And that is what true sexual passion aims at: the fusing of one self with another. Only if we understand this, on Wagner's view, do we grasp the transforming and redeeming nature of sexual fulfilment, and the specific kind of love that is expressed in it. And because of her apprenticeship, in her dream-life among gods, Brünnhilde's passion recoils at first from the existential change that it is about to produce in her.

Brünnhilde is therefore not an intellectualization of erotic love, but the symbol of a real and god-like form of it. As the music slowly brings her down from the cold heights where her divinity was nurtured to the warm place of mortal desire we come to understand that erotic love is not the thing for which Alberich once reached with hungry hands, only to be rejected. Rather it is the most complete expression of our human freedom – a condition in which two people unite in total self-giving. Other relations between adults contain an admixture of calculation and self-interest. This, however, is pure, and therefore involves the greatest happiness as well as the greatest risk. Brünnhilde comprehends and wills the happiness; but being a product of Valhalla, she discounts the risk. She therefore wills

Siegfried's independence, the more to enjoy the free gift of himself that he can, through his adventures, renew.

An important point is at issue here, and is symbolized in Brünnhilde's glorious launching of the post-coital Siegfried in the prologue to *Götterdämmerung*, which is that erotic love, in its true inter-personal form, does not belong in the world of contracts and deals. Its foundation is not a contract but a vow. Contracts have terms, and when the terms are fulfilled they are at an end. Vows do not have terms, and cannot be undone by any calculation. The unity created by them is, as Hegel put it (in his discussion of marriage), a 'substantial unity': not a unity of purpose or place or pleasure but a unity of being.[9] Lovers *dedicate* themselves to each other, and it is in part for this reason that they are so much at risk: to place a commission in another's hands is to risk something; to place yourself in another's hands is to risk everything.

It is this existential dependence that Wagner is putting before us in the love between Siegfried and Brünnhilde. And in her launching of Siegfried into the world of mortals – a world that she has yet to understand – Brünnhilde is exhibiting the sense of renewal that comes with real erotic love. She is no longer one person, but two, and has entrusted her being completely to the other. Siegfried confers on her a feeling of safety, comparable to the safety of the religious devotee in the hands of God. He will return with more gifts for her, but also with the unique and unchanging gift of himself. How can she not feel joy and fulfilment in the thought of this? All this is contained in Brünnhilde's gesture, as she catches sight of him on the horizon and, to a fragment of Freia's motif 22B, waves him on to destruction – a destruction that her abundance of love forbids her to foresee.

The world into which she exultantly sends her lover is not peopled by the free beings who live on mountaintops, among exalted ideals. It is composed of self-interested mortals, and planted in the heart of it is the worm of calculation, the disposition to treat everything, people included, as a means to power. Thus it is that, as Siegfried disembarks from the Rhine at the court of the Gibichungs, the curse motif sounds in the voice of Hagen, alerting us to the great transformation that can occur in a hero who enters the world of competitive passions armed only with his innocence.

Meanwhile Brünnhilde is presented with another moment of transition – the moment when the concerns of the gods, which once she shared, are revealed as meaningless by her mortal love. The new role of the Ring as a love-token has made it impossible for her either to perceive or to be interested in its cosmic powers. In the world of human love all value lies in the moment and not in the eternal scheme of things. And the innocent trust that makes the moment everything cleans the Ring of its curse, if only for that moment. The Ring is returned to its original condition as the gold of the Rhine. (We heard this anticipated in the orchestra when Siegfried emerged from Fafner's lair, toying with this mysterious object whose history was unknown to him, the orchestra reminding us of the joy and lament of the Rhine-daughters.) The dialogue with the distraught Waltraute illustrates the way in which Brünnhilde has put her *will* into her erotic feelings, not so as to forget her past, but so as to reshape it as a preparation for what she now is. Her dismissal of the gods is precisely what is most god-like in her, the thing that establishes the real continuity between the Valkyrie and the wife. In Brünnhilde we see the absolute harmony between emotion and will: what she feels is what she wills, and when her feelings are frustrated her will is frustrated too. Hence, in the terrible scene that follows, when she is overcome by a stranger, to be dragged like Sieglinde into the female cattle market, she sees this as Wotan's punishment. Her will now is for revenge, and when, on being presented at the court of the Gibichungs, she discovers Siegfried, the betrothed of another woman, her feelings of total desolation become focused in a will to destroy.

It is in this last transition, from the woman who has uttered her joyful hymn to 'laughing death', to the enslaved victim of rape and trafficking, that Brünnhilde assumes her real significance. She represents the fate of woman in a calculating world, the ideal cast down and trampled, the sacred object desecrated. And what makes this fate both logical and inevitable is precisely that she had given herself completely. Her desolation, like the joy that it replaces, is an *existential* condition: it is what she now is.

In the world that we know today sex is widely viewed as a commodity, and the act of love as a 'transaction' involving pleasure in the sexual parts – a matter of desire and satisfaction, rather than existential commitment. We find this view already in Freud's *Three Essays on Sexuality*, and shaped as orthodoxy in the writings of Alfred Kinsey. It is embodied in a certain kind of sex-education, which seeks to relieve young people of the burden of shame and guilt, and to open the path to pleasure. If this view of sex were correct then the outrage of rape would be impossible to explain. Rape would be just as bad as being spat upon: but hardly worse. The fact that, in almost all criminal codes, rape is next to murder in the hierarchy of offences, would be a mystery, a hangover from superstitions that humanity is on the way to discarding. And the trivializing of rape is what we find in a world where women are seen as instruments of pleasure, sexual 'objects' from which the subjective essence has been wiped away.[10]

Among the great artists none was more determined than Wagner to remind us of the truth in these matters: to remind us that rape is a crime of annihilation, on a par with murder; that consent in sex is not just a matter of saying 'yes' to a brief transaction, but an existential choice; that sexual fulfilment belongs to the realm of will and personality rather than the realm of appetite; that men are under an obligation to idealize and to protect the women whom they desire, and that shame – shame of the body – is the woman's primary form of protection and the deep expression of her will.[11] Those thoughts, dramatized in Act 1 of *Tristan und Isolde*, are essential to a full understanding of Brünnhilde's symbolic role. As I remarked above, she represents the feminine in its ideal form, the form that men outline in the object of love, in those first moments of need and gift, when the eyes of the future mother look from the unblemished face of the present girl. Through her will and personality Brünnhilde is able to display all that women have to suffer at the hands of men and, as her defences are cut away, she undergoes in her humiliation the spiritual equivalent of the death suffered by Siegmund. Betrayed in her very being she experiences the sense of pollution and worthlessness that haunts the victim of rape, and which explains why rape is not just a kind of theft but an act of annihilation.

In this way Brünnhilde's transition from bride to sex-slave represents, in telescoped form, the fall of woman – of every woman whose love has been given and abused. And, as with the other tragic events incorporated into the story of the Ring, this fall is not some accidental feature of the human condition, but a part of what we are. Just as it lies within a man's love to idealize the other, and to endow her with the attributes that prompt a complete self-giving, so too does it lie within the ways of calculation to move on, to substitute one love for another, to trample on what was once most sacred, and to leave its depleted remnant lying in the dust. This is the work of the Ring, in other words of the forswearing of love of which all of us are capable when power and self-interest require it. And because Brünnhilde's feelings are inseparable from her will, she experiences her annihilation at the hands of Gunther and Siegfried as a cancellation of all that she is. Her reaction is so great only because her being is so great. If it looks like over-reaction, it is because she is an *Übermensch*. Undeniably, however, Brünnhilde, who has been until this moment as credible an ideal woman as art provides, becomes in *Götterdämmerung* both strange and problematic. Is it enough to view her as in that way exonerated from the human norm? I address the question again in Chapter 8.

But there is one last transition, one that it is hardest to understand, since it is effected by music and not by words. At several points in the drama we learn of Brünnhilde's wisdom – the wisdom that comes from her mother, Erda, and which represents woman's rootedness in the cycle of life and her reality, conveyed in the music of Brünnhilde's slow awakening, as the womb of the future. This wisdom is intuitive, an acquaintance with the hidden principle of things, an ability to know without calculation, as a mother knows the feelings of her child. Having been complicit in Siegfried's murder, Brünnhilde in some way recuperates her love for the hero who awakened her, though exactly what she learned from the Rhine-daughters as she wandered by the banks of the river in the night is left unsaid in the drama. All we know is that her wisdom, eclipsed by the unbelievable fact of Siegfried's betrayal, has been restored to her, and what seemed like a betrayal and a rejection is now understood as the work of forces with which Siegfried, in his innocence and freedom, had nothing to do. She rides onto her husband's funeral pyre in affirmation of her love for him, willing not only her own death, but also the death of the gods. And the music persuasively presents her moment of suttee as of such cosmic significance that the gods themselves must perish as a result of it.

Ever since the famous correspondence with Röckel commentators have asked what is achieved at the end of *Götterdämmerung*. I shall address the question directly in Chapter 8. But it is surely clear that whatever is achieved – at the cosmic, the psychic, the political and the moral levels – there is no character that could manage it save Brünnhilde. Her unique combination of will, sympathy and suffering, her indomitable outrage in the face of rape and slavery, her single-minded focus on the other, whether in compassion, love or vengeance, all qualify her for the magnificent and god-like gesture with which she ends her life, reassuming her Valkyrie role without the incapacitating innocence with which she formerly exercised it.

My description of Brünnhilde naturally leads to the question of Siegfried, a character so manifestly conceived as a symbol that no other interpretation seems to make sense of him. But because Siegfried is, for that and many other reasons, such a problem, and indeed for some people an insuperable obstacle to any sympathetic approach to Wagner's drama, I postpone my account of him to Chapter 8. Here I conclude my survey of the symbolism of Wagner's characters with a brief account of Mime, a glance at the Volsung twins and a survey of the demi-gods and nature gods who belong to the primordial flux that Wotan subdued to the rule of law.

Mime is one of Wagner's most masterly creations, a character who perfectly fills his dramatic role, without losing any of his universal significance as a fake. He might have been invented by Dickens or Hugo, so completely does he fill his narrow world with the idioms and obsessions that define him. Unlike his brother, Alberich, who is portrayed as wandering on the fringe of the social world, with no real ties of his own, Mime has raised a companion. And his hope is to dupe this companion into doing what he cannot do, since cowardice and the curse both prevent it. Through Siegfried Mime plans to seize the Ring from Fafner and to wield it as his brother once had wielded it, so as to subdue the race of Nibelungs and to gain power over the world. But this simple and self-interested motive is used in a striking way by Wagner, to dramatize the relation between Nibelheim and the human world. Mime has no free being to assist him: but only a free being can perform the needed task. He is therefore trapped in a strategy of pretence.

Resentment shows itself in the world of human relations in many ways. But one way – the way of manipulation – has a peculiar pervasiveness, which may make it hard to diagnose. In order to use each other for our purposes we cultivate disguises – fake emotions, fake benevolence, even fake personality.

Anyone can lie. It suffices to say something with the intention to deceive. Faking, however, is an achievement. To fake things you have to take people in, yourself included. The liar can pretend to be shocked when his lies are exposed: but his pretence is part of the lie. The fake really *is* shocked when he is exposed, since he had created around himself a world of pretence, in which he himself is included.

In all ages people have lied in order to escape the consequences of their actions. But faking is a cultural phenomenon, more prominent in some periods than in others. Wagner was acutely aware of the way in which true art – art that strives to show the human condition as it is, and to *earn* its redemptive meaning – was being increasingly shadowed by fake art. Sentimentality, cliché, the sugar coating of kitsch around a moral emptiness were becoming familiar to the audiences of his day as they are overwhelmingly familiar to us. And in the character of Mime Wagner provided a symbol of the emotional fake, the person whose unctuous declarations of love and kindness are fuelled by selfish calculation and by resentment at the sight of the virtue that he pretends to love but yearns to annihilate.

Mime's story is an interesting one. When Loge and Wotan visit Nibelheim, he recounts to them how he had once known happiness and freedom, in the days when the Nibelungs, as 'carefree smiths . . . created ornaments for our women, wondrous trinkets, dainty trifles . . . and lightly laughed as we worked'. Wagner does not show this original condition of 'unalienated labour', as Marx would describe it. Instead he presents the transformation brought into Nibelheim by Alberich's Ring, after which all the Nibelungs, Mime included, are enslaved both physically and mentally. They lead the joyless life represented in the motif of the anvils, a life of means without meaning, and always at the back of their minds is the yearning for the love that they have lost, a yearning expressed in the 'suffering love' theme (22B, reshaped as 34A and 34B) that sounds desolately through the percussive rhythm of the factory.

Mime, however, has the intelligence to see an escape route, which is the route of pretence. It is he who crafts the Tarnhelm, the magic covering that enables the wearer to assume any form he wishes. True, he lacks the knowledge required to activate the helmet; but this is surely because he has not made Alberich's journey into the heart of lovelessness, the darkness in his soul being but the reflection of the radiant darkness in his brother's. Escaping nevertheless, when Alberich loses the Ring to Wotan, Mime brings with him into the forest the altered consciousness of the Nibelungs. Truth has been replaced by power as his moral standard, and this is conveyed, first, by the 9/8 smithing theme, the rhythm of which obsessively recurs in the background and, second, by the fake personality that Mime has built for Siegfried's benefit. This fake personality is expressed in Mime's wheedling words; but more completely and revealingly in the waltz-like refrain (107), derived from the smithing theme, with a childish lilt and a relentless repetitiveness that perfectly capture the imprisoned soul of Mime, as he pads around the circle of his pretence, never quite able to take himself in.

Siegfried, who is without guile, does not dismiss Mime's protestations of love as pretences. Instead he is repelled by them. Such is the natural response of the free spirit (the one who 'lives in truth') to the fakes, frauds and sentimentalists among whom he is forced to live. Mime, who weighs all emotions in the scale of calculation, acts as though love can be commanded – 'so mußt du ihn [Mime] lieben!' ('so you must love him [Mime]') – while being unable to express love except in the unctuous phrases of his lilting refrain. These phrases cause the 'yuk!' reaction in Siegfried, as when, outside Fafner's lair, Mime lapses into waltz time to say that Siegfried will remember how Mime loves him; to which Siegfried starts away in rapid 2/2 time, with the words 'Du sollst mich nicht lieben!' – 'You shall not love me!' As Philip Kitcher has put it, Siegfried has an innate sense of honour, which causes him to feel contaminated by the degraded specimen with whom he lives.[12] It is precisely this sense of honour, Kitcher suggests, that leads to Siegfried's downfall – a point to which I return in Chapter 8.

All this is explicitly conveyed in the first two acts of *Siegfried*. But in the music there is something deeper too. Mime's refrain, in which we hear the ceaseless echo of the factory but which also obsessively harps on the theme of love, tells us something important. Real love is difficult, risky and a product of the whole self; fake love is easy and runs through ready-made channels. In this case pretence opens a door into the world of addiction. Kitsch and sentimentality are not only habit forming; they replace real emotions with easy (and therefore valueless) substitutes. They are the buttons which the addict can press in order to be instantly rewarded; hence they drive out the difficult feelings that they imitate. They belong in the world of exchange, the world of substitutes, and are therefore intimately bound up with the original renunciation of love from which the pursuit of dominion began.

Wagner is telling us, therefore, that Mime's fake emotion expresses the same lust for power and the same spirit of calculation that were the ruling principles in Nibelheim. The lie has entered his soul. It is only later, when he has tasted the dragon's blood, that Siegfried fully understands this. Being in touch now with nature he can recognize fake love, even if he has yet to experience the real thing.

Not all Mime's feelings are fakes, of course. His fear is real fear, and in the passage where he tries to teach fear to Siegfried we sense the extent to which, in the world of pure power that has shaped the soul of Mime, fear is an indispensable instrument. Nibelheim is kept in being by fear, the ubiquitous fear of the police state, in which the individual moves unshielded but observed. Mime's fear is part of a general wariness, a sense of being surrounded on all sides by trapdoors through which he might fall to his destruction. This is brought out in the striking encounter between Mime and the Wanderer in *Siegfried* Act 1, Scene 2.

There are those who object to this scene: like that of the Norns in the prelude to *Götterdämmerung*, it seems to be repeating material already fully absorbed by the attentive listener, as though the Wanderer were quizzing the dwarf in order to see whether he had been asleep during the first two parts of the tetralogy. There are three replies to this. The first, and most obvious, is that in these scenes, and in the prelude to Act 3 of *Siegfried*, Wagner is standing back from the drama, helping us to feel its impact as myth, and to glimpse the primordial meaning of the events that we are witnessing. It is as though we see into another dimension, in which this story, which is the story of the world, is repeated forever.

The second, and related, reply has been well formulated by the French philosopher Alain Badiou. Much of the cycle, Badiou points out, consists in some character retelling the story, so as to make it *his own* story. This Fricka and Wotan do in *Die Walküre* Act 2; Mime, Alberich, Brünnhilde and the dying Fafner in *Siegfried*; the Norns and Waltraute in *Götterdämmerung*. Each character's 'subjective position can only be clarified by his running through the telling of the story, and each of these accounts is a unique one that illuminates the story from a new subjective point of view'.[13] To put it another way, the archetypal nature of the story means that in a certain sense it *precedes* the characters who compose it. They are as though awoken to their own nature by the discovery that they fit the contours of the narrative, that this chain of events of which they had unconscious foreknowledge is in fact the story of their life, since it is the story of the world that includes them. The repetitions are therefore of the essence of Wagner's story, a successive winding in of the various spheres of being into the single narrative – the myth – that comprehends them all. Each revisiting of the events also changes them, adds to their comprehensiveness and their inescapability, so as to make entirely plausible the developing sense that Wotan's end is the end of everything.

But, in the case of the encounter between Mime and the Wanderer, there is a third reply that is of greater significance. In this scene Wagner makes use of a favourite device of the Eddas, in which one party triumphs over the other by revealing his rival's ignorance of some crucial matter that he needs to know. In the world of the Old Norse hero knowledge did not come in the form of a scientific hypothesis, but as the key to a mystery. The person with knowledge did not have a superior store of facts: he had a superior range of *experience*, an acquaintance with people, places, things and powers whose workings he understood at first hand. By displaying this knowledge in a contest, he warned the other party that his acquaintance with the world gave him the advantage, and that the other had better withdraw. Thus in *Vafthrudnir's Sayings*, in which Odin tests his wisdom against the Giant Vafthrudnir, the questions take a *cosmic* form – from whence came the earth, the moon, the sun, day and night, winter and summer? – and the answers involve the *naming* of things – 'Wind-cool is he called, winter's father' – showing familiarity with their inner nature.

Mime's questions to the Wanderer are likewise cosmic questions, designed to show that the dwarf is acquainted with places and powers that others may conjure, but which he knows from inside, by the kind of cunning that has come to him through his abilities as a smith – abilities displayed in his supernatural achievement in forging the Tarnhelm. By testing the Wanderer's knowledge of the cosmic order he hopes to claim superior acquaintance with it, but soon discovers that the Wanderer knows the whole scheme of things intimately, revealing in his serene description of the gods that he belongs at the very top of it.

The Wanderer's questions to the dwarf are cosmic only in the sense that they concern the transfer of the divine will to the realm of humans. Mime knows of Wotan's ambitions for the Volsungs since, in his own way, he shares them – though he hopes to achieve through manipulation what Wotan has come to see can only be achieved through renunciation. It is precisely because he treats Siegfried as an instrument to be exploited, rather than a free being, that Mime has lost sight of the crucial fact – which is that only a free being, acting for himself, could hope to overcome Fafner. And only such a being could forge the sword, the symbol of the innocent will, which escapes the curse of the Ring. In other words, the Wanderer's third question to Mime goes to the heart of what Mime is – the smith who has sought to make a free being into his own tool, and therefore lost his only virtue, which is the ability to make tools of his own. Even in his smithing he is 'faking it', and this Siegfried later perceives when he brushes away the solder that Mime has prepared for him, and gets to work on reducing the sword to a heap of filings so as to forge it completely anew. The sword can be forged only by the unalienated labour of Siegfried, and not by the labour of a being who has no real conception of the self-creating act. This fatal flaw in Mime's character was already displayed in his original enslavement: he could forge the Tarnhelm, but could not use it as an expression of his freedom, so that Alberich had no difficulty in taking it from him and making it part of his, Alberich's, *Eigen*.

Two further points need to be made about the wisdom contest. Kitcher and Schacht observe that, through his questions to the dwarf, the Wanderer plants in the scheme of things the information and the motivation that will lead to Siegfried's forging of the sword, but without in any way helping Siegfried to this goal. In other words, the wisdom contest provides Wotan with the means to accomplish his will *for* Siegfried while at the same time withdrawing his will *from* Siegfried. He does not make the mistake that he had made when he planted the sword in the ash tree, in anticipation of Siegmund's need for it. He ensures that the dwarf, in his confusion, will point Siegfried in the right direction. This is an astute observation, which casts light on everything that subsequently happens.

We should also be aware of the role of knowledge in the kind of situation that Wagner is describing. In his great study of envy, Helmut Schoeck assembles a weight of anthropological evidence for the view that, in the conditions of tribal life, useful knowledge is rarely seen as a communal possession. It is a personal acquisition of the individual, to be held close to the breast like a trump card, and played carefully in the game of life. To be known as possessing some store of knowledge is to run the danger – the primary social danger – of envy. In these circumstances the social function of knowledge is less that of contributing to the shared needs of the tribe than that of jostling for power. And the one with knowledge must hide it, lest he provoke envy in his fellows. Likewise Mime's hiding in the forest with his store of enviable skills is a symbol of the fate of useful knowledge, in a world governed by resentment.

The German word for envy – *Der Neid*, which is the title of Schoeck's book – is of wider application than our 'envy', and covers all those feelings of bitterness that are prompted by the knowledge of others' superior virtue, possessions or success. As is clear in the characters of Alberich and Mime, these feelings are a central preoccupation of the *Ring* cycle, and have their own symbol in the dragon Fafner, whose lair bears the name *Neidhöhle* – the cave of envy. Possessions and powers are brought into being by knowledge and skill; but knowledge and skill prompt envy in those who do not possess them. Those who spend generously, who freely display and share their possessions, also risk the envy of those whom they benefit. Possessions and powers are a danger zone, and the safest way forward, for those without creative gifts, is to hoard these things, to hide them from the world and to be ready to fight all those who covet them.

The Giants have strength with which to move and pile the stones that made Valhalla. But they do not have the knowledge that the Nibelungs possess – the knowledge with which to extract the elements from beneath the earth and to forge them into tools. In other words, the Giants have strength without technology, and that is why they fear the Nibelungs and wish to possess the hoard, thinking that this way they will get level with Alberich, by acquiring his technological skills. But skills are not acquired by seizing their product. Having killed his brother for the sake of the hoard, Fafner can do nothing with his acquisition save sit on it: and in this he symbolizes the destiny of property and worldly power in the hands of the uncreative. That which might have been used for the common good is hoarded in a spirit of envy. Resentment freezes the knowledge and the skill that it needs for its own cure. Fafner's transformation to a dragon is the sign of this: the hoard on which he sits represents others' knowledge, others' labour and others' plans. His strength as a Giant is devoted now to the one task of guarding the accumulated power of the Nibelungs, and preventing its use. And, the symbolism implies, just such an accumulation of hoarded power and knowledge lies in the path of every hero, who must free himself of the dead weight of envy that it represents, finding – through the voice of nature that speaks to him in the moment of challenge – the original creative principle. But that creative principle bears a curse that will be activated just as soon as creativity is put to a manipulative use.

The wisdom contest between Mime and the Wanderer serves yet a fur·ther purpose in the drama, which is to emphasize the *temporal* nature of the gods. The world precedes Wotan's government and endures beyond his death. Ancient principles and demi-gods operate in the background, reminding us that the order that Wotan extracts from the *prima materia* of the cosmos lasts only so long as he can maintain it.

Wagner expresses the eternal complexion of the world through an evocative set of symbols. Three of the four primal elements are directly represented: water, by the Rhine-daughters, earth by Erda, fire by Loge. The fourth element, air, is also represented, both in the kingdom of the gods (the 'sky-gods' as they figure in the Icelandic theology) and in the wood-bird. The bird speaks with a kind of primal clarity of things that do not concern her, like the air we breathe, and her pentatonic melody picks up the lullaby of the Rhine-daughters, reminding us that she, like them, personifies the element in which she swims.

The activities that transform the Ur-stuff of the cosmos are also symbolized, in the Ring that turns nature into an instrument, in the sword that turns the raw human being into the free person, and in the spear stripped from the World Ash Tree, which turns fate into law, but which also causes nature to wither and the pool of her wisdom to dry. The Tarnhelm represents a primal force as ubiquitous as any element, the force of *Verwandlung*, or 'Mutabilitie' – the mysterious ability to assume disguises, to change shape, to undergo metamorphosis from one mode of being to another.[14] To control this force is a primordial ambition of humanity and the original aim of the alchemists, for whom the 'lead to gold' transition symbolized every way of seizing control of the natural order. This was the way to outwit the gods, the way in which mortals could rival the immortals and avoid all penalties for their crimes. But the Tarnhelm is also of a piece with the Ring: it makes everything not just changeable but exchangeable. Those who wear it slip out of the overriding human obligation, which is the obligation of the free being to be true to himself, to uphold oaths and commitments, and to regard himself and others equally as ends in themselves.

If you study this collection of symbolic objects long enough – Ring, sword, spear, Tarnhelm – you will see that they comprehend all the ways in which we bend nature to our purposes, and impose conscious planning on the mute ways of fate. Like other magic objects, they are not really objects, since they have a subjective identity of their own. Their individuality mimics that of persons: although broken, the sword is not 'pieces of Nothung', but 'Nothung waiting to be reforged'. The fragments must be filed to powder, so that the oneness and agency of the sword can repossess it. Unlike the hoard that it is used to create, the Ring cannot be divided; hence Fasolt and Fafner are doomed to quarrel over its possession. Magic objects are the signs of the ways in which our deepest needs and longings are imprinted on the world, and hence, like us, they have a soul.

A note needs to be added here, concerning another aspect of the Tarnhelm, since it connects with ideas about economic value, to which I return in Chapter 7. One of the most poetical ideas in Marx's writings on political economy is the claim that, under capitalism, the product of labour eludes the labourer's understanding. The product remains mysterious to the one who fashions it, since he cannot turn this expression of his labour into an item of exchange. Only the owner of the means of production understands the networks that endow the product with its real economic life – its life as an object of exchange. Until seized by the capitalist, therefore, the product remains inert and mysterious. There is a premonition of this idea in the story of the Tarnhelm. Mime, who has the skill and intelligence to forge the helmet, does not know the spell that will activate it. This product of Mime's labour is as much his *Eigen* as the Ring is the *Eigen* of Alberich. But it is a mystery to him. And when Alberich seizes it, and utters the spell that activates its power, it is as though Mime suffers the very same violation of his being that Alberich will shortly undergo from Wotan, when the god lays hold of the Ring.

There are two beings in the cycle whom *Verwandlung* never touches, who are true to each other and themselves throughout their short presence at the centre of the drama, and whose fate is scarcely more bearable than the fate of Shakespeare's Cordelia: the Volsung twins. Unlike the gods and goblins in whose web they are caught, Siegmund and Sieglinde are not tricks of the theological imagination but real beings, whose symbolic significance is that they have no symbolic significance. They are what they are, and what they are is what we should be. Their response to each other expresses the supreme value of life lived for the other's sake. Self-idealization and self-pity are both remote from them, and the possibility of being like them is conveyed by music that proceeds with grammatical inevitability from the first glance of interest to the consummation of love, without the slightest false sentiment. It is precisely these two pure beings, sacrificed for the law, whom the law should be protecting. Yet their being on the wrong side of the law is, paradoxically, the source of their moral grandeur. The last music of the cycle is Sieglinde's, and it takes us back across all the tragic events that have finally ended the reign of the gods, to the moment when this woman showed just why it is that, if there is meaning in the world, it is human beings and not gods who provide it.

Foremost among the demi-gods is Loge, inspired by the Icelandic Lokke or Loki, whose attitude to the gods is conveyed in *Loki's Flyting*, one of the most striking poems in the Poetic Edda. The Prose Edda describes him as 'the first father of falsehood', one who 'has artifices for all occasions; he would ever bring the Aesir [the gods] into great hardships, and then get them out with crafty counsel'.[15] Wagner's faultless characterization provides some of the most important 'binding' music of the cycle – music that ties scenes, paragraphs and motifs together without altering their essential character. While he appears in personified form only in *Das Rheingold*, Loge is a musical presence throughout the cycle. Like Loki, he is a companion of the gods who is also independent of them, prepared to cooperate on terms, but seeing through their divine pretensions. The Eddas hint at a connection between Loki and fire, and Wagner develops this idea: Loge is both fire, as a primal element, and also the mercurial ways of reason. Hence he is bound by no contract to Wotan. Wotan's taming of Loge was an essential move in his assumption of power, since Loge dances at the point of the spear, burning away the runes that have been inscribed there. In just this way our obligations and agreements lapse in time, through the work of legal adjustment and forgetfulness. If they did not do so, then they would accumulate forever and the burden of them would be too great to bear. But although tamed by Wotan, Loge is destined to survive him, and is already, at the end of *Das Rheingold*, meditating the possibility of life beyond the gods.

Cooke suggests that Loge represents the cunning of reason, the ability of the rational being to find a way out of any impasse that has a discoverable exit, and there is truth in this. But it is not the whole truth. The gods come into being in response to human need, and it is we who breathe life into them. But we know that the demands that we make of them are contradictory: they must uphold the law and also evade it; they must love their worshippers and also sacrifice them for their own survival. They depend on other forces than their own will but it is by their will that these other forces exist. Fire, which consumes everything, enables the gods to cover their tracks, to anni-hilate their mistakes and to start afresh in response to all our urgent prayers to them. It is a remedy for insoluble problems, since it gets rid of them without attempting to solve them. But in this way fire will also get rid of the gods. Just as ingenious reasoning led us to invent the gods, so will it lead us to lose faith in them. The same reasoning that gives birth to Wotan will therefore destroy him; and it will do so as soon as the spear loses its power – in other words, as soon as the task of maintaining moral order is bequeathed from god to man.

One other aspect of Wagner's symbolism deserves discussion at this stage, and that is the theme of fate. The leitmotif that is usually described as the fate motif accompanies the supremely solemn moment of Brünnhilde's appearance to Siegmund, when she decides – already giving way to temptation – to announce his death to him. After this the motif assumes a growing importance in the music, being elaborated into the *Todesverkündigung*, and then used to articulate a variety of cadences by way of pointing the music always towards a distant resolution that it does not provide. This musical device introduces an important idea. We human beings understand fate as necessity. The gods understand it as will. But this will is also necessity – necessity become conscious of itself. While this conscious-ness resides in the gods it remains opaque to us: we do not fully grasp it, because we do not grasp it as *ours*. But once we do so grasp it, once we understand that we ourselves are the authors of our fate, we are released from the bondage of it, and the eternal order is at an end. What happens to us now depends upon our own will, and not on the will of the gods.

That vision of fate is brought before us in the scene between Sieg-mund and Brünnhilde, in which human need briefly moves the gods to pity, but only in order to affirm more violently the pitiless decrees from on high. It is brought before us in the prelude to *Siegfried* Act 3, when Erda, who represents an older idea of fate, the idea of a neces-sary order of the universe in which will and consciousness have no place, is confronted by the new idea of fate as the will of the gods – necessity become conscious of itself, so as to appear under the aspect of freedom. And it is brought before us in the prologue to Act 1 of *Götterdämmerung*, in which the Norns are found spinning the rope of fate, as suggested in the Eddas. This scene – again often criticized as a redundancy – is one of the most poetic of Wagner's invocations of the world before the gods. It goes back over the events presented in the previous two operas, but showing them in another light, not as willed by the gods or as suffered by the mortals, but as woven by the fates. We sense that Wotan's rule of law changed nothing in the deeper scheme of things, since it was merely an appropriation of necessity and not an escape from it. The strands of the rope, unwoven, do not tear. It is their weaving together that causes the catastrophe. The Norns do not prophesy the result, but read it from the rope that emerges from their weaving. Hence their growing astonishment that these elements, which before had combined so easily under the law of nature, should begin to chafe against each other.

Only with the forging of the Ring and the god's consequent need for the free and self-made individual is the rope of necessity broken. And the return of the Norns to the primeval mother represents the recoiling of the world from human aims and ambitions, as we free beings emerge alone and full of wonder on the heights. From this point nothing is available to us, save the tragic descent, and whatever we can earn by way of love on the way to our destruction. Fate has been stolen from the Norns, and we ourselves now weave it. But only at the end, with 'Ruhe, ruhe, du Gott!', does the motif of fate resolve.

To understand that final resolution we need to explore some of the philosophical themes that underlie the drama, and also some of the problems posed by the attempt to express them. As we shall see, *The Ring* is not only a work of philosophy, but one that uses music to cast a unique light on the human condition.

7

Love and Power

Wagner's characters are symbols for us largely because they are so much more real, more humanly concrete and more engaging than any mere symbol could be. Yet their story is clearly intended as the story of the world, with all the devices familiar from the creation myths of antiquity, which speak in gnomic terms of huge events and conflicts, glimpsed in the mists of time. Wotan's spear and the missing eye that paid for it point to one such event. Erda and the Norns suggest a primeval order that precedes that of the gods, and no one will ever know quite why the father of the Rhine-daughters entrusted the gold to their keeping instead of looking after it himself. Some commentators find all this absurd – that there should be loose threads of the narrative that cannot be ravelled up. But it is not absurd at all. On the contrary, it is the only way to reconcile a creation myth with the reality that it is supposed to explain. These loose threads can be found in Genesis, in the stories of Zeus, Chronos and Uranus, and in the Vedas. They are what authenticate the creation myth, by setting the past beyond comprehension, except as a projection backwards of things understood now: turtles all the way down. What the myth displays as primeval, occurring before the outset of the human story, is always present, constantly repeated in our fruitless endeavour to cancel the debt of history and begin again.

This thought should be borne in mind as we review some of the philosophical conceptions that are put in play by Wagner's drama, and which lie like archaeological layers beneath the luminous dramatic surface. These conceptions include many that were prominent in the intellectual life of Wagner's Germany: individuality and freedom; law and legitimacy; power and resentment; redemption and the sacred; love and economic value. They are connected in Wagner's drama in an inspired and illuminating way – not as parts of an intellectual argument, but as a vision of life and what matters.

The prelude to *Das Rheingold* evokes a primeval world, lying outside time and change, the Ur-matter of existence, which has yet to be shaped by will. It is the musical equivalent of the 'state of nature', which does not precede history but lies, as it were, beneath it, the unseen depth of an innocence forever lost, because never truly possessed. This world beyond history is filled with currents and eddies which might at any moment break through the mould of changelessness and shape themselves as will. We hear this happening: beneath the unbroken surface of the E flat major triad the horns move in counterpoint, each entering some space as another leaves it. To the undiscerning ear, all is changeless and still, a single chord, spread out over musical space, held constant in root position. But voice-leading and instrumentation ensure that the unisons in this chord are not real unisons; they are points where musical movements coincide, as they hurry on to distant destinations. Beneath its superficial calm the music is beginning to wrestle and break free. Of its own accord the triad becomes animated, until finally bursting forth in an A flat major arpeggio, and incarnating itself as a voice.

In what follows we witness a collision between the serene flow of nature and the agitated demands of the will. Beings with will seek to improve and rearrange things; they wish to turn the flow in their own direction. They seek love and consolation, power and dominion, order and law, and as a means to these ends they need goods for use and exchange. Economic life endows those goods with value and distributes them in payment for our labour. But the process of production is governed by forces that we do not understand and which buffet us like winds from some hidden underworld. These forces were a major topic of wonder and exploration during the century that preceded Wagner's intellectual awakening. 'Political economy' therefore grew as a branch of speculative philosophy, and some aspects of this study are reflected in *Das Rheingold*.

Adam Smith had remarked on a strange paradox – namely, that those things which have greatest value in use, such as air and water, tend to have little or no value in exchange, and this not because they are necessarily abundant or always easy to obtain.[1] Conversely, things with great exchange-value – such as gold and gems – tend to have little or no value in use. And money is the supreme instance of this paradox: it is an object *all* of whose value is concentrated in its power of exchange, and which has no other use whatsoever. In the modern cyber-economy this is made additionally clear, since money is no longer a physical object: it is a ring forged in cyberspace, a closed circle whose raw material is information.

Ricardo and Marx tried to explain the paradox in terms of the labour theory of value, arguing that gold and gems are precious because of the 'socially necessary labour' deployed in their extraction. However, the true explanation has to do neither with labour nor with scarcity, but with the innate structure of desire. For those things that satisfy a natural and recurring need our desire is quickly satisfied; beyond a certain quantity we are surfeited. Such things have a rapidly diminishing 'marginal utility' – water and air being obvious instances. As for money, however, its very volatility, its ability to transform itself into any shape, so as to gratify now this desire and now another, means that its marginal utility hardly diminishes as its quantity grows. And precisely for this reason does it exert its psychological power: the means to all ends, whose hold is endless. Money is the primary instrument of *Verwandlung*, and the thing that we are most disposed to accumulate and hoard.

The prelude to *Rheingold* shows two primal elements, water, and through that water the air (light), which, descending to its depths, is in due course to shine on the gold of the Rhine. The prelude continues to the point of saturation and beyond, so as restlessly to turn away from the surfeit. It is the expression in music of the dwindling marginal utility that pertains to our natural elements, and to the natural use we make of them. In contrast, and expressly singled out as an object of value, is the gold of the Rhine, the shining, glorious thing that has no use but itself, the symbol of all preciousness that would never be exchanged by its foolish guardians. In the falling whole tone over dominant ninth harmony we hear the act of joyful worship – 'Rheingold, reines Gold' – that is the primordial gift of religion, religion in its natural, light-worshipping, sun-blessed, life-endorsing form (14). And the slow, steady poisoning of this motif, as whole-tone turns to semitone and the pure tonal cadence to a pinched chromatic knot, contains the story of *The Ring* (164). From this thing of little use can be forged the Ring, the talisman that remakes value as price, turns praise to resentment and reduces relations of love to relations of power.

The gold of the Rhine therefore possesses two kinds of value, and the passage from one to the other is part of the primordial transformation that we witness at the beginning of *Das Rheingold*. The gold has the value of treasure – of things that are rare, beautiful and enthralling, and which mimic the glory of the sun and the stars. But forged into a ring the gold turns the order of nature towards production, accumulation and exchange, towards the world of the hoard, which is the symbol throughout the cycle of material wealth and the psychological enslavement of those who covet it.

The labour theory of value arose from a philosophical argument of Locke's, concerning the right of property. What, Locke asked, entitles a person to lay claim to a thing as his own?[2] Suppose he takes some unowned stuff and shapes it, as when building a table from the wood of a fallen tree. In doing so he 'mixes his labour' with the wood, and since he has a natural right to his body and its powers, he has an equivalent right to his labour, and therefore to the thing with which he has mixed it. To take the table from him without his consent would be tantamount to slavery, extracting labour without payment.

That argument resurges in transmuted and qualified form in Hegel's defence of private property and Marx's attack on it. For Hegel, property is an objectification (*Entäusserung*) of the will, a realization of freedom in the world of objects. For Marx, property is an 'alienation' (*Entfremdung*) of the will, an eclipse of the subject by the object.[3] Both those competing conceptions are subliminally present in *Das Rheingold*. By forging the Ring Alberich puts his labour, indeed his very being, into this thing that he justly describes as 'my own', 'mein Eigen' (though Wotan promptly challenges him with the shallow legalism that Alberich stole the gold, and therefore cannot own the thing he made from it). The German expression captures the existential nature of Alberich's bond with the Ring. He has *put himself into* this object, which is the expression of his very self. And by cursing the Ring he endows it with his malignant will. The gold of the Rhine thereby acquires value of a third and more potent kind. It is the *Eigen* of Alberich, the distillation of the power that he forged and of the resentment caused by its loss. It is a fetish, alive with the ambitions and yearnings of those who covet it, and thus a symbol of the alienation that comes into the world, according to Marx and the Young Hegelians, through the rule of private property.[4] To put it another way: Alberich's forging of the Ring is the expression of alienated labour, since it springs from the desire for power over others. By contrast, Siegfried's forging of the sword is the realization of freedom, since it springs from the desire to empower the self, rather than to enslave the other.

In the gold of the Rhine, therefore, is encapsulated a vision of economic value in its many forms. There is the pure value of treasure, which in the world of lost innocence shone in the depths of the soul, and which cannot be exchanged, since it has no equivalent in currency. There is the value of money, which permits exchange, substitution and accumulation, and is symbolized by the ever-growing hoard. And there is the value of labour, the *Eigen* of the one who produces, who realizes himself through his work, and who thereby creates a right of ownership. Economic value, so conceived, is both essential to the realization of our freedom, and also a subliminal threat to it.

The forging of the Ring harnesses the latent power of nature, and turns it towards a world imbued by will – a world of rights and claims. But there is a risk attached, namely the loss of the non-economic value that gives meaning to our lives. This non-economic value is what Alberich renounces, when, to the motif of existential choice (17), he utters his curse against love. For love is what happens when people give themselves freely, when I surrenders to I, and when the subject shines forth as the treasure once shone in the depths. This sublime moment, in which the lost beauty of nature returns as self-conscious joy, is what Wagner sets out to portray in the awakening of Brünnhilde to Siegfried. It is also, as the drama shows, a moment fraught with illusion.

The gold of the Rhine appears to Alberich at the very moment when his attempts to obtain love have been frustrated; and it appears as a substitute for love, which can be seized only if love is forsworn. Until seized, however, the gold is merely another aspect of the natural order – it is the treasure that glitters in the primeval world, and which those who play in that world would never think of capturing or owning. They are guarding it only as nature guards her resources, without concern for rational plans. In an important sense the Rhine-daughters are incapable of giving the love that Alberich seeks – for they live in a world that precedes individual existence (a fact symbolized in their triplication).[5] In the world of the Rhine-daughters fatal attachments do not occur, and the free giving of one individual to another has no place. Love, in its higher, personal form, also awaits the theft of the gold. Personal love comes into being because somewhere, in the depth of things, this very love has been renounced.

Thus it is that Alberich, in forging the Ring, creates the only thing that can be given as the price of love: the thing that was obtained by forswearing love. For Alberich, there is no going back on his fatal rejection of love, and henceforth his soul, his identity and his world will all be loveless. Wotan's realm of legal order, we soon discover, is, or becomes, dependent on Alberich's renunciation. The Giants, Fasolt and Fafner, had agreed to build Valhalla only if they could receive Freia, goddess of love and youth, in exchange. To escape the bargain Wotan must find a substitute for Freia that will be acceptable to the Giants – in other words he must find the price of a woman's love. He must price what is priceless. This is captured by Wagner in his inspired transformation of the Eddic tale of Loki and the otter.[6] Freia is hidden by the hoard but, with the eye of love with which Fasolt looks for her, the unpurchasable self-hood of Freia – the look in which her first-person singular resides – continues to appear, until cut off by the thing that represents the price of it, the only thing for which it will exchange. Thus Wotan buys the temporary reprieve, in which he busies himself with the creation of another world – a world in which love and suffering are the dominant principles, and in which human beings pay the continual tax demanded for the upkeep of their gods.

Almost every commentator agrees that the central concern of *The Ring* is the contest between love and power. But there are many kinds of love, and many kinds of power, and Wagner was acutely aware of this. There is a vast and existential distinction between erotic love and the other loves that sometimes grow from it, sometimes compete with it, sometimes are destroyed by it, and this distinction was a pre-occupation of Wagner's throughout his creative life. For one thing, erotic love is jealous, wishes to possess the other uniquely, and can turn to hatred when betrayed – a feature dramatized in the character of Brünnhilde, whose anger has an almost demonic character in *Götterdämmerung*, as in the old *Volsungasaga*.

Moreover, erotic love itself is far from a unitary thing, being a syn-thesis of sexual desire and tender attachment: a fact conveyed by the two parts of the theme associated with Freia (22A and 22B). When Alberich forswears love he does not renounce desire: nor do the Rhine-daughters give any indication that they could offer anything remotely like love to those whom they embrace. To understand exactly what it is that Alberich has forsworn, therefore, involves going far deeper into the philosophy of love than commentators are normally inclined to go.[7] Indeed, at one level, the nature of love is the dominant theme of *The Ring*. One vital part of love, for Wagner, and the thing that distinguishes love from the baser forms of sexual interest, is the focus on the other person, and the irreplaceable value placed on him or her as the true and revealed reason for the lover's own existence. This feature of love is immortalized in the music that weaves together the hearts of Siegmund and Sieglinde, and is encoded in the second part of Freia's motif, 22B. If we were to summarize the meaning of 22B in words it would be something like the 'self-giving of the sub-ject' – the aspect of love that comes into being only with the gift of which individuals are capable: the gift of the self. Love is a relation of existential dependence that must, willingly or unwillingly, be brought to nothing, for we are mortal creatures, and death destroys us utterly. The tragedy of love – real love, that is – is therefore unavoidable.

Alberich has already shown a tendency to reject love in the rapid and self-interested transfer of his sexual interest from one Rhine-daughter to the next – even if what he is seeking from each of them is not just desire but a true *valuing* of his presence, and even if he is being cruelly and unjustly taunted into his final gesture of repudi-ation. At the same time, it is absolutely clear in all of Wagner's dramas, and in his prose writings too, that he believed love to be rooted in sexual feeling, and in the longing that creatures like us, who are both free subjects and embodied objects, feel for each other when troubled by desire.

Whether or not there is real love in *The Ring*, there is certainly unreal love – the love of Mime for Siegfried, for example. There is also calculating love – the love of Wotan for the Volsungs. And there is existential love, love taken entirely into the being of the one who experiences it, like the love of Brünnhilde for Siegfried. But perhaps it is only Brünnhilde's upbringing as a goddess that makes this exalted love a real possibility. Perhaps, for the rest of us, such a love is only an ideal that we strive to match but can never in fact live up to.

The idea of love as a relation between subjects – between beings who can say 'I' – is of critical importance in the philosophy that Wagner encountered as a student. But it also raises questions about love that are addressed in *The Ring*. The first is that of the relation of sex to love. On one, naïve, view of the matter, sexual love is simply sex plus love – that is to say, animal appetite conjoined with, and qualified by, interpersonal affection. There is some evidence that Kant saw it in that way. But it is emphatically not the way that Wagner saw it. For Wagner, sexual love is a specific kind of love, and sexual desire is a relation between free beings, seen in the mutual giving of Siegmund and Sieglinde in the first act of *Die Walküre* and of Siegfried and Brünnhilde in the last act of *Siegfried*.

The fact that sexual love is composed of two contrasting and potentially conflicting psychic elements was a constant preoccupation of Wagner's, from the early *Das Liebesverbot* to the final leave-taking of the erotic in *Parsifal*. In *Tannhäuser* the hero is torn between the sensual delights offered by Venus and Elizabeth's faithful devotion, both of them, in their different ways, intensely erotic. In this fascinating work Wagner's sympathies are with Elizabeth, even if Venus, like the Devil, often has the best tunes. While Wagner never lost his belief in the possibility of a supreme sexual union, in which all the suffering and trouble of existence would be compensated, the later works emphasize that sexual love can move in two directions, only one of which is worthy of us. Alberich reaches for sensual love, and is willing to steal it; but what he renounces is the other thing, the faithful attachment which is achieved, in the cycle, only by Wotan's human children, and then lost as soon as found. Yet it is this other thing that transforms the world, fills it with meaning, and makes suffering worthwhile.

That is not the only great fact that Wagner puts before us in his presentation of sexual love. From the first days of Wagner criticism the claim has been made, often delightedly and maliciously, that the composer was latently homosexual, bisexual, androgynous, even a covert lesbian.[8] This fantasy-ridden line of enquiry has been reworked, in postmodern idiom, by Jean-Jacques Nattiez in his book *Wagner Androgyne*, and no doubt will be reworked again. But it goes nowhere towards undermining the view of sexual love that is presented in Wagner's mature dramas, and also, in fraught and excited form, in his prose writings. Wagner did not take the modern view of sexual love as directed indifferently towards either sex. Sexual love in *The Ring* is emphatically a relation between man and woman; not just between one individual and another, but between two individuals each of whom embodies and represents the other sex, the 'otherness' of the other sex being a crucial factor in how their love is conceived.

Brünnhilde is therefore prepared for her mission in the life of Siegfried by acquiring distinctly womanly virtues. And it is not just a sexual companion that Siegfried is promised or that so many of the other characters long for, but 'love and woman's worth', as Fricka originally expresses it. We may not, now, accept the importance that Wagner places on sexual difference in the relation of erotic love. Nevertheless, not to see that, in a very important sense, the cycle is about women, their destiny and their healing powers is to fail to understand the direction in which its more lyrical passages are moving. It is true that, in a letter to Röckel, Wagner wrote that 'the true human being is both man and woman'. But he explained the point as follows:

> Love in its most perfect reality is only possible between the sexes: it is only as man and woman that human beings can truly love. Every other manifestation of love can be traced back to that one absorbingly real feeling . . . it is only by love that man and woman attain to the full measure of humanity . . . only in this union that the human being exists.[9]

At the same time, as Wagner was aware, and as *Die Meistersinger* and *Parsifal* clearly elaborate, sexual love is *not* the only kind of love, and is apt, when too much leant upon, to give way beneath the weight of our craving. Indeed, this is made explicit in the *Ring* cycle, which shows the idealized sexual love between Siegfried and Brünnhilde to be founded in the same capacity for creative illusion as the world of Valhalla. Moreover, as the music constantly makes clear, the love that endures through all conflicts, which is expressed in the cycle's most moving moment, and which achieves peace and reconciliation after all the disasters, is that between Brünnhilde and Wotan – the father–daughter love which has intruded into all the major turning points in the drama, and which reaches a kind of apotheosis in the fire that burns them both. So what exactly are we being asked to believe about love at the end of the cycle? To that question I return. Suffice it to say that, whatever Wagner is asking us to *believe*, he has presented with extraordinary clarity the fact that love is not a simple thing, and that, in both its forms, sexual love is not the solution but the problem. Desire sets the whole cycle in motion, and love brings it to an end. But both destroy what they find.

There is another and more metaphysical question about love that the drama presents to us, which is the question of the 'identity of the subject'. If what I am is this free being, known to myself in acts of will and subjective feeling, what ensures my identity over time? My body changes, and I could conceivably go to sleep in one body and awaken in another. Or if that is not possible, why is it not possible? When I take responsibility for the past and assert intentions for the future, I speak in the first person, using the word 'I' to link past and future affairs, and assuming identity through time of the subject who is speaking. What entitles me to make that assumption, and what entitles you? In all our relations, love especially, we act, think and feel as though the self endures through time, always the same yet always free. And if we did not think in that way, how would love be possible – love that is founded on the pure giving of the self to the other, not for now only, but forever? Or is this an illusion, a trap into which we are led by language, and notably by that strange word 'I' that Kant placed at the root of the human condition?

The question is not an idle speculation of philosophers only. As I have touched upon at several points in previous chapters, it connects with one of the great mysteries of human life, the mystery that the Germans call *Verwandlung* – the fact that we change in ways that lay waste our intentions, that ruin our responsibilities, that cause those who swear eternal love before long to face each other as strangers. This mystery is central to the understanding of the Tarnhelm, which symbolizes the misfit between the world in which we live and the metaphysics of our thinking. The belief in the absolute identity and individuality of the other, which seems fundamental to our life-plans and to all that we value, is not supported by the endless flow of events: it is a feature of the *Lebenswelt* that has no foundation in the natural order. And even if we can resist the natural flow here and there, our efforts are constantly eroded by the habit of exchanging things, finding substitutes, seeing as a means what was wanted as an end, and undoing our vows in ever newer and more temporary arrangements: in other words by all those habits of lovelessness that are symbolized by the Ring. That, of course, is the story of *Götterdämmerung* and, Wagner implies, it is *this* that is the death of God.

One reason for the impact of Schopenhauer on Wagner was that the philosopher had found a unique way of expressing the conundrum of our assumed identity through time. The *principium individuationis*, the criterion of identity, belongs, Schopenhauer argued, to the world of representation, the physical world in which I exist as one object among others. It is only as located in space and time that I am this one, individual, re-identifiable particular. But what I am in myself is will, the vast and oceanic source of all the desires and needs that trouble me, which is not an individual at all. The idea that I am one thing throughout my life, that I can bind myself in vows of eternal loyalty and take responsibility now for what I did all those years ago – this idea is simply an expression of the illusion under which we are condemned to live, through the mistake of living at all. Needless to say, Wagner read that part of Schopenhauer's philosophy with enthusiasm, since it corresponds so exactly to the experience of Tristan and Isolde, each of whom desires the other as an irreplaceable individual, and each of whom wishes to dissolve into the other as into the primordial night in which there are no individuals, since time and space have been transcended. This is the deepest paradox of the erotic: we give ourselves as individuals, only to enter a condition in which individuality disintegrates and disappears. It is a paradox that recurs in one form or another in all of Wagner's mature works.

Idealist philosophy acknowledges that we are both objects and subjects, both items in the empirical world and free agents, with a perspective on the world that Kant called 'transcendental'. What we are as persons seems, therefore, to bear no clear or explicable relation to what we are as human organisms. We may disbelieve in the gods; but we can give clear sense to the idea of an immortal person, who is not a member of any animal kind. What then is the relation between the person and the organism? Subject and object are constantly competing for the central place in my self-conception, and never seem to be at peace together. Crucial elements of my experience – pain, hunger, lust, sickness – seem to stem directly or indirectly from my animal nature, and yet at the same time to impress on me my apartness from the empirical world, and the reality of the 'transcendental' perspective that I take upon it. I seem to be both the victim of my animal nature and the master of it, and in certain experiences – notably sexual desire – I adopt as a free choice a state of mind that is sincere only when it has the force of an unchosen compulsion. It is as though I live balanced between two competing views of myself, two kinds of motivation, two entirely different conceptions of my nature and destiny. As a free agent in the *Lebenswelt* I am wholly other than the human animal in the order of nature. And yet I am composed of exactly the same stuff.

This aspect of the human condition preoccupied Schopenhauer, in his theory of the *principium individuationis* to which I referred above. It is also placed centre-stage by Wagner in *The Ring*. The mortals in the drama are shown in all their fleshly vulnerability. Death prowls in their wake; they are victims of forced marriage and domestic oppression (Sieglinde), of murder (Sieglinde's mother), of revenge (Siegmund), of the machinations of status and power (the Gibichungs). All these forces invade them from outside, rob them of their peace and freedom, and confine the moments of personal exultation to intense magnificent dreams, as at the brief unions of Wotan's mortal children.

But the tragedy of mortality is yet greater than this suggests. Our animal nature subjects us to the constant invasion and disruption of our loftiest purposes by appetite, distraction and forgetting. The transcendental self never forgets, since it never remembers: it is consciously possessed of its entire past, just as a mathematical proof eternally incorporates its premises. But the thread of rational choice and personal responsibility is hung on mortal chains, and these break, dissolve and bifurcate in ways that we cannot control. The subject is locked in combat with the object, and is constantly overcome by it.

This Wagner dramatizes in the motif of forgetting (156). This is a kind of spell, and relates to the magic potion in *Tristan und Isolde* – albeit with opposite effect. In the old Germanic and Icelandic literature spells have an extremely important role. They show power lying just out of reach of reason. They are symbolic recognitions of the potential that lies dormant in objects, which the free subject reaches for in vain – unless, that is, he has mastered their 'secret'. In Wagner spells have a more focused meaning. They are emblems of the object that most nearly intrudes on us, namely the body, its mortality, and the mutability that it brings. Magic drinks are especially important, since, although they overwhelm us from a point outside our personality, they work from a point within. They remind us that the 'within' of the human person is also the inside of a body. They dramatize the condition of the human person, in which the free subject is constantly overwhelmed by forces that it cannot understand, and which obliterate whole sections of its freedom. And these forces either arise from the body or conscript the body to their purposes. The drink of forgetting obliterates the life project to which Siegfried had attached his personality, and which was to bring him personal fulfilment – namely, union with Brünnhilde. Having begun as a hero of love, he is now prepared as a sacrificial victim. Only as such can he regain the value that he has lost.

Here, I believe, is where Wagner's philosophical anthropology becomes truly interesting, adjusted by the flow of the drama to take account of something really quite extraordinary in the human condition, which is that we recognize mutability and also condemn it, placing on the person an obligation of consistency and continuity that is not achievable in our mortal guise. True subjects take responsibility for failure and forgetting; they reassume their vows, and do not regard them as extinguished by the passage of time or the erosion of appetite. And their forgetfulness and faithlessness are experienced by others not as blemishes which can be cured or compensated for, but as radical defects of character. These vices are objects of blame and also of punishment.

In the extreme case, however, it is as though the personality has disappeared entirely: as though the other has been changed by these defects into something other than himself, since the self – the subject – who undertook the vows has disappeared, taking his personal attributes with him, to be replaced by another person entirely, or maybe by no person at all. When Siegfried bursts through the protecting ring of fire to seize Brünnhilde he wears the Tarnhelm, disguising his identity in order that she will believe that it is Gunther who has claimed her. Wagner states the *Verwandlung* motif, ending on the open fifth on B, to Brünnhilde's fearful question: 'Stammst du von Menschen?' – expressing her sense of the utter strangeness of this apparition. And immediately the motif of forgetting comes in, beginning as when first heard with a strangely spaced C minor triad, which sounds now like the completion of the *Verwandlung* motif: the answering phrase for which it has been reaching all along.

The musical amalgam here connects the material fact of Siegfried's fake appearance with the spiritual fact of his fake reality – of the moral void that he has become since forsaking his only love. The amalgam is strengthened as the act proceeds to its conclusion, and we begin to understand that our forgettings are also disguises, that our very existence as free subjects requires of us a continuity and commitment from which we are condemned by our mortality to hide. And through this hiding we become strange to each other and to ourselves, as Siegfried is shown to be the ultimate stranger in Brünnhilde's eyes when she later meets him undisguised.

Kant argued that rational beings are not merely free, but bound by self-imposed laws, and that the ability so to bind ourselves is what true freedom consists in. But the veneer of personality and selfhood is constantly broken from below by the thrust of animal life, and it is sometimes difficult to resist the view that all our reasons are really rationalizations, ways of representing actions that were wrung from us by the inexorable needs of the animal as though they were products of free deliberation, aimed at the good and issuing from the will.

And even when we can make sense of the idea of reason being not merely in control of a person's actions, but also providing the motive behind them, we have only the vaguest idea how this came about, and by what trick it was that the moral being superseded the animal, and tamed its instincts to a higher law. It is as though, by an enormous collusive effort, people are able to draw a collective veil over their animal natures, and address each other entirely as if appealing to concentrated centres of purely rational choice.

This vision of the essentially compromised nature of freedom is embodied by Wagner in the person of Wotan. The god has resolved to live in freedom, where freedom is interpreted in Kant's way, as obedience to a self-imposed law. To achieve the position of legislator, however, Wotan must rely on natural forces that lie outside the reach of law – the waters of the Rhine and the gold that they harbour, the labour of the Giants, the cunning of fire, personified in Loge, the labour of Alberich through which he imprints his fettered personality on the gold – and at every point in the narrative we discover some other, earlier and deeper act of usurpation that has been necessary in Wotan's rise to freedom. At the same time, this deeply compromised freedom is still freedom, and the element that is missing – the act of sacrifice in which the body and its imperatives are finally scorned and put at nought – is one that no immortal can undertake, and which Wotan himself undertakes only by accepting mortality, first through his proxy Brünnhilde, and then through his own act of renunciation at the start of *Siegfried* Act 3.

The idealist theory of consciousness tries to show how the abstract and universal *Geist* or spirit realizes itself as an individual – i.e. as a self-conscious person. For Hegel, as for Fichte, *Selbstbestimmung* occurs in two spheres: that of 'objective spirit' and that of 'subjective spirit'. Spirit becomes determinate both in the world of institutions and laws, and in the free individual. That which exists objectively as sovereignty and law exists subjectively as self-knowledge and will. Hence Wotan has both these aspects, and the spear on which all oaths are inscribed is both the rule of law that upholds them and the will that intends them. This will shapes the individual, and sets him apart from nature. But since no being, not even a god, can be wholly apart from nature, law and will are subject to mutation. (Loge flickers at the point of Wotan's spear, burning away the runes inscribed there.) The force of law and the force of personal existence are both projected in the character of Wotan. And both involve a defiance of the natural order, a *hubris*, from which punishment must follow. At first Wotan does not understand this. Like the Odin of the Eddas, he wanders the earth seeking knowledge of his fate. But gradually, as the gods become incarnate in the mortals whose dreams they are and whose suffering they have required, they are filled with wisdom, and released from the burden of existence.

Just as love, in *The Ring*, is many things, so too is power, and one of Wagner's philosophical preoccupations is to distinguish legitimate power, which is Wotan's aim in fashioning the spear of government, from the loveless and de-personalized tyranny of Alberich. Wotan's spear is represented by the abstract diatonic scale, which parcels out the space of his cosmic drama. But the spear is constantly changed and distorted through its exercise in the empirical world. It is broken into the pathos of Siegmund's suffering (56), into the frustration of the god who cannot act in this space over which he asserts his futile guardianship (76), into the purity motif of Brünnhilde (95), in which form it relinquishes its transcendental pretensions to become an affirmative melody – the melody of her willed incarnation in the world where she must die. The story of the spear is the story of legal order, which lives not only in the world of human relationships but also in the soul of the individual, constraining and constrained by our desires. The legal order, which makes our vows of loyalty possible, is subject to the same mortal erosion as they are.

The spear confers authority and also qualifies it, by subjecting it to law. This law is natural law, enshrined in the maxim that *pacta sunt servanda*: treaties must be honoured, the maxim made fundamental to International Law by Grotius.[10] We should not be surprised to find such jurisprudential ideas evoked in *The Ring*. From *Tannhäuser* onwards, the Wagner operas show a growing concern with law, as a social force that also shapes the inner life of those who honour it. A great part of what interested the composer in the *Nibelungenlied* and the Nordic Eddas and Sagas was the conception of law and justice contained in them.[11] As his early prose sketch for a Nibelungen drama makes clear, he saw the original poems as by-products of a peculiar power-struggle – the struggle of the Frankish princes to establish their dominion. The poems, he thought, should be read in part as an exploration of the idea of legitimacy and its establishment in a particular stock. It is Wotan, as ruler of the gods, in whom legitimacy resides, or appears to reside. The problem, however, is that the price of this legitimacy is crime – the crime of Alberich against himself, in forswearing love, and of Wotan against Alberich in seizing the Ring (the crime, Alberich says, against all that was, is and shall be).

The association that binds the gods is a free association; that which binds the Nibelungs is coerced. Free association is consensual – if you don't like it, you can withdraw. Coerced association is non-consensual, and no one is free to withdraw. Parties to a free association can render it permanent and trustworthy in a variety of ways, two of which are constantly invoked in *The Ring*: contract, in which terms are implied or stated; and love, in which there are no terms. Free association that is not welded in some such way is an unstable thing and approximates to the state of nature as described by Hobbes. Contract and love both involve a loss of freedom, even though both must be freely engaged in if they are to be genuine, and both are relations between free beings.

Hence neither contract nor love can be commanded. (In English law a coerced contract is voidable.) Mime is abhorrent to Siegfried partly because he endeavours to command Siegfried to love him. And since it is a feature of love that it seeks reciprocity, Mime's wheedling protestations of love towards Siegfried elicit, in the end, a violent reaction, as Siegfried cries 'Du sollst mich nicht lieben!' in answer to Mime's earlier 'so mußt du ihn [Mime] lieben!' The portrayal of this relation – in which the pretence of love is vainly imposed upon an invincible mutual abhorrence – is one of Wagner's psychological master-strokes, all the greater because it is achieved by purely musical means, through the character of Mime's melodic line, in which the obsessive triple time of the smithing theme reappears as an equally obsessive cloying, and through the device of separating inner reality from outward show, as Mime is unmasked by the wood-bird.

Freedom is more irrevocably lost in love than in contract, and this indeed is the paradox of love in its fullest form that, while it can be experienced only by beings who think of themselves as transcendentally free, and therefore able to undertake unspecified obligations, all freedom is at once extinguished in a bond that ties the actions, emotions and destiny of one person to those of another. This complete love and completely un-free freedom exists in *The Ring* only between Wotan's mortal offspring – Siegmund and Sieglinde, and Siegfried and Brünnhilde – and in each case it speedily brings about the annihilation of the parties. Yet in these two mortal loves generous sentiment enters the world of the tetralogy – sentiment that involves a willingness, spontaneous in the case of Siegmund, rather more calculating in the case of Brünnhilde, to make a total gift of oneself.

No political order can be founded on love of that kind, for the very reason that such a love is exclusive and all-absorbing. Indeed love is, in a sense, a threat to the political order, or at best an inner challenge which must be accommodated within a more cogent and universal form of association. This theme was familiar to Wagner from the *Antigone* of Sophocles, and the brother–sister love that there threatens the ship of state parallels the incestuous love of the Volsungs, which threatens the law of the hearth – though in contrasting ways, since Antigone is motivated by piety, which the Volsungs sacrilegiously defy. Like Hegel, for whom the *Antigone* was the paradigm tragedy, Wagner was profoundly touched by this play, precisely because it seems to show self-sacrificing love and political order in radical and insoluble conflict. He saw Antigone's defiance of Creon in the same terms as the plot of *Die Walküre* Act 1, and that of his sketch for *Jesus of Nazareth* (1848/9) – as an illustration of the inexorable conflict and mutual dependence between love and law.[12] And the example is important, since it shows that the 'love versus law' idea is not merely about *erotic* love: a point to which I return.

In a contract people are bound by specific obligations, while remaining free in every other sphere. For the political philosophers of the Enlightenment, therefore, political order could be both justified and reconciled with human freedom, if founded on a social contract, to the terms of which everyone agrees in the state of nature. It was objected that all such theories are myths: there is no such thing as the state of nature, and, even if there were, it is absurd to suppose that human beings would possess, in that state, the necessary ideas whereby to engage in so complex a social performance as a contract. If the social contract theory were correct, therefore, the transition from the state of nature to legitimate political order could never occur.

The answer to that objection is clear from the Wagnerian treatment of myth. A myth represents as a temporal sequence a relation that is not temporal at all but buried in the heart of things. The social contract is not an act that precedes society but a structure contained *within* it: and the same is true of the state of nature. (In just this way lawyers read contracts into relations that were never preceded by an agreement, arguing that a contract is implied by the behaviour of the parties.) To tell the story of an 'original contract' is to lay out as a historical parable a truth that has no history. It is to give what Bernard Williams, following Nietzsche, has called a fictional 'genealogy' of an idea.[13] In just such a way *The Ring* displays in temporal order a timeless truth about society, displaying relations of contemporaneous dependence as though they arose from crucial moments of decision. We could never understand Alberich's theft of the gold in its philosophical meaning if we believed it to be an event that occurred only once, and whose effects are now being documented for our instruction. The theft of the gold (the appropriation of nature in consciousness, in power relations, in exchange) is a constantly renewing process, which at the same time has the inner meaning and the moral identity of a free human choice. And the same goes for Wotan's stripping of the spear from the World Ash Tree, without which law-defying act there could have been no rule of law and no legitimate dominion.

There is, however, a more serious objection to the social contract idea, which was put in a distinctive and powerful form by Hegel.[14] This being who makes contracts, Hegel argued – this free being who willingly renounces some part of freedom for the long-term advantages of society – is not a natural occurrence. He is a social artefact, incapable of existing in the state of nature. His freedom, of which contract is not the lowest but on the contrary the highest expression, comes into being only in society, and each of us wins it only in the course of a prolonged process of conflict and resolution, and a mutual emergence from the state of bondage. How can that be the foundation of society which only society creates? How can we suppose our political obligations to be founded in a contract that only beings subject to political order could conceivably have agreed upon?

Hegel went further, and introduced a striking threefold division into his account of political order. It is indeed true, he argued, that civil society – the totality of free associations – exists through contract, for it is the sphere of contract, the sphere of all those obligations and institutions that arise by mutual consent. But civil society is not in itself a contract, nor is it self-sustaining. It depends for its stability on two other systems of institution-building, neither of which has a contractual foundation: the family, in which the free being is formed from the bondage of love, slowly and painfully separating himself from an obligation that he never contracted; and the state, in which an idea of objective obligation is embodied in law, and given human form in the person of the judge and the ruler. Our obligation to the state, like that to the family, precedes our freedom; and yet this obligation exists objectively, as a legitimate order, only because it permits and fosters that freedom.

Wotan's spear succinctly summarizes Hegel's view of the state. The spear owes its power not to the fact that people have contracted to obey the god who wields it, but rather to the fact that it guarantees agreements, while itself not being a part of them. The treaties engraved upon its shaft indicate the multiple contracts of civil society, in which people put their trust only because they trust that other, higher and independent thing – the law – which will rectify any broken promise.

The spear's power cannot derive from contracts and it cannot be a merely coercive power – a power that people would gladly escape if they could and which they experience as a curtailment of their liberty. For its purpose is precisely to uphold liberty, by enforcing agreements that have been freely made. To put the matter shortly, the spear is a symbol of authority, and owes its power not to any denial of our spontaneous agreements but to its capacity to uphold those agreements and to give them political reality.[15]

This authority, which upholds agreements by transcending them and recasting them as law, accounts for the public aspect of Wotan's rule. Wotan's dominion, expressed in the tranquil Valhalla motif, is one in which law and agreement have replaced coercion and war. Nevertheless, like all dominion, that of Wotan is not self-sustaining.

The peace guaranteed by law is purchased at a price, and the price is that other dominion which, though we banish it to the depth of things, nevertheless constantly fills the air with its gusts of resentment. This is the dominion of the Ring, not the spear.

It is a familiar observation that the motifs of the Ring and of Valhalla are intimately related. The first appears in *Das Rheingold* as a keyless diminished seventh, which works its way by natural steps of rhythm and harmony to the serene D flat major hymn associated with the realm of the gods. The tragedy of Wotan is signified in this transformation. For if it is true that the spear owes its magic to no contract of obedience, whence comes its power? Only from all the trappings of authority symbolized by the castle of Valhalla, trappings which must be purchased, and which therefore require the invention of another kind of power – the power of exchange, the power that comes from assigning a price to things, even to things that are priceless, like 'love and woman's worth'.

Of course, Wotan might have built the castle himself and dispensed with the labour of the Giants. But to engage in those brutal and gigantic actions he would have lost the aspect of authority and the tranquil face of law. This is not a problem for kingship only: all forms of political authority depend upon the ability of the leader or legislator to appear unflustered on the deck in his uniform, calmly steering the ship of state through the waves of fortune.

Hence the endeavour to establish justice – in other words to uphold agreements and to give to each his due – depends upon the huge compromise of justice without which there can be no law. This is all displayed in *Das Rheingold*, which shows in legendary form the process of 'legitimate usurpation', as de Maistre called it,[16] that underlies the rule of law. And the theft that confers on the gods their needed purchasing power depends on Alberich's crime against himself. Just as law-enforcement cannot be acquired by law alone, or the power to uphold contracts by contract, neither can purchasing power be purchased – it must be stolen. This theft has a price – a *natural* price – which is the loss of love. And thereafter, across the peaceful realm of legal order, there blows the chill wind of anguish from the depths.

The philosophers of liberalism saw that this paradox can be overcome only if the obligation to uphold contracts is itself a contractual obligation. That it is not a contractual obligation is the great fact that Wagner dramatizes – along with everything important that follows from this fact, and in particular the division of the world into two parallel and mutually dependent orders, of agreement and coercion, freedom and bondage. The resulting conflict, implanted in the scheme of things, cannot be resolved at the political level – such is the message of Wotan's solemn confession to Brünnhilde in *Die Walküre* Act 2, and of his bequest of the world to the son of Alberich.

But, as the tetralogy shows, and as Wotan gradually comes to see, the conflict *can* be resolved in the individual soul, by the act of renunciation that is the proof of love. This individual solution to a cosmic problem is shown in one of the most beautiful moments of *The Ring*: 'Ruhe, ruhe, du Gott!' Here, when Brünnhilde has finally emerged from her trauma, understood the way in which the world's resentment had taken away her love, and by an act of will regained that love in forgiving both Siegfried and her father, we hear the final triumph of the serene Valhalla motif over the diminished, tritone-filled themes of resentment, as the curse motif is stilled to quiescence, and resolved with the D flat major cushion that Brünnhilde offers to Wotan. (Note the way the tonal argument at this juncture forces the curse motif out of B minor/A minor – which rarely happens elsewhere.)

Wotan's predicament is twofold: first, his inner dependence upon Alberich's theft and all that flows from it; second, his need to stand by the rule of law, which is the ultimate basis of his authority. He can evade his own agreements only by trickery, and for this he needs Loge's help. This process of erosion whereby agreements are slowly burned away is a constant necessity for Wotan. It has a tame equivalent in our laws of prescription and perpetuities, and our statutes of limitations. But it represents the flaw in Wotan's claim to legitimate government. In pursuit of legitimate order he promises Freia to the Giants and the sword of victory to Siegmund; but these promises, on which the destiny of the world momentarily seems to hang, are for that reason subject to mutation, as the necessities of government override their force.

Wotan's predicament would, however, be manageable, were it not for the existence and nature of Alberich. Two decisive experiences shaped Alberich's character: first, the renunciation of love that enabled him to capture the gold, a renunciation which had already taken place, just as soon as he set his mind on rape; secondly, Wotan's theft of the thing in which Alberich's identity had been embodied – his *Eigen*, for which he had exchanged the only thing that enables a person to be at peace with himself. Alberich's curse of the Ring is the curse uttered by all who are separated from their nature – and this separation is pathetically characterized by Alberich's lingering presence beside the dragon's cave, his mind fixed on the thing in which his whole being is contained, waiting to see who next will possess it.

Throughout the tetralogy, therefore, embodied in a variety of motifs and their interrelations, runs the theme of political order: its nature and its price. Wagner is constantly distinguishing the consensual order, ruled by law, and the coercive order, ruled by treachery and violence. And caught between these two orders, frequently defying the one and always threatened by the other, lies the narrow sphere of personal love. This is a sphere of suffering, which has no power to endure or to sustain itself, but which nevertheless contains the sole justification for the rule of law and the act of 'legitimate usurpation' by which the law is founded.

Between the consensual and the coercive order there can be no agreement, as Wotan reminds Alberich outside Fafner's cave. Nevertheless there is a relation of dependence between them, and the tragedy is that this dependence goes one way. All that is fine and beautiful in Wotan's order depends upon the economic penalty, but nothing in Alberich's order depends upon Wotan's achievements, since it is an order of darkness and negation. Wagner said of the descent into Nibelheim that it should convey a demonic delight in destruction:[17] something that we modern people have witnessed in abundance. But we turn away from the terrible truth – the truth that everything we hold as precious, including both love and law, rests on a thin crust above a seething magma of resentment.

In the order willed by Alberich there can be neither trust nor agreement. Hence when Alberich worms his way into the sleep of Hagen, and begs him to be true, the sinister theme of bondage – the Rhine-daughters' cry, poisoned by chromatic harmonies (164) – makes nonsense of the very word 'Treu', which sounds on Alberich's tongue like the distilled essence of treachery. We then understand why Hagen, swearing the oath that Alberich demands, swears only to himself. The order of coercion reigns in Hagen's breast, and it is fitting that when shortly afterwards he summons the vassals to celebrate the double wedding of Siegfried and Gutrune and Gunther and Brünnhilde, it is with the call used to summon them to war.

Wotan confronts the problem of a perished legitimacy. As he gradually discovers, his search for the other, who will be free from the contracts that bind the sovereign power, is self-contradictory. Either the other acts under Wotan's orders and with Wotan's connivance – in which case he is bound as Wotan is bound – or he acts for himself, in which case Wotan is duty-bound to oppose him, as he opposes Siegmund. Only if the free being overcomes Wotan, so as to establish freedom of his own free will, can the crime of sovereignty be atoned for. But if Wotan is overcome the world falls out of governance, and law and contracts are no longer enforced. In a world surrendered to love all oaths, treaties, vows and promises come to nothing. The order of love, so fragile but so full of meaning, depends for its durability on Wotan's rule. And again the dependence goes one way. Siegfried, in pushing Wotan aside, destroys the order that would enable Siegfried to be true to himself.

With the collapse of the objective order of law, therefore, comes the collapse of the inner order of faith and trust. This is part of the meaning of *Götterdämmerung*, which, as I pointed out in Chapter 3, consists of a series of vows – the vow of love between Siegfried and Brünnhilde, of blood-brotherhood between Gunther and Siegfried, of marriage between Siegfried and Gutrune, of vassaldom between the Gibichungs and their retainers – all of which are broken in a cumulative personal disaster, which is also a disaster of cosmic proportions. Wotan's end is therefore Siegfried's end, and in shattering Wotan's spear Siegfried, who is about to discover love, brings about a world in which love will inevitably destroy itself.

The cycle shows the rule of law to be deeply dependent on the machinery of production and exchange. And it shows love, which is a relation between subjects, as fully realized only in our condition as mutable objects, whose freedom might be snatched from us by a spell or a trick, and whose vows are no more durable in the end than the mortal mouths that utter them. These two great facts, which embody the incurable tragedy of the human condition, are symbolized by the Ring, which represents an outlook on the world that disregards the personality of people, and looks upon them as we look upon things. Wagner shows us that this outlook exists at both the personal and the political level, portraying in his evocation of Nibelheim a world that has been voided of love and personality in both their inner and their outer meaning.

But the Ring has this love-denying power in the world of mortals too, since Alberich has, through the curse, imbued it with his own vision of what matters. This is shown immediately in *Das Rheingold*, when the Giants take possession of the hoard. Although the Giants are initially attracted to Freia as a personification of love in its natural form, one of them, Fasolt, is afflicted by her beauty. He cannot, in the end, relinquish her, until her glance – her first-person perspective, her revelation as a free subject – is hidden from view. Only one thing can take away the glance of Freia, namely the thing that was forged by renouncing love. Freia is exchanged for the Ring. Fasolt seizes the Ring from Fafner, with the cry: 'Back, thief! the Ring is mine – it is due to me for Freia's glance' ('mir blieb er für Freias Blick').

The Ring is the spell that undoes love, by dissolving everything desired – even the object of love – in the stream of substitutes. Fasolt's premonition of suffering is verified immediately: he is murdered for the sake of this object which he cannot use. This is not merely because the Ring is *wanted* by Fafner: it is because it has already colonized the soul of Fafner, telling him that the only love known to him – brother love – can be exchanged for something better.

The Ring is the mark and product of a primordial alienation, a loss of the acceptance of life as an end in itself. It casts its spell over all desire and all aspiration, so that everything – the Ring included – is demoted from end to means. That is what Alberich's kind of power amounts to: a *perpetuum mobile* that feeds on itself and knows no point of rest. The forging of the Ring involves, therefore, a universal restlessness, which can be overcome only in the individual soul, by regaining, though at a higher and more self-conscious level, the sense of one-ness that was lost when the natural order was left behind.

(The Ring is therefore a potent symbol of the regime of mass consumption, which is rapidly destroying the natural world. It is one of the oddities of the now standard *Marxisant* productions of Wagner's drama that the natural world is routinely banished from the stage. For this neutralizes one of the most important political messages that the work conveys: namely, that power divorced from love is an ecological catastrophe.) This higher unity occurs through love, which, in the brief moments when it denies the reality of *Verwandlung* and wills its own eternity, re-creates, though in a higher and self-conscious form, the pure act of praise – the *Rheingold, reines Gold* – which is our human salvation.

How are we to understand this profoundly secular idea of salvation? The answer, paradoxically enough, is contained in the idea of the sacred. Certain moments, objects and events are endowed for us with a meaning that could be called 'transcendental'. That is to say, they have a significance that cannot be clearly spelled out in ordinary empirical terms. It is as though another realm of being is revealed to us, a place beyond nature from which a light is shining on the world that we know. It is like this when we fall in love, and the face and body of the beloved become imbued for us with a peculiar radiance – an otherness that seems to contain the secret meaning of our life. It is like this, too when we confront the death of someone loved, and a void opens in the scheme of things through which the vast forms of fate are dimly perceivable. And it is like this at a birth, when we confront the miraculous fact of a new human spirit, entering the world as though from nowhere, catching up at once, so to speak, with the body that has been laid in its path.

These moments correspond to the 'rites of passage' that anthropologists have documented in the life of the tribe – the moments in which the whole tribe joins to affirm its solidarity and which have to do, in some way that may not be clearly understood, with the survival and reproduction of the social organism. But they are also turning points in the life of the individual; and they are connected with moments of memory and anticipation that stand out from the empirical order as though inviting us into a sphere that we call 'transcendental' only because we have no word for it.

The first instinct of the human being is to rationalize these moments as visitations from the supernatural realm, and to populate that realm with beings that possess our own powers and interests in some enhanced and superlative form. Thus arises the belief in gods. And because the gods represent unchanging features of the human condition, the great moments of meaning and destiny that all of us share and which are prepared for us without our help, the gods are 'forever' – they eat the apples of eternal youth, which are symbols of the unending renewal of the community that worships them. It is in the hope of sharing that immortality that we labour on their behalf, building fortifications against our natural scepticism. And by a trick that lies at the very heart of religion, we are persuaded to accept the comfort of society instead of those longed-for apples, and to believe that the magic lies not in the mystical stuff that is eaten in that other world, but in the power that we accumulate in this one. Such is the beautiful allegory that Wagner concocts in the story of the Giants and Freia, and it might seem like the last word concerning the promises of religion.

But it is not the last word at all. Nor does it finally account for the religious need as Wagner conceives it. The old myths related in the Edda are remarkable not only for their rumours of gods before gods, but also for their belief in gods after gods too. Even the gods must die, and their mortal sovereignty is devoted to preparations for their doom. Wagner used this feature of the myth to represent his own conception of the sacred. Instead of seeing sacred actions and events as the points where temporal things are as though lifted into the timeless realm of the divinities and thereby rescued, he saw them as points where timeless sentiments find their temporal presence, and are thereby made real. The 'point of intersection of the timeless with time' is a point in time, not a vision of the timeless. Religion tells us that sacred things contain a promise of our immortality; for Wagner, however, our immortal imaginings become real and significant in the temporal world. The experience of the sacred is an apprehension of our own significance, as beings capable of sacrifice. Redemption does not consist in a release from death, but in the acceptance of death on behalf of a mortal love.

This highly personal idea of the sacred is Wagner's great contribution to the understanding of the human condition. He saw the experience of the sacred as fundamental to consciousness, more basic than the religious ideas that are built from it, and destined to survive the extinction of all religion. We self-conscious beings have learned to understand the world scientifically, to grasp the laws of nature and to see that the explanations offered by religion are as empty as its promises. Our gods have died, and the story of their death is one of the many sub-plots of *The Ring*. The gods are killed by the very thing that created them: the world's consciousness that erupted in us, and whose implacable demands are displayed in the encounter between the Rhine-daughters and Alberich.

But the consciousness that killed the gods did not remove the sacred dimension from our experience. As well as the scientific view of things, consciousness brings into being the self and its freedom. And these in turn bring about another way of seeing the world than the way of science. The world does not lie before us as an inert object of study. It calls to us, addresses us, in moments when time is arrested and our being is at stake. The moment of free commitment, the moment when I am fully myself in an act of self-giving – this has no place in the temporal order as science conceives it. And yet it is the moment that justifies my life, the moment that shows the absolute value of my being the thing that I am. Such a moment is dramatized in the music of the 'look' in *Tristan und Isolde*, and in the uncovering of Brünnhilde in the third act of *Siegfried*.

Subsequent thinkers – notably Rudolf Otto in his influential book *Das Heilige* (1917) – have taken up the suggestion that the experience of the sacred is more basic than religious belief, and an immovable part of the human condition.[18] But nobody has matched Wagner in the attempt to *vindicate* this experience, to show that it is not illusory, even if it is the origin of illusions, and to present our ventures in love and sacrifice as the true goal to which the experience tends. Grasping this is the most important step in understanding *The Ring*. The cycle is an attempt to describe the *Lebenswelt* as though it were the product of the human imagination. And in doing so it isolates and identifies the objects, experiences, times and places where the sacred enters our lives.

There is one other aspect of the human condition that Wagner endeavours to elucidate in the *Ring* cycle, one that was of similar interest to

Nietzsche, who made it foundational to his vision of human society: namely resentment. Like Nietzsche, Wagner saw resentment as an inevitable feature of the human condition – an emotion that pervades our projects, and colours the relations, institutions and perceptions that bring us together. Resentment is something that only a rational being can feel. It is not the same as envy – the desire to possess some good that belongs to another. As I suggested in Chapter 6, when discussing the symbolism of Alberich, resentment involves a relentless need to deprive or destroy, whether or not this brings any other benefit. Alberich resents the Rhine-daughters and their treatment of him and, having seized their gold and forged the Ring, builds therewith a world of distrust, in which resentment is the normal form of intimacy, as between Alberich and Mime. Resentment wants to dominate and subjugate its object: it is restless in the face of happiness until that happiness is destroyed. It is a vigilant, all-consuming passion, and, unlike love, is transferable from object to object (which is why it must win over love in the scheme of things).

Alberich expresses all those aspects of resentment in his night-time encounter with Hagen in *Götterdämmerung*. And through one of the most compelling of *The Ring*'s leitmotifs – the curse – Wagner places implacable resentment at the heart of his drama. This leitmotif is emblematic of the transferable nature of resentment, of its ability to crop up in new and surprising places, meeting all gestures of hope or affection with a fierce repudiating 'No'.

Looking back over recent history it is impossible to doubt the force of resentment in shaping the modern world. In 1849 Wagner already had an inkling of this. The concentration camps and the death camps were then unimaginable. But Wagner's autobiography reveals that he saw in the figure of Bakunin what Dostoevsky described in *The Devils*, what Zola imagined in the Russian exile Souvarine (in *Germinal*) and what Conrad perceived in his communist Professor (*The Secret Agent*), namely the absolute negativity, masked as idealism, that was to regard all people as instruments, regardless of whether they trusted you, regardless of any personal obligations or ties from the past. Thus the nineteenth-century anarchists offered no policy save 'world conflagration' (Bakunin) or 'the destruction of all that is' (the Professor) while Wagner wrote of Bakunin that he insisted 'solely on destruction and ever more destruction'.[19]

I have surveyed some of the philosophical themes that, in my view, are in issue throughout Wagner's drama. They are not treated, of course, as abstract ideas or academic arguments. Rather they are embodied in characters and symbols, and in a narrative that clearly means something more than what it says. In the chapter that follows I consider some of the principal problems of interpretation, before addressing the important criticisms of Nietzsche and Adorno, and making a final attempt to say what the cycle means.

8

Siegfried and Other Problems

The true artist stands back from his work so that it speaks to us directly. The artist who steps forward to moralize does an injustice, not to us only, but also to his characters, who are, by this gesture, deprived of the right to speak for themselves. In giving an interpretation of a true dramatic work we are exploring the characters, and what they symbolize. We are also clarifying the underlying ideas and assumptions that set the context for the drama, so as to show just why these people in this situation deserve our interest and sympathy and just why they have something to tell us. But we are not, or not usually, in the business of extracting a message that can be formulated as a maxim or a recipe for life.

Those observations emphatically apply to Wagner's *Der Ring des Nibelungen*. The drama presents a world and the characters that inhabit it, and it tells us that this world is extrapolated from things that we know. But the work has no simple or explicit moral. Whatever conclusion we may draw from it we must draw through our sympathies, through identifying with the action and the characters, and through understanding that this is how things are. Such is the great claim that Wagner's masterpiece makes on us, indeed: the claim to have given us the world as it is, in its full complexity, by showing what it *would* be, if it were created by our human needs and emotions and not by the laws of physics. The world of *The Ring* is the product of human sentiments. These sentiments are personified as gods and goblins, as giants, demi-gods and primeval forces, but those symbols owe their nature and meaning to the feelings that we discover in ourselves.

This means that, despite the fact, and also because of the fact, that the work presents a wholly imagined world, it must, if it is to succeed, be in every crucial matter true to life – though true in a *general* way, since the characters owe their reality to the human universals that they summarize. Moreover, the drama must excite our sympathies, so that we do not stand back from the narrative as though it were a merely allegorical fairy-tale but instead engage with the characters as believable people.

And here is where we encounter some of the problems. Most important among them is Siegfried. In *Die Walküre* we are introduced to Siegfried's father, Siegmund, the first human being to enter the drama. (Previous characters have been human in their sentiments, but not human in their *being*, since they are projections of our human passions onto a cosmic screen.) Siegmund is a good-hearted but isolated person, who has searched the world for love and never found it, who has fallen time and again into misfortune and hostility, and who, in the vain attempt to rescue a woman from a forced marriage, has created a far worse situation than he found. In his flight he comes across another female victim, this time one who shares his longing for a redeeming affection, and they fall in love. From that moment Sieglinde is everything to him, and he defies all the conventions of society in expressing and acting upon his feelings for her.

Whatever our views of this, they do not cancel our sympathy: thanks largely to the music, we live through Siegmund's pain and know that he acts from a committed devotion. We are then given three views of his conduct – Fricka's, Wotan's and Brünnhilde's. The first is the view of conventional morality and the 'natural law', persuasive but cold; the second is the view of the god who is committed to upholding that morality, but who knows that this can be done only by also defying it, and who in any case strays from it himself. Both see Siegmund objectively, as part of a scheme to which he does not in his heart belong. The third view, Brünnhilde's, comes from sympathy alone, responding to Siegmund as a present and needy individual. She is being shown something whose existence had been previously unknown to her. In this brilliant dramatic stroke Wagner vindicates Siegmund not through denying the morality that condemns him, but through showing the melting heart of a divine visitor, faced with a mortal's doom.

The example creates a striking contrast with Siegfried, who, while just as much an outsider as his father, arouses our sympathy only in those moments when he lays aside his self-centredness and notices that others too have problems. We may excuse his attitude to Mime, since we know that the dwarf is merely using him as a tool. Moreover there is an innate sense of honour in Siegfried that causes him to be instinctively revolted by the dishonourable person with whom he is forced to live. Nevertheless, we also know that a less vacuous youth would have established a certain *modus vivendi* with the only person who has ever looked after him. The forging of the sword would provoke fewer qualms in the audience if it were the act of someone manifestly under threat, as Siegmund was when he took the sword from the ash tree. And his readiness to fight, first with the dragon, then with the Wanderer and then, much later, with Gunther, suggests a pronounced lack of humility in the face of challenge – although again honour, of a kind, might have something to do with it.

Worst of all, of course, is his enthusiastic agreement to the plot to capture Brünnhilde and to force her into a situation from which his father would have rushed to rescue her. Even if the drink of forgetfulness excuses his failure to recognize his wife, even if we make every allowance for the new circumstances brought about by his fall, we surely cannot sympathize with his violent participation in an act of rape and enslavement. Siegfried is rescued from judgement, if at all, only by the deep unconsciousness that sets him apart from the human world, and which is only incompletely explained by Hagen's drug.

Siegfried was the subject of the drama as Wagner originally conceived it, when he sought to rewrite the old *Nibelungenlied* as an allegory of the modern world. Siegfried was to represent the free individual, who overthrows the old and corrupt order of society, but falls victim to the machinations of power. In the rethinking and rewriting of *Siegfrieds Tod* Wagner retained Siegfried's fairy-tale identity. He is the boy who does not know fear; the hero who slays the dragon; the wanderer in the forest who can understand the language of the birds; the innocent master of the Nibelung's hoard who does not know what to do with it. He is the owner of the Tarnhelm through which he can change his shape, and of the Ring, which, if he were interested in using it, would grant him lordship of the world.

He also belongs to a mediaeval society organized by conventions and laws of a kind that we find difficult to sympathize with. The old story, which contains many of the elements of *Götterdämmerung*, including the overcoming of Brünnhilde by force, passes over all the moral difficulties that we now might have, on the understanding that, in this world of feudal ties, making the right alliance is far more important than ensuring the woman's consent to it. And Wagner seized on this aspect in order to dramatize the fall of Siegfried: he wanted his hero to fall just as far as he could, while retaining the inner innocence that wells up as he dies, and washes all corruption away. It is arguably this innocence that traps Siegfried into thinking that Gunther's world is one in which he might be properly honoured, gaining the recognition that makes him at last fully part of things in a stratified society and no longer the bewildered boy from the woods.

In the world of fairy tales things happen without an explanation, and magic lifts the story out of the realm of ordinary events into a place where the price of human action need never be paid. That is not how Wagner uses magic in *The Ring*, or in his works generally. Magic, for Wagner, is always a symbol, a bringing together of events, habits and experiences that belong to the real world, and which can be more easily grasped through the kind of immediacy that magic makes available. It is thus with the drink of forgetting, which represents a process that we all know from the real world, and whose deplorable effects are powerfully summarized in this potion from which the drinker looks up, bewildered, into an entrancing pair of eyes. In a similar way, the *Sühnetrank*, the drink of atonement, that Tristan takes from the hands of Isolde, is not an intervention from some other world, but a symbol of the love that has already overwhelmed the two from within and which they are avowing, in full understanding that matters are now beyond their control.

When using magic in this way, to represent the vast existential elements in a believable life, the artist is obliged to show the lived reality that the magic summarizes, as Wagner does in the love between Tristan and Isolde, in the purity of Brünnhilde protected by the magic fire, and in the conflicts of Wotan embodied in sword and spear. But in the case of Siegfried we have *only* the magic, the drink of forgetting, and nothing to show apart from the appalling effect of it. As a result the character seems to fall apart before our eyes. Of course, there are characters in real life who fall apart in that way; but Wagner wants Siegfried to be the hero of the two works that contain him, and the symbolic representative of the innocence for which Brünnhilde finally praises him, despite the manipulations and power-games that have meanwhile brought him to destruction.

In the end we just have to accept that Siegfried is what he appears to be: not the new man or the artist-hero; not the forger of a freer world or the fitting deposer of a superannuated god; but someone who never quite grows up, an adopted child who is unable to form secure attachments, and who exists fully as a person only by moments, when the armour of his belligerence falls away. At one level Jean Shinoda Bolen is surely right to see *The Ring* as telling the story of dysfunctional families, and of their legacy in the psychology of their members.[1] At this level, Siegfried becomes intelligible, though in a way that clearly unfits him for the larger dramatic role. Bolen ignores, however, the cosmic aspect of the story. Conceived as a symbol of the individual's search for self-knowledge and self-identity in a godless world, Siegfried takes on another character, and it is this other character that interests Wagner.

The supreme moments of transition – such as the forest murmurs, the encounter with the wood-bird, the waking of Brünnhilde and the passage from fear to desire and from desire to love – these are consummate musical explorations of deep and shared states of mind. The last of them, the memory-narrative that leads to Siegfried's death, is perhaps the high point of the entire cycle – the moment when the buried Siegfried emerges in all his child-like wonder from the grave of his forgetfulness, and reclaims his only love. Even the dreadful capture of Brünnhilde on Gunther's behalf can be accommodated if seen in this perspective. For in the course of their lives men regularly betray, abuse or demean their ideal of the feminine, in order to pursue their wayward appetites. What Siegfried does here in a single act the ordinary man accomplishes during a lifetime of compromise. The outrage we feel at Siegfried is a heightened form of the disappointment that we men feel, or ought to feel, with ourselves.

Siegfried's character and emotions are revealed by the music, and although the music of the high-spirited youth is of the open and un-nuanced kind appropriate to his condition, the tonal syntax develops as the drama unfolds, showing that Siegfried is struggling towards a self-knowledge and autonomy that he does not quite achieve. There is another person beneath his impetuous activity, and this other person is less an individual than a universal, composed from the critical moments of transition in the life of Everyman. This other person comes magically to the surface during the forest murmurs in *Siegfried* Act 2, when, as the hero reflects on his lost mother, two chromatic themes, one first heard in association with the tragic fate of the Volsungs, the other connected to Siegfried's questions about his ancestry, give way to the first half of Freia's love motif. We hear Siegfried opening to love – not focused love, but the as yet unfocused desire to be completed by another human being. An enharmonic change into Brünnhilde's key of E major introduces the wood-bird, and there begins an incomparable representation of the sympathy between species. The bird's pentatonic language conveys the innocence not only of the bird, but also of Siegfried, who longs to understand himself as sprung from the same natural order as the bird.

After this enchanting and enchanted episode we have a different view of Siegfried, knowing that the belligerent hero is capable of giving and maturing, even if he himself is only partly aware of this. He has yet to be awakened to himself; but those natural, unmediated feelings that yearn for 'love and woman's worth' are now seeking their object. During his encounter with Brünnhilde, the music is replete with wonder, as Siegfried overcomes his fear, confronts the resistance of the former immortal, and awakens in her the mortal longings that he feels in himself. It is then that, in waking her, he has the clearest vision of his own nature and destiny. He came into this world for this alone – to make a gift of himself, and to receive a gift in turn. It is his moment of greatness – a greatness that matches hers.

The grown-up Siegfried who emerges from Brünnhilde's cave in the prologue to *Götterdämmerung* is someone who has matured through love, and not through trickery. This is the most important aspect of him, since it is the foundation for Brünnhilde's trust. Beneath the belligerence is the innocent heart, which does not know itself, but which has no reason to doubt its own constancy and, as it happens, will never have such a reason, since it will never take the next step towards self-knowledge. Siegfried as Everyman has passed stage 2 of *Selbstbestimmung*, the encounter with the Other, as opponent (the Wanderer), and as lover (Brünnhilde). He now must move on, according to the rules of the dialectic, to stage 3, which is the stage of self-knowledge. As Eliot famously wrote:

> . . . the end of all our exploring
> Will be to arrive where we started
> And know the place for the first time.

But it is just this that Siegfried cannot do. His solitary wanderings in the corrupted world lead to no reflection on himself, no real autonomy of choice, no step beyond the moral void that he becomes, once the mirror held before him by Brünnhilde has been taken away.

Siegfried is not only an abstract Everyman. He is also the vehicle for the great question posed by *Götterdämmerung*, which is the question of *Verwandlung*. The gods whom we worship are true to themselves forever, for that is their purpose – they are the projection into eternity of the principles that govern us in the here and now. Through religious devotion we address unchanging centres of will, in which individuality and identity are maintained through every action. If they let us down, we blame our sins, not their fickleness. (Although of course for a Feuerbachian like Wagner, the gods are in their real essence as fickle as the needs from which they spring: that, indeed, is Wotan's problem.) But the free individual, who launches himself into the world without the benefit of gods, who casts the gods aside and destroys their magic, voids the world of those durable centres of will. He is on his own, committed to being true to his vows, responsible to self and other through every choice, an enduring centre of emotion and will. But mortal beings cannot live up to the standards set by the gods. Even the purest heart can waver in its attachments, and even the most solemn oath can undo itself in time. Such, indeed, is Siegfried's case. And that is what is represented in the transformation brought about by the drink.

It is because of this that we are moved by Siegfried's final recovery of his identity in the narrative that precedes his death. In this remarkable scene Wagner takes us through the entire story of Siegfried in a few pages of vocal score, with music of such vividness and close-knit texture that the effect is like the vision that passes through the mind of a drowning man: beginning, middle and end all come together in a single image of what it means. And what it means in Siegfried's case is Brünnhilde, restored to his inner sight as he dies. Even if Siegfried has remained an abstraction, an Everyman constructed from the universal turning points in human life, his very emptiness lends poignancy to this passage, which represents you and me at the moment of death, opening after all the years of treason and forgetting, to the love that justified our being here.

In a remarkable essay, Robin Holloway has summarized the musical and psychological effect of this passage in words that deserve quotation here, since they are a vindication of Wagner's conception by a writer who is entirely convinced by it:

> The course of *Twilight*, while moving fast through a new and complex story, has managed to bring before us the events and music of almost every salient part of the three preceding operas. Now comes the simplest and most wonderful return, of the long epoch when Brünnhilde was asleep; the boyhood of her deliverer, covering the action of the first two acts of *Siegfried*. It comes neither in the form of a web of allusion like the horns [of the hunting party], nor a reiteration of old obsessions like Alberich [to Hagen]; appropriately for Siegfried, it is pure narration. But his memory is blocked. We have heard him recall how he gained the ring, and that his sword once shattered a spear. Between these and beyond them his memory has to be prompted and stage by stage unlocked. A beautiful three-note motif [183] does this; it is Siegfried's *madeleine*, a horn motif, turning upon itself over tenderly shifting harmony, speaking of nostalgia for time lost, showing that this 'overjoyous' man of action, as Gunther calls him, begins again to reflect and look within himself as he had as a boy when his life lay still before him. Thus it is also the motif of his dawning awareness: as more of his experience is allowed, he possesses himself more fully; land reclaimed from the drugged past and understood for the first time. Finally he repossesses Brünnhilde too. He has grown again to his full stature, a man as great as the woman he awoke or the god he pushed aside. But by the same token this self repossession also means his death, since in his progress towards illumination he will inevitably reveal what will lead to his murder.[2]

Holloway goes on to show how this episode does not merely redeem Siegfried, by restoring his real and continuous identity, but also ties the whole tetralogy together, in 'the farthest-flung arc of memory-architecture ever achieved in music'. Fundamental to this architecture are the two chords that open *Götterdämmerung*, and which we now understand in their full dramatic meaning – pointing backwards to Brünnhilde's awakening, and forwards to Siegfried's death.

There is another pertinent aspect of this episode. In his well-known essay on 'The Sorrows and Grandeur of Richard Wagner', Thomas Mann has this to say about Siegfried's death:

> The overpowering accents of the music that accompanies Siegfried's funeral cortège no longer tell of the woodland boy who set out to learn the meaning of fear; they speak to our emotions of what is *really* passing away behind the lowering veils of mist: it is the sun-hero himself who lies upon the bier, slain by the pallid forces of darkness – and there are hints in the text to support what we *feel* in the music: 'A wild boar's fury,' it says, and: 'Behold the cursed boar,' says Gunther, pointing to Hagen, 'who slew this noble flesh.' The words take us back at a stroke to the very earliest picture-dreams of mankind. Tammuz and Adonis, slain by the boar, Osiris and Dionysus, torn asunder to come again as the crucified one, whose flank must be ripped open by a Roman spear in order that the world might know Him – all things that ever were and ever shall be, the whole world of beauty sacrificed and murdered by wintry wrath, all is contained within this single glimpse of myth.[3]

The passage touches on two vital themes in the *Ring* cycle: the theme of hunting, and the theme of sacrifice. Hunting is portrayed from the outset as the background condition of the human order, with Siegmund driven as quarry into Hunding's house, there to meet the sister who had been orphaned by hunters, and to flee with her into the forest to be hunted as a pair. (The close of Act 2 of *Die Walküre*, with Sieglinde's nightmare of being hunted, set against the approach of Hunding's hounds, is surely without compare as a vision of hunting from the quarry's perspective.) The Valkyries are hunter-gatherers of human flesh, and the great culmination of the tetralogy occurs when Siegfried, hunting with his new companions, recounts the story of his life, and so becomes the quarry. This miraculous scene recovers the victim's innocence at the very moment when he offers himself for sacrifice – so that he offers himself *through* his innocence, thereby undermining the aggression. We are in the world of the hunter-gatherer, where pursuit and worship address the same primordial need, and the death of a victim casts a sacred glow on the assembled tribe.[4]

In *Opera and Drama* Wagner compared the role of the orchestra to that of the chorus in the Greek tragedy. Although this very imperfectly describes his own use of the orchestra in subsequent works, it perfectly fits the technique that the composer uses in order to set a frame around Siegfried as he is led forward to the slaughter. The orchestra is the supremely sympathetic observer of its own sacrificial victim, following his narrative in a kind of subdued awe, leading him on with the gentle gesture that Holloway compares to Proust's *madeleine*, but which might equally remind us of the way in which the sacred bull was once led to the altar, and encouraged to give the sign of acceptance that would summon the sacrificial blow.

In this way Siegfried is lifted out of his disordered life to become the object of a religious sacrifice, on a par, as Mann suggests, not only with the dying and resurrected gods of antiquity, but with Christ himself. In his original prose sketch, 'Die Wibelungen, or World History as Told in Saga' of 1848, Wagner comes close to this interpretation, seeing Siegfried as 'the individualized light or sun-god, who conquers and lays low the monster of ur-chaotic night'. Such, Wagner adds, is the meaning of Siegfried's fight with the dragon, which he compares to Apollo's fight with the serpent Python. Yet, 'as day succumbs to night again, summer to winter, Siegfried is slain at last: so the god became man, and as a mortal man he fills our soul with fresh and stronger sympathy . . . '[5] In the world that Siegfried, in his thoughtless defiance, has created, the world in which the gods are sinking into oblivion, it has fallen to human beings to be the bearers of the world's inner meaning. And, as it was in the Christian story, in which God became human in order to redeem us through his death, the meaning of the world, which once resided in law, now resides in sacrifice. By regaining his purity at the moment of death, Siegfried shows the triumph of love over machination, of the ideal over the real, and therefore of our values over the calculations that constantly erode and replace them. His life then ceases to be his private possession, and becomes an offering on the altar of all our loves and fears.

Mann refers Siegfried's sacrificial death to the old legends of the god who is put to death to be reborn as a saviour. But those legends were themselves the rationalization of something else – of a primordial experience of the sacred. René Girard has made the case for viewing the violent execution of a victim as the root experience from which the sense of the sacred derives. It is this, he argues, that releases human communities from the 'mimetic desires' that tear them apart, by uniting people against a victim.[6] This theory, contentious though it is, touches on something that we all respond to, which is the sense that the sacrificial victim *pays the price* for something, namely for a fault of our own. Hence the sacrificial victim moves us one stage nearer to that precious thing that Wagner wished both to represent and to render possible in his dramas, which is redemption, *Erlösung*, the act that frees us from all the bad things that have beset us, by showing them to be necessary parts of an intrinsically valuable whole. But exactly what this redemption amounts to, if there is no promise of a future recompense, is a deep and difficult question, with which my argument will engage in the final chapter.

Mann's anthropological allusions enable us to look back over the character of Siegfried in another and a more accepting spirit. Siegfried is a hero because he lifts into the light of consciousness all those aspects of our condition that belong to the growth of the free individual. In a way Lévi-Strauss's description of Wagner as the founder of structural anthropology is more completely vindicated in the story of Siegfried than in any other aspect of the cycle. Before Lévi-Strauss's rival, Arnold Van Gennep, wrote his great book on *Les Rites de passage* (1906), Wagner had perceived that human life is built around a series of transitions, and that these transitions have a meaning that is, in the broad sense, religious. (It is precisely this that is the theme of *Parsifal*.) Birth, the passage from adolescence to adulthood, sexual union, death – all are marked out in tribal societies by rituals in which the whole tribe is involved, in an affirmation of collective identity and of the will to endure. Siegfried has entered the world without such a rite of passage – his parents were transgressors, excluded from the moral order, and his birth was the occasion of his mother's lonely death. He is marked out from the beginning as the outsider, the scapegoat, the one who can be sacrificed for the benefit of the tribe. He himself, therefore, is the author of the rites that mark his passage to maturity – the forging of the sword, the slaying of the dragon, the defiance of the father-figure, and the awakening of the bride. His eagerness to be accepted in the community causes him to deviate from this self-created course; nevertheless, he ends as he began, an outsider whose identity is entirely his own doing, the paradigm sacrificial victim.

Wagner's account of Siegfried therefore focuses entirely on the points of transition, with a view to showing their sacred character, but without reference to any social meaning or ceremonial endorsement. They are sacred because they belong to the building of the free individual, whose fulfilment in this world depends upon acts of self-giving. That is what we witness in Siegfried, and it is why moments like the forest murmurs, the encounter with the wood-bird, the exchange with the dying Fafner, and the emergence from Fafner's cave, lost in study of the Ring, touch us in our deepest being – the music is taking us into primordial regions, showing simultaneously the natural order that still murmurs within us and the self-conscious apartness from it which is the gift, and the price, of freedom. It is on the illuminated edge between these two psychic landscapes that we feel the presence of sacred things.

Those who find the character of Siegfried unsatisfactory are rightly troubled by the unconsciousness that obliterates such vast areas of his psyche, and which in many respects precedes the drink of forgetfulness. But the missing consciousness is supplied at another level by the music, which shows a person realizing himself as a free individual by his own efforts alone (which is after all what Wotan required of him) while entirely at the mercy of forces that are hidden from his gaze. And this suggests a solution to another puzzle posed by *The Ring* – the raising of Siegfried's dead hand, so as to withhold the Ring from Hagen. As the miracle occurs the sword motif sounds in the orchestra – a reference to Siegfried's will, which he put into the Ring, first in winning it, then in giving it as a love-pledge to Brünnhilde, and finally in wresting it from her by force. Some part of Siegfried's will survives in this Ring, unpurged by his extinction – namely the part that committed itself to Brünnhilde with an 'eternal' promise, a promise that reaches beyond death. This is why Brünnhilde is already intimate with the miracle, and might even seem to be its author. All else has been extinguished – the winning, the wresting: these were events in time, whose significance has been superseded. Only the bestowing of the Ring in the vow of love lifted it above the order of time and destruction: hence the curse motif did not sound in that passage, and the lovers willingly and exultantly accepted their deaths as they pledged their love, so making clear that – so long as they remain true to this love – the curse cannot harm them. When the dead hand rises, it is to execute the inextinguishable meaning of the vow, and to summon Brünnhilde to death beside her husband. This is the purified remnant of Siegfried's will, from which the dross of mutation has been purged.

The scene reminds us of the meaning of mortmain in law: the will that survives in an object after the conscious life that ordered it has fled. The 'dead hand' survives in our loves too, but only for the shortest time – which is why Brünnhilde must die before the magic of forgetfulness takes over. Siegfried's dead gesture contains everything in him that could have survived as an object of Brünnhilde's love – all that his will had meant by way of gift and renunciation. Brünnhilde's decision to follow him in death we are to understand as a justification for Siegfried's life, of a kind for which 'redemption' was Wagner's favourite name. This word is surely justified by the music, which helps us to perceive the events of Siegfried's life and love under the aspect of necessity, so that freedom and necessity coincide in the soul of the hero, as they coincide in the will of the god.

Questions about Siegfried naturally remind us that not everything is straightforward with Brünnhilde either. As Wotan's Valkyrie daughter, as Siegmund's would-be rescuer and the protector of Sieglinde, as the woman who renounces her godhead for the sake of a mortal love, and who awakens to that love first to resist and then to give in to it – as all these things she is wholly believable and in the highest sense pure. But can we believe that this woman, who ponders each event with a god-like knowledge of its meaning, should be so entirely blanked out by Siegfried's transformation? Could she not suspect a trick, and could she not call upon some reserve of wisdom and sympathy that would give her the insight that she needs? And even if she finds no explanation for the terrible fact that Siegfried no longer knows her, is it in character for her to join in the plot to murder him, and to do so alongside people whom she can only despise and whose motives she ought to suspect? The only answer that I have to those questions is this: Brünnhilde's wisdom as the daughter of Erda is fatally disrupted as she enters the fallen world of mortals, since she is carried into it by force, suddenly aware of what she has lost in losing her Valkyrie powers. On her mountaintop she did not have to face up to her loss. She could rejoice in Siegfried, see him as the idealized husband whom she has imagined from the template given her by Siegmund. That idealized husband does not belong in the real world, and when Siegmund briefly coincided with the ideal, his doing so was dependent on the supreme suffering, the sense of existing at the edge, which transfigured him in the moment of tragedy. Even Siegmund, had he survived to scold Sieglinde for over-cooking the cabbage, would lose some of his transcendent polish. But of such matters Brünnhilde has no knowledge.

Brünnhilde has imagined Siegfried as the man who will always be as Siegmund was on that day of their meeting *in extremis*, and he is sent by her into the world oblivious of the corruptions that prevail there. As she takes leave of him she expresses the wish to be his soul, so as to be one with him in all his adventures. But when she is dragged down after him it is as a being whose soul has been stolen – and stolen, she discovers, by Siegfried. As she says in the great moment of 'Ach Jammer!', in the final scene of *Götterdämmerung* Act 2, her wisdom no longer serves her. She literally cannot comprehend what has happened. All she knows is that her life as a mortal is now a negation, and not a fulfilment, of her previous life as a goddess. For the first time she experiences the feeling of pollution, a feeling for which life on the mountaintop has not prepared her. She condemns Siegfried to death, because his survival seems to her, at that moment, a death-sentence cast on herself. Only later does she come to see that she must die in any case, and that through a new kind of wisdom – the wisdom of forgiveness – she can learn to die as she should.

Putting it that way does not excuse Brünnhilde's murderous

attitude. But it gives a kind of credibility to her resentment, and to the fact that she expresses it through Alberich's music (44): the music of someone who has been robbed of his *Eigen*. She too has been robbed. And her presence in the Gibichung hall is that of a vengeful spectre, a being deprived of all that made her what she was. Only in her final act of reconciliation and forgiveness does she regain her god-like disposition, for only then does she understand that what happened to her happened by necessity, following the choice that she herself once made, to enter the world of mortals for the sake of love.

Two other areas of doubt have impeded understanding of the *Ring* cycle: doubts about the consistency of the story, and doubts about what actually happens at the end. The first set of doubts includes questions like these: why does the Ring, which supposedly confers the power of world-domination, not protect those who possess it? Why does Wotan, having bequeathed the world to Siegfried in a musical gesture of supreme warmth, try to impede the hero's progress towards his goal, retiring in gloom and despair when he fails in this? How does Alberich, having lost the hoard, equip himself with an army that poses a threat to Valhalla, and also seduce a woman with force and gold?

Those doubts might be dismissed as the expression of an ungenerous literal-mindedness. After all, myths and fairy tales extend the reach of human story-telling beyond the possible, without thereby transgressing our sense of the real. As Aristotle argued in the *Poetics*, it is not impossibilities that destroy the narrative, but improbabilities – episodes that are false to the characters and their situation. Thus it is impossible that Fafner should become a dragon, and indeed all the transformations effected by the Tarnhelm take us beyond the reach of possibility, like those described in the *Metamorphoses* of Ovid. But it is entirely probable that Fafner, having use of the Tarnhelm, would turn himself into a dragon rather than, say, an elf, so as to use his dragon's weight and might to stay sleeping on the hoard. Strength and mass, stacking and storing, are the parameters within which his Giant's imagination works, and the idea that he might spend his wealth in search for 'love and woman's worth' would never occur to him. He is a hoarder, not a spender, and wealth, in his hands, is inert and fruitless.

That said, and with due allowance for the inconsistencies that are a necessary part of any myth since they are what distinguishes myth from mere fiction (myth, to repeat, being the story of the eternal present, rather than of an imagined past), we must recognize that there are inconsistencies that demand to be resolved, since their presence detracts from the cogency of the drama. That concerning the Ring itself is the most important. Beginning with Alberich's loss of the Ring to Wotan, through to Brünnhilde's vain attempt to use it to fend off the transfigured Siegfried, the Ring seems to provide its possessor with no help in the hour of need. The only explanation of this must lie in the *kind* of power conferred by the Ring: not an immediate power to defend against assault or danger, but a more insidious power, a form of psychological enslavement. The Ring has power, we might suggest, only over those already disposed to submit to it – those for whom the world is a place of exploitation, and who quickly adopt whatever locks them into this way of thinking. The Ring is a talisman, waved before those who see others as instrumental to their goals and appetites, and who have no 'immortal longings'. Its power over such people is a magic power, and once again magic is being used by Wagner as a symbol of a complex psychological reality that it is easier to dramatize than to put into words.

If something like this is true, then it is immediately clear why the Ring has no power over Wotan, who rules by law and treaty, and who therefore is committed to relations of free agreement with those who form his world. In the moment when he seizes the Ring from Alberich, Wotan acts as a free being, enjoying the power that he has won with the spear, which is the power to administer justice and to claim the obedience of those who live by law. Alberich's power belongs in another realm, where justice has been extinguished. Those who fall into that other realm are subject to the Ring; but free beings, without the lust for domination, are not. When a free being possesses the Ring he does not possess its magic; but he *is* subject to its curse.

When Siegfried emerges from the cave of Neidhöhle, contemplating the Ring, we hear first the Ring motif, and then, as he wonders what the use of this thing might be, the Rhine-daughters' lament, in its original tonal harmony, free from all accretions, and accompanied only by the motif of the Rhinegold. The curse is not heard, and for a moment it is as though we have returned to the realm of nature; the wood-bird, voice of that realm, then sounds in Siegfried's ear.

Siegfried has his faults, as we know. But he neither desires the kind of power conferred by the Ring nor knows how to make use of it. It is inert on his finger, as it is inert on the finger of Brünnhilde. Yet the curse still attaches to it, since it can be purified only by the one who willingly returns it to the Rhine – in other words, by the one who reverses Alberich's renunciation of love for power, by renouncing power for love.

This takes us to the related problem of Wotan's bequest. Not only is it psychologically plausible that Wotan, in relinquishing sovereignty to his mortal offspring, should do so out of love for them, so too is it plausible that he should then resent them for gaining what he has lost. Almost all bequests from people who have worked hard for what they give away are regretted. The power expressed by giving is replaced by powerlessness in the face of the recipient's misuse of the gift. And from this powerlessness proceeds a kind of despair, as the giver wakes up to the waste not of the gift only, but of the life that created it.

But that psychological observation is not the whole truth about Wotan. Whether or not Wagner was influenced in the matter by Schopenhauer, he certainly conceived Wotan as a pure expression of will – a god who exists through acts of will, and who embodies his will in the laws of an ordered universe.[7] Such a god cannot *suffer* his fate; he cannot be the passive recipient of things *done* to him, and cannot in that sense be overthrown by Alberich – not because it is impossible for him to be overthrown by Alberich, but because this is incompatible with his nature as a god. So that if Alberich does succeed in destroying Wotan's rule it has to be because Wotan himself has willed this result. That is the meaning of his bequest of the world to Alberich's son in *Die Walküre* Act 2 – a bequest that is wrestled into being through torment, as Wotan decides to will what seems to be inevitable.

And then, of course, thanks to Brünnhilde's supremely imaginative plan, crystallized from the remains of Wotan's anger, the god discovers that he can make the very same bequest, but this time to one he loves, rather than to one he hates, so that the act of will is not only easier, but more like a fulfilment of his nature than a denial of it. The bequest to Alberich's son implied a loss of sovereignty; the bequest to Siegfried, by contrast, is an affirmation of sovereignty in the moment of giving it away.

Because this act of will is also a renunciation of the world that he has governed, Wotan wills all that pertains to his own end – the hewing of the Ash Tree, the stacking of the logs, even the conflagration, which will be his last order to Loge, except that, with his broken spear, he cannot carry the order through, and therefore relies on Brünnhilde to set the old world aflame with her final gesture. Wotan's renunciation of the world recalls Schopenhauer's advocacy of the renunciation of the will, except that, in Wotan's case, renunciation is itself an act of will, since will is the god's identity.

There is a beautiful logic in all this. Religions are born and they die; but they do not simply dwindle. They die because they will their own end. The life of faith turns against itself, and becomes an act of repudiation instead. That which was once affirmed as orthodoxy is now persecuted as heresy, and as the religion wavers on the edge of the collective consciousness it is as though it were being banished by its own decision. Wotan's bequest to Siegfried, therefore, is conceived and executed in such a way as to affirm Wotan's sovereignty in the very moment of renouncing it.[8]

Problems associated with Wotan naturally impact on the character of Alberich too. Why, after the loss of the Ring, is the dwarf still able to command the Nibelung army, to overcome a woman by force and to reward her with gold, and in general maintain in being the forces of darkness? Of course, it could be that he had his private reserves, which were not brought up from Nibelheim when the gods ordered delivery of the hoard. But there is something deeper at work. Whatever power Alberich enjoyed through the Ring has, in a measure, clung to him. His Nibelung army is the remnant of his mesmerized slaves, who do not dare to rebel because the habit of obedience is so deeply implanted in them by the reign of terror. We should take note of Alberich's condition, as we witness it in the scene outside Fafner's cave in *Siegfried*, and in the dialogue with the sleeping Hagen in *Götterdämmerung*. Alberich's single-minded will to regain the Ring, his monomaniacal devotion to the cause of himself, his air of demonic possession – such things can exert a frightening subconscious influence in any sexual encounter, and maybe Grimhilde was captivated by that malevolently focused gaze, backed up as it was by money and power.

Supposing we can, in those ways, knit up the places where the plot seems in danger of unravelling. We nevertheless have the enormous problem of understanding how it ends. As Röckel put it in a famous letter to the composer, why, given that the Ring is returned at last to the Rhine, must the reign of the gods come to an end?[9] What exactly does Brünnhilde achieve by her self-immolation, and who now is in charge of the world? The original drama of *Siegfrieds Tod* ends, as does *Götterdämmerung*, with Brünnhilde riding Grane onto Siegfried's funeral pyre, after which we witness the rising flood of the Rhine and the return of the Ring to the Rhine-daughters. But in the earlier drama the rule of the gods is thereby restored, and a transfigured Brünnhilde takes a transfigured Siegfried with her to Valhalla, reminding us of the Dutchman and Senta rising skywards at the end of *Der fliegende Holländer*.

The rejection of that ending reflects Wagner's deepening understanding of what has happened prior to Brünnhilde's final gesture, as well as his mature conception of the human world. In his reply to Röckel he admitted that the destruction of Valhalla was not, in any literal reading of the text, entirely necessary, and that a clever lawyer could argue that the conditions had been fulfilled for the renewal of Wotan's reign. Nevertheless, he suggested, the audience would feel the inevitability of the doom of the gods, as Loge had foretold it in the closing scene of *Das Rheingold*.

To understand what Wagner was getting at we must see where the music has got to at the moment when Brünnhilde takes charge of the action. Siegfried's dying words have effectively handed the world over to Brünnhilde: she has been the meaning of it all, and Siegfried's narrative, ending on the fate motif, recalls the first appearance of that half-cadence, when Brünnhilde, on her own initiative, entered the human world. The Valkyrie brought death to Siegmund, since such had the gods decreed. But she received death from Siegmund too, since she was fatally trapped by what she encountered – the human need on which the gods depend for our belief in them.

The German *Noth* captures this reality more effectively than the English 'need'; but neither tells us what we learn from the music, as Siegmund had called out to his father for the promised sword. This epitome of all our heartfelt prayers shows how gods arise: nothing less than a god could answer the great question that the hero throws at the world. But the answer is not to be found in some heavenly realm where abstract principles impose their moral geometry. The answer, if it exists, lies here, now, in the vortex of mortal passion. The Valkyrie is the first divine being to understand this. She is the Christ figure, become mortal through pity.[10]

The fate motif in its original presentation is an incomplete modulation, suggesting the 'elsewhere' to which the hero is summoned. Siegmund, however, turns it into a question, a repeated demand for an answer that the Valkyrie provides, at last, only when the melody has been finally spelled out. (See Ch. 4, Ex (viii) in Appendix.) We hear in this melody the profound fellow-feeling that has invaded Brünnhilde's heart. And we are inwardly aware that nothing else could suffice. This *is* the answer to Siegmund's prayer – not the sword, which belongs with the gods and is as untrustworthy as they are – but the fatal birth of sympathy in an immortal, who is thereby set ineluctably on the path towards her own death. The music of this scene shows that our need for the gods is a need that only we can supply, and that the immortal, the ideal, must take up its residence among us if it is to survive. But by that very fact its survival is put in question.

From that thought it is a small step to the recognition that henceforth the world is in our hands: it is up to us to make sense of it, to seek and find the answer that our need requires, and to maintain in being, on whatever heights can be reserved for it, the ideal towards which we aspire, and through which we might be in some way reconciled to our fate. Yet we are born into a poisoned world, the very world that the gods required for our devotion. The rest of the drama is taken up by this thought.

In the two stories of Brünnhilde and Siegfried, which are one story only by moments, we see the way in which the sacred and the ideal are captured by the personal – through the forging of self-identity, and through love offered unconditionally in the heights of erotic desire. We must remake the world through our own self-affirmation, in just the way that Siegfried remakes the sword as his own, so that it ceases to be a gift of the gods. But we are no more trustworthy than the gods from whom we have freed ourselves. After all, they were our own creation, marked by all the failings that define our lot. We have inherited the fallen world that we created in our need for them, the world in which calculation, manipulation and *Verwandlung* undermine all relations of trust and love.

The action of *Götterdämmerung* takes place after the gods have retired from the scene – all we know of them now we know by hearsay, as the last messenger from the eternal arrives on the mountaintop to plead for their survival. The world that they have bequeathed is in our hands: it is up to us to rescue our ideals, and the music is in the business of showing this. At every turn we confront the curse of Alberich, the resentment planted deep in the human psyche by the machinations of power. Only by placing the moment of dedication above the calculating and scheming that our situation otherwise requires, do we free ourselves from the curse. This rescue must be won by each of us. It was an illusion to think that the gods would do it for us, and the illusory nature of our old beliefs is exactly what Brünnhilde acknowledges, in the supremely tranquil setting of 'Ruhe, ruhe, du Gott!' All the loose ends of life, all the damage suffered and inflicted, can be knitted into a consoling totality in retrospect, when seen in the light of renunciation.

What is accomplished, therefore, when Brünnhilde leaps with her horse into the flames, is the reaffirmation of what really mattered, those supreme moments that the music now iconizes and wraps together in a symphonic whole. We hear the world of the gods fall away, carried down by its weight of sorrow. And we hear the moments of love and gift rise above it to take their place as the only possible fulfilment of the individual life. There is no way that the gods can survive, since they are now only a memory. The return of the Ring to the Rhine symbolizes Brünnhilde's recognition that this is so. As the Rhine-daughters take the Ring, and the sin of calculation is washed away, we hear again Sieglinde's blessing of Brünnhilde, and we recognize that those moments of sacrifice are all that we have.

Such is the message distilled in the music, and Wagner was surely right to reply as he did to Röckel, that the music was a sufficient explanation of the ending. Throughout *Götterdämmerung* the burden of the world has been removed from the gods and assumed by humans. And the humans, Siegfried included, are not up to it. Only the former goddess can win through to a proper understanding, and in doing so she takes the drama of the gods into herself, knowing that it must find its conclusion in her. Hence her death, which is also a renunciation, is the death of the gods. But we are not bereft, for our greatness remains, in those deeds of sympathy and gratitude that are our sole vindication.

That is not the last word, however, for there is another aspect to Brünnhilde's final immolation. The music leads her through the sequence already used by Erda to invoke Brünnhilde's wisdom, in which the purity and the fate motifs form the links of a chain. During this passage Brünnhilde addresses not the dead Siegfried but her father, Wotan, expressing her final acknowledgement that Siegfried had been prepared as a sacrifice to the need of the God. This aspect of Siegfried's life is suddenly more important to Brünnhilde than all her empty praise of her faithless lover's greatness: what, after all, did he do, to earn the epithet of a 'hero', if it was not this – to fit the role assigned to him by the divine need? But this need is also her need: both she and Wotan were seeking a way out from the curse, Wotan through the hero's action, Brünnhilde through his love. And both have sacrificed the hero to their need, Wotan by provoking Siegfried to break the spear of government, Brünnhilde by arranging her lover's death. Siegfried enters again the sacred space reserved for the sacrificial victim. Through his death he has reconciled Brünnhilde and her father. That is surely the musical import of the sequence that accompanies Brünnhilde's mysterious words, and which resolves all its accumulated tension in 'Ruhe, ruhe, du Gott!' Wagner's memory architecture recuperates not the love of Siegfried and Brünnhilde only, but all the loves explored and vindicated in *Die Walküre*, loves founded in sympathy and self-sacrifice for the sake of the future. It recuperates the love between Wotan and Brünnhilde, her compassion for Siegmund, and the love and gratitude of Sieglinde, whose blessing now shines on them all.

9

Retrospect

But is that not just a cheat? Is it not identifying the meaning of life with the good bits, and then puffing those good bits up so that the bad bits are reduced, by contrast, to a price that we can afford? There is a long line of critics, beginning with Nietzsche, who have dismissed the Wagnerian magic as a kind of manipulation. Wagner's great conceptions, they argue, do not tell the truth about our condition: they falsify it. And the music, with its urgent accents, is part of the deception, injecting unjustified emotion into situations that, judged in themselves, are too thin and schematic to merit our concern. Nietzsche even argued that the whole idea of redemption, conceived in Wagner's way, is a denial of life and an invocation to decadence. In the third essay of *The Genealogy of Morals*, devoted to the demolition of asceticism, he ridicules *Parsifal*, wondering whether the composer had not intended the work as a kind of satyr play, a grotesque sequel to *The Ring*. And in *The Case of Wagner* he sets out to demonstrate the diseased quality of the Wagnerian hero, who is not a hero at all but a decadent human being.

Nietzsche also argues that there is an *aesthetic* disaster that ensues, when such a character is made central to a large-scale music drama. The goal of Nietzsche's book is to reject Wagner's moral vision, and also to suggest that the attempt to build that vision into a sustained work of art leads to music that is fundamentally sick. The moral faults of the vision translate directly into aesthetic faults in the music, and at the same time an immersion in the music involves a corruption in the soul of the listener, whose psyche is jeopardized by this surrender to a polluted ideal.

In opposition to Wagner's claims for his art, Nietzsche argues that the composer is really a 'miniaturist', that his musical techniques are incapable of generating real development, and that the whole thing is a kind of confidence trick, a simulation of musical life, which ignores the real source of music in rhythm and dance. He also argues that the heroic in Wagner is a sham. His characters need to be unmasked, to be deprived of their mythic costumes and returned to the bourgeois context from which they have been lifted into legend. Wagner's portentous music does not offer his characters redemption, since it merely disguises the fact that they are the ordinary sick refuse of nineteenth-century society – as far from tragic grandeur as Flaubert's Emma Bovary. The Wagnerian drama is a species of 'counterfeiting', in which the heroic passions and vast deeds reveal themselves, when held up to the critical light, as thin wisps of sickly passion, puffed up by musical bombast. The promises of 'redemption' and 'transcendence' depend on the forgery conducted by the music, and the fact that these promises are taken so seriously by so many is indicative of the equally decadent and counterfeit nature of the surrounding culture.

Nietzsche associates the Wagnerian musical process with a 'degeneration of the sense of rhythm'. In *Contra Wagner* – the fragments collected in Turin in 1888 – he takes this criticism further, connecting Wagner's *'endlose Melodie'* with the rhythmic disintegration, as he perceived it, of the music – its inability to *dance*. He illustrates the point through an image that occurs also in *The Case of Wagner*:

> One walks into the sea, gradually loses one's secure footing, and finally surrenders oneself to the elements without reservation: one must *swim*. In older music, what one had to do in the dainty, or solemn, or fiery back and forth, quicker and slower, was something quite different, namely, to *dance*. The measure required for this, the maintenance of certain equally balanced units of time and force, demanded continual *wariness* of the listener's soul – and on the counter-play of this cooler breeze that came from the wariness and the warm breath of enthusiasm rested the magic of all *good* music. Richard Wagner wanted a different kind of movement; he overthrew the physiological presuppositions of previous music. Swimming, floating – no longer walking and dancing.[1]

According to Nietzsche Wagner's music only *pretends* to the emotions that it claims. Hence the dramas themselves fall apart. The characters are real only by moments, and only in those histrionic gestures that reveal Wagner's art to be the art of the showman. True drama, Nietzsche holds, is not in that sense theatrical, and it is precisely Wagner's mastery of the theatrical idiom that disqualifies his dramas from bearing the meaning that he wishes for them: to put it another way, they are not dramas but melodramas. Wagner is an actor, and everything he does is devoted to *effect*, even though there is no dramatic content in terms of which the effect could be justified. It is only by moments that the magic works. But, in a famous passage, Nietzsche turns that criticism around, acknowledging that some of those moments, at least, are not mere theatre, but sparks of lyrical insight without compare in the history of music:

> There is a musician who, more than any other musician, is a master at finding the tones in the realm of suffering, depressed, tortured souls, at giving language even to mute misery. None can equal him in the colours of late autumn, in the indescribably moving happiness of the last, truly last, truly shortest joy; he knows a sound for those quiet, disquieting midnights of the soul, where cause and effect seem to be out of joint and where at any moment something might originate 'out of nothing'. He draws most happily of all out of the profoundest depths of human happiness, and, as it were, out of its drained goblet, where the bitterest and most repulsive drops have finally and evilly run together with the sweetest. He knows that weariness of the soul which drags itself, unable to leap or fly any more, even to walk; he masters the shy glance of concealed pain, of understanding without comfort, of the farewell without confession – indeed, as the Orpheus of all secret misery he is greater than any; and some things have been added to the realm of art by him alone, things that had hitherto seemed inexpressible and even unworthy of art – the cynical rebellion, for example, of which only those are capable who suffer most bitterly; also some very minute and microscopic aspects of the soul, as it were the scales of its amphibian nature: indeed he is the master of the very minute. But he does not *want* to be that![2]

Take away those moments, however, and what remains? A great work of counterfeit: fake transcendence, fake characters, fake emotions, and – in the end – a fake redemption offered without cost by

Parsifal, the 'pure fool'. None of this is believable, since none of it comes from the heart – it is all icy abstraction, rooted in the Hegelian conception of music as a vehicle for the 'Idea'. Thus 'everything that ever grew on the soil of *impoverished* life, all of the counterfeiting of transcendence and beyond, has found its most sublime advocate in Wagner's art . . . '[3]

Although Nietzsche does not explicitly say so, I suspect that he regarded the Wagnerian 'redemption' as a kind of cliché, an idea worn thin by too much use, brought into the later dramas only because the characters, lacking the will and integrity that make true tragedy possible, have to be content with 'redemption' as second best. Hence Nietzsche's ironical comment, regarding the placing of a wreath on the composer's grave by the German Wagner Society, on which were inscribed the last words of *Parsifal*: 'Redemption for the Redeemer': 'Many (strangely enough) made the small correction: "Redemption from the Redeemer". One breathed a sigh of relief.[4]

Yet, as the now well-known letter to Peter Gast of January 1887 illustrates, *Parsifal* was, for Nietzsche, a shattering experience, an entirely *genuine* expression 'of sympathy with what is seen and shown forth that cuts through the soul as with a knife . . . Has any painter,' Nietzsche asks, 'ever depicted so sorrowful a look of love as Wagner does in the final accents of his Prelude?' Clearly then, his attacks on Wagner did not cure him of the enchantment, and we are left wondering how sincerely he meant them.

There is truth in Nietzsche's claim that the Wagnerian characters do not always live up to the metaphysical and moral burdens that the composer places on them. Only every now and then – alone in the forest, confronting the Rhine-daughters, dying in a long-delayed access of consciousness – does Siegfried represent the tragic truth of human freedom. Nevertheless, the real test of Wagner's achievement lies with the music. Nietzsche's question to Wagner could be put simply thus: in engaging with this drama am I surrendering something of myself that I should be withholding? Or am I, as Wagner wants me to believe, entering a sacred place, in which music shows the true meaning of the witnessed events, and thereby elicits order and reconciliation in the feelings of the observer? Can I through this music achieve the peace and quiescence that the Greeks sought through tragedy, and which we moderns must seek through a new form of art – the 'art-work of the future' that will replace religion not by refuting it, but by doing its work, and doing it better?

In many ways Adorno's criticisms echo those of Nietzsche, although expressed in more consciously political terms. Adorno was understandably influenced by the catastrophe of the Holocaust and all that it meant concerning the roots of German nationalism. But he was also profoundly affected by his experience of Hollywood and the rising idiom of film music, much of it making use of stock effects and musical clichés that have their origin in Wagner. He saw the popular culture of America not as a liberation but as a new kind of enslavement, a way in which addictive forms of entertainment extinguish the search for inner freedom. He dismissed both jazz and film music as 'musical fetishes' – cheap effects that provide unreal emotions towards cliché-ridden situations. He saw Wagner's music in many ways as an anticipation of the worst kind of blockbuster film score – a way of inflating empty dramas with bombastic sequences that have no intrinsic musical logic, no ability to survive outside the peculiar context of the accompanying scenario. Like Nietzsche, he saw the Wagnerian hero as a fabrication, and the idea of heroic love as a fantasy through which we try to compensate for life in a world of debased and commercialized distractions. Only because of the inflated contrivances of the music do we accept any of this as believable.

Several commentators try to by-pass those criticisms, by following Shaw in seeing the drama as a political allegory, advocating a politics of innocence, a new order of purity in which all will be equal and no one will exert dominion over anyone else. On this view, the Wagnerian hero is justified by the immense political task that has been entrusted to him, from which the tragic love moments are mere distractions, given more prominence by the music than they really deserve. So long as we confine our attention to *Das Rheingold*, forgetting that this work is a mere prelude to the drama, this interpretation gains a foothold. However, even if Wagner was originally inspired by the revolutionary ideas of Feuerbach, he was too astute a thinker to be taken in by the utopian politics that Shaw and others read into the final drama. In a programme note for *Götterdämmerung* Bernard Williams put the point well:

The problem . . . is not that the *Ring*, as it proceeds, simply avoids politics. It is rather that the hope for a politics of innocence is what it centrally rejects. If one wants transportable philosophical conclusions from *The Ring* – and Wagner himself insisted that one should not want any such thing – one of them will be that there is no politics of innocence, because nothing worth achieving can be achieved in innocence. Only in the depths, where nothing has been imposed on nature or wrested from it, is the trusty and true. Siegfried is as near to pure nature as any active human being can be, and he eventually achieves nothing but disaster. Wotan does achieve many things, but in deep lack of innocence. Forced back from doing (in *Rheingold*) to manipulating (in *Walküre*) to leaving Siegfried free, he chooses to accept his own end in the hope of achieving something by purely innocent means – that is to say, by leaving everything to a purely innocent agent. *Götterdämmerung* shows how this does not work, and, particularly through the incident of the Rhinemaidens' refusal of the ring, why it could not work. Human action is significant only if it expresses knowledge, and knowledgeable action is already distanced from pure innocence.[5]

As Williams says, there is no 'transportable conclusion' – or at least, none that can be contained in a simple formula. *The Ring* does not argue for a thesis: it shows us what we are, and so helps us to understand, through sympathy, what is at stake in our moral choices. The real question that any lover of this great work must confront is not whether it offers true conclusions, but rather whether it affirms or denies the life that we have, which is *all* that we have.

As we have seen, Wagner was influenced in this matter by his conception of Greek tragedy. Like many readers of the Greeks, Nietzsche included, he was struck by the extraordinary sense of reconciliation that radiates from the Greek tragic stage. The audience lives through the destruction and death of noble and commanding characters; witnesses the fate of cities and families hanging by a thread; observes the most dreadful reversals of fortune; and all of this presented as a kind of necessity, a destiny that cannot be averted. And yet somehow the result is not only beautiful but serene. The audience is raised by the dreadful events to another level of being, in which the fear of death has been transcended and human life reaffirmed in the knowledge of its fleetingness. Explanations of this remarkable experience have been forthcoming since Aristotle, whose view of tragedy as a 'purgation' of pity and fear still has a certain following. But Wagner was the first thinker fully to grasp that the tragic experience is akin to, and derived from, the ritual heart of religion. Suffering, as portrayed in tragedy, is both ritualized and sanctified. The tragedy shows human beings on the edge, on the verge of nothingness, who can nevertheless snatch greatness from the jaws of destruction. They do this by displaying the worthwhileness of what is about to be taken away – the absolute value of life and love, revealed in the moment of their annihilation.

Nietzsche's complaint, that Wagner's characters, returned to the modern context where they belong, are no more capable of tragic grandeur than Emma Bovary, surely shows a disregard for what art can do, and indeed for what Flaubert did for Emma. Suppose we were to return Oedipus and his children to their context, to see them merely as the most famous dysfunctional family in fiction, and to place their well-known moments of distinction, as when Oedipus stabs out his eyes or Antigone buries her brother, in the context of the ordinary and no doubt sordid machinations of day-to-day life in Thebes. Would they not appear then, as Nietzsche says of Wagner's characters, as 'five steps from the hospital'?[6] Tragedy does not deny the ordinary and the sordid. But it takes the turning points of human life and frames them as religious sacrifices – it is a 'making sacred' of those moments when we must pay the full cost of being what we are. It is not absurd to give to these moments the name that Wagner clung to when attempting to summarize their power – *Erlösung*, or redemption. He did not mean that word in its Christian sense, as invoking the promise and the purchase of a better life to come. He meant it as a description of the religious rite itself, and hence of the moment of transcendence on the tragic stage: the moment when life is shown to be intrinsically worthwhile, exactly when it is engulfed by the ambient nothingness.

But this raises the question of whether the tragic experience is still available to us. Can tragedy still speak to us, in a world without religion? Wagner's answer was an emphatic yes. And in this he showed a deep philosophical awareness of what is at stake for us. Modern people, he believed, are living beyond the death of their gods: such is precisely the background assumption of *The Ring*. And this means that we live with an enhanced awareness of our contingency – of the fact of being thrown down in the world without an explanation. And yet, just as much as our forebears, we are social beings, accountable to each other, susceptible to guilt and shame. We are compelled by our own social nature to praise and blame, love and hate, reward and punish. We are aware of the self, as the centre of our being; and we try to connect to other selves around us. We are accountable persons, and the process of winning freedom and personality leads us to confer those gifts on others. We see each other as beings with a more than worldly destiny, even if there is no world for us save this one.

In other words the life of the free and accountable person remains, for us, the focus of meaning, and its many aspects are symbolized by Wagner in the leading characters of *The Ring*. If we shift from that focus, and turn our attention instead to the human organism, then we might be tempted to see the belief in freedom as no more than a misreading of the impersonal forces that govern us. We might begin to reimagine our condition in purely objective terms, as though subjectivity and its gifts were illusions and the *Lebenswelt* no more than a dream. Religion was an antidote to that kind of cynicism. It encapsulated the ideas of freedom and personhood, and presented them in mythical form, offering a kind of metaphysical guarantee of our apartness. Wagner set out to capture that way of thinking in the character of Wotan. But sceptical modern people have no such easy way to reassure themselves. Science has removed us from the central place in the scheme of things that once we occupied, and persuaded many of its devotees that the 'eternal in man' is an illusion, maybe even a destructive illusion. No god will come down, now, to rescue us. If we are to be lifted from our cynicism, so as to believe in the freedom and dignity of the human being, it is we ourselves who must come to the rescue.

This, for Wagner, is the task of art – the task bequeathed by the death of our gods. Art must show us freedom in its immediate, contingent, human form, reminding us of what it means to us. Even if we live in a world from which gods and heroes have disappeared, we can, by imagining them, dramatize the deep truths of our condition, and renew our faith in what we are.

Wagner was a child of his time, and it is not surprising if that idea of the redemptive task of art emerged over time from another, and more time-bound, conception. The first truly Wagnerian drama, *Der fliegende Holländer*, tells the story of a lonely and accursed man, a wanderer on the face of the earth, who will be offered the death that he longs for and the transfiguration that rewards it, only if he meets the woman who is prepared to sacrifice herself in order to redeem him. Variants of that story can be found throughout the literature of romanticism, and it was Wagner's distinctive contribution to use it to shape an ideal of the feminine, and to embody that ideal in vivid and appealing characters – notably in Senta and Elizabeth, in Eva and Isolde. This idea of the redeeming woman, of the *Ewig-weibliche* who lifts the man from his futile quests and offers him at last a consolation that is both sexual and metaphysical, begs for a psychoanalytic explanation, and there are many tedious commentators who have rushed to provide one. But it is emphatically *not* the idea of redemption that is expressed in *The Ring*. Although Wagner's obsession with the feminine, and with the sexual act as a union of opposites, is still present in the relation between Siegfried and Brünnhilde, it is precisely this aspect that – glorious music apart – carries the least conviction for the modern audience. *The Ring* shows Wagner thinking beyond his life-long fixation with the redemptive role of woman in sexual love, so as to consider love in its entirety.

The great turning point of the cycle occurs when Brünnhilde is stirred to sympathy by the encounter with Siegmund's love, and it is the sacrifice brought about through her act of compassion that is the heart of *The Ring*. The sacrifice of Siegfried, hero of the erotic, is an earth-shaking moment, for all the reasons given by Robin Holloway and Thomas Mann. But it is an episode between the two apotheoses of Brünnhilde, the first in sleep, the second in death. It is the first of those that is the turning point of the drama, and it is a moment purged of all traces of erotic feeling. The Valkyrie has been moved by sympathy, she has been blessed in a transcendent burst of gratitude by a human woman, and she is being dedicated to the future by a father, full of paternal love for her. And when, at the end of the cycle, the music takes over, and we understand that these cosmic events are really moments in the life of all of us, it is the recollection of Sieglinde's blessing that brings quietus. In other words, it is sympathy that heals the cosmic wound. And in showing this through a succession of tragic moments, in each of which some aspect of our freedom is the occasion for heroic suffering, Wagner's great work fulfils its promise. By purely artistic means, and with no reference to the transcendental, it consecrates the short life that is ours.

'We must learn to die,' Wagner wrote to Röckel, 'and to die in the fullest sense of the word; fear of the end is the source of all lovelessness.' Only if we learn to die in a spirit of acceptance can we live in a spirit of love. Loving means giving, and giving is a relation between persons, who act from the conscious pursuit of another's interest, and by the willing renunciation of interests of their own. To reach the condition in which this kind of giving is possible, human beings had to pass through a long prehistory.

Wagner divined the truth about that evolutionary prehistory and presented a matchless summary of its psychic legacy, in the demi-gods and goblins of *The Ring*. He showed the emergence of law-governed freedom in the form of cosmic moments: the theft of the gold, the stripping of the spear, the forging of the sword, the kiss of love in which the self is awakened and also awakened to its death. In that way he dramatized the discontinuity between the world of the moral person and the dark Eden that preceded it.[7] And he showed in dramatic form the process of *Selbstbestimmung*, whereby freedom, sovereignty and accountability are won by each individual through conflict, self-knowledge and love.

He showed how our conceptions of the transcendental and the immortal hold the *Lebenswelt* in place, and how they are constantly eroded by greed, resentment and doubt. He dramatized the great moral truth, that we must value others intrinsically, and protect our loves and commitments against substitution and exchange. And he saw that it is precisely the fear of death, the desire to hold on at all costs to our worldly schemes for power and status, that has created a world in which we abandon what we love, in which we treat as a means what exists in reality only as an end, and in which we lose our way in the mists of *Verwandlung*. He showed that the emergence of the person from the natural world is not a biological fact but a spiritual drama, and that all of us are caught up in this drama and fulfilled or destroyed by our way of engaging in it.

Destruction does not mean death: on the contrary, it is the fear of death that destroys us, since it destroys the openness to love. At the same time Wagner saw that without our ideals we are destroyed in any case: only by idealizing our condition do we take possession of what it offers. The *Lebenswelt* that was built from our great illusions, but which contains the secret of personal freedom – the secret that was hidden on the mountaintops and which each of us must discover for himself – can be recovered as a personal possession, but only through the conscious pursuit of the ideal. The world that is dramatized in *Siegfried* and *Götterdämmerung* is a world of ideals without illusions, in which individuals are in charge of their lives and bound to make a mess of them. Nevertheless it is a world full of meaning, and we understand this because we are presented with those sacred moments in which human beings and their emotions transcend the world of calculation to become exemplary and pure.

In describing these moments as sacred I am consciously evoking a concept that we owe above all to Wagner – the sacred conceived as an aura attaching to the great transitions and existential choices, the aura that sets them apart from nature, as visitors from another sphere. This aura arises spontaneously in the experience of the self-conscious being, and is inseparable from the I to You encounter that shapes the *Lebenswelt*. The awe that we feel at the great moments of sacrifice and resolution in the *Ring* cycle is proof enough that we are by nature turned towards the sacred. And it is our openness to these moments that enables us to come away from the Cycle with a sense of profound spiritual comfort, knowing that life in this world is worthwhile.

Wagner is not trying to persuade us that sacrifice is the meaning of life. Rather, as in the Greek tragedy, he is showing through represented acts of sacrifice that life has another meaning than the pursuit of status and power, and that it is our ability to accept death that makes this meaning real to us. He is showing, through the sacrificial moment, that there are things in all our lives that are sacred, and which vindicate what we are. That, ultimately, is what the Wagnerian 'redemption' means.

This is not the 'love panacea' mocked by Shaw. Love is significant for Wagner because it is the symbol of something else, which is the ability of human beings to discount their own interests, to stand up against the omnipresent forces of destruction and to act from a vision of intrinsic value. It is not erotic love only that has this character, and indeed if there is one lesson to be taken from *The Ring* it is that erotic love is love in its most dangerous form, the form in which we are most likely to betray our ideals and in which our ideals can turn on us and take their revenge. The ecstasy of erotic love is paid for by the fatal flaw of jealousy and by those coiling inner hatreds conveyed by the motif of murder (171).

As important is the love between parent and child, a love that is foreshadowed in Siegmund's desire for Sieglinde and hers for him. Nobody who feels the *drama* of the twins' encounter can fail to recognize that their life of deep sorrow makes sense only as a preparation for the new life that is to spring from it. And the mystery of *Die Walküre* is that this very act of preparation, in which human mortality is not only the precondition of sexual union but also its meaning and its vindication, is necessary also in order to renew the life of the immortals. Our sacrificial loves are the true source of the golden apples – such is the ultimate meaning of Freia's motif in all its many forms. And it is the meaning also of the scene between Brünnhilde and Sieglinde, when the Valkyrie finally involves herself completely with the unborn child, and hands over the broken fragments of the sword – a god's dishonoured promise, which can be redeemed only by a man.

At the end of *Die Walküre*, after all these tragic conflicts have been not so much solved as dissolved in Brünnhilde and are now held in solution in her, the drama returns to the same emotion: the emotion of the 'womb of time'. The idea that this secret, lying in the heart of the world and awaiting discovery, is the fruit of an obscure cooperation between god and man, in which the destiny of each is equally at stake – that the unawoken wisdom of the world should have arisen by an invisible hand from transactions in which god and man, immortal and mortal, were equally necessary and equally compromised – this idea, and its astonishing realization in music that brings magic wonder and heart-rending grief inextricably together, provides one of the two most sublime moments of *The Ring*, and one whose authority, artistic, moral and metaphysical, cannot be questioned.

This sublime moment at the end of *Die Walküre* reaches forward to its equally sublime companion at the end of *Götterdämmerung*. The great outpouring of forgiveness and acceptance with which Brünnhilde accomplishes her death is directed equally to Siegfried, the lover who betrayed her, and to Wotan, the father whose predicament made this betrayal inevitable. The only previous vision of peace that the cycle contains is that in which father–daughter love was wrapped in forgiveness and consecrated to the future. But yet more important, the concluding music of the cycle seems to say, is the love for the unborn, for what is yet to be, that welled in the breast of Sieglinde, and was poured out in gratitude on the self-sacrificing goddess who stooped to rescue a mortal and her unborn child.

This complex vision of love and its place in the life of the person is presented to us in moments of sacrifice. Siegmund is sacrificed to Fricka's outrage; Brünnhilde is sacrificed twice, once in sleep and once in death, in one case looking forward to love, in the other case obeying it. Siegfried is prepared as a sacrifice from the very beginning, and killed in the most profoundly religious moment of the drama. And in the final immolation the gods themselves are burned on the altars that we raise to them. Sacrifice is not the *moral* of the story, but the means by which it makes its moral known. By presenting sacrificial moments in artistic and fictional form, Wagner argued, the Greek tragedy captured what was once the prerogative of religion.[8] It presented a purifying ritual, in which life is remade as a vehicle of the ideal. The audience was to see through the death to the heroic grandeur of the free being who confronts it. That is the central mystery of sacrificial religion; it is also, for Wagner, the imaginative core of the work of art – of his own art, as much as the art of the Greek tragedians. It is the 'concealed deep truth' that religion hides from us, and which art reveals in symbols. In *The Ring* that deep truth is conveyed as in no other work conceived in modern times.

Appendix

Alan Dunning (see Appendix to Heise, *The Wound That Will Never Heal*) identifies 178 leitmotifs, some of which have embryonic versions and variants; my own researches suggest 186 or more. Dunning and Heise are an excellent resource, since the motifs are written out in musical notation, identified in all their occurrences, and translate immediately into sound at the touch of a mouse. One word of caution, however, which is that – partly for reasons of presentation – many of the motifs are not given their full harmonic context. A motif like the curse (45), for example, cannot be separated from the harmonic process that moves both with and against the melodic line. In what follows I give most of the leitmotifs that seem to me to deserve to be singled out, followed by the examples explicitly referred to in Chapter 4.

The names often given to the leitmotifs vary, as do the accounts of their meaning. I have given them names where I can, and also noted here and there the names and the descriptions given by others, notably by Cooke, in his introduction to the Solti recording, by J. K. Holman in his *Listener's Companion and Concordance*, by Newman in *Wagner Nights* (reissued as *The Wagner Operas*) and by Julius Burghold in the edition of the poem published by B. Schott's Sons in Mainz, around the end of the nineteenth century. The Schott edition contains tables of all the leitmotifs then recognized by commentators, and marginal notes identifying each of their appearances.

1

Primal nature.

2

2A

2B

Two nature motifs, associated with the Rhine.

3

3A

3B

Waves of the Rhine (2A and 2B diminished).

4

Rhine-daughters: Woglinde's lullaby. (The descending whole-tone interval at beginning and end anticipates **14**.)

5

Rhine-daughters: Flosshilde's warning.

6

Rhine waves: descending version of **3A,** using a diminished seventh in place of a major triad as harmonic base.

7

Alberich's clumsy wooing. Cooke: Alberich.

8

Wellgunde's taunt ('Heia! Du Holder!'). Diminished fifth and fifth in apposition. (Cf. **45.**)

9

Alberich's distress ('Wehe, ach, wehe!').

10

The rape taunt ('Greife nur zu …').

11

Alberich's cry: 'Fing' eine diese Faust!' (10 varied).

12 and 13

Nature motion (Cooke) and Rhinegold.

14

A: Rheingold!　　　　　**B. Heiajaheia!**
Two motifs, described by Cooke and Holman as Rhinegold, and the
Rhine-daughters' joy in the gold.

15

Swimming motif.

16A

The world's mastery.

16B

The Ring, forged from two chords, the 'curse chord' (F sharp, A, C, E), (cf. **8** and **45**), and the diminished seventh on D sharp.

17

Entsagungsmotiv (renunciation). More appropriately: existential choice. Wagner himself wrote '*Entsagung*' in the first sketches of the score.

18

Valhalla.

19

Wotan's spear.

20

Love's longing for fidelity.

21

'... herrliche Wohnung, wonniger Hausrath'.
Burghold: *Weibmotiv*: love in its domestic aspect. Cooke: domestic bliss. Holman and Newman: love's enchantment.
Sung by Fricka to express her longing for a home from which her husband would not seek to wander.

22

Freia's gift of (erotic) love: **A**, in its sensual aspect; **B**, in its devoted and tragic aspect. **A** is sometimes prolonged in these and similar ways:

B is prolonged in many ways. See, for example, **59** below. When the Giant Fasolt expresses his desire 'to win a woman, winsome and gentle, who will live with us poor creatures', **22A** and **B** are combined in a new way. Ernest Newman aptly writes that 'Wagner here lays the gentlest of hands on the uncouth giant who has a strain of tenderness in him' (*The Wagner Operas*, London, Putnam, 1961, p. 463):

23

The Giants.

24A

Fasolt's demand that Wotan keep faith. Sometimes called 'irrevocable law'.

24B

Fasolt: What you are, you are only through contracts. Continuation of **24A**.

25

Treaty motif. (Variation of **19**, closed at both ends.)

26

A **B**

Freia's apples. (Derived from **18A**.) (**B** is an ironical diminished version, given to Loge.)

27

Heise: Godhead lost. Prolongation of **26B**.

28

Froh. (Variation of **26**.)

29

Donner (not exactly a leitmotif, unlike **49** below).

30

Loge (up by fourths, down by fifths). This motif occurs first at quarter-speed to Fafner's warning to his brother against Loge's untrustworthiness, suggesting that it is more about deception than Loge's other aspects. It has a large role in *Götterdämmerung*, notably as an accompanying figure to Siegfried's Rhine Journey and his subsequent exploit in passing through the flames to capture Brünnhilde.

31

Loge's flames.

32

Magic fire.

33

Introduced by Wotan to the words 'You don't know Loge's art'. Usually called the brooding or scheming motif, since it is associated in this connection with Mime. Cooke argues that it is derived from 16, the Ring, as in this occurrence:

34

Sometimes called the motif of woman's worth, since introduced to the words 'woman's loveliness and worth', sung by Loge, and often associated with the deep need for the feminine, as in Wotan's words to Freia: 'Let youth return to us'. Usually used, as here, to articulate the cadence from the subdominant seventh to the dominant in the minor.

J. K. Holman (*Wagner's 'Ring': A Listener's Companion and Concordance*, Pompton Plains, NJ, Amadeus Press, 1996, p. 121) writes of this theme that it is 'one of the drama's most pervasive musical ideas. The falling scale of six notes, which recurs more than forty times in the course of the tetralogy, is always readily identifiable. It is also among the most plastic, formless, and intriguing phrases in *The Ring*. We often hear it as a cadence, a kind of closing attached to quite different ideas or music.' To Cooke it is a second form of **17**, the renunciation motif, 'which often occurs as a mournful cadence, expressing futility' (see example **84** in his introductory discs). It is indeed described as the renunciation motif by Burghold, who places it side by side with **17**, as another version of the same idea, which it brings to closure with a fitting cadence. Robert Donington writes that the phrase 'conveys a mood not unlike that of the "renunciation" motif: it speaks of grief and destiny; it also speaks, not in all but in some of its harmonic and dramatic contexts, of acceptance and resignation' (*Wagner's 'Ring' and Its Symbols: The Music and the Myth*, London, Faber and Faber, 3rd edn, 1974, p. 85). When Alberich in Nibelheim confronts his divine visitors, the words 'alles was lebt soll ihr entsagen!' ('all that lives shall renounce it [i.e. love]') it is to the accompaniment of this motif. And the motif accompanies Siegfried's Rhine Journey, at the point where joy begins to be polluted, and a mist of hatred descends.

A. E. F. Dickinson, in a comparatively early attempt to catalogue the motifs, refers to this theme as 'powerlessness', and gives an impressive list of its occurrences in confirmation (*The Musical Design of 'The Ring'*, Oxford, OUP, 1926).

35

Nature-weaving motif, introducing a prolongation of **22A**, representing the natural call of sensual love, and immediately following Loge's first statement of **34**.

36

A   **B**

Diminution (**A**) and augmentation (**B**) of **22B**, during descent into Nibelheim.

37

Smithing motif. Related, though perhaps not significantly, to **14B**.

37A

Servitude motif: profiling the descending semi-tone (i.e. **9**).

38

Tarnhelm – *Verwandlung* motif.

39

The power of the Ring. (Amalgam of **37A** (=**9**) and **14B**.)

40

The hoard.

41

Dragon motif: semi-tone, tritone and major seventh dramatized, but sterile.
Holman: Serpent. Donington: 'Fafner as the enormous backward pull (or inertia, or resistance to change) of the unconscious'.

42

This accompanies Alberich's humiliation. Probably not a motif.

43

Loge's sarcasm.

44

Alberich's resentment, and resentment generally. The syncopations become more complex and the harmonies denser as the cycle proceeds.
Holman: hatred; Cooke: resentment; Newman: annihilation.

45

The curse.

46

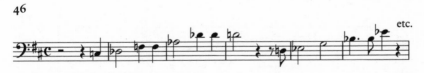

Motif also associated with the curse, important in the prelude to *Siegfried* Act 2.

47

Erda (=2B in the minor).

48

The doom of the gods. (Inversion of **47**.) Sometimes invokes, or concludes in, **34**.

49

Donner's thunder: 'He da! He da, he do!'

50

etc.

The rainbow bridge.

51

Wotan's great idea: the sword.

52

Wotan's defiance: 'So grüß' ich den Burg!'

53

The Rhine-daughters' lament for the gold.

54

Wotan's storm (the shake of the spear, **19**).

55

Donner's lightning, variation of **49**, which (together with its harmonic elaboration) becomes significant in Sieglinde's nightmare.

56

Siegmund (the spear interrupted).

57

Siegmund's exhaustion. Perhaps not a motif. (Cf. **42**.)

58

Sieglinde.

59

Love motif, derived from the second half of Freia's motif, **22B**.

60

Siegmund's chivalry ('Unheil wende der Wunsch von dir!'). Variation of **58**.

61

The sorrow of the Volsungs.

61A

Version of **61**, introduced in *Siegfried*, and thereafter crucial to the narrative.

62

Hunding.

63

Associated with 'hearth and home' by Hunding, with Hunding's honour by Fricka, and with Mime's inhospitable hearth by the Wanderer. Holman calls this 'rights', Cooke 'Hunding's rights'. Rather, it signifies the desire and need for respect, even among those who cannot offer it.

64

Volsung suffering, though Heinrich Porges, reporting Wagner, calls it a Sieglinde motif (*Wagner Rehearsing the 'Ring'*, tr. Robert L. Jacobs, Cambridge, CUP, 1983).

64A

The race of the Volsungs.

65

Holman: bride's lament; Newman: the maiden's grief. The distress of the girl whom Siegmund vainly tries to save. Also occurs when Fricka accuses Wotan of abandoning the race of the gods (*Die Walküre* 2, i).

66

'Wälse!'

This octave drop extracted from 51, Wotan's great idea, and 52, the motif of Wotan's defiance, and thereafter associated with Nothung, as in this setting of 'Ein Schwert verhiess mir der Vater – ich fänd' es in höchster Noth', which repeats 52, more or less exactly:

67

The triumph of Siegmund and Sieglinde.

68

Siegmund's love song ('Liebe und Lenz Lied').

69

Sieglinde's tenderness: variation of **22B.**

70

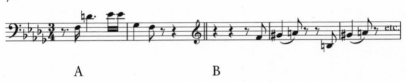

A   B

Longing. Newman: bliss. **B** = longing, **A** = the bliss that fulfils it.

71

Entwining. (Brother and sister remember.)

72

Ride motif.

73A

Ride of the Valkyries. Riding more generally.

73B

Subsidiary Valkyrie motif.

73C

Valkyrie laughter and cry ('Hojotoho!').

74

Anger motif, associated with Fricka, but not only with her. Cooke identifies the melodic line here as a figure that occurs in all Wagner operas, and which in some way represents the obstacles between an intention and its fulfilment, or, more poignantly, the attachment to false idols, which creates a barrier between agents and their true ideals. (See Deryck Cooke, 'Wagner's Musical Language', in Peter Burbidge and Richard Sutton, eds., *The Wagner Companion*, London, Faber, 1979, pp. 225–68.)

75

Fricka's indictment. (Another variation of **22B**.)

76

Wotan's frustration. (Derived from 19.)

77

Wotan's frustration (the spear in pieces).

78

Wotan's revolt or despair (*Verzweiflung*). The chord on which this ends is entirely new and looks forward to *Götterdämmerung*. The E double flat is the first minim of the curse, which now sounds. (Grammatically speaking, the chord is the first inversion of a D flat seventh plus minor ninth over a C natural pedal.)

79

Agitation (*Unruhe*) motif. Heise, Cooke and Newman: the need of the gods. The motif has two parts: the first occurs alone when Brünnhilde's horse Grane enters in a state of exhaustion in *Die Walküre* 3, i; the second is identical with **76**. The two occur together in altered form in the contrapuntal peroration to *Die Walküre* 2, ii.

80

Wotan's first bequest.

81

Wotan's anger: first motif.

82

Wotan's anger: second motif.

83

Hunding's pursuit.

84

The fate motif.

85

Todesverkündigung: the announcement of death. (Burghold calls it the *Todesklage*, the lament of death.) The melody ascends through an octave while the bass descends through an octave, creating an eerie sense of opening out, as though to reveal a great emptiness.

86

Siegmund's resistance. Related to **76**, Wotan's frustration.

87

Sieglinde's dream. (Borrowed from Liszt, Faust Symphony.)

88

Wotan's grief. (Brooding.)

89

Siegfried as hero.

90

Sieglinde's blessing. (Also called 'redemption', among other things.)

91

Wotan's reproach. Not exactly a motif.

92

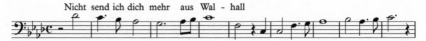

Wotan's judgement: **76** and **85** combined in sequence to make a new melody. Porges tells us that Wagner wanted no tenderness (*Weichheit*) to enter Wotan's voice as he sings the notes of **85**: the memory of grief contained in the melody should here be secret.

93

Valkyrie fugue (from **85**).

94

Brünnhilde faces judgement. **93** slowed down and brought to closure, and with it **85**, which has been looking for closure from the first announcement of death. Porges writes of this: 'An effect of inexpressible tragic sadness was created by the bass clarinet's melody, which so movingly conveys the mood of the moment, the anxiety, the expectancy. Its performance requires a blending of profound emotion with, if I may so express myself, impressionable calm (*plastische Ruh*), attainable only if the crescendo and diminuendo are made to sound absolutely spontaneous and natural' (p. 72).

95

Called 'Brünnhilde's pleading' and also (by Burghold) 'Volsung-love', but to my mind best described as Brünnhilde's purity motif. Derived by octave displacement from 19.

95A

Prolongation of 95, though preceding 95 in the score, conveying Brünnhilde's god-like dignity. Cooke and Holman call this 'Brünn-hilde's reproach'.

96

Brünnhilde's gentle response to Wotan's anguish: derived from 76.

97

Variation of 96.

97A

Growing out of **97**.

98

Sleep motif.

99

Brünnhilde's appeal to Wotan. Widely known as the sleeping Brünnhilde motif, or sleeping nature motif, on account of its subsequent use.

100

Wotan's farewell. Cooke and Holman: Wotan's love for Brünnhilde.

101

The ring of magic fire.

102

Crafty Mime: three motifs extracted from 9 and 14.

103

Mime's glee. The first half of this motif is also associated with Alberich's insolent threats in *Das Rheingold*. Synthesis of Valhalla and Loge, in a fantasy of longed-for power. Has been called the arrogance of power (*Machtdünkel*) motif.

104

Siegfried's horn call.

105

Frustration, associated with both Siegfried and Mime. Cooke: Siegfried's anger; Holman: youthful energy.

106

Mime's Nibelung nature. Based on 37.

107

False sentiment: Mime's 'altes Starenlied'.

108

The voice of nature in Siegfried. Sometimes called 'longing for love' (*Liebessehnsucht*). Reminiscences of **100** and **22B**. Wagner said this should 'sound as out of a dream' (Porges, *Wagner Rehearsing the 'Ring'*, p. 83).

109

The first suggestion of birdsong, accompanied by **22B** and woven into **108**.

110

Freedom, *Wanderlied*.

111

Freedom, second motif.

112

The World Ash Tree. One of several contenders for this title. See **114**, **146** and **147** below.

113A

The Wanderer, first motif.

113B

The Wanderer, second motif.

114

Sometimes called 'the power of the gods', though also, when preceded by **19**, the World Ash Tree motif. (Derived from inverting **19**. See also **79**.)

115

Variant of **63**, associated with the Wanderer: claiming a temporary home. Related also to **163**, the 'oath of atonement'. The three motifs are all connected with household, piety and honour, and therefore with the aspect of the moral life over which Fricka stands as guardian.

116

Hallowed contracts (guarded by the spear).

117

Mime's glee. Prolongation of **37**.

118

Siegfried's labour.

119

Nothung. (Falling octave, plus augmented triad.) From **51** and **52** via **66**.

120

Siegfried's smelting song; four semi-motifs.

121

Associated with Mime's craftiness.

121A

Extension of **121**.

122

Siegfried's forging song.

123

Siegfried's praise of Nothung. (Possibly not a motif, but reappears in the Siegfried Idyll.)

124

Fafner as dragon. (Transformation of **23**.)

125

Fafner motifs. A is derived from **41**.

126

The free hero. (Based on **110**.)

127

Forest murmurs. (Related to **12**.)

128

Wood-bird motifs.

129

More of the same.

130

Wood-bird. (Related to 4.)

131

Crafty Mime: variation of 102. Holman: false flattery.

132

Siegfried's joy.

133

Wotan's summons to Erda. (Based on **22B**.)

134

World inheritance motif: Wotan's second bequest. (Porges calls it the redemption theme, which seems to have been Wagner's own term for it. Burghold calls it *Siegfried-Liebe Motiv* – Siegfried-love motif.)

135

Wotan teasing Siegfried: satirical memory of **134**.

136

Siegfried's fear.

136A

Later version of **136**, expressing Siegfried's confusion in the face of Brünnhilde's reticence. In both versions the first bar is derived from **61**, and Porges therefore describes this motif as the sign that the blood of the Volsungs is stirring in Siegfried (*Wagner Rehearsing the* 'Ring', p. 111).

137

Brünnhilde's beauty. This ends in a version of 34. As does this:

137A

The final version of 34, and an elaboration of the last three bars of 137. Burghold describes **137A** as the *Hingebungsmotiv* – the devotion motif. It occurs, however, in the course of Brünnhilde's accusations directed at the faithless Siegfried, as she says 'Er zwang mir Lust und Liebe ab' – 'He wrung from me pleasure and love.'

138

Brünnhilde's awakening. To Cosima, Wagner remarked 'Do you know what I was thinking of in that great arpeggio at Brünnhilde's awakening? Of the movement of your fingers in a dream, when your hand glides through the air. That's why I am still not satisfied with it.' (Diary, 20 July 1870.)

139

Siegfried stands before Brünnhilde.

140

O Heil der Mut - ter, die mich ge- bar!

Love-salute. (Derived from **22B**.) Burghold: delight (*Entzückung*).

141

Brünnhilde's maternal love for Siegfried, associated with **137**. Cooke and Holman: love's ecstasy.

142

Brünnhilde's sense of her unsullied nature. (Inversion and adaption of **99**, with **99** in the bass.) Cooke and Holman: immortal beloved.

143

Brünnhilde addresses Siegfried as 'hoard' and life of the world. Cooke and Holman call this the world's treasure motif.

144

Brünnhilde and Siegfried united. (Has been called the *Liebesbund-motiv.* Cooke: love's resolution; Holman: laughing at death.)

145

The rope of destiny. (Variant of **6**.)

146

Motif associated with the World Ash Tree. (Variant of **18**.)

147

A------------------------------------ B------------------
Norns. A recalls **85**, while B recalls **101**.

148

The Norns sing of fate.

149

Siegfried's manhood. A broader version of 104.

150

Brünnhilde's womanhood.

151

Love's delight. (Cooke relates this to 143, and calls it 'heroic love', while Burghold calls it *Gattenliebe* – 'spouse love'.)

152

The Gibichungs. A family of motifs built around these two.

153

A, variant of 152A, associated with Hagen. B, Hagen's definitive tritone.

154

Gutrune's first motif.

155

Gutrune's second motif. Called 'seduction' by Cooke, and 'plotting' by Holman, perhaps refers to Gutrune's part in Siegfried's downfall, and also more generally.

156

Forgetting. Cooke and Holman describe this as 'the potion'.

157

Gibichung hospitality motif. One of many uses of the falling fifth, representing Gunther and Gutrune, and the falling tritone (bar 4), representing Hagen. Cooke and Holman call this 'friendship'.

158

A related motif, called *Gastfreundschaft* ('guest-friendship') by Burghold.

159

Gutrune in seductive mode. Holman calls this 'Gutrune's deception'.
Variant of 158

159A

Gutrune motifs, derived from 159

160

Siegfried rowing, amalgamation of 14 and 104.

161

Blood-brotherhood: three motifs.

162A

Oath motifs, also associated with the sword Nothung: see 66.

162B

Cooke and Holman: honour. Extension of 162A.

163

Oath of atonement. A descending-third motif, like 63 and 115: this is more a quirk of style than a cross-reference, though connected in each case with Fricka's vigilance, as noted under 115.

164

Hagen's watch (from 14 and 39).

165

Hagen's envy.

166

Diminished version of 93: Valkyrie motif given to Waltraute and Brünnhilde.

167

Brünnhilde's longing to be reconciled with Wotan.

168

The logs of the World Ash Tree, piled ready for the conflagration. The bass taken from **114**.

169

Brünnhilde's anger, and anger generally; related to **76** and also to **179** below. Burghold calls this the *Unheil* (mischief) motif. Newman: Brünnhilde's calamity; Holman: betrayal; Aldrich: tangled threads of fate (Richard Aldrich, *A Guide to the Ring of the Nibelungen*, Boston, Mass., 1905).

170

Hagen's brooding.

171

Sometimes called the murder motif, but first heard when Alberich raises with Hagen the prospect of their inheriting the world.

172

Dawn on the Rhine. **B** is called 'Grim Hagen' by Holman, and has a separate life in what follows.

173

Gutrune's welcome. Called the *Verlockungs* (allure) motif by Burghold.

174

Gibichung home motif and horn-call. (Variant of **159**.)

175

Hagen's summons to the vassals.

176

The Gibichung vassals.

177

Wedding march, loosely based on 174. Holman: vassal's greeting.

178

Betrayal. Related to 162B.

179A

Brünnhilde's anger. Full version of 169.

179B

Hagen's tritone joined to Brünnhilde's anger joined to Gunther's fifth: bass figure in the betrayal scene and frequently thereafter.

180

The oath on Hagen's spear. (Fifth and tritone prominent, the 'curse chord' in the accompaniment.) Cooke: the swearing of the oath.

181

The Rhine-daughters' second lament.

181A

More of the same.

182

Siegfried lost.

183

Remembrance.

184

Siegfried's death.

185

Siegfried, truest of traitors. (Based on 140.)

186

'Ruhe, ruhe, du Gott!'

Examples, Chapter 4.

Ex (i) 22B modulating from C sharp minor to C minor (and onwards).

Ex (ii) 22B completed in a rising arch.

Ex (iii) Wotan's farewell.

Ex (iv) The fate motif: two harmonizations.

Ex (v) Sleeping Brünnhilde surrounded by fire.

Ex (vi) Brünnhilde to Siegfried: 'vernichte dein Eigen nicht!'

Ex (vii) The question cliché: Spohr, *Faust*.

Ex (viii) *Todesverkündigung*: answering phrase.

Notes

I INTRODUCTION: THE WORK AND THE MAN

1. Max Graf in *Richard Wagner im 'fliegenden Holländer'*, 1911, and Otto Rank, *Die Lohengrinsage*, 1911, both discussed in Isolde Vetter, 'Wagner in the History of Psychology', in Ulrich Müller and Peter Wapnieski, eds., *Wagner Handbook*, tr. John Deathridge, Cambridge, Mass., Harvard UP, 1992.

2. Theodor Adorno, *Versuch über Wagner*, Suhrkamp Verlag, 1952, 1974; tr. Rodney Livingstone, *In Search of Wagner*, London, New Left Books, 1981. For more German reactions to the Nazi connection, both pre-war and post-war, see H.-K. Metzger and Rainer Riehn (eds.), *Musik-Konzepte 5: Richard Wagner: Wie anti semitisch darf ein Künstler sein?*, January 1999.

3. See also, for some Oedipus platitudes, the article by Lindsay A. Graham, 'Wagner and *Lohengrin*, a Psychoanalytic Study', *Psychiatric Journal of the University of Ottawa*, vol. 3/1, March 1978, pp. 39–49.

4. Barry Millington, *Wagner*, London, Dent, 1984.

5. For the reception by the French intellectual left in recent times, see Philippe Lacoue-Labarthe, *Musica Ficta*, Paris, Titres, 1991, and Philippe Godefroid, *Richard Wagner, l'ecclésiaste anti-semite*, Paris, L'Harmattan, 2011.

6. Michael Tanner, *Wagner*, Princeton, NJ, Princeton UP, 2002; Bryan Magee, *Wagner and Philosophy*, London, Penguin Books, 2001, and *Aspects of Wagner*, 1968, 2nd edn, New York, OUP, 1988.

7. For an exacting survey of Wagner's distortions, half-truths and lies see John Deathridge's short biography in John Deathridge and Carl Dahlhaus, *The New Grove Wagner*, London, Macmillan, 1984.

8. For a brilliant demolition of the Boulez–Chéreau *Ring* see Tanner, *Wagner*, the chapter on 'Domesticating Wagner'.

9. Deryck Cooke, *I Saw the World End: A Study of Wagner's 'Ring'*, London, OUP, 1979.

10. 'Über die Benennung "Musikdrama"', *Musikalisches Wochenblatt*, 8 November 1872.

11. George Bernard Shaw, *The Perfect Wagnerite: A Commentary on the Niblung's Ring*, London, 1898.

12. Heise's work, *The Wound That Will Never Heal*, can be found online at Wagnerheim.com.

13. Robert Donington, *Wagner's 'Ring' and Its Symbols: The Music and the Myth*, London, Faber and Faber, 3rd edn, 1974; J. K. Holman, *Wagner's 'Ring': A Listener's Companion and Concordance*, Pompton Plains, NJ, Amadeus Press, 1996; M. Owen Lee, *Wagner's Ring: Turning the Sky Round*, New York, Limelight Editions, 1988; Philip Kitcher and Richard Schacht, *Finding an Ending: Reflections on Wagner's 'Ring'*, New York, OUP, 2004.

14. Heinrich Porges, tr. Robert L. Jacobs, *Wagner Rehearsing the 'Ring'*, Cambridge, CUP, 1983.

2 HISTORY AND CULTURE

1. Ludwig Feuerbach, *The Essence of Christianity*, 1841, tr. Marian Evans (George Eliot), London, John Chapman, 1854.

2. Wagner, *Judaism in Music*, p. 261. Ernst Raupach's *Der Nibelungenhort* appeared in 1834.

3. Fouqué was a lifelong friend of Wagner's literary uncle, Adolph, and therefore as close as any literary figure came to being a friend of the family in Wagner's youth. The influence of Fouqué's *Sigurd* over the scenario for the *Ring* has been analysed by Elizabeth Magee, in an important book documenting Wagner's researches in Dresden during the early 1840s, and subsequently during the drafting of the poem. See Elizabeth Magee, *Richard Wagner and the Nibelungs*, Oxford, Clarendon Press, 1990.

   It is to Fouqué that we owe the story of the water nymph Undine, which Wagner was reading aloud with Cosima on the eve of his death in Venice (see *Cosima Wagner's Diaries*, 2 vols., eds. M. Gregor-Dellin and D. Mack, London, Collins, 1978–80). Fouqué's story was turned into operas by E. T. A. Hoffmann and Albert Lortzing. Other versions of the tragic water-nymph idea appear in *The Little Mermaid* by Hans Christian Andersen and in the fairy tales of Jaromír Erben. Jaroslav Kvapil adapted the latter's tale of Rusalka, as the basis of another and more famous opera by Dvořák.

4. Wagner's use of the Icelandic sources has been explored by previous writers, notably by Donington in *Wagner's 'Ring' and Its Symbols* and by Deryck Cooke in *I Saw the World End: A Study of Wagner's 'Ring'*, London, OUP, 1979. We also know in detail what Wagner studied in the period leading to the composition of the poem. See again Elizabeth Magee, *Richard Wagner and the Nibelungs*.

5. For this and many more such examples see E. O. G. Turville-Petre, *Myth and Religion of the North*, London, Weidenfeld and Nicolson, 1964, pp. 85–6.

6. See especially the essays in Mircea Eliade, *Myths, Dreams and Mysteries: The Encounter between Archaic Faiths and Contemporary Realities*, tr. Philip Mairet, New York, Harper and Row, 1967.

7. See Bryan Magee, *Wagner and Philosophy*, pp. 25ff.

8. Richard Wagner, *My Life*, tr. Andrew Gray, ed. Mary Whittall, Cambridge, CUP, 1983, p. 260.

9. See the full account of Wagner's immersion in the tales and poetry of the German Middle Ages given by Volker Mertens, 'Wagner's Middle Ages', in Ulrich Müller and Peter Wapniewski, eds., *Wagner Handbook*, tr. John Deathridge, Cambridge, Mass., Harvard University Press, 1992, pp. 236–68.

10. It is worth noting that Wagner is credited by Lévi-Strauss as the founder of structural anthropology: the first thinker who saw that human communities depend on ordering their world according to changeless patterns. See the preface to *Le Cru et le cuit*, Paris, Plon, 1964.

11. Richard Wagner, *Zukunftsmusik*, 1860, in *Richard Wagner's Prose Works*, tr. William Ashton Ellis, ed. Bryan R. Simms, London, Kegan Paul, 1894, p. 318.

12. Paul Bekker comments that, for Wagner, consonants were the life-blood of poetry: *Wagner: Das Leben im Werke*, Berlin and Leipzig, Deutsche-Verlags-Anstalt, 1924, p. 252.

13. See the discussion by Carl Dahlhaus in John Deathridge and Carl Dahlhaus, *The New Grove Wagner*, London, Macmillan, 1984, pp. 151–2, and Chapter 4 below. See also the analysis of the passage from Wotan's dialogue with Fricka in *Das Rheingold* Scene 2, in Werner Breig, 'The Musical Works', in Müller and Wapniewski, *Wagner Handbook*, pp. 445–7, and Wagner's marginal jottings for the rhythmic values of Siegfried's 'Aus der Wald fort', reproduced by Ernest Newman, *The Wagner Operas*, London, Putnam, 1961, pp. 408–10.

14. See, for example, *Cosima Wagner's Diaries*, vol. 1, entry for 1 July 1872, in which Wagner notes the resemblance between Darwin and Schopenhauer.

15. Michael Ewans points to the parallel between the prophetic terror of Sieglinde and that of Cassandra before the palace of Agamemnon (*Wagner and Aeschylus: The Ring and the Oresteia*, London, Faber, 1982). It is worth pointing out that imagery from hunting, and the terrors of the quarry, is constantly in the background of the *Oresteia*, as it is of *Die Walküre*. See the illuminating account of the *Oresteia* by Pierre Vidal-Naquet, in J.-P. Vernant and Pierre Vidal-Naquet, *Mythe et tragédie en Grèce antique*, vol. 1, Paris, Éditions François Maspero, 1972, ch. 6.

16. For the influence of this play on Act 3 of *Die Walküre* see Ewans, *Wagner and Aeschylus*.

17. On what Wagner took from Greek literature generally see Hugh Lloyd-Jones, 'Wagner', in *Blood for the Ghosts: Classical Influences in the Nineteenth and Twentieth Centuries*, London, Duckworth, 1982, pp. 126–42, and Ulrich Müller, 'Wagner and Antiquity', in Müller and Wapniewski, *Wagner Handbook*. On the influence of the *Oresteia* see Ewans, *Wagner and Aeschylus*.

18. See Ewans, *Wagner and Aeschylus*.

19. Richard Wagner, *The Art-Work of the Future*, tr. William Ashton Ellis, Lincoln, Nebr., University of Nebraska Press, 1993, p. 165.

20. Ewans, *Wagner and Aeschylus*.

21. G. E. Lessing, *Briefe die neueste Literatur betreffend*, no. 17, 16th February 1759.

22. 'Religion und Kunst', 1880, in R. Wagner, *Gesammelte Schriften und Dichtungen*, 2nd edn, 10 vols., Leipzig, 1887–8, vol. 10.

23. Wagner wrote, in *My Life*, p. 510, that it was on reading Schopenhauer that he understood his Wotan for the first time.

24. Wagner's later account of Bakunin and his philosophy is well worth reading: *My Life*, pp. 384–7. It shows an insight into and revulsion towards the moral exorbitance of the Russian anarchist movement worthy of a Dostoevsky or a Conrad; but it is not necessarily true to what Wagner felt at the time.

25. In *The Wound That Will Never Heal* Paul Heise interprets the cycle as an allegorical presentation of Wagner's original Feuerbachian worldview. I will discuss Heise's interpretation in Chapter 5.

26. This remark occurs in the highly influential review of Beethoven's Fifth Symphony which appeared anonymously in the *Allgemeine musikalische Zeitung*, 1808.

27. G. W. F. Hegel, *Aesthetics: Lectures on Fine Art*, tr. T. M. Knox, Oxford, Clarendon Press, 1975, vol. 2, p. 890.

28. A. Schopenhauer, *Die Welt als Wille und Vorstellung* (*The World as Will and Representation*), tr. E. J. F. Payne, Indian Hills, Colo., Falcon's Wing Press, 1958, vol. 2, p. 448.

29. Ibid., p. 455.

30. Ibid., p. 456.

31. Ibid., p. 449.

32. See Ludwig Wittgenstein, *Philosophical Investigations*, tr. G. E. M. Anscombe, Oxford, Basil Blackwell, 1953, Part 1, section 293.

33. I have defended this view at length in *The Aesthetics of Music*, Oxford, Clarendon Press, 1997, and assume, for present purposes, an intuitive understanding of what it means.

34. T. S. Eliot, *Four Quartets*, London, Faber, 1944, 'The Dry Salvages', V, ll. 28–9.

35. Wagner, *Zukunftsmusik*, p. 317.

36. Ibid., pp. 319–20.

37. See Curt von Westernhagen, *Richard Wagners Dresdener Bibliothek, 1842–1849*, Wiesbaden 1966; Elizabeth Magee, *Richard Wagner.*

38. The story of the composition of *The Ring* is fascinating, and has been pleasingly told by Ernest Newman, *The Wagner Operas*, pp. 393–450.

3 THE STORY

1. Ernest Newman, *The Wagner Operas*, London, Putnam, 1961. Originally published as *Wagner Nights* this book has exerted a well-deserved influence over subsequent conceptions of what Wagner was attempting in *The Ring*.

2. Snorri Sturluson, *The Prose Edda*, tr. A. G. Brodeur, London, 1929, pp. 143ff.

3. Robert Donington, *Wagner's 'Ring' and Its Symbols: The Music and the Myth*, London, Faber and Faber, 3rd edn, 1974, p. 98.

4. The music of this passage, which is a consummate illustration of Wagner's ability to amalgamate words and music in a single rhythmical pulse, has been illuminatingly discussed by Jack M. Stein, in *Richard Wagner and the Synthesis of the Arts*, Detroit, Wayne State UP, 1960, pp. 84–5.

5. In the Eddic poem the Wala prophesizes the doom of the gods, tells of the World Ash Tree (Yggdrasil), where the three Norns make laws and cast the fates of mortals, and describes the Valkyries, who collect the dead heroes for the defence of Valholl.

6. That suggestion is the cornerstone of the interpretation of the cycle offered by Philip Kitcher and Richard Schacht. See *Finding an Ending: Reflections on Wagner's 'Ring'*, New York, OUP, 2004.

7. The method of composition of this beautiful passage has been interestingly analysed by Robert Bailey. See 'The Method of Composition', in Peter Burbidge and Richard Sutton, eds., *The Wagner Companion*, London, Faber and Faber, 1979, pp. 296–300.

8. G. B. Shaw, *The Perfect Wagnerite: A Commentary on the Niblung's Ring*, 4th edn, London, Constable, 1923, p. 97. Theodor Adorno, 'Wagner's Relevance for Today', *Essays on Music*, tr. Susan H. Gillespie, ed. Richard Leppert, Berkeley, University of California Press, 2002, pp. 598–9. The theme is absent from the sketch for *Die Walküre*, a fact that leads Curt von Westerhagen to hypothesize that it was conceived in connection with the end of *Götterdämmerung*. He even rather brilliantly detects it as an 'inner voice' in one of the sketches for *Siegfrieds Tod*. See Carl von Westernhagen, *The Forging of the 'Ring': Richard Wagner's Composition Sketches for 'Der Ring des Nibelungen'*, tr. Arnold and Mary Whittall, Cambridge, CUP, 1976, p. 106.

9. Donington, *Wagner's 'Ring'*, p. 170 – numbering of motifs as in my Appendix.

10. Cf. here Simone Weil's idea, that God must withdraw from the world, if he is not to destroy it. See *Gravity and Grace*, tr. Arthus Wills, with an introduction by Gustave Thibon, London, Routledge, 1952.

11. See Newman, *Wagner Operas*, pp. 426–7.

12. Hermann Broch, *Einige Bemerkungen zum Problem des Kitsches*, 1933, in Ute Dettmar and Thomas Küpper, *Kitsch: Texte und Theorien*, Stuttgart, Reclam, 2007.

13. Heinrich Porges, tr. Robert L. Jacobs, *Wagner Rehearsing the 'Ring'*, Cambridge, CUP, 1983, p. 103.

14. *Cosima Wagner's Diaries*, 2 vols., eds. M. Gregor-Dellin and D. Mack, London, Collins, 1978–80, vol. 1, entry for 15 August, 1869.

15. See ibid., entry for 19 May 1869. I discuss the theme in Chapter 4 below. For speculations as to Wagner's original plans for it see Gerald Abraham, 'Wagner's String Quartet: An Essay in Musical Speculation', *Musical Times*, August 1945.

16. Ibid., entry for 15 September 1871.

4 HOW THE MUSIC WORKS

1. See again the illuminating discussion of this declamation in Jack M. Stein, *Richard Wagner and the Synthesis of the Arts*, Detroit, Wayne State UP, 1960, pp. 84–5. On Wagner's immaculate sense of the syntactical congruence of music and speech see the examples discussed by August Halm, *Von Grenzen und Ländern der Musik*, Munich, G. Müller, 1916.

2. See Carl von Westernhagen, *The Forging of the 'Ring': Richard Wagner's Composition Sketches for Der Ring des Nibelungen*, tr. Arnold and Mary Whittall, Cambridge, CUP, 1976, pp.16–17.

3. See William Mann, 'Down with Visiting Cards', in John DiGaetani, ed., *Penetrating Wagner's Ring*, London, Associated University Presses, 1978.

4. Wagner himself commented upon this transformation, in *Über der Anwendung der Musik auf der Drama*, 1879 (in *Gesammelte Schriften und Dichtungen*, 2nd edn, 10 vols., Leipzig, 1887–8, vol. 10. pp. 189–90), tr. Antony Peattie as *The Application of Music to Drama*, 1986. The passage is summarized in Ernest Newman, *Wagner as Man and Artist*, London, John Lane, 1925, pp. 238–9.

5. See Constantin Bräiloiu, *Problems of Ethnomusicology*, tr. A. L. Lloyd, Cambridge, CUP, 1984, pp. 250–51.

6. See my essay on this topic in *Understanding Music*, London, Continuum, 2009.

7. *Report to the German Wagner Society*, 1871, discussed in Carl Dahlhaus, 'Wagner's Place in the History of Music', in Ulrich Müller and Peter Wapniewski, eds., *Wagner Handbook*, tr. John Deathridge, Cambridge, Mass., Harvard University Press, 1992, pp. 110–11.

8. Cooke, CDs of leitmotifs. Cooke's elegant and suggestive account has been taken forward by Alan Dunning, whose catalogue of the motifs and description of their embryonic forms, provides an appendix to Paul Heise's *The Wound That Will Never Heal*. Following Dunning's account online (at Wagnerheim.com) provides an invaluable aid to understanding *The Ring*, since the leitmotifs are both written out and presented in audio form as MP3 files. My own list of leitmotifs in the Appendix differs slightly from Dunning's.

9. Thus for Paul Bekker leitmotifs should be seen primarily as harmonic ideas, spelled out horizontally. See *Wagner: Das Leben im Werke*, Berlin and Leipzig, Deutsche-Verlags-Anstalt, 1924, pp 279–81.

10. See my *Death-Devoted Heart: Sex and the Sacred in Wagner's Tristan and Isolde*, Oxford, OUP, pp. 105–9, where I give some of the reasons for this.

11. Alfred Lorenz, *Das Geheimnis der Form bei Wagner*, 4 vols., Berlin, 1924. On the relevant approach to functional harmony see H. Riemann, *Elementar-Schulbuch der Harmonielehre*, Leipzig, 1906.

12. Patrick McCreless, *Wagner's Siegfried: Its Drama, History and Music*, Ann Arbor, UMI Research Press, 1982; Robert Bailey, Norton score of the Prelude and Transfiguration from Wagner's *Tristan und Isolde*.

13. It does in fact matter, philosophically, whether we call the result 'representation', 'imitation' or 'expression', even if it does not matter for the purposes of this chapter. See my *The Aesthetics of Music*, Oxford, OUP, 1997, chs. 5 and 6.

14. Deryck Cooke in *I Saw the World End: A Study of Wagner's 'Ring'*, London, OUP, 1979, ch. 3.

15. Ernest Newman, *The Wagner Operas*, London, Putnam, 1961, p. 460.

16. McCreless, *Wagner's Siegfried*.

17. Friedrich Nietzsche, *The Case of Wagner*, Leipzig, 1888, Section 9. I answer Nietzsche's criticisms in the last chapter.

18. The work was begun in an exemplary way by Deryck Cooke, and I refer the reader again to the CD set mentioned at the beginning of this chapter.

19. On the metaphysics of the curse, and on the act of cursing as hovering between the illocutionary and the perlocutionary, see the penetrating study by Andreas Dorschel, 'Entwurf einer Theorie des Fluchens', in *Variations*, 23, 2015, pp. 165–73.

20. The point is developed by Deryck Cooke in 'Wagner's Musical Language', in Peter Burbridge and Richard Suttons, eds., *The Wagner Companion*, London, Faber, 1979, pp. 230–31.

21. Theodor Adorno, *Versuch über Wagner*, Suhrkamp Verlag, 1952, 1974; tr. Rodney Livingstone, *In Search of Wagner*, London, New Left Books, 1981.

22. See Robert Bailey, 'The Structure of *The Ring*', *Nineteenth Century Music* 1, July 1977, p. 50.

5 UNDERSTANDING THE STORY

1. See my argument in *The Soul of the World*, Princeton, NJ, Princeton UP, 2014.

2. J.-J. Nattiez, *Wagner Androgyne*, tr. Stewart Spencer, Princeton, NJ, Princeton UP, 1993.

3. G. B. Shaw, *The Perfect Wagnerite: A Commentary on the Niblung's Ring*, 4th edn, London, Constable, 1923, p. 28.

4. Ibid., p. 41.

5. Ibid., p. 75.

6. Paul Heise, *The Wound That Will Never Heal*, available at www. wagnerheim.com, p. 581.

7. Mark Berry, *Treacherous Bonds and Laughing Fire: Politics and Religion in Wagner's Ring*, London, Ashgate, 2006.

8. Robert Donington, *Wagner's 'Ring' and Its Symbols*, 3rd edn, London, Faber and Faber, 1974.

9. Ibid., p. 264.

10. Cooke, *I Saw The World End*, pp. 31–2.

11. Ibid., p. 32. For the Freudian version, equally impotent as criticism, see Robert L. Jacobs, 'A Freudian View of *The Ring*,' in DiGaetani, *Penetrating Wagner's Ring*.

12. See 'Religion und Kunst', 1880, in R. Wagner, *Gesammelte Schriften und Dichtungen*, 2nd edn, 10 vols., Leipzig, 1887–8, vol. 10.

13. Jean Shinoda Bolen, *Ring of Power: The Abandoned Child, the Authoritarian Father, and the Disempowered Feminine. A Jungian Understanding of Wagner's Ring Cycle*. San Francisco, Harper, 1992.

14. Edward Westermarck, *The History of Human Marriage*, London, Macmillan, 1891; *The Origin and Development of the Moral Ideas*, London, Macmillan, 1906.

15. Richard Wagner, *Prose Works*, vol. 2: *Opera and Drama*, Lincoln, Nebr., University of Nebraska Press, 1994, §240.

16. Philip Kitcher and Richard Schacht, *Finding an Ending: Reflections on Wagner's Ring*, New York, OUP, 2004.

17. Ibid., p. 44.

6 CHARACTER AND SYMBOL

1. The most vivid account of Loki's character is *Loki's Flyting*, which can be found in *The Elder Edda*, a selection translated from the Icelandic by Paul B. Taylor and W. H. Auden, London, Faber, 1969, pp. 133–43.

2. Kitcher and Schacht, *Finding an Ending*, pp. 138–9.

3. See Joachim Köhler, *Richard Wagner: The Last of the Titans*, tr. Stewart Spencer, New Haven, Conn., Yale UP, 2004, p. 324.

4. Richard Wagner, *The Wibelungen*, in *Prose Works*, vol. 7: *Pilgrimage to Beethoven and Other Essays*, tr. William Ashton Ellis, Lincoln, Nebr., University of Nebraska Press, 1994, pp. 275–6.

5. Max Scheler, *Das Ressentiment im Aufbau der Moralen*, tr. W. W. Holdheim as *Ressentiment*, with an introduction by L. A. Coser, New York, Schocken Books, 1972.

6. One of Wagner's most important insights concerns the connection between property and shame. Alberich's shame as the Nibelungs deliver his property to Wotan, Fricka's shame as the hoard is piled in front of Freia, Wotan's shame in losing in this way the property that he so shamefully acquired – all these experiences, delicately and convincingly conveyed by the music, exhibit the way in which property penetrates the sense of self. What I am is what I own, and through ownership I am exposed to the eyes of others.

7. Helmut Schoeck, *Envy: A Theory of Social Behavior*, 1966, reissued Liberty Fund 1987.

8. See the contrast between Wagner in *Tristan* and Schiller in *The Maid of Orleans*, discussed in my *Death-Devoted Heart: Sex and the Sacred in Wagner's* Tristan und Isolde, Oxford, OUP, p. 42.

9. G. W. F. Hegel, *The Philosophy of Right*, tr. T. M. Knox, Oxford, OUP, 1952, p. 111.

10. The fact that a view is widespread does not prevent it from being false, and in *Sexual Desire* I set out to show just why that view is wrong in almost every particular.

11. The nature of bodily shame has been persuasively analysed by Max Scheler, *Über Scham und Schamgefühl*, 1913, in *Gesammelte Werke*, vol. 10, Berne, Francke, 1957. See also the speech of Potone, Plato's sister, in 'Phryne's Symposium', contained in R. Scruton, *Xanthippic Dialogues*, London, 1991, reprinted South Bend, Ind., St Augustine's Press, 2005.

12. I report here a conversation with Kitcher.

13. Alain Badiou, *Five Lessons on Wagner*, tr. Susan Spitzer, with an afterword by Slavoj Žižek, London, Verso, 2010, pp. 116–17.

14. See the penetrating discussion of this idea and its place in the history and literature of Europe by Andreas Dorschel, *Verwandlung: Mythologische Ansichten, technologische Absichten*, Göttingen, V & R Unipress, 2009.

15. Snorri Sturluson, *The Prose Edda*, tr. A. G. Brodeur, London, 1929, p. 41.

7 LOVE AND POWER

1. Adam Smith, *The Wealth of Nations*, 1776, Book 1, chapter 4.

2. John Locke, *Second Treatise on Civil Government*, 1690, chapter 5.

3. I am caricaturing an extended argument, to be found in *The Philosophy of Right* (Hegel) and the *1844 Manuscripts* (Marx), but which will be sufficiently clear, I hope, in what follows.

4. Marx retained this aspect of his early argument, and elaborated it in the chapter of *Das Kapital* devoted to 'the fetishism of commodities'.

5. Why three, however? Three Norns, three Rhine-daughters, three times three Valkyries – some argue that this is the way that goddesses are counted. (See Robert Graves's extravaganza, *The White Goddess: A Historical Grammar of Poetic Myth*, London, Faber and Faber, 1948.)

6. Cooke describes the use of this legend in *I Saw the World End*.

7. Philip Kitcher and Richard Schacht (*Finding an Ending: Reflections on Wagner's Ring*, New York, OUP, 2004) being honorable exceptions. See their chapter 16.

8. The literature here, beginning with the notorious publication of Wagner's 'Letters to a Seamstress', by Daniel Spitzer in 1877, is vast, and summarized by Isolde Vetter in 'Wagner in the History of Psychology', in Ulrich Müller and Peter Wapnewski, eds., *Wagner Handbook*, tr. John Deathridge, Cambridge, Mass., Harvard UP, 1992, pp. 125–9. For the bisexual, covert lesbian theory see Heinrich Pudor, 'Richard Wagners Bisexualität', *Geschlecht und Gesellschaft*, 2/3, 1907, pp. 140–44.

9. Richard Wagner, letter to Röckel, 25/26 January 1854.

10. H. Grotius, *De jure belli ac pacis*, 1625.

11. The legal, republican and litigious nature of Icelandic society was commented on in medieval times. See the *Patrologia Latina*, and also Rémi Brague, *La Loi de Dieu*, Paris, 2004, p. 336, n.2.

12. See the discussion of the Sophocles play in Richard Wagner, *Prose Works*, vol. 2: *Opera and Drama*, Lincoln, Nebr., University of Nebraska Press, 1994, §§265–71.

13. Bernard Williams, *Truth and Truthfulness: An Essay in Genealogy*, Princeton, NJ, Princeton UP, 2002.

14. G. W. F. Hegel, *The Philosophy of Right*, tr. T. M. Knox, Oxford, OUP, 1952, pp. 156–7.

15. Compare Thomas Hobbes's argument, that the sovereign, who owes his authority to the social contract, is nevertheless not a party to it: *Leviathan*, 1651.

16. Joseph de Maistre, *Essai sur le principe générateur des constitutions politiques*, Paris, 1814.

17. Curt von Westernhagen, *The Forging of the 'Ring': Richard Wagner's Composition Sketches for Der Ring des Nibelungen*, tr. Arnold and Mary Whittall, Cambridge, CUP, 1976, p. 42.

18. I have elaborated on this thought in *The Face of God*, London, Continuum, 2011.
19. Richard Wagner, *My Life*, tr. Andrew Gray, ed. Mary Whittall, Cambridge, CUP, 1983, p. 388.

8 SIEGFRIED AND OTHER PROBLEMS

1. Jean Shinoda Bolen, *Ring of Power: The Abandoned Child, the Authoritarian Father, and the Disempowered Feminine. A Jungian Understanding of Wagner's Ring Cycle*, San Francisco, Harper, 1992, see earlier, Chapter 5. It is worth mentioning the view of Philippe Ariès, who saw Siegfried as the archetype of the adolescent, a fitting hero for a society that regards adolescence as the high point of human life. See the astute description in *L'Enfant et la vie familiale sous l'ancien régime*, 2nd edn, Paris, Seuil, 1973, p. 19.
2. Robin Holloway, 'Motif, Memory and Meaning in *Twilight of the Gods*', in *On Music: Essays and Diversions*, Brinkworth, Claridge, 2003, p. 47.
3. 'The Sorrows and Grandeur of Richard Wagner', in Thomas Mann, *Pro and Contra Wagner*, tr. Allan Blunden, London, Faber and Faber 1985, p. 100.
4. See the exploration of this theme in Walter Burkert, *Homo Necans: The Anthropology of Ancient Greek Sacrificial Ritual and Myth*, tr. Peter Bing, Berkeley, University of California Press, 1983.
5. Richard Wagner, 'Die Wibelungen, or World History as told in Saga', in *Prose Works*, vol. 7: *Pilgrimage to Beethoven and Other Essays*, tr. William Ashton Ellis, Lincoln, Nebr., University of Nebraska Press, 1994, p. 275.
6. René Girard, *La Violence et le sacré*, Paris, Gallimard, 1972.
7. In his autobiography Wagner reports that, discovering Schopenhauer's philosophy, he understood his Wotan fully for the first time (*My Life*, tr. Andrew Gray, ed. Mary Whittall, Cambridge, CUP, 1983, p. 510). In other words Schopenhauer gave the philosophical backing to a position to which Wagner had already been led by his own artistic thinking.
8. Philip Kitcher and Richard Schacht make an ingenious suggestion in *Finding an Ending: Reflections on Wagner's Ring*, New York, OUP, 2004. As they see it, Wotan intends Siegfried to inherit the world, but without Wotan in any way assisting him, since to assist him is to implicate him in the curse and all the pollution that has flown from it, as Wotan inadvertently implicated Siegmund. Hence the wisdom contest with Mime, in which the Wanderer lays the ground for Siegfried's forging

of the sword without in any way instructing him. And hence the encounter on the mountain, when the Wanderer provokes Siegfried's anger and then, to his own surprise, feels angry in his turn. Out of his anger the Wanderer then challenges Siegfried, says things that perhaps he never intended to say concerning the history of the sword, and finds himself attacked and overcome, his spear broken and his rule at an end. He has relied on Siegfried's uncouth nature to engender the irrational conflict from which Siegfried will emerge as victor, with no help from the person who desired this end. Wotan has intended not to intend what he desires, and he has succeeded! The existence of such far-reaching 'second-order' intentions is precisely what sovereignty requires.

9. Röckel's question in a letter of 1853 is repeated in Wagner's reply of 25 January 1854, contained in *Richard Wagner's Letters to August Roeckel*, tr. Eleanor C. Sellar, Bristol, 1897.

10. Cf. Girard, 'Nietzsche and Contradiction', *Stanford Italian Review* 6, nos. 1–2, 1986, pp. 53–65. Girard adds: 'Instead of joining the collective murderers of Siegmund, as she must do, as she always does, she tries to save Siegmund. Like Antigone, she threatens the power of Wotan because she destroys the unanimity of the lethal circle and she herself must become the victim. This is as quintessentially Christian as the intervention of Elizabeth to save Tannhäuser when the knights form a violent circle around him' (pp. 54–5).

9 RETROSPECT

1. F. W. Nietzsche, 'Nietzsche Contra Wagner', in *The Portable Nietzsche*, ed. and tr. Walter Kaufmann, New York, The Viking Press, 1954, p. 166.

2. Ibid., p. 163.

3. Ibid., p. 183.

4. Ibid., p. 182.

5. Bernard Williams, *On Opera*, New Haven, Conn., Yale UP, 2006, ch. 9.

6. Nietzsche, 'Contra Wagner', section 9.

7. There have been creditable (though in my view not yet credible) attempts to overcome this discontinuity, notably that given by Philip Kitcher, in *The Ethical Project*, Cambridge, Mass., Harvard UP, 2011. To address this matter would take me far from my present task, but I have said something about it in *The Soul of the World*, Princeton, NJ, Princeton UP, 2014.

8. Richard Wagner, *The Art-Work of the Future*, tr. William Ashton Ellis, Lincoln, Nebr., University of Nebraska Press, 1993, p. 165.

Index

Wagner's operas and other works are mostly indexed under the heading 'Wagner, Richard: works', but the *Ring* cycle itself has its own main heading of '*Ring of the Nibelung*, the cycle' and each of the four operas comprising the cycle also has its own main heading. Page references in *italics* indicate musical examples.